Dynamics, Mediation, Mobilization

Media and Cultural Memory

Edited by
Astrid Erll · Ansgar Nünning

Volume 41

Dynamics, Mediation, Mobilization

Doing Memory Studies With Ann Rigney

Edited by
Astrid Erll, Susanne Knittel, and Jenny Wüstenberg

DE GRUYTER

The open access publication of this book was funded by the Open Access Publication Fund of Goethe University Frankfurt am Main.

ISBN 978-3-11-143443-8
e-ISBN (PDF) 978-3-11-143927-3
e-ISBN (EPUB) 978-3-11-143943-3
ISSN 1613-8961
DOI https://doi.org/10.1515/9783111439273

Library of Congress Control Number: 2024943780

Bibliographic information published by the Deutsche Nationalbibliothek
The Deutsche Nationalbibliothek lists this publication in the Deutsche Nationalbibliografie; detailed bibliographic data are available on the internet at http://dnb.dnb.de.

Cover image: Joep Leerssen
Typesetting: Integra Software Services Pvt. Ltd.

www.degruyter.com

Acknowledgements

This book would not have been possible without its more than fifty outstanding authors. They were all immediately enthusiastic about the idea of a new encyclopedia of memory studies "with Ann Rigney," and willing to contribute their chapters at very short notice.

We are also immensely grateful to Myrto Aspioti from De Gruyter, who strongly supported the idea of this very special book, as well as to Eva Locher and Stella Diedrich, who helped us in the process of making it.

We could not have edited this book without the utterly competent and unfailing help of Bilyana Manolova.

Last but not least, we would like to thank the Open Access Publication Fund of Goethe University Frankfurt am Main for generously supporting the open access publication of this book.

Astrid Erll, Susanne Knittel, and Jenny Wüstenberg
Frankfurt, Utrecht, and Nottingham in July 2024

Contents

3 Mediation and Remediation

4 Life and Afterlives of Memory

5 National and Transnational Memory

6 The Matter of Memory

7 The Agency of the Aesthetic

8 The Memory-Activism Nexus

Astrid Erll, Susanne Knittel, and Jenny Wüstenberg
Introduction: Doing Memory Studies with Ann Rigney

What does it mean to 'do' memory studies 'with Ann Rigney'?[1] The answer to this question has several dimensions: First of all, it entails a number of theoretical, conceptual, and methodological choices. It means research with an understanding of memory as the outcome of cultural representations and their circulation, and thus a particular focus on the role of literature, media, and the arts, on their historical dimensions and political implications, in producing and transmitting memory. It also means paying close attention to the dynamics of memory and the interplay between remembering and forgetting, convergence and contestation, to questions of mediation and remediation, and to possibilities of mobilization of and through memory.

Key to Rigney's approach to memory research is the notion of the agency of the aesthetic, the ability of culture to shape experience and memory. Crucially, Rigney conceives of cultural memory not as made in one go, but as the outcome of multiple and ongoing acts of remembrance in different forms and media. Memory is remediated time and again across multiple platforms, traveling between words, images, and performances, and from the news media to the arts. Rigney's work shows how memory filters experience through cultural forms and media technologies; that events have a slow-release impact in the form of the stories that are told and retold about them; that words and images are agents capable of mobilizing people.

Developing approaches to memory over a period of more than thirty years, Rigney has given the field of memory studies a number of key concepts that have

---

1 Memory studies is a well-established field of inquiry. Over the past three decades, it has developed and taken shape through a multi-voiced polylogue. Approaches from sociology, anthropology, history, literary studies, media studies, psychology, political and cultural studies – to name only some of the major disciplines – have come together to address the field's key question about the presence of the past. For fundamental studies on collective and cultural memory, see the works by Maurice Halbwachs (1994 [1925], 1941, 1997 [1950]), Pierre Nora (1984–1992), and Aleida and Jan Assmann (J. Assmann 2011 [1999]; A. Assmann 2011 [1999]). *The Collective Memory Reader* (Olick et al. 2010) provides an intellectual history of the field of memory studies. For ongoing research, see the journals *Memory Studies* (SAGE, since 2009), *Memory, Mind & Media* (Cambridge UP, since 2022), and the *Memory Studies Review* (Brill, since 2024); for research with a particular focus on the medial and cultural dynamics of memory, see the volumes of the *Media and Cultural Memory* series (De Gruyter, since 2004).

become 'household terms,' forming its discourse and identity. The "dynamics of memory," the "mediation and remediation of memory," and "the memory-activism nexus" are examples of such felicitous coinages that will be elaborated and carried to new shores in the individual chapters of this book.

Methodologically, doing memory studies with Ann Rigney implies a close reading of particular memory materials – from novels to street signs, and from revolutionary calendars to documentary films – and the bringing-together of such materials as new archives of memory. Importantly, Rigney's work showcases the importance of an ecological approach that does not only study discrete or isolated objects of remembrance but also considers and analyzes the networks within which they operate and become meaningful (or lose their meaning), always with an eye to the interdependencies and interactions of the material and the symbolic. Tracing the dynamics of memory across national and cultural contexts, across time, and, importantly, across media and discourses, crucially also entails comparative and longitudinal perspectives. Finally, it means an openness to and embracing of the interdisciplinarity of memory and memory studies.

There is another, more practical dimension to 'doing' memory studies 'with Ann Rigney.' It refers to a particular style of conducting research and building a research community. Rigney is not only conceptually highly generative, inspiring new and established researchers and providing them with useful tools to address their own questions. She also plays an active role in ensuring the transgenerational life of memory studies as a scholarly field. As a 'founding mother' of the Memory Studies Association, she has been instrumental in building a professional organization that is innovative, global, inclusive, and well-governed. Throughout her career, she has worked closely together with PhD candidates and Postdocs, in research groups, in editing projects, and in many other forms of academic mentorship. Rigney's engaged mentorship is 'formative' in the best sense of the word: It shapes researchers' thinking and writing style in a way that brings out the best in their academic personalities and projects. Curiosity about and respect for approaches from other regions and disciplines is part of her academic style, and this openness and her constructive ways of 'bringing-together' have formed memory studies into an enormously hospitable academic community.

This book is a *liber amicorum* as well as an invitation. It honors Rigney's achievements in chapters written by her students, colleagues, and friends. At the same time, this book is meant as a building block for the future of memory studies. It is conceived as a new encyclopedia of memory research that takes stock of the field's most important concepts and current developments and sets the research agenda for the coming years. It invites researchers to this field in a series of short accessible chapters that present key concepts of memory studies and show how these can be applied and developed further.

Doing Memory Studies with Ann Rigney is arranged in eight sections that are dedicated to eight major research areas of memory studies, all of which were either developed or significantly shaped by the work of Ann Rigney. The book begins with the fundamentals of memory studies in debates around history and narrative. It moves on to questions around the dynamics of memory and its mediatedness, to the life and afterlives of memory, national and transnational memory, the agency of the aesthetic, and, last but not least, to the memory-activism nexus.

Section 1: "**History, Narrative, Memory**" starts with a debate that is both foundational for and ongoing within contemporary memory studies. An important strand of the field's roots goes back to discussions emerging in the 1960s about the narrative properties of historical writing and historical consciousness. In his *Metahistory: The Historical Imagination in Nineteenth-Century Europe* (1973, 2), Hayden White notoriously argued that an historical work is not a transparent window onto the past, but merely a "verbal structure in the form of a narrative prose discourse that purports to be a model, or icon, of past structures and processes in the interest of *explaining what they were by representing* them." This new understanding of 'history' as a human construction within changing presents, which turns the past into stories, paved the way for the emergence of 'memory' in academic discourse. Making the past present through narrative clearly was not only the work of historians and historiography, but also of family conversations, rituals, literary works, or popular films. Yet, this recognition also raised uncomfortable questions about the relationship between fact and fiction.

In *The Rhetoric of Historical Representation*, Ann Rigney (2002 [1990], 16) offered a literary historian's view on this debate. Studying three historical narratives of the French Revolution, she asked: "How is the historian-narrator to go about representing this complex, collective event through the medium of a finite, linear narrative discourse? And what is even more problematic: how is he to render these different events as a coherent whole which has a particular significance?" Rigney thus paved the way for the study of history and historical writing from the vantage point of literary studies. To the 'rhetoric of historical representation' she would add further felicitous terms, such as "imperfect histories," i.e. the "chronic imperfection that distinguishes history from literature" (Rigney 2001, 2), or the "improper historian," refuting the misconception that "'history' *tout court* must be where the real historians are at" (Rigney 2007, 150).

Starting from the vantage point of today's interdisciplinary memory studies, the chapters in this section address the still heated debates around history, narrative, and memory. The section opens with Wulf Kansteiner, who revisits and updates the controversies from a theory of history perspective. He discusses narrative structure and emplotment, the difference between facts and interpretation, the uses of comparison and the limits of representation, concluding with "five suggestions for good memory management." Daniele Salerno contributes a semiotician's understanding of history, memory, and "the stories we remember by." He revisits the writings of Vladmir Propp and Algirdas Julien Greimas as well as the famous debate between Hayden White and Reinhart Koselleck, and delineates the nexus of memory, narrativity, and narrative schemata. Sarah Gensburger thinks about what it means to engage with recent history as an "improper historian." She addresses the terrorist attacks in Paris on 13 November 2015 from the perspective of a sociologist, looking empirically at grassroots memorializations of what would almost immediately be turned into 'an historical event,' and highlighting the role that narratives played in the process.

Literary historian Joep Leerssen discusses in greater depth what much of Ann Rigney's early work on history and narrative revolves around: memories of the French nation. Starting from Ernest Renan's famous question "what is a nation?," Leerssen scrutinizes the palimpsestic memory policies of Louis-Philippe in 1830s France. He concludes that the "chronology of the nation is not when its Remembered Things took place, but at what moments in time their remembrance was culturally activated." Moving to nineteenth-century Ireland, historian Guy Beiner discusses a compendium of speeches by Irish protesters in order to show how certain acts of memory prepare the ground for future remembrance. Beiner calls this phenomenon "prememory," thus introducing another key term for the study of history, narrative, and memory. Aleida Assmann brings us back to the present and the "crisis of transnational solidarity." To approach the "divided narratives" underlying many current memory wars, she proposes a distinction between "story" and "script," and considers how toxic and destructive scripts can be overcome by more creative and productive scripts.

Section 2: "The Dynamics of Memory" revolves around the central insight that cultural memory is not static but is constantly in flux, shaped by myriad social, political, geographic, environmental, and technological contexts. Criticizing the long-dominant "lieux de mémoire" approach in memory studies, Ann Rigney argued that "collective memory is constantly 'in the works' and, like a swimmer, has to keep moving even just to stay afloat" (2008a, 345). Rather than understanding memory as a fixed repository of the past, then, it is conceptualized as an active process involving continual negotiation, (re)mediation, and interpretation. Rigney has supplied us with a whole host of generative concepts that help us systematically analyze these dynamics. To name just a few examples, she has written about the "stickiness of stories" – the notion that certain cultural narratives have a lasting impact on collective memory and historical consciousness, sometimes transcending their original contexts (Rigney 2008b, 2016). She has explained the "differential memorability" of events or figures, where some are more likely to be remembered over the long-term than others (Rigney 2016). And she has referred to the uneven distribution of attention and resources devoted to various narratives about the past through the linked notions of "plenitude and scarcity in the production of cultural memory" (Rigney 2005).

In this section, authors in the fields of history, sociology, comparative literature, political science, anthropology, cultural studies, and psychology build on Ann Rigney's understanding of memory as a dynamic process and contribute perspectives from their own research. Jeffrey Olick opens with a consideration of "the Dynamic Turn," arguing that the "move from products to processes" has been central not only to our conceptualization of memory, but in contemporary cultural studies more widely. It challenges us to confront the tensions between "permanence and change." In her chapter, Marianne Hirsch revisits her concept of "postmemory" in the light of Rigney's call to move beyond traumatic histories. Hirsch thus considers how "hopes and dreams that were destroyed [. . .] can be made present again in the liquid time of dynamic memory." Ido de Haan uses the case of the sensational publication of a new book about Anne Frank to illustrate the political economy of memory as a key dynamic in which the Holocaust has acquired "gold standard" status in political struggles as well as in studies of memory. Jenny Wüstenberg engages with the notion that "memory secretes meaning over time [. . .] through a process of sedimentation," and proposes a "memory-geology nexus" that can help overcome a division between culture and nature in memory studies, as well as develop a sense of "timefulness." William Hirst picks up on Rigney's concern with how collective memory forms and circulates through lived experience, extending her culturalist approach with a focus on "flashbulb memories" – recollections of the circumstances around emotionally charged public episodes, such as September 11. He argues that flashbulb memories have a significant impact on differential memorability and collective identity indices of events. Sophie van den Elzen discusses the "eccentric agency" of female writers and artists who worked to remember chattel slavery over two centuries. She thereby shows how peripheral mnemonic dynamics contributed to the "vortex" from outside the center, developing their own, autonomous, gravitational pull. Antonius C.G.M. Robben takes us to the ESMA in Argentina to underscore the dynamic nature of seemingly static traumatic "sites of memory," which are in fact re-narrated and re-signified as competing groups seek to fix their meaning in time and place. Finally, Susannah Radstone engages in an experiment in memory work – a productive merger of analysis and self-reflection – that revolves around memories of food and spaces for sharing it. She thereby heeds Rigney's recent call to surface joy and hope in narratives that connect past, present, and future.

Section 3: "Mediation and Remediation" brings together major directions of media memory studies. Ann Rigney was one of the first memory scholars to emphasize that media not only stores, but also circulates cultural memory (Rigney 2005). The section's title refers to a collection of essays edited by Astrid Erll and Ann Rigney (*Mediation, Remediation and the Dynamics of Cultural Memory*, 2009), which brought together (new) media theory with questions of memory, emphasizing how acts of 'mediating again' – across time, space, and available media technologies – create and stabilize cultural memory.

When the field of media memory studies emerged, it was considerably shaped by Alison Landsberg's study *Prosthetic Memory* (2004), and it is indeed Landsberg who opens this section with a discussion of 'prosthetic memory,' raising the question how cinema and mass culture can lead to the "mobility or transportability of memory." The challenges that the digital era poses to the study of mediated memory are at the heart of the subsequent chapters. José van Dijck offers a tongue-in-cheek reconstruction of the "platformization of a [i.e. Ann Rigney's] scholarly legacy." More seriously, though, van Dijck's example points to a key process of memory in the digital age: its inevitable dependence on, emergence from, and shaping through digital platforms. In the following chapter, Rik Smit critically theorizes "the platformization of memory" and argues that platforms are today's "dominant infrastructures for and actors in the keeping, selection, production, and circulation of human experience and knowledge carried in media forms."

The role of artificial intelligence in present memory culture is addressed by Anna Poletti. Focusing on AI in the remembrance of Andy Warhol, Poletti emphasizes the "desire to have a non-human intelligent collaborator" as well as the significant amount of human labor that goes into the datafication, training, and computation of AI. Gerardine Meaney introduces "cultural analytics" as a tool for memory research. She argues that when facing an age of digital platforms and AI, the "theoretical models developed by cultural memory studies, with their emphasis on process, change and collectivity, are potentially among the most useful at our disposal." Laura Basu rounds off this section by reminding us that news media unfold agency not only in processes of cultural remembering, but also of forgetting. She argues that the news coverage of the global financial crisis of 2008 and its aftermath created a "media amnesia," in which the banking crisis was forgotten and transformed into a public debt crisis.

Section 4: "Life and Afterlives of Memory" provides diverse examples of how to 'do' literary, cultural, and media history within a memory studies framework. 'Life' and 'afterlives' are key terms for longitudinal approaches to cultural memory. In Ann Rigney's *The Afterlives of Walter Scott* (2012a), 'afterlives' emerge as a long-term perspective on the remembering and forgetting of an author and their works. Studying literary afterlives means delving deeply not only into textual, but also medial, social, and material histories. Together with Kiene Brillenburg Wurth, Ann Rigney defined comparative literature as a field that focuses on *The Life of Texts* (2019), thus endowing it with a pronounced emphasis on questions of cultural memory.

The section opens with a chapter by Astrid Erll who discusses "five lessons" from her research on the *longue durée* afterlives of the Odyssey. These are: the possibility of cultural loss, the significance of transcultural memory, the agency of transtemporal translation, the entanglement of analogue and digital memory media, and the benefits of 'reading backwards.' Rosanne Kennedy takes the concept of 'afterlives' from literature to the memory practice of apology. She discusses the activist afterlives of Australia's National Apology to the Stolen Generations in 2008, which demonstrate that only "the substantive implementation of Indigenous self-determination, rather than the forgetting imagined by 'turning the page on the past,' is what must come after the apology." Tashina Blom's chapter continues the discussion of activist afterlives, turning to the cultural memory of protest slogans. Using 'No Pasarán' as example, Blom shows that adaptability, ambiguity, and aesthetic appeal are "the three key ingredients that determine whether a protest slogan" will "stick around and become a carrier of cultural memory."

Kiene Brillenburg Wurth turns our attention to an understudied question: that of music as part of cultural memory. Her discussion of the lives and afterlives of two popular songs (*The Windmills of Your Mind* and *Les moulins de mon cœur*) shows that "distributed creativity" is key to understanding (not only) musical memory across time. Mads Rosendahl Thomsen reflects on questions of memory, being, and eternity through the lens of posthumanist fiction and philosophy, showcasing the "fascination with extraordinary memory" in films such as *Blade Runner* (1982) or novels such as Alan Glynn's *The Dark Fields* (2001). Claire Connolly discusses afterlives engendered by a particular textual form: the footnote. Using the example of Charles Robert Maturin's Gothic classic *Melmoth the Wanderer* (1820), she asks the compelling question "how a footnote remembers". Connolly argues that Irish writers of the Romantic period used footnotes to "mediate memory for a divided society, bringing print culture into proximity with a palpable and varied community of knowledge". The section closes with Marek Tamm's mnemohistorical approach to the afterlives of the St. George's Night Uprising (1343) in Estonian cultural memory. Tamm underlines the important insight that "mnemohistory allows scholars to move beyond the (although still important) question of 'what really happened' to questions of how particular ways of construing the past enable later communities to constitute and sustain themselves."

Section 5: "National and Transnational Memory" brings together contributions that revolve around the ways in which memory circulates and is articulated within and across national borders. The chapters in this section draw on the concept of "transnational memory," which advocates for us to move "beyond methodological nationalism," that is, for us not to regard the nation-state as the primary "container" for remembrance practices. In their path-breaking volume on *Transnational Memory*, Chiara de Cesari and Ann Rigney argue that "a critical rethinking of scale and of the unspoken hierarchies of scale implicit in our research practices is one of the core challenges of a transnational approach" (de Cesari and Rigney 2014, 18). Nevertheless, the national framework remains a crucial arena for memory work, and Rigney's work on everything from memory icons, reconciliation, apologies, monuments, citizenship, activism, audiovisual memory, and hope (Rigney 2008a, 2012b, 2018b, 2018c, 2022) has demonstrated how memories are articulated and circulated to construct and reimagine the nation, as well as transnational communities and solidarities.

Anthropologist Chiara de Cesari fittingly opens the section by reconsidering transnational memory in the light of scholarly and "real-world" developments a decade on. She argues that while transnationality continues to offer a fruitful pathway to studying memories beyond national boundaries, it has been crucially expanded by critical attention to decoloniality, digitality, and memory activism. Nicole Immler, who specializes in cultural studies, examines how memory matters to justice, focusing in particular on how the legacy of Dutch slavery has been negotiated in intergenerational and thus transformative terms. Sociologist Vered Vinitzky-Seroussi applies the lens of transnationality to mnemonic practices that emerged in response to Covid-19. She traces the circulation of white flags, yellow hearts, and postal stamps as commemorative mechanisms, but contends that this pandemic – like previous ones – may not stand much of a chance of becoming a mainstay of our collective memory. Stijn Vervaet, an interdisciplinary East European Studies specialist, analyzes Croatian visual and performance artist Sanja Ivekovic's engagement with female Yugoslav partisans. His study of the articulation of feminism and internationalism through traditions of antifascism showcases how local, national, and transnational scales can be entangled in complex ways. Margaret Kelleher, who focuses on Anglo-Irish literature, contributes an essay on Yeats' Nobel Prize as an evolving mnemonic event and practice. She utilizes the double meaning of "articulation" in order to understand how the Nobel both "brought to expression" Irish national identity and "connected" it transnationally. The diffusion from the Baltic to Hong Kong of the social movement practice of creating a human chain is the focus of Eneken Laanes' contribution. Laanes, a scholar of comparative literature, discusses how the memory of struggle against authoritarian rule and occupation in Estonia, Latvia, and Lithuania was redeployed and transformed when it was used thirty years later, on the other side of the world, in a case of "minor transnationalism".

Section 6: "The Matter of Memory" explores the intersection of cultural memory and materiality. Cultural memory is deeply intertwined with material objects, places, and traces, as well as technologies and bodies. Objects are endowed with meaning and affect through memory practices, but they also possess an inherent "liveness" and agency, and they influence cultural memory in often unanticipated ways. Objects, remains, or traces can acquire testimonial force and 'speak' as evidence of violence and trauma. While the entanglement of memory and things has always been part of the literature on memory, recent work in memory studies has begun to pay more attention to the complex ways in which things participate in and shape acts of remembrance, to reconsider the distinction between subject and object of memory, and to conceptualize materiality in relational and ecological terms.

The material dimension of memory plays a central role in Ann Rigney's work, and she has contributed significantly to developing a materialist memory studies. Crucially, Rigney argues for an ecological approach that "shifts attention away from discrete artifacts towards the continuous interactions between humans and non-humans, between mediations and materialities, within particular social and physical environments" (Rigney 2017, 475–476). Bringing together perspectives from literary and cultural studies, history, religious studies, and anthropology, this section takes Rigney's materialist and ecological approach, especially her 2015 article "Things and the Archive: Scott's Materialist Legacy," as a point of departure.

In the opening chapter of this section, Liedeke Plate sketches a framework for a new materialist memory studies from a literary and cultural studies perspective. She argues that conceptualizing things as co-agents of memory calls for a radical rethinking of some of the methodological premises underpinning memory studies. Following on from this, Maria Zirra's chapter sketches such a new materialist approach in her discussion of art reviews in South African literary periodicals from the 1960s. Taking inspiration from Karen Barad's feminist new materialist concept of diffractive reading, Zirra explores what happens in the encounter between the researcher and the magazine as a "resistant" object of/in memory. The following chapters then turn to the question of how to approach difficult material heritage in various post-conflict and post-colonial contexts. Barbara Törnquist-Plewa explores how post-war generations in Western Poland grapple with the things – furniture and other household items, as well as postcards or schoolbooks – left behind by the former German owners of their houses. This "unwanted heritage," Törnquist-Plewa argues, not only generates affective responses and produces new memories, but also connects people across generations and cultures, setting in motion transcultural memory work between Poles living in these areas and German expellees and their families.

Birgit Meyer reflects on how "provocative objects," as she calls them, catalyze meaningful change in the construction of collective memory, specifically the belated memory of Germany's colonial past. She focuses on a collection of sacred items belonging to the West-African Ewe people that are on display at the Übersee-Museum in Bremen, and which form a crucial node in unpacking the role of missionaries in German colonialism. In his chapter on the Valley of Cuelgamuros (formerly known as the Valley of the Fallen) in Spain, Francisco Ferrándiz proposes the concept of "necrotoxicity" to describe how certain funerary designs – specifically the underground necropolis at the site that houses the remains of more than 30,000 bodies – can become a poisonous and divisive memorial legacy. Ferrándiz reflects on the difficulties of "de-commemorating" such toxic material heritage, specifically in a context where the site is still partially controlled by neo-Francoist associations and right-wing religious and political groups.

From such figurative toxicity we move to literal toxicity in the form of the material legacy of racial capitalism and environmental racism along the River Road between New Orleans and Baton Rouge, Louisiana, USA, which is the focus of Lucy Bond and Jessica Rapson's chapter. This area, often referred to as "Cancer Alley," has a layered history of violence stretching from the plantation past to the petrochemical present, a violence which is erased or glossed over in the contemporary heritage discourse. Bond and Rapson show how art can counter this erasure by remembering both human and more-than-human victims of (slow) violence, and thus construct a critical-ecological-mnemo-history of the area. The section concludes with Rick Crownshaw's reflection on the advantages and pitfalls of adopting redistributive models of human and non-human agency and recalibrations of scale in environmental memory studies. Taking Claire Vaye Watkins' novel *Gold Fame Citrus* (2015) as a case study, he explores the role and agency of aesthetic artifacts in making environmental devastation, and human responsibility for it, memorable while remaining attentive to the ecological interconnections between text and world.

Section 7: "The Agency of the Aesthetic" revolves around the role of aesthetics, and aesthetic *form* in particular, in generating memorability. Key to cultural memory research is the idea that cultural forms have *agency* and actively shape and structure experience. As Rigney shows in her 2021 essay "Remaking Memory and the Agency of the Aesthetic," aesthetic forms have the ability to make the past memorable and relevant. This agency of the aesthetic comprises repertoires, and cultural modes (e.g. memoir, drama, documentary), as well as narrative genres (e.g. melodrama, romance), and involves the use of media technologies (e.g. print, photography, social media). There are various ways in which artworks generate memorability. One is by "representing less familiar events through the lens of more familiar ones" (Rigney 2021b, 13), a hallmark of multidirectionality as theorized by Michael Rothberg (2009). However, Rigney argues, art also serves to defamiliarize and unsettle established notions of the past, which helps us remember repressed or forgotten aspects of the past.

The authors in this section approach the question of memory and the agency of the aesthetic from the perspective of literary, medieval, and Celtic, as well as performance studies, covering a range of aesthetic forms from film to lyric poetry, novels, visual art, and theater. The section opens with Michael Rothberg's discussion of the role of multidirectionality in generating memorability and reconstructing broken or repressed mnemonic linkages. Rothberg takes as his case study Pınar Öğrenci's 2022 essay film *Aşît* [The Avalanche], which deals with suppressed histories of violence against Armenian and Kurdish minorities in Turkey. Rothberg shows how, at a formal level, the film creates multidirectional constellations that help surface and make memorable suppressed histories of violence, while at the same time remaining conscious of the limits of mnemonic repair.

Susanne Knittel's chapter focuses on the multigenerational family novel as one of the paradigmatic literary genres of cultural memory. Drawing on critical insights from perpetrator studies and ecocriticism, she argues that such novels can negotiate questions of complicity and implication in multiple histories of violence against humans and non-humans at different scales. Continuing with the theme of generations, Stef Craps explores the problem of "environmental generational amnesia," i.e. the idea that each generation takes their own experience of the state of the environment as a norm, "forgetting" that this environment is degraded compared to the experience of previous generations. Literature and the arts, Craps argues, can play a crucial role in recovering and remembering lost or about to be forgotten environmental knowledge and fostering a deeper, emotional connection to nature beyond intellectual understanding.

Jesseka Batteau's chapter focuses on Dutch trans author Lucas Rijneveld's award-winning novel *The Discomfort of Evening* (2020), which presents the stark reality of Protestant life in the Netherlands from the perspective of a ten-year-old girl. Through its unique poetic language, intertextual and paratextual references, and focus on loss and vulnerability, Rijneveld's novel, Batteau argues, has the potential to unsettle the dominant masculine cultural narrative of secular liberation and thus make visible unseen lives and identities.

Next, Ann Dooley reflects on the status and agency of lyric poetry in collective memory and memory studies. Her case study of the early Irish nature lyric highlights its resurgence in contemporary Irish culture both in elite literary forms and as a tool in popularizing social movements. Moving backwards in time from a contemporary Irish frame to a medieval one, she then argues for a historical reevaluation to reveal the conflicted group identities embedded within the lyric's origins. Staying within the Irish cultural sphere, Emilie Pine explores the relationship between theatre and memory, examining how theatrical performances embody both individual and cultural memory through actors' recollections and the inherent repetition of performances. Taking Deirdre Kinahan's play *An Old Song, Half Forgotten* (2023) as an example, she argues that theater actively creates new cultural memories by engaging audiences in the co-production of meaning and remembrance, thereby bridging the gap between personal and collective histories.

The section concludes with Andreas Huyssen's discussion of the legacy of Adorno's *Aesthetic Theory* (1977) in light of the challenges art faces in today's conditions of neoliberal commodification. Focusing on four concepts relating to the agency of the aesthetic – autonomy, art activism, transnational reciprocities, and the intersectionality of sedimented timelines – Huyssen argues for a renewed understanding of art's role in resisting neoliberalism, transcending national boundaries, engaging with historical trauma, and reshaping perceptions of time and memory in a global context.

Section 8: "The Memory-Activism Nexus" features chapters that bring social movement studies into sustained conversation with memory studies. The "memory-activism nexus" is Ann Rigney's term (Rigney 2018a, 2021a, see also Daphi and Zamponi 2019a). It helps distinguish three aspects of memory and activism: first, "memory activism" (how grassroots actors shape public memory); second, "memory of activism" (how societies remember contentious struggles of the past); and third, "memory in activism" (how social movements tap into past narratives and repertoires to identify and mobilize). In her typically tongue-in-cheek style, Rigney proposed the acronym "MaMaMia" as a shorthand for the memory-activism nexus. Under this umbrella a research program has thrived, in part due to projects and conferences instigated via the "Remembering Activism" (ReACT) ERC grant (2019–24). In the process, Rigney and her collaborators have called for memory studies to shift from a focus on trauma to one on hope and solidarity (Rigney 2018a, van den Elzen 2024), have helped us understand the dynamics of the "re-framing" and "re-signifying" decommissioned monuments (Rigney 2023), and have written about activists' use of archives (Salerno and Rigney 2024), images (Smits and Ros 2021, Rigney and Smits 2023), and sounds (Rigney 2022, Salerno and van de Warenburg 2023) in their memory work (see also Rigney 2020).

Social movement scholar Priska Daphi opens this section with an overview of the memory-activism nexus, arguing that while it has helped us better understand a diverse set of phenomena, more interdisciplinary dialogue between social movement and memory scholars is called for. Stefan Berger, a historian of labor movements, shows how Rigney's insights on the mnemonic grounding of solidarity can be practically employed, reporting on the efforts of German trade unions to harness memory politics strategically to citizens' awareness of the achievements of the labor movement and to improve levels of support for unions in the present.

Like van den Elzen, digital sociologist Samuel Merrill draws on the metaphor of a "vortex," but applies it to develop an understanding of how state and market forces influence civic activism through repressive actions both in analogue and digital arenas. Moving further into the digital realm, historian Thomas Smits examines the role of generative artificial intelligence in changing the visual memory of protest, thereby rethinking both the memory of and in activism.

Cultural and media scholar Amza Reading brings disability studies into the picture and asks how the memory-activism nexus would be illuminated through memories of autistic and disability activism. Maria Grever, a historian, returns to Rigney's research on protests around monuments by discussing the controversial case of a statue celebrating the Dutch colonial past. Building on Hannah Arendt's insights in *The Human Condition* (1988 [1958]), she proposes distinguishing between "monuments as work" and "monuments as action" in order to understand their varied position in mnemonic contention.

The final chapter, written by two members of the ReACT team, considers "activist afterlives." Duygu Erbil and Clara Vlessing use the French anarchist Louise Michel, as well as (on a more personal note) Ann Rigney herself, as examples of how a life full of activity becomes mediated and remediated via multiple channels as they form part of the canon of memory sites.

*

The more than fifty entries that follow constitute an encyclopedia of current approaches to collective and cultural memory. In their sum, these short chapters are a testament to the vitality, multi-disciplinary traction, and generativity of a field of inquiry that Ann Rigney's work has shaped in myriad crucial ways over several decades. Memory studies continues to help us understand the intricate intersections between time, culture, and politics – and Ann Rigney will no doubt continue to be central to this process.

1 History, Narrative, Memory

Wulf Kansteiner

History, Memory, and Historical Theory: Five Ideas for Good Memory Management

History and memory got off to a rocky start. Academic historians went on the offensive when they recognized during the memory boom of the 1980s that people's historical consciousness is shaped by popular culture not historical research. Memory culture, they alleged, with its relentless focus on the present was all about feelings and identity and lacked factual and moral integrity. In their perception, history, in contrast to memory, holds the past in high regards, has an unmatched ability to detect new facts about the past, and hence maintains a sensible and sensitive relationship between past and present (Megill 1998). History, unlike memory, conducts itself with professional and ethical integrity and offers a valuable service to society.

The special attention affluent Western societies paid to memory in response to the World Wars and the Holocaust was just one challenge historians faced four decades after the Nazis' demise. Several years before memory culture became an important concern of politicians, media professionals, artists, and academics, the historical profession was provoked by a group of critics, including some from the historians' own ranks. Armed with an assortment of narratological and linguistic analytical tools, the critical theorists argued that historians render life meaningful by crafting stories that spell out the continuous relevance of the past for the present. Generating historical facts constitutes an important component of historical practice but in terms of intellectual accomplishments and social relevance the generation of facts takes a backseat to the generation of narrative explanations. To put it in a nutshell, the post-structuralist critics accused historians of producing memory instead of history.

Since the 1970s, the stone of contention between historians and historical theorists has been the precise relationship between facts and narrative interpretations. For post-structuralist critics such as Roland Barthes, Hayden White, and Frank Ankersmit there exists an inexpungeable gap between historians' most important accomplishment, i.e., the creation of compelling narrative interpretations of the past, on the one hand, and the generation of facts reflecting statements about small-scale events, on the other hand. About specific events historians can often reach consensus by applying the tools of their trade including rigorous source criticism. But the large-scale narrative trajectories of historical writing tying these facts together do not emerge piecemeal from archival research; they are imposed onto the factual record and reflect historians' conscious and unconscious ethical and political priorities. Here is the historians' profound dilemma as it presents itself from the critics' perspective: historians take pride in, and receive considerable social recognition for, safeguarding the truth of history but the narrative trajectories of their writing, that render academic publications relevant and attractive to a larger audience, are mere inventions. In that sense, the stories crafted by historians have the same epistemological status as fictional stories, even if historical stories consist of actual events (Gangl 2023).

Most historians and some historical theorists entertain different notions about academic historical work. They assume that the incremental compilation and interpretation of facts according to the rules of the discipline result in an intellectual edifice that can claim factual integrity for all its components, including all layers of its narrative structure (Rüsen 2017). Given their ethos as guardians of the historical truth, historians have resented being called mere storytellers. In the second half of the twentieth century, historians were thus caught in a perfect storm challenged by post-structuralists in academia and a dynamic popular memory culture rendering the past enticing in film and television.

On the theory side, two analytical terms deserve special attention, i.e., White's concept of emplotment and Ankersmit's elaboration of the process of colligation. White ascertained that historians arrange events, whose existence they can prove, in the shape of overarching narrative plots that do not arise from the historical record (White 1973). These narrative trajectories, Ankersmit added, often take the form of highly condensed interpretive concepts, i.e., colligatory concepts, that capture a myriad of past events in a programmatic, narrative nutshell (Ankersmit 1983). The colligatory concepts appear all the more natural and factual the more they circulate in academic publications and popular memory culture. Think "World War I," "World War II," "The Holocaust," "Decolonization," and "The Anthropocene." For White and Ankersmit, the events grasped by these concepts can be responsibly emplotted and colligated in many different ways. Alternative emplotments and colligations likely set into motion different ethical, political, and aesthetic dynamics without necessarily losing their factual integrity. "The Great Western Wars," "The Military Triumph of Communism," "The Bloodlands" – all viable candidates with other interpretive implications than currently dominant colligations (see for instance Snyder 2010).

On the memory side, concepts abound that highlight the ethical implications of cultural strategies of making sense of the past and encourage academics and citizens to take responsibility for the ways they interpret the past. The institutionalization of memory studies at the end of the twentieth century began with explorations of national memory culture, inadvertently naturalizing national and even nationalistic sites of memory as the default setting for social memory processes (Nora 1989). At the turn of the twenty-first century memory studies pivoted to the study of transnational memory in response to the transnational circulation of memory media and memory templates. Initially, the transnational turn in memory studies adopted an unabashedly optimistic view of the ethics of memory hoping that transnational sites of memory, for instance an increasingly globalized memory of the Holocaust, would help establish a self-critical, human-rights-focused memory regime (Levy and Sznaider 2006). In recent decades, the optimism captured in concepts like cosmopolitan memory and prosthetic memory gave way to more somber acknowledgements of the political impact of transnational mnemonic entanglements (Rothberg 2019; De Cesari and Rigney 2014; Berger and Kansteiner 2021). The multidirectional, conflictual nature of twenty-first century memory practices, exacerbated by digital media, can have many political consequences, including empowering nationalist, right-wing movements which, ironically, thrive in transnational cultural settings (Hoskins 2018).

Ann Rigney is one of few scholars who has excelled in both fields of study and whose work exemplifies the considerable intellectual cross-fertilization between historical theory and memory studies. At the beginning of her career, Rigney contributed path-breaking analytical readings of professional historical writing and provided the advocates of a linguistic turn in historical studies with a much-needed empirical foundation for their expansive theoretical claims (Rigney 1990). Later in her career she helped invent the new research field of memory studies, exploring the media of memory, the transnational dynamics of memory, and the interdependence between political activism and memory (De Cesari and Rigney 2014; Rigney 2018a). However, both as a historical theorist and as a memory scholar Rigney retained a great deal of curiosity about the work of historians and their efforts to perceive the past on its own terms. In contrast to other proponents of the linguistic turn, she remained intrigued by the prospect that the historical record, painstakingly reconstructed by historians, might impose limits on its professional interpretation (Rigney 2001). Emplotment choices might contain a decisive epistemological component, even if the veto power of the sources regarding their proper emplotment is difficult to identify in the finished narrative product.

The post-narrativist turn in historical theory in the 2010s has confirmed Rigney's intuition. Post-narrativist philosophers of history have raised compelling questions about the analytical axioms of the linguistic turn in historical studies. For a carpenter equipped with a hammer everything looks like a nail; and for a cultural critic looking at the world through narratologically-tinted glasses every text looks like a narrative. With that thought in mind, the post-narrativist philosopher of history Jouni-Matti Kuukkanen has suggested that the proponents of the linguistic turn have misidentified the type of text that professional historians produce. For Kuukkanen historians are in the business of crafting compelling arguments about a wide range of topics, including the complex social, cultural, psychological, economic, and political dynamics that propel human societies past and present. He therefore concludes that as exercises in intellectual reasoning the publications of historians can be ranked according to their ability to abide by the rules of informal logic and convince an audience; their assessment should not be reduced to questions of aesthetic taste and moral preference (Kuukkanen 2015).

Hoping to provide a robust set of criteria for the rational assessment of professional historical writing, Kuukkanen zooms in on a given text's colligatory concepts. He maintains that colligatory concepts can be rated according to how well they semantically-metaphorically relate to the events under description. In addition, there are good reasons to prefer concepts that integrate more data points into a coherent argument and appear relevant to a larger segment of history than competing concepts. Finally, Kuukkanen appreciates originality and therefore favors compelling concepts that have not existed previously (Kuukkanen 2015). In principle, Kuukkanen's criteria should allow us to determine the argumental integrity and communicative efficiency of competing concepts such as "The Holocaust" and "The Bloodlands."

The post-narrativist turn in historical theory indicates that not all emplotments, arguments, and concepts are created equal in epistemological terms. Concepts may be more or less successful at gathering historical data, imbuing them with meaning, and providing them with an argumental purpose. Nevertheless, even for post-narrativists, the relationship between data and their interpretation remains prone to a great deal of subjective interference. A set of data points can be integrated with the help of professionally viable concepts that reflect different political, aesthetic, or moral objectives and may nevertheless attain similar levels of logical and epistemological validity. Apparently, facts do not determine which narrative or argumental masters they are made to serve.

For the time being, historical theory and academic history remain areas of unsettled knowledge. We are not exactly sure what historians do when they write histories. Do they argue, narrate, or describe? Perhaps there exist different types of history that should be assessed according to different sets of criteria depending on a given text's structure and primary objective (Kansteiner 2021b). But a closer look at the triangle of history, memory, and historical theory indicates that history and memory have more in common than assumed and that historical theory provides useful guidelines for responsible memory management.

The historian's dilemma and the unsettledness of history as a field of knowledge also apply to memory. Cultural memory narrates and argues, and memory, like history, relies on intellectual practices of emplotment and colligation. Therefore, the elasticity of the relation between facts and interpretations causes many mnemonic complications. To begin with, we certainly often wish that factual integrity would determine the ethical integrity and communicative effectiveness of a given memory-political intervention. We wish, for example, that Vladimir Putin's unappetizing visions of Russian collective memory would already be widely discredited by the egregious factual errors they contain. But that is unfortunately not the case. In many theaters of memory politics, ideological preferences and entertainment value trump epistemological integrity any day. Moreover, Putin's lies could be fact-checked and corrected, and he would likely be able to patch together a then factually accurate but still ethically repulsive and ideologically effective justification of his war crimes. In addition, the distance between facts and interpretations in memory culture also cuts the other way. One could argue, for instance, that it did not diminish the ethical integrity of some early attempts to raise awareness for Nazi crimes that said attempts operated with inflated numbers for the victims murdered in Auschwitz.

And then again, in some mnemonic settings facts do apparently resist specific emplotments, even when launched with the best of intentions. Take Danish memory culture as an example. Danish academics and journalists have tried valiantly to give Danish Holocaust memory a self-critical turn and have it play the same cosmopolitan tune as Holocaust memory across Western Europe. But in a country that is transnationally scripted as a shining exception to the bleak Holocaust story, with a population happily lingering in self-praise, the fact that 90% of Danish Jewry survived the Holocaust has successfully derailed all cosmopolitan initiatives. Time and again the more disturbing details concerning the economics of Danish rescue and the role of the SS occupiers have run afoul a heroic self-image bolstered by an exceptional rescue record. Even with hindsight it is difficult to determine what factors weigh heavier in the mix, the encouraging facts or the interpretive desire for self-praise (Bak 2024).

These examples indicate that the cultural contexts within which facts matter are socially constructed. The realm of law provides a suitable example. In a functioning legal system, facts matter. Donald Trump's lies about his net worth have had important financial and mnemonic repercussions because the collective memory of Trump as a successful business tycoon lost some of its luster. Advocating for memory arenas within which facts make a difference, all the while acknowledging the factual underdetermination of history and memory, I suggest the following guidelines for responsible democratic memory management in the twenty-first century.

(1) Get your facts straight. If we want to build memory cultures that honor facts we need to protect them. That requires historical research and applies to all platforms of media memory including social media and AI generated content.

(2) Differentiate between facts and interpretations. That is a challenging undertaking because in history and memory we constantly conflate facts and interpreta-

tions. Take the colligatory concept of the Holocaust as an example. That Nazi perpetrators and their collaborators murdered approximately six million Jews is a fact. That that event constitutes an unprecedented historical occurrence requiring special acknowledgement in memory culture is an interpretation, a reasonable and well-intentioned interpretation but an interpretation nevertheless that cannot be proven as fact. There exist other interpretations of the same events that are also reasonable and well intentioned and democratic societies should excel at tolerating a large variety of reasonable interpretations.

(3) Develop explicit comparisons. We make sense of events that concern and irritate us by comparing them to other events even if the axes of comparison are often not sufficiently acknowledged in a given mnemonic intervention (Rothberg 2009).

(4) Be transparent about the moral values and ethical codes informing your interpretation of past events. Since they are not facts, interpretations are always based in values. They are advanced in the service of national interest, democratic institutions, human rights, gender equality, animal rights, material equality, global justice, social peace and reconciliation, protection of the environment, and many other reasonable or unreasonable values. Transparency as to values and axes of comparison empowers audiences to partake in democratic deliberation about memory politics.

(5) Explicitly define applicable limits of representation. The transition from analogue-electronic media ecologies to digital media ecologies has changed the perception of limits of free speech, as the Digital Services Act and laws against Holocaust denial illustrate. In a specific institutional setting, limits of representation may pertain to willful lies or violent or otherwise unethical speech, including right-wing memory culture. The protection of limits implies processes of social exclusion through censorship and criminal prosecution. Hence, limits of representation are blunt yet powerful tools of social forgetting requiring democratic legitimacy (Kansteiner 2021a).

In the end, memory's factual underdetermination and interpretive malleability is a glass half full rather than half empty. If memory was beholden to the facts of history, we would be doomed to repeat the mistakes of the past. As Ann Rigney taught us, memory is also a realm of utopian hope (Rigney 2018a).

Daniele Salerno
Stories We Remember By: Narrativity and Memory-Making

"A maximum amount of meaning in a minimum number of signs" [le maximum de sens, dans le minimum des signes] (Nora 1997, 38) – in Pierre Nora's description of sites of memory Ann Rigney (2005) identifies one of the manifestations of a principle of scarcity that shapes memory-making in two ways. First, both individuals and groups grapple with limited cognitive capacities for remembering. Second, semiotic formats are unable to encapsulate the phenomenological totality of a past event or experience. Consequently, information must be selected and organized in order to be transmitted over time. This selection and organization enable an event to align with specific forms of expression (e.g., writing or visual) and discursive genres (e.g., history or testimony), turning it into a meaningful story for a future audience. This story can be repeated, translated into other languages and other media and transformed through its transmission. At times, an event, as a story, becomes a model for shaping the narration of other events, whether they occurred earlier or later. These phenomena show how memories rely on the use and recycling of a set of semiotic forms and narrative schemata. Such schemata facilitate the transformation of collections of incidents into recognizable and specific stories infused with meaning, ready to be transmitted over time. This chapter delves into the exploration of these schemata.

The anthropologist and linguist Vladimir Propp was among the pioneers who identified common schemata in seemingly diverse narratives. In the 1920s, Propp gathered one hundred different folktales and demonstrated that, underneath the hood, they share the same engine. Propp described this engine as a schematic template made up of a limited number of roles and narrative sequences. In the reuse and recombination of the same building blocks, such a schema generates a corpus of different stories that are recognizable as the tradition of Russian folktales.

Propp's methodological approach resonates with different analytical perspectives that emerged during the twentieth century. In linguistics (e.g., Lucien Tesnière's theory of syntax), semantics (e.g., Charles Fillmore's frame semantics), literary criticism (e.g., Kenneth Burke's dramatistic pentad) and artificial intelligence (e.g., Roger Schank's script theory), many scholars have worked on the idea that we can use a limited set of elements to describe a vast array of meaning-making productions (Eco 1986, 178; Salerno 2021). Here I will focus on the field of narratology and, more specifically, on the model elaborated by the semiologist Algirdas Julien Greimas.

According to Greimas, humans understand the world and events in terms of transformation processes. This perception shapes the organization of all discourses. Greimas used the term 'narrativity' to describe this overarching principle of discourse organization. He asserted that beneath the surface distinctions among stories, there exist "more abstract and deep organizations that have an implicit signification" (Greimas and Courtés 1982, 209). Combining Propp's model and Claude Lévi-Strauss's structural study of myths, Greimas conceptualized 'narrations' as sequences of transformations that interconnect networks of actants. On a deep level of the story, actant roles include for example the subject of the action, the object of the action – which embodies also the value contended in the narration – and an anti-subject. On a more discursive and figurative level, these positions are occupied by distinct actors along a series of transformations. For instance, in the context of an epic tale, a hero (e.g., Frodo) serves as the Subject, a coveted artifact (e.g., a magical ring) as the Object, and a villain (e.g., Sauron) as the Antisubject in the narration. A series of actions then transform the relationship between these three actants along the stories.

But if narrativity is the organizing principle for all discourses, we can extend this methodology to non-fictional texts and practices. This idea prompted Bruno Latour in the 1970s to build on Greimas's model (Latour and Fabbri 1977; Latour 2005), creating his actor-network theory for the analysis of scientific practices and texts. Latour's theory stands out as one of the most successful examples of adapting the semiotic theory of narrativity to non-fictional domains. Following this same logic, in the 1970s narratologists and historians engaged in discussions around the use of narratological tools for analyzing historical writing. In fact, if fictional and historical writing share similar linguistic forms, then similar methodologies can be employed for their analysis.

Hayden White in *Metahistory* (1973), applied a formalist approach to the analysis of the deep structures of historical writing. According to White, the notion that "the historian 'finds' his stories, whereas the fiction writer 'invents'" them (White 1973, 6) obscures the role of imagination and creativity in the historian's use of language. In White's perspective, historical work is "a verbal structure in the form of a narrative prose discourse." Histories "combine a certain amount of 'data,' theoretical concepts for 'explaining' these data, and a narrative structure," which present events as having occurred in times past (White 1973, ix). White identifies five distinct levels, with the first being a set of events arranged chronologically, termed the level of the chronicle. The second level, known as the "story," involves historians organizing events within a process. Each event gains significance based on its placement in the story, determined by the historian. For instance, the assassination of Julius Caesar could be represented either as the culmination of the Roman Republic or as the inception of the Roman Empire. These initial levels involve the selection and organization of data extracted from raw historical records. Historians will seek to elucidate them through the remaining three levels identified by White: emplotment, argument, and ideology. Emplotment entails the type of narrative the historian selects to imbue events with overarching significance. Within his framework, White identifies four primary modalities: Romance, Comedy, Tragedy, and Satire, although other genres such as the Epic can also shape the narration. For instance, the assassination of Julius Caesar could be depicted as the tragic end of the Roman Republic after five centuries. Or, alternatively, it can be depicted as the genesis of the epic of the Roman Empire. The argumentative explanation views the event(s) as specific occurrences of general historical laws, relying on deductive reasoning. White analyzes various philosophies of history and elucidates the argumentative structures that underpin their approaches. Conversely, the explanation by ideology pertains to the historian's stance on the ethical significance of past events for the present, historical change, and the notion of 'progress.' Historiographical styles bring all these levels together in a consistent way. In his theory, White reconceptualizes historical writing as grounded in a poetic act. It is this conceptual move that paves the way to the analysis of historical writing and historiographical styles through the lens of narratology and the literary theory of tropes.

White dismisses from his theory any concern about the alignment between narratives and historical evidence or documents (the so-called "extralinguistic truth"). This is in contrast with the approach elaborated by Reinhart Koselleck. In 1970, Koselleck organized the symposium "Geschichte und Geschichten" [History and Histories] to bring together historians and narratologists for discussions on the relationship between "History" and "stories." In his contribution, Koselleck (2004 [1985]) accepts the principle that historical writing and fictional narratives share the same forms. Nevertheless, he repeatedly emphasizes that historical sources "provide control over what might not be stated" (Koselleck 2004 [1985], 111). This posits a sort of negative realism as a fundamental rule that governs historical writing that contrasts with White's position.

According to Koselleck, in historical writing, an event takes shape through the selection and combination of a series of incidents. The historian structures the event by delineating a 'before' and an 'after,' and gives this segment in the historical continuum a plot with its sequences and actors. However, events always emerge from the interplay of contingent facts and the enduring presence of certain underlying forms. These forms are supra-individual, intergenerational, and transhistorical. For instance, general categories of actors, such as the State, the Nation, or the People, manifest in different histories and contexts, embodied by distinct specific (historical) actors (Koselleck 2004 [1985], 255–275).

This debate constitutes the conceptual core of Ann Rigney's *The Rhetoric of Historical Representation: Three Narrative Histories of the French Revolution* (1990), a "literary study of historical writing," in which Rigney explores the narrative strategies employed by historians. Rigney compares three different accounts of the French Revolution written sixty years after the event by Alphonse de Lamartine (1847), Jules Michelet (1847–53) and Louis Blanc (1847–62). Rigney demonstrates that representing historical events is not merely about *reproduction* but about *signification*: producing meaningful stories of what happened in the past. The way historians assign a name and figurative thickness to actors in the narration takes center stage in Rigney's analysis. For instance, the masses of people that gathered, marched, and rioted in the streets of eighteenth-century France might have been referred to as crowds ('foules') or the People ('le Peuple'). This lexical choice has fundamental implications for the meaning of the narrative. In the former case, the historian represents an accumulation of people acting without political intention that needs to be controlled or dispersed. In the latter case, it becomes a proper Subject (in the actantial model) of the narration and, consequently, in the History of France. The actor 'le Peuple' is imbued with values, capable of actions and intentions. Even though a crowd logically never truly represents the entire population of France, when referred to as 'le Peuple,' it comes to symbolize the Nation in its entirety and gains the ability to speak on behalf of it. This narrative arrangement yields tangible social and political consequences within the political structure of the Nation. The People challenges the king and, in essence, contests and claims back sovereignty itself. The historian structures and shapes its actors according to a specific grammar and inscribes the event, and its constituent actors, into History.

This actorial type – 'le Peuple' – as the Subject of the History of France takes on various discursive forms. These extend well beyond the historical writing and the narratives of Michelet, Blanc, and Lamartine. It materializes in visual representations, such as Eugene Delacroix's *La Liberté guidant le peuple* (1830) and within the monumental squares of Paris. It also resurfaces in contemporary media discourse, especially when the concepts of 'the People' and 'the Nation' need to be invoked to embed an event in collective memory (Wertsch 2021). More recent examples include the portrayal of crowds as 'the People' in French media coverage in 2015, following the terrorist attack on the satirical magazine *Charlie Hebdo*.

On its frontpages, the newspaper *Le Monde* emphasizes the memorable nature of the event. On the January 9 frontpage (Figure 1), *Le Monde* portrays a group of people mourning and demonstrating and draws parallels to 9/11 terrorist attacks in the US. On 13 January, the same newspaper features an image of a group of individuals during the 11 January Republican marches gathered around the statue in Place de la Nation (Figure 2). The picture draws on the composition

Figure 1: Frontpage of *Le Monde*, 9 January 2015.

Le Monde

Mardi 13 janvier 2015 · 71ᵉ année · N° 21769 · 2,20 € · France métropolitaine · www.lemonde.fr —   Fondateur : Hubert Beuve-Méry

C'ÉTAIT LE 11 JANVIER

Place de la République, à Paris.

▶ Du jamais-vu : 3,7 millions de Français et 44 chefs d'Etat ont défilé à Paris et dans tout le pays

▶ Hollande a rempli son rôle de rassembleur. Sarkozy et Marine Le Pen se sont exprimés dès lundi

▶ Faut-il un Patriot Act à la française ? Le durcissement du dispositif antiterroriste est en cours

▶ Syrie, Iran, Russie : la diplomatie française n'envisage pas de révolution stratégique

▶ Selon les historiens, le 11 janvier sera une journée fondatrice de la République

▶ ÉDITION SPÉCIALE DE 24 PAGES

ANALYSE

LA TENTATION D'UN PATRIOT ACT À LA FRANÇAISE

PAR JACQUES FOLLOROU ET FRANCK JOHANNÈS

Rien de pire, pour le droit, que ces moments d'intense unanimité, que cette vague d'émotion qui submerge la raison. Or, le code pénal a les plus grandes difficultés à revenir en arrière. Les mesures exceptionnelles prises en temps de crise s'ancrent à jamais dans les textes : peu à peu, les procédures dérogatoires prennent le pas sur le droit commun. Faut-il un Patriot Act à la française, après les tueries de Charlie Hebdo et de la porte de Vincennes ? Le lobbying des policiers, c'est de bonne guerre, à commencer pour faire oublier les failles du dispositif et réclamer plus de moyens.

Une réunion à l'Elysée consacrée à la sécurité intérieure devait avoir lieu lundi 12 janvier, mais l'idée même de « guerre au terrorisme » est inquiétante. Elle est entrée dans le droit positif aux Etats-Unis sept semaines après le 11-Septembre, par une résolution du Congrès. Elle consacre « la notion d'"ennemis combattants illégaux" », rappelle Mireille Delmas-Marty, professeure au Collège de France. Des personnes qui ne bénéficient ni des garanties du droit pénal, parce que ce sont des ennemis, ni de celles des prisonniers de guerre, parce que ce sont des combattants illégaux. »

▶ LIRE LA SUITE PAGE 14

LE REGARD DE PLANTU

Boulevard Voltaire

C'EST QUI VOLTAIRE ?

Claude Lanzmann : « Oui, la France sans les juifs n'est pas la France »

TRIBUNE

« Hyper Cacher » au fronton d'une grande surface juive de la porte de Vincennes ! Heureux comme Dieu en France ! Aucun doute : les chalands qui fréquentaient ce magasin considéraient l'emploi du mot « cacher » non seulement comme un slogan publicitaire, mais comme une fière revendication identitaire dans un monde paisible.

▶ LIRE LA SUITE PAGE 21

Algérie 190 DA, Allemagne 2,50 €, Andorre 2,40 €, Autriche 2,40 €, Belgique 2,20 €, Cameroun 1 900 F CFA, Canada 4,50 $, Côte d'Ivoire 1 900 F CFA, Danemark 20 KRD, Espagne 2,50 €, Finlande 4 €, Gabon 1 900 F CFA, Grande-Bretagne 2,30 £, Grèce 2,80 €, Guadeloupe-Martinique 2,40 €, Guyane 2,80 €, Hongrie 950 HUF, Irlande 2,50 €, Italie 2,50 €, Liban 5 500 LBP, Luxembourg 2,20 €, Malte 2,50 €, Maroc 15 DH, Pays-Bas 2,50 €, Portugal cont. 2,50 €, La Réunion 2,40 €, Sénégal 1 900 F CFA, Slovénie 2,50 €, Saint-Martin 2,80 €, Suisse 3,50 CHF, TOM Avion 450 XPF, Tunisie 2,50 DT, Turquie 5 TL, Afrique CFA autres 1 900 F CFA.

Figure 2: Frontpage of *Le Monde*, 13 January 2015.

of Delacroix's painting to shape the crowd as 'the People' (a process that Greimas called 'actorialization,' Greimas and Courtés 1982, 8). It shows how *La Liberté guidant le peuple* is a powerful example of a narrative evolving into a model. By gaining recognition, spreading widely, and inspiring imitations, the painting transcended its initial historical context and became a potent visual schema. It is utilized in different contexts to shape crowds as narrative actors that audiences can recognize as 'the People.' In the realm of visual language, Delacroix's painting is referred to as an 'icon' (Hariman and Lucateis 2007; Rigney and Smits 2023). An image that has turned into an icon does not only serve as a conveyance of historical content, such as representing or commemorating a specific event. As a model, it can be repurposed to depict new (historical) events, as seen in the Republican March of January 2015.

In the picture of people that ascended the statue in Place de la Nation (Figure 2), this small group somehow symbolizes the French people as a whole. The headline reads: "it was January 11," rhyming with the initial frontpage that references September 11 (Figure 1). Between January 9 and January 13, 2015 *Le Monde* constructs in its frontpages a Proppian narrative arc in which the People, as the Subject of a historical event, battles for its values and triumphs with the elimination of the enemy. The January 13 frontpage captures a glorifying moment intended, within media discourse, to etch this occurrence into the annals of history (note the use of the past in the title). By referencing different events and employing various schematic templates, *Le Monde*, in images and writing, pens the narrative of the *Charlie Hebdo* attack and its aftermath into the collective memory and history (or at least an initial draft of it).

I would like to address two final questions that deal with the ontological and epistemological nature of schemata. The first question pertains to the issue of truth. If historical, fictional, and media narratives all utilize the same schemata, does this imply an equalization of their 'value of truth'? This query has been central in discussions surrounding the epistemology and ethics of and in historical writing (refer to Dominick LaCapra (2001) and the critiques raised by Carlo Ginzburg (2012) against White). The answer is no: asserting that historical writing and fictional narratives, as well as history and memory, share the same semiotic systems does not imply an alignment in their rules of (good) formation, as these rules differ across distinct domains of discourse.

The second question revolves around the 'real existence' of these schemata. Schemata are undeniably methodological tools, which Astrid Erll (2022) has recently proposed to investigate under the label of "implicit collective memory." By identifying schemata, scholars create maps of the cultural and mnemonic universes. However, it is essential to recognize that maps should never be confused with the territories they seek to chart. Identifying actants can be likened to marking isobars on a map; while they do not have a tangible existence, they serve as tools to capture an aspect of reality. The investigation into the nature of 'reality' constitutes an interdisciplinary endeavor within cognitive narratology (Herman 2003). By examining the "relations between perception, language, knowledge, memory, and the world" (Jahn 2005, 67), cognitive narratology conceptualizes narrativity not merely as an inherent quality of texts or cultural artifacts but rather as a fundamental modality of thought (Bruner 1991). Individuals utilize cognitive templates to process experiential data in a "narratively organized way" (Pisanty 2012, 262, my translation). Narrativity, in this sense, emerges as a structure resulting from the interplay between embodied cognition and the social environment. It serves as a 'tool for thinking' that, among other things, enables individuals and societies to remember despite and through the principle of scarcity.

Sarah Gensburger

Narratives at my Doorstep: Researching Memory as an "Improper Historian"

1 Introduction

During the night of 13 November 2015, the most murderous terrorist attack in Paris history took place. The event was immediately referred to as "historic" by journalists, politicians, and historians. Some even went so far as to call it a turning point in French history. It followed an earlier attack on 7 January of the very same year which targeted the satirical newspaper Charlie Hebdo, and which had also been immediately described as a new historical mark.

I am not a historian but a sociologist of memory. More importantly in this case, I happen to live on boulevard Voltaire in front of the Bataclan Concert Hall and close to the restaurants of the 10th and 11th arrondissement which were targeted on 13 November. My two children, who were still very young at the time, were attending a school located halfway between the Bataclan and the Charlie Hebdo offices. The day after the attack, I was shocked, of course, but I still did my usual end-of-the-week grocery shopping. And on 16 November, as on any other Monday, I dropped my kids off at school.

This personal experience led me to decide to become an "improper historian," following Ann Rigney's beautiful expression, and to postpone the qualification of the event as "historical." Instead, as a proper sociologist, I looked empirically at the grassroots memorialization of it. In doing so, I studied the many written cards, pictures, drawings, objects and other 'things' that people brought to the sites of the attacks in the immediate aftermath, and for several months. Here, and again following Ann Rigney's steps, I observed the memory sites of my neighborhood not for themselves but as a way to grasp the "dynamics of remembrance" (2008a) and the way it relied on the remediation of pre-existing narratives to make sense of the current event. In this chapter, I will take stock of the social study of these narratives on my doorstep. What stories have people told in this dynamic grassroots memorialization process? Where does the narrative of the event start and end?

2 Researching narratives on my doorstep

How can we research the narrative impact of an event? As early as the morning of 14 November, the pavement and the pedestrian walks of my neighborhood had instantly been filled by 'things,' cards with messages, pictures and drawings, figuring people's readings of the recent event. I decided to dedicate my initial research to this material manifestation of narratives. First, I did ethnographic observation around these grassroots memorials to document how these narrative products came to life. Second, I conducted interviews with visitors and passersby. Considering that "in practice, of course, people rarely talk about 'history' as such" (Rigney 2007, 150), I started the conversation with practical, and in fact material questions: from "do you often come here?" to "when (or where) did you write this message?," and others of this type.

In some ways, I considered these grassroots memorials as "textual monuments" in the same way literary scholars have been considering books. In fact, several novels were brought to these sites of memory and left there as a commemorative tool. The most prominent one was Ernest Hemingway's *A Moveable Feast* (1964). Indeed, in the French translation, its title is *Paris est une fête* ["Paris is a celebration party"]. Because of this, Hemingway's book quickly became a textual symbol of the spirit of resistance Parisian people have been practicing, for example through keeping the coffee terraces alive despite the fact they had been targeted and had become sites of murder. And, on the first anniversary of the event in November 2016, it was the very picture of Hemingway's book cover, taken one year before on this very same location, that a street artist chose to paste on the walls of the building close to the Bataclan concert hall as an act of commemoration (Figure 1).

In January 2016, already, the neighborhood had hosted the first anniversary of another major terrorist attack – the one against the satirical newspaper Charlie Hebdo, which is located in the exact same district. This commemoration took place on the Place de la République where the massive grassroots memorial born after the January attack had just been revivified by the November one. At the center of the square, a giant screen displayed some photographs meant to embody the event to be remembered (Figure 2). The French government and the administration of the City of Paris had decided not to show images of the event itself but of some of its grassroots commemorations, that is, messages and people writing them, literally building a "textual monument."

Since then, this grassroots memorial was remediated again, this time in the form of a permanent commemorative artefact. In July 2016, through the decree n° 2016–949, the French government created a "national medal for the recognition of victims of terrorism." The medal presents a literal materialization of the grassroots memorial of the Place de la République: "The center is edged with a blue band bearing the inscription "République Française," and on the silver circle at the center is a representation of the statue of the Place de la République."

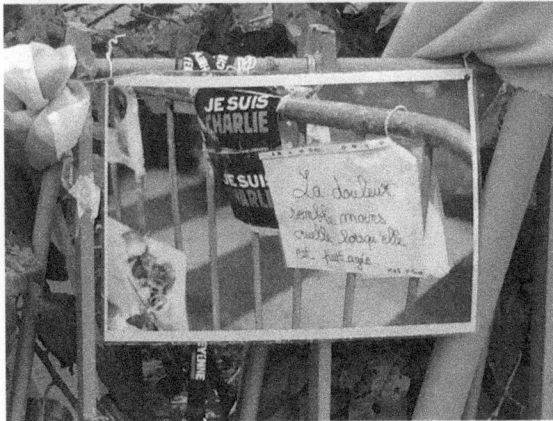

Figure 1: November 13, 2016. **Figures 2 and 3:** January 2016 © Sarah Gensburger.

3 Grassroots memorialization as remediation of narratives of terrorism

The dynamics of remediation had already played a major role in the construction of the grassroots memorials themselves. Narratives of other terrorist attacks were very present in the textual monuments built by the thousands of messages people left on the sites of the 2015 terrorist attacks in Paris, located mainly in front of the Bataclan and on the Place de la République.

Of course, the temporal and the spatial proximities between the two events – they took place the very same year and in the very same district – explained that speaking of the Charlie Hebdo attack was considered by a lot of people as a relevant narrative to tell their reaction to 13 November. This trend is even more present after January 2016 and the anniversary of the first attack. In front of the Bataclan, some months ago, someone hung laminated photographs of messages on the park's railings (Figure 3). The messages figuring in these photographs referred to Charlie Hebdo through the iconic motto "Je suis Charlie" [I am Charlie]. However, beyond this immediate local connection between January and November 2015, these grassroots memorials as textual monuments have told a lot of other stories of terrorist attacks. Some people came to these sites to tell the story of the victims of terrorist attacks which had just taken place or to commemorate others which had happened several months or sometimes years before. In January 2016, Ankara had just been hit twice. As a reaction, a poster told the story and showed the faces of the victims of an attack which took place in October 2015 in Ankara (Figure 4). On 19 January, someone wrote "I am Ouagadougou" on a white paper and pasted it on a gigantic pink painting about "Love" which had been brought there several days earlier (Figure 5). And yet another terrorist attack had taken place four days ago on 15 January in Burkina Faso.

On Tuesday 22 March 2016, the region around Brussels was hit by three bomb attacks, two inside the airport and another in the subway. In the following days, the grassroots memorial of the Place de la République was filled with messages about Brussels. As can be seen in Figure 6, the messages represent a double reference to the Brussels attacks and to the Charlie Hebdo one, through the use of the "I am Bruxelles" slogan and the typography designed originally as a popular reaction to the Charlie Hebdo massacre. On 12 June 2016, a shooter entered a popular gay nightclub in Orlando, Florida. Figure 7 shows a drawing that combines different references to the Charlie Hebdo attack, to the Brussels one and, through the rainbow flag to the recent homophobic massacre. Here, the memory dynamics create a composite textual and visual monument made of multiple remediations. With my colleague Sylvain Antichan, we spoke to a young couple who came this

Figures 4 and 5: © Sarah Gensburger.

very day to leave a banner made of paper that read "The more you kill us, the more we will love each other" (Figure 8).

The man, aged 26, and the woman, aged 23, were both philosophy students. They had moved to Paris in September 2015 from Portugal (she is Portuguese, and he is Belgian-Portuguese) and they now live in the 18th arrondissement. They said that they were particularly sensitive to issues around LGBT rights. They had come in response to the attack in Orlando and brought the banner. They chose the place to hang it with care. The man wanted it to be hung next to the Belgian tribute, as though it was an echo of his own national belongings. This was the first

Figures 6 to 8: © S. Gensburger.

time that either of them had come here to leave a tribute after an attack. For the attacks in Brussels, the young man said he had been "too involved," he "called people" and "didn't even think" (of coming here). For Paris, in November, "we had just arrived" in the capital. They had made their banner "an hour ago, in a park near the Archives" (The French national archives being nearby the square), and they "brought the supplies from home." To which event does this banner refer to? What kind of narratives is it a textual monument of?

4 The other "historical" nature of event: from rupture to continuity

The grassroots memorialization on my doorstep has relied on numerous other reme-diations of past narratives. Among the cultural memory which was mobilized at these sites, the ones of the two World Wars have been the most prominent. On 18 June 2016, for example, the iconic figure of Anne Frank appeared on different mes-sages suddenly displayed on the base of the statue at the Place de la République, stress-ing one more time the textual dimension – Anne Frank has become known worldwide as the author of a book, her diary – of this narrative remediation (Figure 9).

These sites of memory serve as locations from which to observe the dynamics of memory. This latter process turns out to be a continuous narrative remediation rather than solely a product of trauma and the definition of boundaries between the before and after of the event.

This study of the narratives on my doorstep confirms Maurice Halbwachs's claim in the *Legendary Topography of the Gospels in the Holyland* (2008 [1941]), in which he considered the pilgrims' narratives as stories of social continuity rather than of historical discontinuity (Gensburger 2019b). In the light of the above, the historical nature of the event is very different from the one usually considered by the commentators. The event is historical not because it marks the limit between before and after but because the way people make sense of it is embedded in pre-existing narratives of the past and will, on its turn, inspire new remediations in the future.

Since the 2015–2016 sequence, this grassroots memorialization I studied on my doorstep has itself become a cultural memory reference. In March 2020, while the grassroots memorials had long disappeared from both the Place de la Répub-lique and the Bataclan concert hall, I witnessed its reenactment. On this day, on my way home, I saw an ephemeral memorial brought back to life along the square in front of the concert hall (Figure 11). Taken by surprise, I asked around and quickly learned that it was the set for a TV series, for which the set designer

Figures 9 and 11: © S. Gensburger. Figure 10: © with the courtesy of Clémence Boussicot and the team of the TV show "En thérapie".

and her team recreated artefacts left at this very spot five years earlier. The 'fake' messages, flowers, and photographs have now taken the place of the authentic ones and look more real than life. From the interview with the set designer I conducted, I then learned that the artefacts were fabricated from images preserved by the media since 2015 (Figure 10). The place in which they are displayed lends these counterfeits an almost greater veracity than that of the originals, which have now become 'tributes,' to use the official term, and which are kept in boxes in the Archives de Paris following the City of Paris' decision to collect them for "history" (Gensburger and Truc 2020). This case study illustrates one more time the importance of studying memory sites not mainly for themselves but as a way to understand "the cultural dynamics in which they function" as Ann Rigney already demonstrated (2008a).

Joep Leerssen
The Nation Facing Its Memories

The nation, whatever that is, is nothing if not a mnemonic community. In his seminal 1882 lecture "What Is A Nation?" [Qu'est-ce qu'une nation?], Ernest Renan phrased it in words that after 150 years are still authoritative: the strongest bonding agents in a self-defining national community are the collectivized memories, both painful and glorious, of having suffered together and of "having achieved great things together" [avoir fait de grandes choses ensemble].[1] But as Ann Rigney (2018b) was among the first to point out, memories can divide as well as unify, become a locus of dissent. With this insight in mind, the study of nineteenth-century nation-building throws into relief many attempts to negotiate these divisive memories. In many cases, the strategy is to draw the public's attention away from awkward historical narratives altogether, and to replace these with a shared sense of a co-inhabited territory. To couch this in the opposition first used in Lessing's *Laokoon* (1766): the temporal and narrative *Nacheinander* [one-thing-after-another] of the nation's history becomes the spatial and visual *Nebeneinander* [one thing-next-to-another] of the nation's homeland. That was the agenda of the Irish romantic nationalist Samuel Ferguson, a conservative, protestant unionist, who in the 1830s sought to replace the grievance narratives of Catholic writers, recalling colonial injustice, with a shared love of the green fields of the common fatherland; a strategy that is still drawn on in Northern Irish politics (Leerssen 1996).

The principle is perhaps best exemplified by the policies of Louis-Philippe in 1830s France. The large square between the Tuileries and the Champs-Elysées was the locus of multiple, mutually inimical memories palimpsestically inscribed by the country's successive regime changes since 1789. Originally named in honor of Louis XIII, it became the place where the French Republic performed its public executions-by-guillotine in the 1790s, a memory that itself was suspended under

---

1 Renan's (1882) lecture is a classic in the theory of national identity, as a first and very powerful formulation of "voluntarism": national identity comes into being, not as a direct result of underlying cultural, social or geographic features, but on the basis of the people's acceptance of such features as meaningful in their self-identification as a nation. Those who view Renan in the frame of ethnic essentialism (to which, as an Oriental scholar, he was undoubtedly prone), may be surprised by this voluntaristic anti-essentialism. His "What Is a Nation?" should be understood in the context of debates around Alsace-Lorraine, which had been recently annexed by the German Reich on the basis of historicist and essentialist arguments, and, as Renan and other French intellectuals argued, against the will and the French national self-identification of the inhabitants.

Napoleon and exorcised by the restored Bourbon monarchy after 1818. As the Bourbons sought to return to a status quo ante, they erased all traces of the 'guilty' regimes that had intervened between 1789 and 1815 and re-erected an equestrian statue to Louis XV on the fateful site with a "Chapel of Expiation" nearby. The postcolonial and identitarian 'statue wars' of the last twenty years (trenchantly analyzed, again, by Rigney, 2022) are a pale imitation of the ones that raged in nineteenth-century France (Agulhon 1977).

Simply repressing inconvenient memories proved impossible. Literature, especially, opened up mnemonic spaces that, unlike the thoroughfares of Paris, were almost impossible to police. Stendhal evokes, in *Le Rouge et le Noir* (1830), how the proscribed recall of Napoleon remained a clandestine inspiration; the chansons of Béranger relate how an army veteran reverently keeps an ancient, battle-worn tricolore hidden under his bed, and after Napoleon's death on St. Helena the publication of the diaries of his physician in 1824 brought the Emperor back to mind everywhere. After the fall of the Bourbons in the 1830 revolution, the return of Napoleon's remains from St. Helena, to be re-interred in the Invalides, became one of the first national re-interments that the century, with all its pantheons, is so strongly characterized by. The return of this particular repressed was an act of religious mass fervor, and the arrival of the hearse in Paris was marked by a characteristic statement on Louis-Philippe's part. The King welcomed back the emperor in the name of a higher unity: "I receive and welcome this on behalf of France" [je le reçois au nom de la France] (Martineau 1990).

This is an act of pure Hegelian sublation, *Aufhebung* in all three senses of the word (abolition, storage, and lifting up). Napoleon's reign has been put to an end and laid to rest; his corpse will be enshrined, reverently stored in its new mausoleum in the Invalides; and the conflict between the successive incompatible regimes (monarchy, republic, empire) is transcended and lifted up to a higher plane, that of the ideal and eternal nation 'France.' Louis-Philippe attempted a similar sublation when he set aside the Pavillon Gabriel in the north wing of the Versailles palace to house a historical museum dedicated to the glories of French history from tribal days to the present, irrespective of constitutional regime (Figure 1). Much as the transcendent use of "on behalf of France" foreshadows Michelet (the historian who saw French history as an unfolding manifestation of the nation's true essence (Rigney 1990)), the mural inscription "To all the glories of France" [A toutes les gloires de la France] anticipates Renan's idea of "having achieved great things together." But whereas Renan's assertion in 1882 is about the bond between truncated France and its lost provinces of Alsace and Lorraine, Louis-Philippe's is about a France divided by its successive revolutions.

Figure 1: North wing of the Versailles façade (Pavillon Gabriel) with the Royal Chapel.
Image: Janmad (https://commons.wikimedia.org/wiki/File:Chapel_and_Gabriel_Wing_Palace_of_Ver
sailles.JPG), "Chapel and Gabriel Wing Palace of Versailles", slightly cropped by author, CC BY 3.0,
https://creativecommons.org/licenses/by/3.0/legalcode.

Such a policy was more difficult when it came to that fraught place between the
Louvre and the Arc de Triomphe. The Cologne-born architect Jacques-Ignace
(Jacob Ignaz) Hittorff was commissioned to drastically redesign what was hence-
forth to be called, significantly, the Place de la Concorde. Concord? In Gandhi's
words, that "sounds like a good idea"; in 1830s France it was at best aspirational.
In order to achieve that sense of concord Hittorff's design abolished all temporal
references in favor of spatial ones. Two huge fountains on the oval's focal points
evoke the aquatic aspects of France: the country's coastlines and its rivers. In the
middle, an Egyptian obelisk was placed (donated as a diplomatic gesture by Mu-
hammad Ali Pasha), in a publicity stunt that demonstrated the transport *tour de
force* of the French navy with its new paddle-steamers, and that indicated the
country's imperial ambitions in North Africa (France was in these years engaged
on the colonial conquest of Algeria).

Around the square were placed eight statues of personified cities: Bordeaux,
Brest, Lille, Lyon, Nantes, Marseille, Rouen, and Strasbourg. They function almost
as signposts: pointing at distant places by displaying them as a *signifiant*. The co-
presence of these eight *signifiants* (seated statues of female municipal deities)

symbolically draws the various outlying corners of France into the Place de la Concorde as a unifying focus of the country as a whole (Schneider 1977).[2]

And so Space is used to suspend Time, ousting it from the identitarian frame. Even so, memories have crept into the Place de la Concorde. The city statue of Rouen, rumored to mark the place where Louis XVI had been guillotined, became a point of congregation for diehard monarchists. After the German annexation of Alsace-Lorraine in 1871, the city statue of Strasbourg gained a new symbolical function for *revanchistes*, and was repeatedly draped in black as a sign of mourning.

Louis-Philippe's entire program of sublating and defusing the divisive memories of the past ended in failure during the 1848 revolution. His reconciliation of Empire and Monarchy as jointly acting "on behalf of France" may have anticipated Michelet's view of French history; but it was Michelet who anticipated his 1848 overthrow by evoking, at the beginning of his *History of the French Revolution* (1847), the non-presence of the Republic in the public spaces of Paris (Rigney 1990). No memorial, he wrote, perpetuated the memory of that Revolution, except maybe by way of an absence: the empty space of the Champ de Mars. At that juncture, Michelet resurrected the one, awkward national memory that had been repressed even more deeply than that of Napoleon, and that had not been sublated into the *juste milieu*'s *idée de la France*: the Revolution, including its Jacobins. Unmentionable as that Revolution had become, Michelet hailed it as "the arrival of the Law, the resurrection of Rights, the response of Justice" [l'avènement de la Loi, la résurrection du Droit, la réaction de la Justice]. The Second, Third and Fourth Republics re-adopted, in 1848, 1880 and 1946, the Revolutionary *Liberté, Égalité, Fraternité* as the state's official motto. There was more than mere mnemonic symbolism in this: the Conseil Constitutionnel in 2018, in recognizing *fraternité* as a constitutional principle, derived from it the state's duty to extend solidarity to migrants regardless of their legal status (Pascual 2018).

When Renan wrote about the unifying power of shared memories, he referred to the more subversive and divisive ones only as bygones which needed to be laid to rest: the Albigensian Crusades and the wars of religion had to be forgotten and overcome, he wrote, for a nationally French memory to become possible at all. In an almost deafening silence, he omitted any reference to the much more recent, much more traumatic Parisian Commune. It had perpetuated a radical, Jacobin memory and had itself after 1871 become as unmentionable as the Jacobins had become after 1800. It had taken Michelet and Louis Blanc to retrieve the

---

2 Hittorff was to repeat that symbolism in his much later design of the Gare du Nord, festooned as it is with statues symbolizing the different cities now connected by the railway lines radiating out from the train station, with Paris at the centre of this world-configuration.

memories of that earlier event; the Commune was to be recalled in ways altogether more diffuse, more complex, more illicit.

To shift the spotlight back from France to Ireland: it too had had its radical revolution – the 1798 United Irish uprising – which after its repression had become unmentionable, and which, like the French one, was recalled by way of cultural defiance in the 1840s – with a poem significantly entitled "Who fears to speak of '98?" In Irish nationalism, the insurrectionists of 1798 have been half-sublated into the national memory: partly as the founders of a republican-separatist tradition which is reverently invoked by the state that gained its independence in 1922, partly, much more incommodiously, also as the harbingers of a physical-force resistance which was adopted by the IRA's paramilitary and terrorist war against the British state in Northern Ireland.

The unmentionability of such episodes is first and foremost a sociopolitical one. It falls to the creative imagination, in the sanctuary of cultural production, to engage with such incommodious topics: from Walter Scott coming face to face with the 1745 insurrection in *Waverley* (1814) to Thomas Pynchon thematizing (well before it was adequately addressed by historians) the Herero genocide in *V.* (1963; cf. Weisenburger 1982). Ann Rigney has repeatedly drawn attention to the pioneering role of the literary imagination in extending the field of vision of cultural memory. Empathetically *imagining* the past is a very important aspect of "how a cultural community mentally processes its past" (to recall Huizinga's definition of history[3]); and this is done, not by factualist archival research but by creative minds in cultural production. It is a recursively-nested, iterative activity: an important part of the past was how it confronted its past. Each time we remember something we recall the previous time we remembered it; and historical 'forgetting' often takes the form of assuming that we, now, are the first to remember something for the first time.

Memories are always recursively multiplied. While culture has a special role to play in confronting and engaging with the awkward and incommodious parts of the past, rendering them imaginable, it also has a privileged function in disseminating memory. Rigney (2012a) has coined the idea of procreativity: the power of artworks to 'go forth and multiply,' to spark off other creative (or mnemonic) instances in the course of their own dissemination. The memories of 1745, of 1792, of 1798, of 1871 were not only retrieved, but also perpetuated and dissemi-

---

3 Huizinga (1929, 102). In the original: "Geschiedenis is de geestelijke vorm, waarin een cultuur zich rekenschap geeft van haar verleden." My translation is free and compressed but does justice, I think, to the idiomatic and semantic complexities that Huizinga himself discusses.

nated through cascading cultural relays, in what Rigney calls the "social life of texts" (Brillenburg Wurth and Rigney 2019).

What does that mean for the historians who deal with nation-building? Recent studies have demonstrated that historical memories in national movements operate, not as a static presence, but as a complex dynamic process, alternating between states of latency and salience and shifting intermedially and transnationally (Leerssen 2022). Nonetheless, memories in nationality studies still seem to be seen as one-dimensional, mere signposts across history pointing straight at the events that gave rise to them. Their mediated and cascading nature tends to be elided from the analysis, or else subjected to a debunking "invention of tradition" approach (Hobsbawm and Ranger 1983) where their mediated subjectivity is placed at odds with historical factuality. What historians could learn from Memory Studies, and from Ann Rigney's work, is that memories *are* facts, and that their dynamic, ongoing, self-replicating presence in the sphere of culture is not a by-product of political events but a mental ambience in which events gain their meaning. The chronology of the nation is not when its Remembered Things took place, but at what moments in time their remembrance was culturally activated, and how these activations functioned either as unifying or divisive agencies in the nation's recalled past or in its social fabric.

Guy Beiner
Orating Prememory from the Dock

Memory is distinguished by its backward gaze, reconfiguring the past for present purposes, but it also subtly entails an imaginative forecast – a "prememory" that sets the ground for future remembrance. In its rudimentary form, prememory signifies "premediation," defined by Astrid Erll (2009, 114) as "the use of existent patterns and paradigms to transform contingent events into meaningful images and narratives." It allows us to explore further the ever-developing "dynamics of remembrance" outlined by Ann Rigney, in which texts hover between persistence and malleability, exhibiting monumentality while also morphing "into the many other cultural products that recall, adapt, and revise them in both overt and indirect ways" (Rigney 2008a, 349). Functioning as what the psychologist Frederic C. Bartlett labelled "schemata" for constructing new recollections (Bartlett 1995 [1932], 199–214), prememory in this structural sense is about how earlier representations of memory influence remembrance of subsequent events.

There is also another, more personal and emotive form of prememory, which calls attention to the agency, as well as the anguish, of historical figures seeking to be remembered posthumously. Expectations of how history will be recalled, as well as anxieties over how it may be misremembered or even forgotten, surface already during historical events, informing later mnemonic remediations (Beiner 2014a). Use of prememory in both these meanings is apparent in Irish political traditions of republican martyrdom that deliberately mobilized memories of condemned rebels in order to inspire future generations to participate in struggles for national independence, which in turn were also remembered along similar lines.

The functions of prememory are exemplified in *"Guilty or Not Guilty?": Speeches from the Dock, Or, Protests of Irish Patriotism*, a compendium of biographical notices and courtroom speeches by "the men who fill the foremost places in the ranks of Ireland's political martyrs" (anon. 1867, 6). First sold individually as penny pamphlets, the speeches were compiled into a cheap booklet that became an instant bestseller upon publication in 1867 (Elliott 2003, 176–180). By the time of its first American publication, a decade later, *Speeches from the Dock* had already been reissued in Dublin through twenty-three editions (1878). This number would more than double before the end of the century, making it "one of the most influential books in 19th century Irish nationalist literature" (Boyce 1986, 14–15), with a circulation that "almost certainly exceeded that of any other Irish nationalist work ever published" (Donnelly 1996, 53).

The volume was produced by the Sullivan brothers – three siblings from the small southern town of Bantry in county Cork who rose to prominence as nationalist politicians and writers (Tally 2004): Timothy Daniel (T.D.) and Donal Baylor (D.B) Sullivan authored the biographical entries and Alexander Martin (A.M.) Sullivan provided supplements. Notably, A.M. was the editor and proprietor (to be succeeded by T.D.) of the *Nation*, a newspaper founded in 1842 by Young Ireland as the principal organ for Irish cultural nationalism. Indeed, it has been claimed that through the journalism of the *Nation* and the multiple reprints of *Speeches from the Dock*, he effectively "helped create the Irish popular concept of nationalism" (Foster 2001, 6).

Being devout Catholics and affiliated with the rise of an Irish parliamentary party in Westminster that advocated for Home Rule, the Sullivans promoted a constitutional Catholic nationalism that was at odds with the revolutionary militancy of the separatist Irish Republican Brotherhood, commonly known as the Fenians. Yet, despite professed objections to the use of physical force, they recognized the political capital to be gained from supporting amnesty for Fenian prisoners. *Speeches from the Dock* was originally issued as part of a campaign that elevated three condemned prisoners – accused of causing the death of a policeman during a post-rebellion prisoner rescue operation on English soil – into the "Manchester Martyrs," whose executions would be commemorated annually in mass demonstrations (Beiner 2014b, 204–207). All subsequent editions were augmented by additional entries on imprisoned Fenians (including among them Irish-Americans who had participated in the 1867 rebellion) as well as an extended section on the Manchester Martyrs that featured the speech made by A.M. Sullivan when prosecuted for organizing a mock funeral demonstration in their memory.

Replacing the early modern genre of moralistic "last speeches," in which capital offenders acknowledged their guilt prior to the execution and accepted that justice was being done at the gallows (Kelly 2001), the unrepentant patriotic speeches were scathing indictments of British rule in Ireland. This would seem to correspond to a growing popular nationalist sentiment, although, in seemingly seeking to democratize politics, the Sullivans – who were upwardly mobile middle-class Victorians – confined the nationalist canon to men of respectable social standing, excluding social radicals and women (Goldring 1993, 52–56). The collation of speeches congealed into a "sub-genre of Anglo-Irish literature" that inspired others to make similar statements when brought to trial (Dolan 1976; Harlow 1993). The literary critic Lucy McDiarmid has pointed out that the inherent intertextuality of the volume "links the patriots across the years, and the continuing sequence of linked speeches serves as an accumulating collective memory of political resistance and confirms the tradition" (McDiarmid 2001, 448).

Republished in countless editions, the book has remained in print to the present day. In an extended edition prepared in 1945, the hardline republican writer John Joseph O'Kelly (using the Gaelic version of his name – Seán Ua Ceallaigh) updated the scope of the anthology to cover the period up to the Irish War of

Independence (tactfully ending in 1921, ahead of the ensuing civil war in which O'Kelly had objected to the Anglo-Irish Treaty and the establishment of the Irish Free State). Incrementally, *Speeches from the Dock* presents a lineage of political martyrdom, enshrining a revered genealogy of Irish nationalism (Akenson 2011, 46). The perpetuation of a pattern, by which successive generations of aspirant leaders sought to be remembered though emulating illustrious predecessors, places importance on origin. Hence, there is particular value in identifying the urtext, or archetype, which shaped subsequent memorialization.

Speeches from the Dock opens with an entry on Theobald Wolfe Tone, claiming that "No name is more intimately associated with the national movement of 1798 [. . .] He was its main-spring – its leading spirit" (anon. 1867, 11). Tone was prominent among the founding members of the United Irishmen, Ireland's first republican movement, but he was not – as is too often mistakenly assumed – the leader of the 1798 rebellion, Ireland's primary embodiment of the Age of Revolution (he petitioned the Directory of the French Republic to send an invasion fleet to support the insurgents, only to arrive on board a French warship after the rebellion had been suppressed, when he was arrested and court-martialed). His apotheosis into the nationalist pantheon was launched after Young Ireland and their leading poet Thomas Davis called attention to Tone's neglected grave in Bodenstown, county Kildare (erecting a memorial stone in 1843). Subsequent interest among Fenians developed from 1873 into a tradition of annual commemorations through which the site ultimately became a Mecca for nationalist pilgrimages (Woods 2018). With his memory further exalted in 1898, during the widespread centennial commemorations of the United Irishmen, by the early twentieth century Tone would be retrospectively recognized as the "Father of Irish Republicanism." Although the Sullivans awarded him pride of place in the opening of the volume, their reproduction of the brief statement read at his court martial (taken from the *Life of Theobald Wolfe Tone* published by his son in 1826) is overshadowed, by the fourth entry, dedicated to a more junior United Irishman – Robert Emmet, whose speech "has eclipsed all other speeches from the dock, and now stands as a point of comparison for the others" (Dolan 1976, 155).

Emmet, who led an aborted brief insurrection attempt in 1803, was catapulted into immortality following his execution and the initial circulation of his courtroom oration, which poignantly appealed to contemporary romantic sensibilities, as reflected in poetry and prose (Connolly 2020, 16–18). The scene of him defiantly delivering his memorable words from the dock was captured in iconic visual representations (O'Donnell 2003, 117, 121, 146; see also Figure 1) and from 1806, when first enacted by an Irish woman at the New York Theatre, the speech was repeatedly performed on stage to the delight of Irish audiences on both sides of the Atlantic (Geoghegan 2002, 269). Of the various versions in circulation, the

Sullivans chose to reproduce the adulatory text from his most influential biographer, the Catholic nationalist Richard Robert Madden, whose "Life and Times of Robert Emmet" (first published in 1846 and shortly after serialized in the *Nation*) was the main source for popularizing the legend that raised Emmet into a hallowed republican martyr (Elliot 2003, 4, 133–140, 176).

Figure 1: The cover of an 1890 edition of *Speeches from the Dock* (Dublin: M. H. Gill & Son) featuring Robert Emmet's courtroom oration.

In 1914, Pádraic Pearse delivered a set of commemorative addresses that venerated Emmet's legacy as "the memory of a sacrifice Christ-like in its perfection" and commended his speech as "the most memorable words ever uttered by an Irish man" (Pearse n.d., 69–70). Conscious imitation of Emmet would lay the foundation for subsequent memorialization that would turn Pearse into the preeminent martyr of the 1916 Easter Rising (McCarthy 2017). As the model for all subsequent patriotic speeches, and a yardstick by which they would be evaluated, Emmet's oration was clearly a prememory template for generations of revolutionaries who sought to follow in his footsteps and to be similarly remembered.

Prememory, however, is not just a later-day retrospective appropriation of earlier memory that generates new memory. In crafting his speech, Emmet attempted to designate how he would be remembered:

> The man dies, but his memory lives. That mine may not perish, that it may live in the respect of my countrymen, I seize upon this opportunity to vindicate myself from some of the charges alleged against me. When my spirit shall be wafted to a more friendly port – when my shade shall have joined the bands of those martyred heroes who have shed their blood on the scaffold and in the field in defence of their country and of virtue, this is my hope – I wish that my memory and name may animate those who survive me (anon. 1867, 42)

Concerned that he would not be appropriately honoured, Emmet made a plea to be remembered on his own terms: "let no man attaint my memory" (anon. 1867, 46). Recognizing that in his own time this was not possible, he consigned himself to forgetting in the hope that his memory would be rehabilitated in the future, as famously expressed in his closing statement:

> I have but one request to ask at my departure from this world, it is – THE CHARITY OF ITS SILENCE. Let no man write my epitaph; for as no man who knows my motives dare now vindicate them, let not prejudice or ignorance asperse them. Let them and me rest in obscurity and peace; and my tomb remain uninscribed, and my memory in oblivion, until other times and other men can do justice to my character. When my country takes her place among the nations of the earth, then, and not till then, let my epitaph be written. (anon. 1867, 47)

Kevin Whelan has observed that this use of a "future perfect tense" was "a carefully crafted piece of oratory pitched not to the contemporary moment but to an ever-unfolding future, and to those who would complete and perfect his republican vision" (Whelan 2003, 51).

Tracing the recycling of memory is an elusive task. Even as Robert Emmet consciously strived to shape his own memory in the mould of a martyr for Ireland – a prememory that would consecutively shape the memory of others who aspired to be similarly honoured – he too was drawing on a prememory of republican martyrdom that preceded Wolfe Tone and the other United Irishmen executed in 1798 (most notably the brothers John and Henry Sheares, whose speeches were reproduced by the Sullivans immediately before Emmet). As a Protestant, Emmet did not have a personal attachment to cultural memory of Irish Catholic traditions of martyrdom from earlier periods. Instead, Emmet fashioned his memory after the northern Presbyterian United Irish protomartyr William Orr, who was tried and executed in 1797, ahead of the preparations for rebellion. In a declaration issued prior to his execution, which appears as the second entry in *Speeches from the Dock* (after Tone), Orr sought to contradict "certain alleged confessions of guilt" that he feared would tarnish his reputation, "which is dearer to me than life," and voiced the expectation that "all my virtuous countrymen will bear me in their kind remembrance" (anon. 1867, 26). Consequently, in preparation for the 1798 rebellion, "Remember Orr" was adopted as a motto by the United Irishmen (Beiner 2013).

The bold rhetorical proclamations of impenitent radicals, facing condemnation and seeking the vindication of posterity, conceal a nervousness as to whether this exculpation will be eventually attained. More generally, apprehensions of being remembered negatively, and the desire to be remembered sympathetically, express an angst of 'pre-forgetting.' If memory is affirmed by prememory, its self-confidence is perforated with concerns of pre-forgetting. Yet, rather than being a hindrance, the ambivalent tension between memory and forgetting that is encoded into memory as it is constructed and repeatedly reconstructed ultimately sustains remembrance.

Aleida Assmann

Divided Narratives and the Crisis of National Solidarity

1 Introduction

Due to the pandemic, the exacerbation of political extremism, economic recession, and ecological problems, in many nation-states the social solidarity has
come under severe stress. In this contribution I will focus on yet another cause
for the loss of national cohesion that has to do with a division of national narratives and historical memories within a society. This topic has acquired a new urgency in many countries in which the citizens are in a deep conflict about their
national self-image.

Here is an example. Every year on January 26, Australians celebrate their national bank holiday. This date goes back to the arrival of the first British fleet of
prisoners in Sydney Bay in 1788 under Captain Arthur Phillip. While "Australia
Day" is traditionally celebrated by the White population as the beginning of the
history of modern Australia, it is celebrated by the Indigenous population as "Invasion Day." From an Aboriginal perspective, it does not make sense and is even
offensive to promote the national narrative that Captain Cook "discovered" and
took possession of their island, which had been inhabited by their ancestors for
60,000 years. And although the facts are well known to historians, Australia's violent colonial history hardly features in the official narrative (Maddison 2023; Kennedy 2023). Unsurprisingly, every year the official celebrations on Australia Day
are accompanied by protests that are joined by more and more White Australians. Over the years, perspectives and symbols in these celebrations appear to
have become more inclusive. Aboriginal representatives speak, there is a traditional smoking ceremony, and the Sydney Opera House is decorated with the colors of Indigenous art. But there are no signs yet that the national narrative is also
becoming more inclusive: the Voice to Parliament Referendum for Aboriginal &
Torres Strait Islanders was defeated. It called for three phases of reform: "Voice,
Treaty and truth-telling about Australia's colonial history."[1]

---

1 https://theconversation.com/explainer-australia-has-voted-against-an-indigenous-voice-to-par
liament-heres-what-happened-215155

2 (Hi)story, narrative, script

Ann Rigney has made an important contribution to the construction of historical narratives in the nineteenth century (Rigney 2001; 2002 [1990]). In addition, Benedict Anderson (1983) introduced the broad term "imagined community" to point to the importance of a collective self-image of the citizens of a nation. For Anderson, this self-image is not a mysterious entity but the product of cultural practices such as reading the same newspapers in a world of shared cultural references. Political imaginings are not only immaterial constructs but also social facts (fait social) in the sense of Émile Durkheim. Historical events are formatted as collective memories that shape collective self-images and create cultural spaces, but also have the capacity to trigger violence and unleash wars.

In order to get a more precise hold on the vague concept of "collective memory," I propose here a distinction between a "story" and a "script." All stories that we tell each other are plot-based and have, as Aristotle already pointed out, a beginning, a middle and an end. This simple insight is also reflected in the children's song: "At the end of a rainbow you find a pot of gold / at the end of a story you find all has been told." This closure of stories is not a trivial insight. Stories can be summed up in a sentence like this one: "A man travels the world over in search of what he needs and returns home to find it." Stories gain their charm and coherence from their ending; it is this structure that makes them memorable and apt for retelling. In their literary form, closed stories are open to multiple interpretations.

Scripts works differently. They are often a collective construction and convention, built on a belief that is shared by those who are part of it. The script is not only *told* within a group, it is *lived by* a community. It anchors people in a specific past which gives meaning to their lives and offers them a clear vision of their future. American examples of such a script are the concept of "Manifest Destiny," the "American Dream," or Trump's promise to "Make America Great Again." While a story can be exciting or instructive; a script provides meaning and motivation for the individual and for the collective. Another term for script is "myth," if myth is defined as a "foundational story." It is pointless, as historian David Blight (2020) has emphasized, to generally condemn and dismiss the term myth for collective narratives. What is urgently needed, however, is the distinction between creative and destructive scripts, in other words: scripts founded on historical lies or historical truth.

> Some myths are needed because they support a good and important cultural orientation. Others are founded on vicious lies and are such powerful instruments of hatred and political mobilization that they set up great parades, whether on the Reichstag grounds in Nuremberg, on the streets of Charlottesville, or other places in this country. (Blight 2020)

The distinction between the closed "story" and the open "script" also allows us to better distinguish between a past that has ended and a past that is still ongoing. Which of the historical scripts are considered to have expired, and which are a legacy that is still supported? What is held to be past and over with for one group may be ongoing and still present for another group. "The past is never dead, it's not even past," wrote William Faulkner in his novel *Requiem for a Nun* in 1931 (229). James Baldwin echoed Faulkner forty years later, when he wrote in one of his essays:

> White man, hear me! History, as nearly no one seems to know, is not merely something to be read. And it does not refer, merely, or even principally, to the past. On the contrary, the great force of history comes from the fact that we carry it within us, are unconsciously controlled by it in many ways, and history is literally present in all that we do. (1998, 713–714)

In order to get a better understanding of this "great force of history," it is important to pay more attention to scripts and their power to shape collective memory and prescribe what is to be remembered and what is to be forgotten. There are crucial questions to ask: What kind of society do such scripts/myths support? Who is empowered by them and who suffers from them? What kind of a future do they open and whose future do they obstruct? And most importantly: How can toxic scripts be ended and overcome?

3 Repairing the past – a new American script?

The possibility of overcoming toxic narratives and creating a new national narrative is succinctly summed up in two lines of Amanda Gorman's powerful poem that she recited on the occasion of President Joe Biden's inauguration on 20 January 2021:

> [. . .] being American is more than a pride we inherit
> It's the past we step into, and how we repair it.

Two words from these lines are crucial: "pride" and "repair." Everywhere in the world, pride is an essential ingredient of national memory. In 2002, President Bush issued a new educational program called "We the People," following the advice of Bruce Cole, Chairman of National Endowment of the Humanities. He argued that the country was in need of a new script. "People increasingly are forgetting what shaped their past and led to a national identity. When a nation fails to know why it exists and what it stands for, it cannot be expected to long

endure." For Cole, it was the task of the humanities "to tell us who we are as a people and why our country is worth fighting for" (Fuisz 2009, 113).

With pride as its powerful gatekeeper, memory is always highly selective and strongly averse to acknowledging and including shameful parts of one's history in the collective memory. This traditional mode of framing national memory, however, has ceded more complex and more dialogic forms of memory. Admitting negative events can have the positive effect to build new relations and create bonds of solidarity with victims of racial violence.

What can be meant by repairing the past? One thing is certain: the past cannot be changed. But it can be interpreted in various ways, and, even more importantly, it can be acknowledged or it can remain unacknowledged. There are different aims and goals in remembering that may go together: one is to remember *in order not to repeat*; another is to remember *in order to repair*. It is a sign of hope that many democratic societies in the last decades have learnt that remembering and working through a dark past can actually lay the ground for solidarity across social groups in the future. Facing and remembering their history has helped societies to become more attentive to their diverse makeup and to effectively terminate toxic narratives together with the values that they endorsed.

A visible step in this direction was taken by President Joe Biden at the centenary commemoration of the Tulsa lynching massacre – a historical episode in which a White mob had killed many Black people, burnt 1,200 houses, and left 10,000 people of a flourishing community homeless and terrorized. On 1 June 2021, Biden was the first American president to ever attend such a ceremony of mourning. These were his words:

> for much too long the history of what took place here was told in silence and cloaked in darkness. But just because history is silent it does not mean that it did not take place. While darkness can hide much, it erases nothing. Some injustices are so heinous, so horrific, so grievous, they can't be buried no matter how hard people try. [. . .] We can't choose to learn what we want to know, and not what we should know. We should know the good, the bad, everything. That's what great nations do. They come to terms with their dark sides, and we're a great nation. The only way to build a common ground is to truly repair and rebuild. I come here to fill the silence because in silence wounds deepen and, painful as it is, only in remembrance do wounds heal. We just have to choose to remember. We memorialize what has happened here in Tulsa so it can't be erased.

In dictatorships, history and memory are isomorphic, as it is up to the head of the state to define both as in Putin's Russia. But even in democracies there can be impediments and obstacles that obstruct the search for historical truth. Democracy, equal justice and the mutual recognition of the members of society are at stake if one part of the society does not want to learn about the crimes of their ancestors. Biden's attempt to rescue this memory of White racial violence from total oblivion was answered by others with vehement rejections. Donald Trump called Biden's attempt "a crusade against our history." He was joined by Republican parents and lawyers who are fiercely preventing the teaching of this history in American schools. In Oklahoma, for instance, where the massacre took place, a new law forbids teachers dealing with historical materials that might raise feelings of uneasiness, remorse, or anxieties among their students. As events like those of Tulsa are being banned by state censorship, for some affected members of the society, the American dream is morphing into an American nightmare.

Whether white Americans will eventually embrace the black perspective of their shared history remains an open question. "We believe that understanding our nation's past is critical to finding a way forward on a range of contemporary issues," said Bryan Stevenson (2021), founder and executive director of the Equal Justice Museum and Memorial in Montgomery, Alabama. "We're proud that the Legacy Museum can play a vital role in helping people learn American history that's often not taught and empower everyone to build healthier communities."

Today, we live in a time of transition in which many societies are engaged in renegotiating their troubled past. Colonial monuments are toppled and new museums arise. The time has come to learn more about silenced historical episodes and to promote a more self-critical and responsible approach to the shared national history. But whether a more inclusive view of the shared history will eventually be embraced and become also a shared national memory is another story. In a democracy, this decision is an open question and remains ultimately in the hands of the voters.

2 The Dynamics of Memory

Jeffrey K. Olick
Memory in Motion: The Dynamic Turn

According to Ann Rigney, both lay and scholarly approaches to memory often adopt a model of what she calls "plenitude and scarcity" (2005). In this view, memory is "something fully formed in the past" that it is subsequently a matter of "preserving and keeping alive" (2005, 12). "Memory," Rigney writes, "is conceptualized as something that is always imperfect and diminishing, a matter of chronic frustration because always falling short of total recall" (2005, 12). As such, loss or change in memory is seen as pathological, which is one reason psychologist Daniel Schachter (2001) famously wrote of such processes as the "sins" of memory.

It is strange how persistent this view of memory has been. There has indeed long been an alternative view that reverses the value of persistence. Where some have stood under the banner that whoever "forgets" the past is "condemned" to repeat it (Santayana), others have argued that too much memory can be "the gravedigger of the present" (Nietzsche). Many memory scholars thus quote Jorge Luis Borges's (1962) short story, "Funes, the Memorious," about a boy who suffers greatly, ultimately fatally, from the inability to forget. Despite this, however, "plenitude and scarcity" is deeply embedded in our culture, which at least since what Merlin Donald (2010) has called "the exographic revolution" (the invention of external media for storing information about the past) has been particularly – and not entirely to the good – concerned with mechanisms of storage and retrieval and the completeness and accuracy of representation. The prevalence of this understanding of memory has been supercharged in the digital era with its misnamed emphasis on computing, which is more commonly nothing other than ever more sophisticated mechanisms for sorting, storing, and retrieving more and more information. The concern over storage and retrieval – and hence over plenitude and scarcity – is also enhanced by the neurological challenges posed by the increasing prevalence of old age for people who have had exponentially more diverse experiences and who have processed vastly more "information" in the course of their lives than those in previous eras.[1]

Indeed, neither storage and retrieval nor plenitude and scarcity accurately describes what psychological and cultural science know about memory. Funes's apocryphal malediction is a death sentence, after all, because the ability to sort,

---

[1] The emphasis on storage and retrieval is also shaped by the increasing emphasis on *memory that* over *memory how* that, according to Ian Hacking (1995), is a key feature of the transformation to modernity.

ignore, and forget is essential to life; Funes is thus crushed under the weight of his perception's infinitude and its permanence. Normal people, in contrast, do not perceive every aspect of a situation, do not "store" every aspect they perceive at the moment, and handle different kinds of perception in different ways. Indeed, the very term "memory" is a rather crude reduction of vastly different processes that operate both independently of each other and in different fashions, including not only the coding of semantic and episodic phenomena, but the acquisition of motor skills, emotional responses, and perceptual learning (Donald 2010). The imagery of "storage" is also misleading not simply because it emphasizes sufficiency and completeness, but because its representation of a memory trace as a static thing that has a particular location in the brain is false: memory traces are more reinforced patterns of neurological association rather than content loading of particular cells or structures; dynamism rather than stasis, process rather than location, are more of the essence, since there is no permanent location of a memory trace (Rosenfeld 1987; Sutton 1998). Retrieval, by the same token, has been shown by both psychologists and, at least since Halbwachs (1992), sociologists, to take place in the present. Why something is remembered in a particular way at a particular time and in a particular place is always an interaction between engrained dispositions (which never produce exactly the same result) and present circumstances and perspectives (which are always changing); such mnemonic productions are, moreover, shaped as much by what came between the past and the present as by either end (e.g. through reinforcement, repeated reinterpretation, interference and overwriting by intervening events, etc.). Retrieval is thus a misleading term as well, since the process is as much the result of change over time and novel circumstances as it is of preservation; change is normal rather than abnormal.

For her part, much in line with the best work since Halbwachs, Rigney has pursued "a social-constructivist approach that takes as its starting point the idea that memories of a shared past are collectively constructed and reconstructed in the present rather than resurrected from the past" (Rigney 2005, 14). Consistent with the repudiation of memory traces as specific and fixed locations in the mind, she also critiques the emphasis within cultural memory studies on "sites" of memory: "The metaphor of the memory site," she argues, "can become misleading if it is interpreted to mean that collective remembrance becomes permanently tied down to particular figures, icons, or monuments. As the performative aspect of the term 'remembrance' suggests, collective memory is constantly 'in the works' and, like a swimmer, has to keep moving even just to stay afloat" (Rigney 2008a, 345). As Rigney's close collaborator, Astrid Erll, has put it, "all cultural memory must 'travel', be kept in motion, in order to 'stay alive', to have an impact both on individual minds and social formations" (Erll 2011a, 12). For Rigney, the resultant shift from "sites" to "dynamics" in memory studies also "runs parallel to a larger shift of attention within cultural studies from products to processes, from a focus on cultural artifacts to an interest in the way those artifacts circulate and influence their environment" (Rigney 2010, 346). This shift from sites to dynamics is thus a harbinger, or part of, a wider cultural transformation, even if lay – and even some professional – vocabularies have not kept pace, burdened with both the vocabulary and fantasy of sufficiency and permanence.

As a literary scholar, it is not surprising that Rigney finds narrative essential to her dynamic view of memory. "Arguably," she writes, "all other forms of remembrance (monuments, commemorations, museums) derive their meaning from some narrativizing act of remembrance in which individual figures struggle, succumb, or survive" (Rigney 2010, 347). She even goes so far as to argue that literary form is better suited than other narrative forms like history or memoir to capture the fluidity and "recursivity" of memory dynamics: "The freedom to invent information, and not merely structure it [. . .] gives to fiction a flexibility which is absent in other forms of remembrance . . ." (Rigney 2010, 347). Fictional versions of the past, she argues, may be more durable than ones that strive for accuracy. This is because, she argues, "literary texts exemplify the fact that memorial dynamics do not just work in a linear or accumulative way. Instead, they progress through all sorts of loopings back to cultural products that are not simply media of memory [. . .] but also objects of recall and revision" (Rigney 2010, 352). According to Rigney, then, "Once cultural memory is seen as something dynamic, as a result of recursive acts of remembrance, rather than as something like an unchanging and pregiven inheritance, then the way is opened to thinking about what could be called 'memory transfer'" (Rigney 2005, 25). And this operation is not, as scholars – and certainly as advocates – of heritage sometimes imply, unchanging.

Memory thus travels, flows, crosses, and exchanges, and continually revises itself, though always in dialogue with both its past and present. And it is, moreover, clearly not merely a product of individual minds. As Aleida Assmann has written, while "Autobiographical memories cannot be embodied by another person, they can be shared with others." And,

> Once they are verbalized in the form of a narrative or represented by a visual image, the individual's memories become part of an intersubjective symbolic system and are, strictly speaking, no longer a purely exclusive and unalienable property. By encoding them in the common medium of language, they can be exchanged, shared, corroborated, confirmed, corrected, disputed, and even appropriated (Assmann 2008b, 50).

The importance of this reframing should not be underestimated: cultural memory scholarship is coming for the vaunted solipsism of the liberal subject. For his part, Michel-Rolph Trouillot, in a rather scathing critique of contemporary memory politics, has argued that "the attribution of [. . .] [the] liberal self to states, ethnic groups and nations is a major condition of possibility of collective apologies as late modern rituals," rituals which he characterizes as "abortive" (Trouillot 200, 185). And, in a reverse direction, since at least Halbwachs's implication that there are no individual memories without social frames, that liberal self itself is now up for reconsideration. The collectivist and narrativist approach to memory articulated so clearly by Rigney makes clear how.

Even though I am a sociologist, I can certainly appreciate Rigney's, Erll's, and Assmann's emphasis on literary form, in which the author has the space to play with linearity and causation. Within that world, however, it is important to recall, of course, as Proust argued so clearly, that literature's ability to represent the dynamism of memory more often works behind the backs of even the most brilliant writers. As Proust put it in his essay *Contre Sainte-Beuve,* "What intellect restores to us under the name of the past, is not the past" (Proust 1954, 19). According to Proust, this is because "as soon as each hour of one's life has died, it embodies itself in some material object [. . .] and hides there. There it remains captive, captive for ever [SIC], unless we should happen on the object, recognize what lies within, call it by its name, and so set it free" (19). Indeed, Proust adds, "it is not merely that intellect can lend no hand in these resurrections; these past hours will only hide themselves away in objects where intellect has not tried to embody them" (21). Given these allusions to death, captivity, and resurrection, the connections to later discourses of haunting or the spectral in memory studies is not entirely surprising.

While I too, then, am particularly concerned with the circulating supply of meanings, which often work on, and behind the backs of, both writers and ordinary people, however, I do so with a somewhat different – though by no means antagonistic – set of references and procedures. For social scientists (sociologists and anthropologists in particular), narratives function as, through, and alongside what Émile Durkheim (1974 [1898]) originally theorized as "collective representations." To be sure, these "representations" can include, or be structured as, narratives and other constituent elements of literary and other forms of story. But for his part, Durkheim was mostly interested in norms and symbols, which in his view are the constituent elements of social order. More so than his legatee Halbwachs, Durkheim maintained a clear distinction between what he called "individual representations" and "collective representations," though he located both in the mind of the individual (hence his famous model of Homo Duplex). Norms and meanings function as the building blocks and mechanisms of social order because people learn to think with them, and to forget that they are not themselves the source of these ideas. For Halbwachs, in his elaboration of this approach more directly to the phenomena of memory, collective representations are the frames of even the most individual memory, which combines both the individual and the collective. But they are not limited to narrative.

How, then, do collective representations circulate beyond narratives? Or, put differently, how can the theory of collective representations contribute to "the dynamic turn" Rigney identifies? The Durkheim/Halbwachs theory of collective representations has had numerous later versions and adaptations, perhaps most important in the work of Serge Moscivici (2001) on "social representations," which has been introduced into and elaborated in memory studies by Brady Wagoner (2015) and others, and in my view deserves a wider audience than it has so far received. More directly relevant to the dynamic turn, however, is, in my opinion, the epidemiological approach of Dan Sperber (1985).

While Durkheim located both individual and collective representations in the minds of individuals, Sperber recognizes that collective representations operate both within human minds and as "public representations in the environment of brains." For Sperber (1985, 74), "There exists [. . .] no threshold, no boundary with cultural representations on the one side, and individual ones on the other." The central question, then, is not whether representations are purely individual or purely collective, internal or external, ideal or material, but how they circulate. Rather, it is "why are some representations more successful in a human population, more contagious, more 'catching' than others?" (Sperber 1985, 74). Sperber thus characterizes his approach as an "epidemiology of representations." The overlaps with Rigney's, Erll's, and Assmann's dynamic view of memory are thus more than apparent.

My purpose in calling attention to this particular framework, however, which has not so far been much present in contemporary memory studies, is not to convince of its particular value or to outline its detailed implications, which would require much more space. Rather, it is merely to point out how poignant Ann Rigney's articulation of the move from products to processes that constitutes a dynamic turn in contemporary cultural studies is, and how widespread. It is also, it seems to me, further evidence of how central our inquiries into memory are as part of this important shift. While memory studies has sometimes been captive to the model of storage and retrieval and plenitude and scarcity, more than most phenomena memory forces us to confront the tensions of permanence and change. Memory studies, this body of work makes clear, is of the essence, as evanescent as that might be.

Marianne Hirsch
The Dynamics of Postmemory

In much of her recent work, Ann Rigney has powerfully reconceptualized our understandings of cultural and collective memory as a dynamic practice, rather than a static storehouse and as a process of circulation, transmission, community building through "an exchange of memories," (Rigney 2005, 15) rather than a series of sites and monuments that unchangingly and continuously recall a memorable past. As a process and practice, it is shaped by structures of mediation and remediation: "To the extent that cultural memory is the product of representations and not of direct experience, it is by definition a matter of vicarious recollection" (Rigney 2005, 15). These are structures that in her single-authored and collaborative publications, Rigney has carefully analyzed through examples from public commemoration, literature, and art.

There are deep resonances here with my own work on postmemory, resonances I would like to explore by reflecting on the temporal dynamics of postmemory (Hirsch 2012). A distinctive feature of Ann Rigney's conception of memory dynamics is that, unlike so much of the work in the field, including my own, it does not specifically focus on trauma and what has come to seem as its inevitable haunting return. Thinking about time as a form of traumatic return has in large part displaced conceptions of time as linearity, progress, and futurity but, without denying the effects of traumatic histories, Rigney contests these conceptions of time from different and more future-oriented directions.

Postmemory is indeed a "vicarious" form of recollection, a product of transgenerational mnemonic transmission of powerful collective experiences – catastrophes such as war, genocide, and extreme violence, but also transformative political movements such as coups, revolutions, and uprisings. Descendants of survivors of these monumental events re-experience them not as memories, but as postmemories; they are belated, mediated, temporally and qualitatively removed.

Postmemory describes the relationship that the "generation after" bears to the personal, collective, and cultural trauma or transformation of those who came before – to events that they "remember" only by means of the stories, images, and behaviors among which they grew up. But these events were transmitted to them so deeply and affectively as to *seem* to constitute memories in their own right. Postmemory's connection to the past is thus not actually mediated by recall but by imaginative investment, projection, and creation – by what Robert Jay Lifton has called "formulation" (Lifton 1979, 152).

In recent years, neuroscientists have substantiated these accounts by showing how trauma, specifically, can be transmitted across generations epigenetically. Thus parental trauma can be encoded in children's DNA structures, making them more vulnerable to traumatic and post-traumatic stress symptoms. Although this research is in its very beginnings and not yet conclusive, it does corroborate the accounts of members of what the writer Eva Hoffman has called the "postgenerations."

And yet, I have argued, the family is not the exclusive site of this powerful form of transfer. Family life, even in its most intimate moments, is imbricated in a collective imaginary shaped by a shared archive of stories and images, by public fantasies and projections. These inflect the dynamics by which individual and familial memories are transmitted. And this archive is often framed as familial, even if it exceeds the family frame. And yet, the temporality of mnemonic transmission is not uni- but multi-directional.

As Rigney so rightly suggests, different cultural artifacts and practices, aesthetic and institutional structures, tropes and technologies, mediate the complex psychology of postmemory, as well as the continuities and discontinuities between proximate and more distant witnesses. Across the globe, contemporary writers, filmmakers, visual artists, memorial artists, and museologists have forged an aesthetic of postmemory. They have sought forms through which to express the gaps in knowledge, the fears and terrors, that ensue in the aftermath of trauma, the excitements and disappointments that follow revolutions. Some of these tropes and artistic strategies have been remarkably consistent, constructing a global memory and postmemory aesthetic that both bridges and occludes political and cultural divides. The wall of photos at the Museo de la Memoria in Santiago, Chile, recalls similar walls in memorial museums in Phnom Penh, Paris, Amsterdam, and New York. Lists of names recall victims of the Holocaust, the Vietnam War, the 11 September 2001 bombings, and more. Memorial artists like Horst Hoheisel have worked in Germany, Argentina, and Cambodia; Daniel Libeskind in Berlin, Stockholm, and New York. Their memorial sites are dominated by idioms of trauma, loss, and mourning, invoking tropes of absence and silence, unknowability, and emptiness. They tend to rely on archival images and documents, highlighting ghosts and shadows, gaps in knowledge and transmission. They use projection, reframings, recontextualization. They juxtapose or superimpose past and present, without allowing them to merge.

What are we to make of the remarkable aesthetic continuities in the arts of postmemory across the globe? The challenge of allowing connections between divergent histories and the structures of transmission they engender to emerge is to avoid obscuring important historical specificities and particularities. But there is another challenge as well, and that is, amid the aesthetics of loss and mourning, to make space for memories of resistance, activism and the anticipation of change – to mobilize memory and postmemory oriented not only to the past but also toward a more hopeful future. To demand accountability and justice, as, for example, do the groups of mothers who walk or sit in squares from Buenos Aires to Istanbul, memorializing their disappeared children by holding photographs of them from a time before their violent disappearances or deaths. These photographs acquire new meanings every time they are held up counterintuitively to demand that their subjects, long dead, be brought back alive. In the words of the Argentinian madres: "Reaparición con vida."

In collaboration with Leo Spitzer, I have sought to define such a potentially reparative aesthetic through a notion of "liquid time" derived precisely from archival photographic images and the work of photo-based artists and my reflections here build on this earlier collaborative work (Hirsch and Spitzer 2019; 2023). Archival images are powerful media of postmemory both as remnants from a powerful past and as historical actors whose role in mobilizing what Rigney terms "memorability" also shifts as they circulate over time (Rigney 2016).

It might seem counter-intuitive that a still photograph would be open to multiple temporalities and possibilities, rather than immortalizing a single instant in time. In *Camera Lucida*, Roland Barthes famously wrote that "The photograph does not call up the past. [. . .] Not only is the photograph never, in essence, a memory [. . .] but it actually blocks memory, [and] quite quickly becomes a counter-memory" (Barthes 1981, 61). It does so through its power to occlude other forms of recollection. And yet, for Barthes, photography performs the inexorable passage of time. "By giving me the absolute past of the pose (aorist)," he writes, "the photograph tells me death in the future" (1981, 65). Indeed, Barthes sees time itself as a photographic punctum that confronts what he terms the "this will be" with the "ça a été," the "this has been." Photographic time is thus both sequential – the record of singular moments irrevocably past – and recursive, evolving in haunting returns and after-effects. These powerful "emanations" of the past in the photograph that Barthes discusses through the "punctum" open a way to see time's affective dimensions, available in photography as forms of nostalgic, melancholic memory. (Barthes 1981, 80, 82, 91). Indeed, for Barthes the photograph itself remains the same: static, unaltered, and unalterable. What changes is its effect on us, our response to it, what, dynamically, it brings forth from the past. But is the photograph static? Isn't it also contingent and, as such, malleable? If it is, then it would also allow us to re-envision the history from which it emerges, and to discover within it different possibilities and potentialities.

Walter Benjamin's notion of the "optical unconscious" presents photographs in this contingent way, evoking minute invisible elements in the photographed scene that the camera can bring to visibility. "The camera introduces us to unconscious optics as does psychoanalysis to unconscious impulses," he writes (Benjamin 1969, 237). The camera can reveal what we see without realizing it, just as psychoanalysis can uncover what we know without knowing that we do. The optical unconscious disturbs and expands conscious acts of looking and the smooth surfaces of photographic images. As images circulate, their unconscious does as well.

We can look at a photograph not only from the perspective of the photographer who controls the lens and shutter, or the institution that sponsors the photographic event, but also from that of the photographed persons at the time of the event and, perhaps, even from that of their descendants or correspondents, later, at different moments of retrospection. By unsettling the power and authority of the photographer over the image, a multiplicity of meanings can emerge from the encounter of different subjects, at the time of the image's making and subsequently. We might thus argue that the photograph anticipates a future viewer who will see in it what we could not detect at the time of its making. As Benjamin writes:

> No matter how artful the photographer, no matter how carefully posed his subject, the beholder feels an irresistible urge to search such a picture for the tiny spark of contingency, of the here and now, with which reality has (so to speak) seared the subject, to find the innocuous spot where the immediacy of that long-forgotten moment the future nests so eloquently that we, looking back, may rediscover it. (Benjamin 1931; 1999, 510)

It is this act of looking back that defines the "liquid" temporality of postmemory. The photographer Jeff Wall, in a 2007 essay on "Photography and Liquid Intelligence," bases his reflections about the "liquid intelligence" of the analog photograph on the darkroom process in which both the photographic film and the photosensitive paper onto which the film's negative image is subsequently projected is immersed in a liquid developing solution. There, each can change, often in subtle and unexpected ways, before being chemically "fixed" – again through immersion in liquid – into perpetuity. Wall wanted to complicate the pervasive view of photography as an inexorable apparatus and tool of ideological power and domination, a medium of representation which, when "fixed into permanence," embodies a "dry," and thus unalterable optical and technological "intelligence." Instead, in highlighting its "liquid intelligence" – its fluidity – he reveals the emanating connection of the photograph to nature and water: the contingencies, possibilities, potentials, and affective registers inherent in the process of image-making. In what we, therefore, want to think of as "liquid time," photographs continue "developing" when they are viewed and reviewed by different people in different presents. "Unfixed," remediated in the work of memorial artists, they remain open, active, dynamic, acquiring new meanings and associations in new circumstances, or returning to potential meanings they contained before they were immersed in the fixing solution.

How, when we look at photographs from places and times lost through violence and displacement, can we access those contingencies and potential alternative meanings? Such a fluid and multi-temporal reading displaces the retrospective gaze, shadowed by a known and predetermined outcome, that has dominated critical approaches to images of past violence, dislocation, war and genocide, as well as the canon of memory studies. It inspires us to think even further back: to the event itself and to the time before the shutter click that extracted the image. How would this dynamic rewinding alter the image and enlarge and multiply its temporalities? Might it mitigate the inevitable return of trauma? The liquid time of photography as a medium of memory and postmemory leaves space for what Ariella Aïsha Azoulay has called "potential history" – not just what was, but what might have been, and what might potentially be.

Thus archival photographs show us not only the past in which they were taken, but, through liquid time, also the present and the futures contained in that past, futures that their diverse subjects may have envisioned when they stood facing the lens. Breaking out of entrenched memories and returns of traumatic pasts, we can attempt to recuperate the lost resistances, hopes and dreams that also shaped these images – hopes and dreams that were destroyed, but that can be made present again in the liquid time of dynamic memory. This, indeed, is the spirit of Ann Rigney's work on memories of activism and of memory activism oriented toward a future that is and has always been present.

Ido de Haan

The Political Economy of Memory

In January 2022, the publication of *The Betrayal of Anne Frank: A Cold Case Investigation*, written by the Canadian author Rosemary Sullivan, caused quite a stir (Sullivan 2022). Based on research by a 'cold case team' led by a former FBI agent, Vince Pankoke, the book claimed to have identified the person who betrayed the hiding place of the Frank family, causing their arrest, and consequently the demise of the girl who became the most prominent symbol of the Holocaust, Anne Frank. As the accused was Jewish, the research team hesitated to publish his name, but as the initiator of the research project Pieter van Twisk declared, consulting a rabbi, who said the truth should prevail, convinced the team to reveal his identity with "85 percent certainty." (Wertheim 2022) Both the book and the international marketing campaign supporting its publication heavily focused on the meticulous detective methods deployed to reveal the identity of the supposed traitor. As Pankoke declared in the CBS *60 Minutes* documentary which aired at the time of the publication, he was leaning on "decades of experience and intuition" as a detective when he used the "cold case playbook" of following leads and looking for clues. The book showed pictures of the investigative team, studiously leaning over documents, of a display of names and photos connected by red lines, and of a digitally produced map of all the places in Amsterdam mentioned in the sources studied by the cold case team (Wertheim 2022).

Soon after the publication, the story of the cold case team unraveled. Not only did it become clear that most, if not all, of the information presented in the book was already known, but also that the accusation leveled against the supposed traitor was unfounded. After a group of Dutch historians published a devastating review of the research of Pankoke and his team, the Dutch publisher decided to pull the book, recalling the copies already delivered to the bookstores and apologizing to the family of the accused for the suffering the book might have caused. That policy was not followed by the American publisher HarperCollins, or any of the other twenty publishers worldwide, who profited from the fact that the book was a commercial success (Wallet 2022).

The upheaval around Sullivan's book on Anne Frank can be seen as a confirmation of the familiar observation that the memory of the Holocaust continues to dominate the public debate on recollections of the past. Moreover, the remembrance of the Holocaust is often reduced to a pious reference to Anne Frank. Innumerable are the versions of her diary – ranging from scholarly editions to graphic novels and musicals – as are the accounts of her life before, during and after her hiding in the Annex, the recollections of the people who knew her (or claimed to have known her), the stories about who betrayed her (with Sullivan's only the last in a long line of speculations about it), the accounts of those who want to draw attention to their Holocaust story by connecting it to her name ('the other Anne Frank'), and the lessons that can be drawn from her life. An equally respectable number of books has by now been published on the 'Anne Frank phenomenon' itself – generally critical of the commercialized, universalized, aestheticized, and anaesthetized nature of Anne Frank as a topos in Western and global postwar cultural memory (e.g. Barnouw 2018; Kirshenblatt-Gimblett and Shandler 2012). Both its all-pervasive presence and its deeply problematic nature make it unavoidable to reflect on the meaning of Holocaust memory within the wider context of the dynamics of memory.

In fact, the episode in Holocaust memory narrated above reveals dynamics of cultural memory that hitherto have remained undertheorized and which perhaps can most aptly be conceptualized as the political economy of memory. While the *politics* of memory are by now familiar terrain, the *economic* perspective in memory studies is often reduced to the materialist question *cui bono*, focused on the competition of victims, clashing for recognition of their traumatic experience, reparation of their losses, or support for their present and future material, territorial, or political claims (Chaumont 1997; Marwecki 2020). In the most cynical version of this line of argument, Holocaust memory is framed as the product of a 'Holocaust industry,' geared to justify the policies of the state of Israel and its continuous support by the American government – an argument that all too easily engages familiar antisemitic tropes about Jews, money and secretive political control, perverting at the same time the metaphor of the Holocaust as an instance of industrial killing (Cole 2000; Finkelstein 2000). Even if the publication of *The Betrayal of Anne Frank* clearly involved profits – and losses – the economic dynamics are not fully acknowledged by an account of material interests.

A more productive perspective is to analyze the dynamics of memory itself in terms of a political economy, in which, as Karl Marx famously claimed, "it is not the consciousness of men that determines their existence, but their social existence that determines their consciousness" (Marx 1904 [1859], 11). Translated to the context of cultural memory, one might argue, as Ann Rigney did, that "cultural memory is the outcome of a fundamentally non-egalitarian process" defined by "differential memorability" (Rigney 2016, 79). The crucial notion Rigney introduces here is that cultural memory should not be conceptualized in terms of storage and retrieval, but as a social process, defined by scarcity, in which interested parties – victims, perpetrators, bureaucrats, activists, lawyers, historians, etc. – compete as entrepreneurs for the use of a limited set of sites, objects, and models of memory. It means that "cultural memory evolves, not just through the emergence of new memorial languages, but also through the recycling and adaptation of old forms in new situations" (Rigney 2005, 22). The recycling of "old forms" is then further conceptualized as 'premediation' of experiences which resonate with available templates, creating tensions because "the desire to recall, the availability of information, and the availability of suitable models of remembrance do not always coincide" (Rigney 2005, 22). Yet another mode of recycling is 'remediation': the transfer of objects of established mediations to new media, claiming to provide a more direct, less mediated access to past experiences, while at the same time questioning, and thus drawing attention to the mediated nature of all forms of cultural memory (Erll and Rigney 2009a).

These mechanisms are clearly visible in the example above: the iconic memory of Anne Frank and her betrayal reinforce an already powerful template of commemoration, yet its remediation by a shift to criminal forensics provoked a rebuttal from historians who contested the validity of the forensic mediation. As Rigney rightly points out, familiar sites of memory, like the Annex and its inhabitants, "are constantly being reinvested with new meaning . . . [and] can be said to function as a principle of economy in cultural memory, helping to reduce the proliferation of disparate memories and providing common frame-works for appropriating the past" (Rigney 2005, 18). Thus, remediation as an "ongoing symbolic reinvestment" shapes a competition not just between conflicting memories of the past, but also between mediators and their disciplinary toolboxes (Rigney 2005, 21). In the case of *The Betrayal of Anne Frank: A Cold Case Investigation*, the author and the research team clearly delved into the repertoire of forensic science, profiting from the 'CSI-effect' and the forensic turn as a result of which the entanglement of criminal investigation methods and moral reckoning have become such a powerful rhetorical mix (Byers and Johnson 2009; Gessat-Anstett and Dreyfus 2017). Yet high stakes became big losses when historians argued, that by their account, the forensic methods produced no valid results. Moreover, the credits the cold case team claimed by adding a list of historians who supposedly had certified the outcome of the cold case research became a deficit when the list turned out to be fraudulent. Also, the lavish subsidies for the project from the Amsterdam city council turned out to be unaccounted for. Yet all of this happened without fundamentally undermining the mediation of Anne Frank as a commercial asset.

The partial collapse of the cold case investigation thus demonstrates that not all investments in cultural memory pay off. Yet at the same time, it challenges a paradox of collective remembrance Rigney proposed. Although sites of memory function as a principle of economy by creating a shared point of reference for disparate memories, at the same time "consensus ('we all recollect the same way') is ultimately the road to amnesia . . . it is ironically a lack of unanimity that keeps some memory sites alive" (Rigney 2008a, 346). Also here, political economy helps to elucidate what is at stake: the items that circulate in cultural memory are positional goods – like the exemplary calm beach, its value diminishes when demand is rising (Hirsch 1977). Their mnemonic value depends on the number of users and the varieties of use: a lot is good, too much inflates its worth. If anyone can claim the topos of Anne Frank, its value becomes subject to diminishing returns. This also applies to the proliferation of mediations. Even if the introduction of a forensic perspective in *The Betrayal of Anne Frank* fueled the contestation, in the end it diminished the iconic worth of the remembrance of Anne Frank by turning it into a cynical ploy to gain attention and to make a lot of money.

By extension, this might also be an issue for memory studies itself. As Gavriel D. Rosenfeld observed, memory studies itself seemed to have become a booming industry, and "as any casual observer of economics knows, all booms are temporary. Following periods of rapid growth, emerging industries inevitably crest" (Rosenfeld 2009, 123). Borrowing the economic vocabulary introduced by Rigney, the boom might be explained by an ongoing symbolic reinvestment in Holocaust memory. As a result, it becomes very difficult for memory scholars not to discuss the Holocaust. Even the study of multidirectional and traveling memory, demonstrating how Holocaust memory offered a template for decolonial and post-slavery memory, tends to converge all forms of memory studies into derivatives of Holocaust memory studies, and to convert Holocaust memory studies into the gold standard of all forms of memory study (Rothberg 2009).

And in the end, when Holocaust memory becomes the measure of all things, one shouldn't be surprised that it is used to account for all kinds of injustice. The recent debates ensuing in response to the 7 October attacks demonstrate how the memory of the Holocaust is used as a template, not only to interpret the killing of Jewish Israelis, but also to reinforce the condemnation of mass violence against Palestinians – as if the slaughter of human life can only be acknowledged when it can be equated with the barbarity of the Holocaust, even when that taints the memory of its actual victims. (Bashir and Goldberg 2019; Mishra 2024).

Jenny Wüstenberg
Digging Up Mnemonic Fossils

1 Introduction

A continuous focus of Ann Rigney's work has been explaining how memory changes over time and how that change is negotiated through different kinds of – human and other – actants. She has long been concerned with the *gradual* workings of memory, through different media and remediations, and should therefore be regarded as one of the foundational theorists of the new paradigm of slow memory. In her keynote address on the occasion of the first meeting of the transnational COST Action on "Slow Memory: Transformative Practices in Times of Uneven and Accelerating Change"[1] in 2022, Ann Rigney argued that "culture as memory [. . .] secretes meaning over time," acting through "slow-release," and accumulating "over time through a process of sedimentation." She was making the point that cultural memory changes at a (sometimes maddeningly) slow pace, and that slowness is thus a fundamental dynamic with which memory scholars need to contend. Around the same time, Rigney was grappling with the mobilizations around colonial and racist monuments, suggesting that one of the reasons they become foci of dissent is that they are "structurally anachronistic" and "last relics of an older regime." She also called them "mnemonic fossils," (Rigney 2022, 21) in the same article.

What struck me were the multiple geological metaphors Rigney employs here. This essay seeks to explore and spin further this generative connection between geology and memory by thinking through the different ways in which sediments and fossils relate to cultural remembrance. Taking inspiration from Ann Rigney's "memory-activism nexus," I propose a "memory-geology nexus" that encapsulates *mnemonic fossils, memory* in *fossils,* and *memory* of *fossils.* While I build on Rigney's metaphorical use of geological memory, I also consider the literal ways in which the past is recorded in the ground and how the unearthing of fossils is remembered in the Anthropocene.

---

1 https://www.slowmemory.eu/

2 A memory-geology nexus?

The memory-activism nexus (see Daphi, this volume) has helped scholars of remembrance and of social movements find common ground, and it has demonstrated that two phenomena that not long ago were regarded as quite unrelated in fact interact and overlap through multiple mechanisms. According to Rigney, "there is a feedback loop between these different practices, meaning that an integrated approach to their interplay over longer periods of time is needed" (Rigney 2020, 707). Moreover, the notion of a nexus has helped us understand that we are not dealing with a "linear progression from past to present to future," (Rigney 2018a, 372) but rather an intricate set of temporalities.

Since the "geologic turn" (Ellsworth and Kruse 2012) in the humanities and social sciences, several recent works have challenged conventional historical categories and dividing lines between the human and non-human (Chakrabarty 2021; Wood 2019; Tsing et al. 2017), as well as critically reexamining the relevant scholarly disciplines as themselves infused with racialized, colonial, and slow violence (Yusoff 2024; Nixon 2011; Bond et al. 2017). More specifically, attention to the memory-geology nexus can fruitfully highlight the complex ways in which memory studies and earth sciences speak to each other. First, both memory studies and geology are fields fundamentally concerned with explaining change. An ongoing challenge for students of memory is to "understand better the dynamics whereby collective memory can be revised and remade in response to changing social conditions and changing social imaginaries" (Rigney 2021b, 12). Geology, in turn, is above all interested in the powers of transformation that come with the passage of (deep) time. As Marcia Bjornerud writes so evocatively: "rocks are not nouns but verbs – visible evidence of processes: a volcanic eruption, the accretion of a coral reef, the growth of a mountain belt. Everywhere one looks, rocks bear witness to events that unfolded over long stretches of time" (Bjornerud 2018, 8).

Second, both geology and memory studies are fundamentally committed to relationality. They stress that the material traces of the past, though they may seem singular or unique, must in fact be regarded as part of complex networks. Thus, "monuments never stand alone" (Rigney 2022, 14) but are part of a relational web that spans different media, and are underpinned by multiple remediations. In the same way, it would be misguided to analyze a fossil find in isolation; fossils are in fact traces of a past Earth system, made up of "a number of reservoirs or spheres, which are linked to each other via complex feedback loops or fluxes that cycle energy, water, and various elements [. . .] These fluxes ensure that a change made in one reservoir will flow through and affect the entire system" (Hannah 2021, 14).

Third, both fields rely strongly on archives and both must contend with their inherent incompleteness. Michael Hannah compares the fossil record to a chain-link fence; the analogy works just as well for cultural archives:

> The fence is strong, durable, and full of holes. The fossil record is strong: we have recovered many, many fossils. It's durable: no one (despite repeated efforts) has ever been able to prove it inconsistent. [. . .] But like the chain-link fence, the fossil record is full of holes, and it's important to understand why these holes exist. (Hannah 2021, 29)

Geologists need to be cognizant that not all organisms are capable of being preserved and not all environments are suitable for preservation, as well as that species with low numbers of individuals or a limited geographical distribution are less likely to be preserved as fossils (Hannah 2021, 30–31). Memory scholars must keep in mind that our knowledge about the past is limited by unequal abilities and access to the technologies needed to record information for the future, as well as by social relations that powerfully determine who gets to decide what is recognized as significant. Historical traces of marginalized peoples are less likely to be preserved. Nevertheless, even a small selection of cultural artifacts can tell us a great deal about cultural eras, just like "index fossils" can tell us a lot about geological ones (Bjornerud 2018, 26).

Their joint interest in explaining change and in viewing the world in relational terms, and their reliance on archives of different kinds suggests that memory scholars and geologists should be able to find a common language. So what can they learn from each other?

3 Mnemonic fossils

Ann Rigney uses the term "mnemonic fossil" almost pejoratively to mark a previously significant cultural symbol as outdated. It is a metaphor expressing that memory has become "fossilized," is no longer "alive" for contemporary culture. A mnemonic fossil has entered a state of dormancy, though this does not mean that it cannot reemerge as significant. Thus, Cecil Rhodes may have become a mnemonic fossil in that nobody seemed to care any more about his service to the British empire. But subsequently, his continued presence in the memoryscapes of Britain and South Africa became a focal point for anti-racist mobilization. What "mnemonic fossil" encapsulates is therefore the dialectic nature of such material and located objects – it is precisely their ability to command respect in a bygone era – their structural anachronism – that makes their continued presence appear as a barrier to cultural change and thus a target for protesters. Studying the history of counter-memorial mobilization alerts us to the fact that the "contesting of mnemonic fossils" merely "provides the capstone to a slow process of transformation" and that memory actually "crabwalks toward the future" (Rigney 2022, 21, 34). The fossil is accordingly not the only concept from geology that might help us make sense of the slow-release dynamics of memory. We might imagine the slow washing away of a rockface that leads to a fossil find and thereby revolutionizes scientific knowledge as a metaphor for the many minor and invisible actions of activists that then enable a "moment of madness" (Zolberg 1972) where "suddenly" everything shifts. Or, we might analogize what Laura Ann Stoler has conceptualized as "aphasia" (Stoler 2011; Rigney 2022) – the notion that large parts of human history have been left out of our narratives because we simply did not recognize them as relevant – to our inability to grasp the importance of particular fossils or mineral traces. This may be simply because nobody knew they existed or because scientists could not grasp them within existing scientific paradigms or with the technologies available at a given time. In the case of the ecological past, important pieces of the story have been occluded by the sediments of time and natural forces. In human pasts one might say that this happens by processes of "cultural sedimentation" – of slow overlaying by cultural narratives that are deemed more relevant, though new developments could also gradually wash away and reveal long-forgotten pasts. What "mnemonic fossils" and "sediments" help us with as memory scholars, then, is to find an evocative language to get a feeling for the often unspectacular, but over long stretches of time immensely powerful, workings of cultural change.

4 Memory *in* fossils

If the term "mnemonic fossil" draws on geology to help us express *metaphorically* what is happening in cultural memory, thinking about "memory in fossils" points to a way of thinking about what the ground holds *literally* that is of relevance culturally. The advent of the Anthropocene challenges memory studies to begin to think ecologically, rather than merely socially. As Stef Craps writes, "humanity's geological agency and the nature and extent of the changes we have wrought on the Earth system raise problems of scale for the human imagination" (Craps 2018, 499). One way to expand our imagination is to learn more about the fundamental ecological processes in which we have meddled since the beginning of human history – with ever-increasing speed and force. The minerals and sediments that have accumulated over mega annums (millions of years before the present day) not only hold information about past life on earth, they also make up the building materials and provide the energy that powers our current lifestyles. Humans have truly become both movers and creators on a geological scale: by conservative estimates, 30 trillion tons of Earth material have so far been used or discarded by human beings, most of it since the 1950s (Zalasiewicz 2020, 26).

Getting a sense of the sheer time, complexity, and luck that was needed to create these resources and preserve fossils may help us develop a sense of "timefulness" – including a "feeling for distances and proximities in the geography of deep time" (Bjornerud 2018, 17). Among other things, this may support the creation of some humility given how briefly homo sapiens has been around and how utterly dependent our existence is on the species that came before us – right back to the very first life forms. The collaborative monument "∞Blue" at the Eden Project in Cornwall (UK) pays homage to cyanobacteria and their role in changing the nature of our planet three billion years ago by continuously blowing rings into the atmosphere (Figure 1). Developing such a sense of timefulness through creative means is important not just to develop greater care with using or transforming natural assets, but also because it can help us connect to our world deep into the future when our current actions will form a distinct and unprecedented layer

Figure 1: "∞Blue (2018) by Studio Swine, Eden Project." Photo: Jenny Wüstenberg.

of sediment with novel index fossils embedded. As paleobiologist Jan Zalasiewski writes, "the incorporation of plastics into the sedimentary record – that is, into far-future rock strata – is significant in demonstrating the geological character of this modern material" (Zalasiewicz 2020, 25). Thus, cultural memory is being encased in what David Farrier calls "future fossils" (Farrier 2021) and just like "mnemonic fossils," they may vanish from view and become obsolete – though we never know whether they might surface and gain new resonance.

While the analogies to geological processes, then, alert memory scholars to the "slow release" of culture, seeing fossils and rock layers as cultural traces of non-human and human inhabitants of the Earth breaks down barriers between species, de-centers human stories, and simultaneously spotlights the extraordinary impact of humans as the most dangerous organism that has ever roamed the planet. Though anyone confronted with the damage humans have already wrought would rightly feel anxious, it is important to remember that the geological record also holds evidence of less destructive human ways to live on the planet. In this sense, it is an archive that "may become a future resource for alternative narratives" (Rigney 2024), opening up the potential for (cross-species) solidarity.

5 Memory *of* fossils

This third component of the memory-geology nexus prompts us to ask: How are the study of geology and paleontology and their scientific insights culturally recollected and which aspects are forgotten? How is the geology as a discipline itself implicated in colonialism, racism, dispossession, and extraction? What are the dynamics of our societal memory of fossils and sediments? Our cultural fascination with life-turned-rock dates to before the creation of public natural history museums. After all, the iconic Mary Anning made her living collecting fossils that were in high demand from a nascent tourist economy. And almost from their inception, geology and its sub-fields created their own memorial culture – the collecting of specimens for scientific study went hand-in-glove with their exhibition and staging, framed by narratives around exploration, curiosity, and the control of nature and human "others" that lies at the heart of the effort to rule the planet. Thus, established museums of natural history, which every modern state has acquired, are very much implicated in creating the superstructure that helped legitimate the exploitative character of human-non-human relationships. As I argue elsewhere, the dominant "memory culture of extinction" tends to steer us towards mourning the loss of individual species represented by fossils and specimens – e.g. of the Dodo – rather than communicating what past extinction events represented in the fossil record can tell us about our past and present ecological impact and responsibility (Wüstenberg forthcoming; see also Heise 2016).

However, a different kind of memory culture of geology has also developed – one that opens up scientific knowledge to a broader audience and may even succeed in providing non-expert access to "deep time." One example is that "golden spikes," which mark the boundary between geologic time periods, in some places have become popular tourist destinations. For instance, "the type section of the Permian-Triassic boundary is in China, and to celebrate, the government developed monuments, gardens, and an interpretive centre to help geo-tourists understand the importance of the place" (Hannah 2021, 55). The golden spike as a mnemonic device has already been remediated in multiple ways – including as a graphic novel.[2] Another example is the success of high-budget documentaries such as Netflix's "Life on Our Planet," which chronicles all major mass extinction events and links past species to those still present, zipping back and forth on a (now maybe slightly more imaginable) timeline. Finally, geology already has some monumental sites of memory, like the "Felsenwelt" in the Swiss city of Luzern. This is an underground experience that takes the visitor deep into a mountain and (with the help with projections and sound) pinpoints traces of long-gone geological eras in the rock.

6 Conclusion

There are multiple axes of interaction between memory and geology, indicating once again that the division of nature and culture is no longer tenable (though really it never has been). Not only does the language of fossilization and sedimentation – sometimes punctuated by volcanic rupture – provide an evocative way to think about the slow-release workings of memory. Considering the ways in which the past is recorded in the rock and how this can be made to resonate in human memory culture seems essential given the contemporary threat facing our Earth systems. If nothing else, maybe the memory-geology nexus can help us devise ways to expand our cultural repertoires to include a sense of "timefulness," creating publicly-accessible and affective connections to deep time. The challenge is to identify with past life on Earth and to regard ourselves as considerate ancestors to future beings.

---

2 https://tamingtime.de/

William Hirst

Flashbulb Memories as Sites for Collective Memories

1 Introduction

In her essay *Differential Memorability and Transnational Activism: Bloody Sunday, 1887– 2016*, Ann Rigney (2016) brilliantly highlights two pressing issues in the study of collective memory: (1) their differential memorability and (2) the nature of their circulation. She mainly addresses these concerns as they apply to cultural memories – the books, films, art works, and large-scale commemorative practices that preserve memories for generations. I want to narrow in on what she refers to as the "first phase" of collective memory formation and circulation, the time in which the memory is a "lived" experience. Much can be gained by examining this early stage of collective memory formation. I want to illustrate this point by look-ing at *flashbulb memories* (see also Erll and Hirst 2023).

Flashbulb memories (FBM) involve an emotionally charged, often consequen-tial public event that unfolds within a limited timeframe. They are not memories of the public event itself, but memories of the circumstances of learning of the public event. People do not form flashbulb memories around every emotionally charged, consequential public event. I do not have a flashbulb memory of the confirmation of the conservative Supreme Court Judge Samuel Alito, though the confirmation was no doubt consequential, in so many ways. I have only what psychologists would call a *semantic* or *event memory*.

But on occasion, people do form FBMs. Most Americans, for instance, can readily tell you where they were when they learned about the attack of 11 Septem-ber 2001 (Hirst et al. 2009; 2015). And most French citizens can tell you where they were when they learned about the Charlie Hebdo attack (Gandolphe and El Haj 2016). The special nature of such flashbulb memories is well-recognized. Televi-sion commentators will often stress the consequentiality of an event by saying that people will remember where they were when they learned about it – not just for weeks or months, but for the rest of their lives. The general public, not just academics, find FBMs of great interest. People enjoy sharing their flashbulb mem-ories with others (Neisser 1996).

On the surface, FBMs might not be viewed as relevant to the study of collec-tive memory, since they are essentially autobiographical, not collective. After all, the FBM I have of 9/11 differs from the FBM of every other American. If one is interested in collective memories, why not study memories that people share? Additionally, FBMs have a limited temporal horizon. People may talk about their FBMs to family members, friends, acquaintances, and even strangers. They may even be passed down from one generation to the next. One study found that 89% of the generation born after 9/11 knew their parents' FBMs of 9/11 (Meyler et al. 2024). But it is unlikely that a parent's FBMs of 9/11 will be known to their great-great-grandchildren.

Ulric Neisser (1982) provided insight into why FBMs may be relevant to students of collective memory when he noted that FBMs mark the rare occasion in which personal history intersects with History writ large, that is, when the autobiographical intersects with the collective. In this way, FBMs might provide a foundation on which collective memories of the precipitating event might be built.

2 A primer on FBMs

The psychological study of FBMs began with Brown and Kulik (1977). They not only coined the term *flashbulb memories*, but observed that it is surprising people would form FBMs of public, emotionally charged, and consequential events, when it is the event itself that is necessarily emotionally charged and consequential and not the circumstance of learning of it. They argued that FBMs are distinctive enough that there might be a "special memory mechanism" at play (Brown and Kulik 1977). According to the people they surveyed, unlike most autobiographical memories, their FBMs were accurate, vivid, elaborate, and confidently held, not just for a short period of time, but, presumably, for a lifetime.

One major task of psychologists interested in memory is to uncover the mental mechanisms by which memories are formed and retained. As a result, they took Brown and Kulik's (1977) claim about a special mechanism seriously and sought additional support (see Hirst and Phelps 2015, for a review). Specifically, inasmuch Brown and Kulik relied on self-reports, a number of psychologists tested their claim about the long-term accuracy of FBMs using a test-retest methodology. Participants in these studies reported their FBMs, usually within a week of the precipitating events and then months or years later. The assumption was that the initial report was accurate; the question was: Are the recollections months or years later consistent with the initial report? Participants believed with great confidence that FBMs were accurate, but when their second report was compared to the first report, in most studies, inconsistencies were found. For instance, Hirst et al. (2009, 2015) found that, when asked about the so-called canonical features of their FBMs of 9/11 – the who, what, how, where, and when –

their American participants accurately recalled only 61% of these features after a year. However, when asked to report on a scale from 1 to 5 how confident they were in their memories, their average rating was 4.3, even after 10 years. The widely accepted conclusion of those studying FBMs is that no special memory mechanisms may be needed to account for the characteristics of FBMs.

3 FBMs, community-specificity, and collective identity

Brown and Kulik (1977) also observed that FBMs were community-specific. In their study, Black participants reported having FBMs of the assassinations of John F. Kennedy, Martin Luther King, Jr., and Malcom X, whereas White participants only held FBMs of the assassination of Kennedy and, to a lesser degree, King. Few White participants reported FBMs for Malcolm X. Subsequent research reinforced this finding. For example, in one study, French citizens reported a FBM of the death of their former President, François Mitterrand, whereas French-speaking Belgians did not (Curci et al. 2001). It would appear, to follow-up on Neisser (1982), FBMs are an occasion in which personal history insects with History writ large, but only for affected communities.

Importantly, not only are FBMs community-specific, but they are also widely held within a community. In their study of FBMs, Hirst et al. (2015) found that 99.5% of their American sample reported possessing a FBM after 10 years. Similarly, 98.8% of Brown and Kulik's (1977) participants reported a FBM for the assassination of Kennedy.

When considered together, these two observations suggest that FBMs can serve as a marker of community membership. That is, they can ground not just personal identity, but also collective identity. It is not simply that every person who identifies strongly as an American will possess a FBM of, let's say, 9/11, but that a failure to possess a FBM of 9/11 would suggest a weak identification with the US, even if one is a US citizen. In one survey, for instance, respondents rated a fictional character without a vivid 9/11 FBM as identifying less as an American than a fictional character with a vivid 9/11 FBM (Cyr et al. 2023). They did not expect a Briton to necessarily have a 9/11 FBM. Along the same lines, respondents to another survey thought that a person with progressive dementia who could no longer recollect their FBM of 9/11 was, as a result, losing their identity as an American (Merck and Hirst 2022).

4 FBMs and collective memory formation

These varying characteristics of FBMs provide a foundation for the formation of collective memories for the precipitating event in various ways.

First, the linkage between one's personal story and a public event makes the public event more memorable and perceived as more important. Information is more memorable if one can relate it to one's self (Rogers et al. 1977).

Second, because of their bearing on collective identity, people feel an obligation to remember their FBMs. The same may also apply to memories of the FBM-eliciting event. As with FBMs, people's memory for the precipitating event is usually not extremely accurate or detailed (Hirst et al. 2009; 2015), but having a FBM of 9/11 ensures that you remember that the events of 9/11 occurred.

Third, perhaps because of their role in collective identity construction, people talk to others about their FBMs (Neisser 1996). They involve strong emotions, and people like to talk about emotionally charged events (Rimé 2009). Perhaps more importantly, people like to talk about events that had a strong impact on themselves, and, in the case of FBMs, their collective identity (Ochs and Capps 2009). It is not dissimilar to people getting together and realizing that they had all gone to summer camps in their youth. Inevitably, they will end up recounting to each other their summer camp experiences, establishing a common bond.

Fourth, and related to the previous point, because one has a FBM of, let's say, 9/11, one can say "I was there" and as a result can serve as a witness to the event (Hirst et al. 2022). Of course, most individuals were not 'there' in the same way as someone who was at Ground Zero on 11 September was there. Most Americans may only have witnessed it by watching it unfold on television. However, because they lived through the event – and have a FBM of doing so – they have an epistemic relation to the event that differs, for instance, from what might be expected from historians hundred years from now, even if they watched the same television programs.

Finally, because FBMs are community-specific and because they provide an epistemic quality to a memory that differs from a cultural memory acquired many years thereafter, one needs to be hesitant about claims about the transnational character of collective memory, at least in some instances. Yes, they can travel across national boundaries, a point Rigney (2016) and others have stressed. But one needs to recognize that even as memories circulate across national boundaries, the memory held by an affected community differs qualitatively from the memory of those who live outside the affected community. The case of 9/11 is interesting in this regard. The unfolding events of 9/11 were immediately broadcast live across the world. And, interestingly, people across the globe report FBMs of 9/11 (Curci and Luminet 2006). Moreover, 9/11 has become the focus of a large number of films, novels, and other cultural products that also cross national boundaries. Indeed, in order to stress the transnational character of 9/11, the September 11 Memorial Museum in New York begins their exhibition with recordings of people across the world recounting their 9/11 FBMs.

But, as the discussion above underscores, the function of these FBMs for an American differs from that for a German or a Turk. For the American, it is critical as an American to have a FBM of 9/11 in order to be a good American. As noted, this might be one reason that Americans assign high confidence ratings to their memories of 9/11. If they want to view themselves as a good American, then their FBMs of 9/11 must be elaborate, vivid, and accurate. The German's and Turk's identity as a German or Turk does not rest on their possessing a FBM of 9/11. They can be a good German or Turk even if they cannot recollect where they were when they learned of 9/11. This may be one of the reasons the confidence Germans, for instance, have in their FBMs has declined over time (Echterhoff and Hirst 2006).

5 Final thoughts

Ann Rigney has masterfully considered the differential memorability and circulation of cultural memories. I have tried to stress that the need to consider the early stage in which "collective memories" are still part of one's autobiography. To be sure, as time passes, and the memories cross many generational boundaries, transforming themselves from "lived" memories to "cultural" ones, personal recollections become less relevant. Nevertheless, they create the foundation on which these more long-lasting collective memories can be built. The presence of a FBM makes the memory of the event more memorable, more essential in confirming one's collective identity, more epistemically authoritative, and more distinctly community-based. Of course, not all enduring collective memories have elicited FBMs in the public as they unfolded. But FBMs are means of propelling a collectively experienced event into the collective memory of a community.

Sophie van den Elzen

Eccentric Agency: Women 'Remembering' Chattel Slavery

1 Introduction

One of Ann Rigney's memorable conceptual metaphors is her description of cultural memories as a "self-perpetuating vortex of symbolic investment" (2005, 18). Sites of memory, she argues, are not at all holdovers from the past whose relevance slowly erodes (the "plenitude and loss model" (Rigney 2005, 12), but instead are constantly invested in as people attentively engage with new cultural representations of stories from, and about, the past. This cultural model for the study of vicarious memory at first seems counter-intuitive, as Rigney points out, as it accords rather little agency to past events. Over time, media-based and cultural mechanisms in the present, such as artists' relationship to formal traditions, the drive towards repetition, and the "agency of the aesthetic" (Rigney 2021b), become increasingly important factors in the dynamic patternings of cultural memory. Rigney's naturalist image of a vortex of currents, which not only maintains a balance of impersonal opposing forces but begins to exert its own, independent drawing power, provocatively illustrates how shifting constellations of existing stories and models both maintain the cherished and produce the new. The seeming gravitational pull of sites of memory (the "weight of history") is in fact the result of a dynamic cluster of active forces.

Striking as the naturalist first half of the image is, the more abstract second half is equally important. Though the vortex is self-perpetuating, investments in it are not: the powerful cultural forces called up in the vortex are the result of people's continuous efforts. As Rigney writes, sites of memory "elicit intense attention" on the part of people participating in remembrance (2005, 18), and individual investments of attention and creative effort can leave significant and often unexpected marks in the cultural record. Ultimately, it is this space for the agency of individual expression that makes this model electrifying – sites of memory are charged with creative, social, and political possibility. Picking up on this thread of Rigney's work, I would like to use this occasion to reflect on the power of what, in keeping with the logic of her metaphor, one might call "ex-centric agency": investments of memory work that work obliquely to the center of the vortex, or resolutely miss the point. What part do they have to play in the construction of memory, and where and why might we want to look for them? I will discuss three examples of eccentric agency among women recalling the historical institution of chattel slavery over the past two centuries. Ana Araujo has chronicled how since the 1990s, there has been an increasing drive around the world to create public, official, and institutional memories of the kidnapping and enslavement of Africans (2020), and the ways in which the African diaspora has pioneered new modes of representing this history. My cases represent other engagements with this world history, which also shape its legacy in the Western world, including the personal, the appropriative, and the libidinal, involving different women's attempts to think together histories of race and gender.

2 Idiosyncratic selections: the archives of Anne Knight

The first case of eccentric agency worth considering is that of personal archiving. Archiving has long been overlooked as a practice of political activism (see also Salerno and Rigney's 2024 volume), as its effects work in a different, generally much longer timespan than more ostentatious actions often associated with protest. Yet as the case of Anne Knight illustrates, despite being an undervalued or even criticized individual undertaking, it has powerful potential to shape memory down the line. Knight (1786–1862) was a small-town Quaker and one of England's most radical voices both for the abolition of slavery and for the equality of women. In keeping with social and religious gender expectations of her circle, she did not speak in public until later in life, choosing to support the cause of antislavery by gender-appropriate activities such as contributing to fundraising bazaars and driving petitions. In her sixties, two events catalyzed her development of a more public persona. In 1840, she attended the World's Antislavery Convention in London, where she witnessed the participation of women delegates from the US as well as the fierce debate this drew. In 1848, she was on one of her regular visits to Paris, when revolution overthrew the July monarchy and paved the way for immediate abolition in the French colonies. Seeing this, she became convinced that the year could prove a window of opportunity for women's rights, and she became a public advocate for the cause.

When she made this transition, she relied on an archive of anti-imperial, abolitionist, and feminist materials which she had been amassing since the 1820s. She excerpted relevant tracts in her notebooks and rearranged and recombined quotes and information in deliberate ways, in order to have them printed onto colorful labels to attach to her correspondence, or to hand out in the form of little pamphlets from a workbag which she was to carry on her hip. Within her familial and coreligionist transatlantic antislavery circles her efforts were intensely scrutinized and denounced as embarrassing to the antislavery campaign: they were thought to miss the point at several levels. Her intensified efforts took on a different significance in Paris, 1848. She began consistently introducing herself as a living link between the emancipatory struggles of the enslaved and of women, and she reprinted her labels in the French feminist press. These included, for instance, the following text:

> That Which Is
> *Young women of the Gauls* had the right to make laws, they were *legislators.*
> *African women* have in some tribes, *the right to vote.*
> *Anglo-Saxon women* participated, in England, *in the legislature.*
> *Women of the Hurons*, one of the strongest tribes in North America, formed a *council, and the elders followed their advice.*
> See, in antiquity and with people who have been barely civilized, women enjoyed rights which modern peoples refuse them, in the countries where Christianity reigns, *where universal brotherhood is proclaimed, without distinction of sex.*
> We fight for liberty!

As this historically far-reaching and, for the period, cosmopolitan statement suggests, Knight mobilized decades of her personal memory work at a crucial moment in time. In the context of the Parisian women's rights campaign of the late 1840s, Knight's efforts made a concrete contribution: she helped to contextualize women's striving in a broader world-historical movement for emancipation, rather than a French Republican frame. Viewed over the long term, the eccentric agency she exerted in her memory work of selecting, preserving, recombining, and reprinting, bore rare fruit.

3 Multidirectional projections: the productive reception of Hiram Power's *The Greek Slave*

A second form of eccentric agency worth considering is that which, with Michael Rothberg, one might call "multidirectional projection." As Rothberg explored in *Multidirectional Memory* (2009), the stories of marginalized groups can serve both as catalysts and as models that allow stories of an unconnected marginalized group to take shape. This process is made explicit on the rare occasions that people explicitly compare histories, but rather than a fringe phenomenon, this deliberately eccentric move is an engine of what Rigney, in her study of the reception of Walter Scott, terms "productive remembrance" (2012a). The transatlantic feminist reception of Hiram Powers' sculpture *The Greek Slave*, considered the most well-known American sculpture of the nineteenth century, illustrates this force, as throngs of viewers projected onto her white marble their own world-historical concerns (Fig. 1).

Figure 1: Hiram Powers' *The Greek Slave.* From the Washington National Gallery of Art's collection. Wikimedia. https://commons.wikimedia.org/wiki/Category:The_Greek_Slave#/media/File:Hiram_Powers,_The_Greek_Slave,_carved_1846,_NGA_166484.jpg. https://creativecommons.org/publicdo main/zero/1.0/legalcode.

Completed in 1844, *The Greek Slave* depicts an Orientalist, fantastical scene from the Greek War of Independence (1821–1829). It shows a nude young woman who stands with her arms bound in chains. She is about to be sold into a Turkish harem, but her demure gaze and the locket and Christian cross draped over her discarded clothing indicate her chastity, stoicism, and inner resistance. As Joy Kasson has detailed, Powers and his agents provided copious commentary and documentation to manage audiences' attitudes towards the nude, as well as the titillating subject matter of Oriental sex slavery, which was a popular theme in the West at the time (1990, 48–51). Nevertheless, in its reception in both the US and the UK, where it was displayed in the Crystal Palace Exhibition of 1851, the statue provoked mnemonic associations and a powerful productive reception of its own. Disregarding the professed Greek reference of the work, *Punch Magazine* commented on the irony of this statue's furore against the backdrop of the intensifying struggle against slavery when it published a cartoon of a "Virginian Slave, Intended as a Companion to Powers" (Kasson 1990, 66). The record of prominent women's response to the sculpture is especially intriguing. Abolitionist Lucy Stone described her epiphany upon viewing the statue as emblematic of womanhood as a whole needing to be freed, with a delicate chain of historical associations directing her to redouble her efforts for the women's cause, as well as that for the enslaved. Meanwhile, English poet Elizabeth Barrett Browning used the "alien Image" to direct attention from the Greek context to that of the West: "To so confront man's crimes in different lands / with man's ideal sense/ [. . .] Catch up in thy divine face not alone / East griefs, but West, and strike and shame the strong / by thunders of white silence, overthrown" (ll. 7–14). Browning recontextualized the work in a tradition of Anglo-American philanthropy, and with her gendered description of "man's crimes" and the passivity of the female subject also questioned the gender dynamics of this history.

Possibly less susceptible to the sculptor's intended male gaze, women projected onto the image alternative histories. They saw reflected in it their own perceptions of historical parallels between the position of women and that of the enslaved, in the case of Stone, as well as the question of women's role in nineteenth-century moral reform, in the case of Browning. The overwhelming popularity of the sculpture was rooted in these eccentric multidirectional gestures, which lent it its power.

4 Defiant appropriation: Kara Walker's artistic reflections

The imaginative legacy of chattel enslavement has not at all abated, as descendants of its victims and its perpetrators continue to contend with its world-historical effects. The final gesture of eccentric agency I would like to consider here is that of defiant appropriation, which contemporary artist Kara Walker displays throughout her work and artistic reflection. Her carnivalesque silhouetted animations, sometimes presented as life-sized installations, play with the plot conventions and stereotypes of nineteenth-century melodrama and historical media to present grotesque, often scatological tales of violent Southern plantation life. Rather than engaging in an outright collision with nineteenth-century forms, Walker intimately appropriates them, producing unsettling satirical works which are dense with social and psychological critique. Her 2014 colossal sculpture of a sphinx with stereotyped African-American facial features and a knotted headdress may serve as an example of these aspects of her work. Fashioned from white sugar, it commented on the slave-powered sugar industry, and Walker simultaneously invoked both obscure nine-teenth-century confectionary art and modern-day sexual stereotype as she titled it *A Subtlety, or the Marvelous Sugar Baby.*

By appropriating near-obsolete media, Walker visualizes how her imagination of entanglements of race and gender is steeped in historical plots and conventions. In this ultimately highly personal artistic expression, sometimes verging on exhibitionism, she simultaneously probes the collective historical imagination to question how deep the roots of cultural stereotype and received tradition reach. As she wrote in a typescript displayed at her 2022 exhibition "A Black Hole is Everything a Star Longs to Be":

> "No, no, don't do that" [the intellect] seems to say "Yee-haw! Jes'you try n' stop me!" is the reb's reply

> "How," you might be inclined to ask, "do you get from a slave mistress to a *yankee/reb*?" Simple, they're all in me or their shadows have been in me at some point or another– stroking me up and stabbing me in the head.

Walker's polarizing work passionately engages with the history of enslavement, but at an angle which appears directly at odds with contemporary attempts to create a common language of national commemoration. Her art arrestingly visualizes a wider dynamic of defiant appropriation, another form of oblique memory work worth considering when pondering the further reaches of mnemonic actors' symbolic investment.

The vortex is a phenomenon of what is known as "turbulent flow." Rather than smooth layers and steady streams, its centrifugal power is created by the enduring frictions of contrary forces. In this essay, I have reflected on memory dynamics that are eccentric, and contribute to the vortex by exerting their power outside of the center, at an angle or even in collision course. Idiosyncratic selections, multidirectional projections and defiant appropriations are clear examples of such forces. Attending to them brings into view a broader sense of the agency of "intense attention" to sustain memory.

Antonius C.G.M. Robben
Transmutations of an Argentine Site of Traumatic Memory

1 Introduction

"This is all?," the German tourist said when we entered a building marked *Clandestine Detention, Torture and Extermination Center*. In 2010, I joined a guided tour in Buenos Aires of the Officers' Quarters of ESMA where five thousand disappeared captives had been detained and assassinated during Argentina's last dictatorship. What irritated the German tourist was that the ESMA didn't resemble the Nazi concentration camps she had seen on school visits.

The Navy Mechanics School or ESMA (Escuela Superior de Mecánica de la Armada) was a complex of over thirty buildings in the city of Buenos Aires where naval non-commissioned officers were trained. There were dormitories, classrooms, dining rooms, an infirmary, a chapel, and so forth. The building that housed the Officers' Quarters (Casino de Oficiales) was converted in 1976 into a secret detention center for captured guerrilla insurgents that were trying to achieve a social revolution by violent means since 1973 and political opponents of the military regime that had in March 1976 overthrown the civilian government of Isabel Martínez de Perón, the widow and successor of the populist leader Juan Domingo Perón. After the fall of the dictatorship in 1983, the acronym ESMA became a synonym for the Navy's secret detention center located in the Officers' Quarters (Figure 1) (Naftal 2021, 71–76).

ESMA is today a nationally and internationally recognized site of memory. This was not so when it was identified in 1976 as a place suspected of detaining disappeared captives. Memory sites and collective memories are dynamic, as Ann Rigney (2008a, 345–346) has argued: "collective memory is constantly 'in the works' and, like a swimmer, has to keep moving even just to stay afloat (because) the canon of memory sites with which a community identifies is regularly subject to revision by groups who seek to replace, supplement, or revise dominant representations of the past as a way of asserting their own identity." In the case of ESMA, such revisions were driven by changing civil-military relations, repeated state interventions, and human rights activism. I agree with Ann Rigney (2008a, 348) that memory sites are dynamic because of re-narrations and changing memory practices. Nevertheless, this scholarly view does not coincide with the understanding of people competing about the representation of the past at memory sites. They regard memory dynamics as a political struggle that will eventually be decided in immutable memory sites.

Figure 1: Officers' Quarters at the Navy Mechanics School (ESMA) in Buenos Aires, Argentina. Credits: photo by author.

This chapter focuses on how ESMA was repeatedly re-narrated during the aftermath of the military regime by competing groups that tried to impose a hegemonic meaning on ESMA. ESMA's different designations awakened different remembrances of the memory site among survivors, and evoked changing mental associations among the site's visitors and Argentine society at large. The interaction between different collective memories and the accompanying designations turned ESMA into a dynamic site of traumatic memory that competing groups tried to crystalize into a petrified memory of the past.

2 From unofficial detention center to extermination center

A fact-finding mission by Amnesty International, conducted in November 1976, mentioned ESMA as one of seven Unofficial Detention Centers in the province of Buenos Aires where disappeared Argentine civilians might be held captive. The mission was obstructed by the dictatorship and ridiculed in the censored press, but the visit of the Inter-American Commission on Human Rights (ICHR) in September 1979 was taken seriously. The ICHR stated in its report that the commission had been informed about secret locations that were called concentration camps. The inspection of ESMA was inconclusive. The mystery was solved years later. The ESMA captives had been moved to a former spiritual retreat of the Catholic Church on a small island called *Silence*. In an official reaction to the ICHR report, the Argentine government stated that the commission's failure to find any disappeared detainees was proof that the secret centers did not exist.

More solid evidence was provided in October 1979 by three former captives who had been sent into exile after spending several years at ESMA and testified in the French parliament. They presented the facility's ground-plan and identified its personnel and captives. The three ex-disappeared called ESMA a "concentration and extermination camp" (Martí et al. 1995, 10). There was the implicit suggestion that genocide was taking place in Argentina.

Argentina's defeat in April 1982 in the Falkland/Malvinas War with Great Britain increased the protests against the dictatorial regime. Human rights marches and labor protests hastened its fall and a return to democracy in December 1983. The new government immediately created a truth commission to investigate the whereabouts of the disappeared. The commission located 340, what they called, Secret Detention Centers. This term did not match the traumatic experiences of the ex-disappeared, such as the three exiled captives who had testified in France in 1979. More detailed information was revealed when nine junta members were put on trial in April 1985. They were sentenced to lengthy prison terms in a verdict that identified ESMA as a Clandestine Detention Center.

The conviction of the junta commanders, and especially the subsequent prosecution of hundreds of middle-ranking officers, rapidly deteriorated the already tense civil-military relations. Several mutinies by army personnel took place, which resulted in two laws in 1986 and 1987 that ended the trials. The presidential pardons and amnesties of 1989 and 1990 appeased the armed forces but were a blow to the human rights movement that in response decided to concentrate its efforts on the collective memorialization of the military's state terrorism and crimes against humanity.

The amnesties and pardons of 1989 and 1990 had been promulgated by President Carlos Menem to improve the civil-military relations and pacify a polarized Argentine society. The strategy ended when Navy Captain Francisco Scilingo confessed in 1995 that he had participated in two death flights at which sedated ESMA captives were dropped from a plane flying over the Atlantic Ocean. Large street protests erupted, and the human rights movement launched in December 1997 the plan to construct a memory park in Buenos Aires. President Menem tried to regain the political initiative by passing Decree 8/98 on 6 January 1998 that ordained the relocation of ESMA's personnel and equipment to the Naval Base of Puerto Belgrano. According to the decree, this move would have great symbolic value and show the Argentine people's desire for reconciliation. The decree also contained a devastating decision: the Ministry of Defense would demolish the entire complex of over thirty buildings to create a park. Within days, two relatives of disappeared persons filed a constitutional appeal against the decree and proposed to declare ESMA a cultural patrimony similar to Auschwitz.

Clearly, President Menem had overplayed his hand. The human rights movement regarded his reconciliation policies as means to undo Argentina's collective memory of a brutal dictatorship. The movement launched several proposals for national memory sites and encouraged initiatives from neighborhood and grassroots organizations throughout Argentina. By 2009, there were already two hundred memory sites in the city of Buenos Aires alone, including ESMA. ESMA's memorialization was embraced by five former captives who met in 1998 to share their traumatic experiences and put them in print. They compared ESMA to a Nazi concentration camp. Parallels were drawn between the treatment of the inmates, the selection of captives for forced labor, and the systematic killing of detainees (Actis et al., 2001, 296–297). This comparison helped other former captives and relatives of the disappeared to make sense of their traumatic experiences and made them regard ESMA as a concentration and extermination camp.

The killing of disappeared persons was by then described as genocide by former captives and the human rights movement, but the Argentine state and society were not ready to draw this far-reaching conclusion. Elsewhere I have explained why there was no genocide in Argentina (Robben 2018, 179–190). What my argument boiled down to was that people were assassinated for what they did or for what they were believed to have done or might do, but not for who they were.

On 13 February 2001, the Argentine Supreme Court ruled that the complex of buildings on the ESMA grounds could not be demolished because that would destroy valuable criminal evidence about the still unresolved disappearances. Several plans were proposed through the years, including a golf course, a polo field, a lake, luxury apartments, and a memory museum, until President Menem's successor, Néstor Kirchner, decreed on 24 March 2004 that ESMA, as the country's largest clandestine detention center, would be converted into a memory museum.

In the following years, two names circulated in the human rights movement: Clandestine Detention and Disappearance Center and Clandestine Detention, Torture and Extermination Center. Although the designations were used interchangeably, they represented different views. The first term emphasized the individual suffering of the disappeared whose death had not yet been established. It assumed the activist position that disappearances are ongoing crimes. The second term suggested that the disappeared had been assassinated as members of a group condemned to genocidal extinction, and that they should be memorialized in permanent sites of memory, such as ESMA.

Argentina's Supreme Court derogated in June 2005 the amnesty laws of 1986 and 1987, and ruled in July 2007 that the presidential pardons of 1989 and 1990 were unconstitutional. The released military and police, including the junta commanders, were now prosecuted again. The renewed trials revealed the magnitude of the disappearances that were described by human rights lawyers as genocide.

In November 2007, the *Museum of Memory* was established at ESMA's former Officers' Quarters and inaugurated in May 2015. The Museum applied in 2021 for a World Heritage status, arguing that ESMA "is nationally and internationally recognized as the most prominent symbol of the illegal repression carried out and coordinated by the dictatorships of the region on the grounds of the enforced disappearance of persons" (Naftal 2021, 155). This initiative aimed to congeal the dynamic memory process and create a permanent memory site whose meaning would become hegemonic after UNESCO's stamp of approval. In September 2023, UNESCO decided that ESMA would become a world heritage site under the name *ESMA Museum and Site of Memory – Former Clandestine Center of Detention, Torture and Extermination*. This designation seemed the end of a long trajectory pursued by the human rights movement. However, Argentina's newly-elect vice-president Victoria Villarruel, an apologist for the military dictatorship, suggested in November 2023 that the ESMA should become a school again. This radical move would turn back time and erase ESMA as Argentina's most prominent site of traumatic memory.

3 Final remarks

The growing recognition of Argentina's ESMA as an emblematic extermination center confirms Ann Rigney's insight that memory and activism are deeply entangled (2016), and that memories are shaped through the re-narration and re-naming of traumatic places. The laws that dismissed the charges against police and military in 1986 and 1987, and the amnesties and pardons of indicted and convicted perpetrators in 1989 and 1990, ended the massive human rights protests of the 1980s that had demanded the prosecution of the perpetrators of torture, disappearance, and assassination. The human rights movement shifted its strategy from accountability to memorialization. Whereas memorialization had before been rejected as accepting the death of the disappeared, it was valorized in the

1990s as a way to instill the acknowledgement of past atrocities in Argentina's collective memory. This memorialization strategy opposed the military's denial of those atrocities by creating memory sites like ESMA, and by divulging the testimonies of surviving captives. These former inmates narrated their experiences in a language common to Holocaust narratives and compared ESMA to a Nazi concentration camp. This correspondence was reinforced in ESMA's official designation as an extermination center and helped shape Argentina's collective memory about the military dictatorship.

The struggle over ESMA's name was waged in the full awareness that designations have political consequences. Step by step, ESMA's national prominence as a site of traumatic memory was reinforced when in the mid-2000s the systematic disappearances were described as genocide. Genocide was the only crime that was on a par with the collective trauma of the disappearances. Once this memory politics proved successful, it was taken abroad by convincing UNESCO that ESMA represented similar sites of traumatic memory in other Latin American countries and was therefore worthy of becoming a World Heritage site.

Susannah Radstone

Citrus: An Experiment in Memory Work

1 Introduction: memory work

This chapter focuses on an experiment in a variety of memory research called memory work, prompted by Ann Rigney's call for memory studies to explore a spectrum of memories that includes not only suffering and trauma, but hope and happiness, too (Rigney 2018a). My memory work takes its lead from a research practice that falls somewhere between the scholarly and the creative.

Collective or individual memory work involves exploring and analyzing memories produced as part of the research process. Memory work practitioners have deployed various methods, both to prompt remembering and to analyze memories. These include writing, reading aloud in a group and then collectively analyzing memory stories that have been prompted by a theme (Haug 1987),[1] working individually or in groups with memories prompted by photographs from the family or personal archive (Kuhn 1995; Kuhn 2007; Spence 1986)[2] and producing memoir-like reflexive writing that binds together memories and analysis (Fraser 1984; Kuhn 1995; Steedman 1986). The latter method is deployed in my own experiment.

Like autoethnography, memory work involves self-reflection to research the relations between self and society (Adams et al. 2014, 2). Memory work often straddles the boundary between research and practice and, like autoethnography, the primary research object of memory work is the researcher/s themselves. The specificity of memory work lies, however, in its focus on researchers' memories, which the method takes as its raw material for a mode of analysis informed by the insights of memory studies. Memory work takes two of the central tenets of memory studies as its starting point. In memory work, memory is approached as anything but a transparent record of the past, and memory – personal memory – is understood to be permeated by cultural genres, modes, and regimes. Focusing on absences, contradictions, figures, and tropes, memory work reveals memory's entanglements with culture and politics.

The concept of memory work was introduced into memory studies via Frigga Haug's book about collective research into women's memories (Haug 1987). Mem-

---

1 For an account of doing memory work by means of writing, sharing, and analyzing themed memory stories, see Clare and Johnson 2000.
2 For an account of doing memory work with photographs see Kuhn 2007.

ory work has been shaped, too, by oral history research that has tracked cultural genres, plots, and tropes as they inform personal testimonies (Chamberlain and Thompson 1998; Passerini 1987). Passerini demonstrates that even personal memories are made up of diverse shared materials – a finding echoed in the psychologist Mark Freeman's understanding of memory as "a curious amalgam of fact and fiction, experiences and texts, documentary footage, dramatizations, movies, plays, television shows, fantasies, and more" (Freeman 2002, 199).

In the 1980s in the UK, a number of developments in the disciplines of cultural studies and history also played their part in shaping memory work practice. Interest in the memories of "ordinary people" was spurred both by Gramscian Marxism's focus on finding the "good sense" within "common sense" (Hall 2017) and the commitment of radical history groups to the exploration of local and community memories. Under these influences, and led by Stuart Hall, explorations of memory at the Birmingham Centre for Contemporary Cultural Studies (Popular Memory Group 1982) eventually resulted in a research group undertaking its own memory work (Clare and Johnson 2000).

Tracking relationships between visual media – particularly film and photography – and memory has proved particularly productive for memory work. Beginning with an understanding that the conventions of family photography are entangled with the politics of representation, feminist-oriented memory work has re-worked (Walkerdine 1991) or analyzed (Kuhn 1995) photographs from the family album to gain distance from their cultural/political normativity. This memory work revises the memories – and sense of self – associated with the images that are its focus. Kuhn's memory work goes beyond tracking the permeation of personal memories with remembered still or moving images. By analyzing the part played by films in her own memories, Kuhn reveals both that our individual memories meld the personal with the cultural and that the activity of remembering mediates shared cultural resources in line with the desires, contingencies, and particularities of the present (Kuhn 1995, 105–121).

The memory work outlined above provides memory studies with a wealth of insights into the relationships amongst memory, identity, culture, and politics, as well as into the part played by the present in the shaping of memories. Notable however, and all too understandably, particularly in feminist memory work (Haug 1987) and in memory work that has explored the injuries of class (Steedman 1986) and "race" (Khawaja 2022), has been the common focus on difficult and painful memories. The experiment that follows treads a different path. In focusing on memories of hope, my memory work follows Rigney's call for memory studies to extend its range beyond explorations of suffering and trauma, to include research into positive and joyous memories (Rigney 2018a).

While writing, I became aware of an experience best likened to swimming against the tide, as I sought to stay with my theme of hope and avoid slipping into the mnemonic modes of elegy, mourning, and grief. Experience – including remembered experience – is multi-dimensional and laden with diverse affects, so it is hardly surprising that my memories of hope emerged entangled with sorrow as well as with joy. As Ann Rigney reminds us, however, those genres and tropes of mourning and trauma have been dominant in my own research area of cultural memory studies (Rigney 2018a). In the experiment that follows, I have sought to explore hopeful memories, aware, all the while, of a psychical/cultural/scholarly propulsion towards plotting and figuring my associations in terms of grief, mourning, and unhappiness. I offer my exploration in the hope that it will encourage others to expand the corpus of memory work by undertaking their own experiments.

2 Citrus: remembering hope

During the weeks following moving house, hungry, tired, and with bodies and souls in disarray, my partner Felicity and I found ourselves frequenting Citrus, an unassuming family-run Sri-Lankan buffet restaurant on a street corner in North Fitzroy, only a ten-minute drive away from our new house. We're not the first to have discovered Citrus. A friend's daughter told us we should go and when we first walked through the door, the hubbub of conversation on the warm, curry-scented air met us like an embrace and – for me, at least – a home-coming. That Sunday night, it looked to us as though the whole of North Fitzroy was there: Large multi-generational family groups sharing what looked like a regular Citrus get-together, couples sitting more quietly at the smaller tables near the windows, big groups of younger people restoring themselves at the tail end of their weekends. And now we were there too – all of us gathered together, enjoying, and maybe, like me, feeling comfort, feeling joy.

To gather and eat at one kind of Indian restaurant or another has been a part of my life for almost as long as I can remember. On one never-to-be-repeated occasion, sometime in the 1960s, mum, dad, me, and my sister visited The Great India Restaurant on Lower Sloane Street, near our council flat, for what must have been our first and only Indian meal *en famille*. But Dad didn't like the food and although the restaurant (established in 1958) is still there today, we never went back. But for me, like so many in London and across the British Isles, this was the beginning of a lifetime of evenings spent around the tables of London's Indian restaurants. As I plot the lines and loops of my decades across the map of London's Indian eating places, I'm remembering too that from the 1970s onwards, those restaurants, with their gentle colored lights and intense aromas, became our everyday, here-and-now utopias.[3] My group of friends inhabited a hopeful milieu inspired by feminism, cultural studies, and psychotherapy. Of course, we didn't always agree on everything and there were tensions and break-ups. Even so, in hindsight, our gatherings around those Indian restaurant tables seemed to prefigure the egalitarian and kinder world envisioned by the often ill-fated struggles of the past – a world that our own politics placed just within reach – or so we hoped.

From 1971, the budget-friendly Diwana Bhel Poori House in Drummond Street, near Euston Station welcomed the hungry – some just off, or *en route* to Euston Station's trains, others pouring out of the regular political meetings held at the vast nearby Friends Meeting House, and still others heading to, or away from protest marches. Others were simply there for dinner before going home, comforted by Diwana's warm dosas, sambhars, pooris, and chats – all dishes that we Londoners were beginning to know and love.

In the early 1980s, we cultural studies students began to learn why it mattered to describe the seventeenth century's ill-fated English uprisings collectively as a revolution, rather than a civil war. We learnt, too that the radical groups that led those uprisings, including the Levellers, the Diggers and others, were forerunners, in some sense, of the political protesters of the 1970s and 1980s. Accepted as a mature student into the inaugural year of the first ever undergraduate cultural studies degree at what was then North East London Polytechnic (NELP), my co-students and I began our studies in 1980. This was the year following Margaret Thatcher's election as prime minister – a significant year in which to remember those radicals who had seen and allowed us to glimpse the possibility of another England. Together, we studied feminism and psychoanalysis and so much more, all inflected through Stuart Hall's subtle and hopeful Gramscian quest to unearth fragments of good sense within the common sense that had now produced Thatcherism (Hall 2021 [1988]). In dark times, we learnt Gramsci's motto of "pessimism of the intellect, optimism of the will" (Gramsci 1977 [1920], 188), or, following Ann Rigney, to choose hope over despair (Rigney 2018a).[4] But together, we glimpsed something else, as well. At NELP, our lecturers taught us about the English Revolution, Freud, Marx, and Gramsci, colonialism and feminism with generosity and passion, treating us students – many of us mature students close to them in age – as co-travelers. But in those years, it felt as though we were doing more than just learning about the radi-

---

3 On Asad Haider's account (Haider 2020) Gramsci was not a supporter of utopian thought. I am not drawing on Gramsci or Stuart Hall, here.

4 In remembering the Gramscian thought that we were taught, I am also now aware of Ann Rigney's careful advocacy of hope over optimism (Rigney 2018a).

cal politics of the near and more distant past and studying contemporary cultural studies' readings of those politics. In seminar rooms and bars, on intense away weekends, in our relationships, in my housing co-op, and when we gathered in our favorite Indian restaurants, it felt as though in the act of gathering together, we were living out – even if fragmentedly – some part of the visions about which we were learning.

In the mid-1980s, it was in other Indian restaurants that we – Amal Treacher Kabesh and I and other close friends – would gather. Amal and I had met at NELP, introduced by our adored gay philosophy lecturer Peter Horne and, having launched into a love affair, we had recently moved into a beautiful new housing co-op flat. Amal, who was to become a brilliant and inspiring feminist scholar of the afterlife of the Egyptian Revolutions, was, like me, doing a PhD at the time. After days at our desks, we would head around the corner, to our beloved Belash Restaurant. With its glorious street-front of pillars, arches, and colored lights, and its ornate interior, the Belash reminded me, more than anything, of childhood visits to Battersea Park's mysterious and fabulous grotto – a remainder of the 1951 Festival of Britain's attractions. The Belash's adornments – like those of most of the UK's "traditional" Indian restaurants – can't be unpicked, I acknowledge, from the orientalist and imperial fantasies of India that we and our fellow students had learnt to recognize and that were coming to be challenged by the time of the 1951 Festival (Heinonen 2015). But the lights, the colors, the scents, the deliciousness, and the manager's warm, welcoming, and fatherly smile created, too, an accessible utopia at the end of our street where we would recover from our writing – or failure to write – over dishes of brinjal, dhal and sag.

On other nights, our new friends Pauline and Farhad would invite us to their house for dinner, where, in their glass-walled conservatory filled with the glow of colored hanging lamps, Farhad would bring his deep and brimming pots of curry to the table. There, amongst the lights and the scents, and safe from the night, the conversation turned more easily to how it felt – as an Anglo-Egyptian or Parsi-Indian – to be treated as "other," and the political and psychotherapeutic possibilities for mitigating those dynamics. On yet other nights we would gather at our new Stoke Newington haunt. Owned and run by the inimitable visionary Das Sreedharan, Rasa embodied Das's vision of supporting Kerala's economy by keeping the local cuisine he remembered and had learnt from his mother alive and in the hands of Keralan women. At Rasa, with our hopes still alive and now mingled with Rasa's, my friends and I celebrated our special days until I left London.

One night, sitting in Citrus after dinner, Felicity asked me why I ate more than usual when we had dinner there. Was it because second helpings were free, she wondered. Well – perhaps! But maybe it's also because each spoonful of dahl and rice and chutney carries with it *so much* of what I've written about, here.

Maybe I'm trying to fill myself up with those familiar tastes in the hope that if I eat enough, the loved friends with whom I gathered for so many years – some of whom have now died – will re-appear at this far-flung table, encouraging me to eat just another piece of pappadam. But, tempting as it is to finish this chapter on this elegiac and somewhat mournful note, that ending would emphasize only a part of the story. As Ann Rigney has argued, memory studies' tendency to foreground trauma and suffering has been at the expense of a focus on happier memories (Rigney 2018a) and may be contributing to a constraining public discourse on memory and identity (Rigney in McIvor et al. 2017, 182). So, the ending I'm choosing, here may prove harder to write because it is grounded in happier memories (Rigney 2018a, 370) and because it attempts to contribute to nascent understandings of "the communication of such things as joy, hope, and aspirations for a better world across generations" (Rigney in McIvor et al. 2017, 182).

I am writing this chapter at a women's writing retreat, held at the Tauhara Centre, that sits above Taupo's vast, volcanic lake on Aotearoa/New Zealand's north island. Tauhara's quiet, its simple accommodation, lake views, grassy paths, abundant veggie gardens and generous and delicious food combine to make it one of the most beautiful places I have ever been. For some decades now, a group of academic women have been gathering regularly at Tauhara for week-long retreats, providing generous, kind and insightful support to each other in their daily writing endeavors. In Tauhara's entrance hall, an information book and faded black and white photographs of the Centre's founders tell the story of Tauhara's origins in a shared hope for a better, kinder, and more supportive way of life. Not all who gather at Tauhara will share in its founders' spiritual beliefs. But to share food at Tauhara's tables, and to sit and talk and laugh with the other women gathered here, is to witness and remember its founders' hopeful vision made manifest in the here-and-now.

As Ann Rigney reminds us, "[w]hether a private or a collective matter, recollection is not a matter of stable 'memories' [. . .] Instead, it is an active and constantly shifting relationship to the past, in which the past is changed retrospectively in the sense that its meaning is changed" (Rigney 2005, 17). It starts to make sense, then that it took Ann Rigney's essay about celebratory commemorations of the Paris Commune (Rigney 2018a) and this gathering of women at Tauhara to draw out the hopeful rather than the more pessimistic potential of the memory fragments that my Citrus dinners have been prompting. From the vantage point of *this* present, the early 1980s that I'm remembering, emerge as hopeful student days, when, with the help of our teachers, and inspired by their mentor, Stuart Hall, we learned to believe that good sense might be present, even at the heart of Thatcher's Britain and that all is never lost. In that Melbourne restaurant, similarly perhaps, to during the feasts that have marked remembrance of the ill-fated Paris Commune, "communal pleasure [became] a carrier of memory" (Rigney 2018a, 376). At Citrus, each spoonful of curry now tastes of times when our gatherings prefigured a world inspired by the often-failed struggles and dreams of those who had lighted our way.

Recently, Felicity and I – along with many others – were invited to my Melbourne friend and literary studies scholar Mridula Nath Chakraborty's home to celebrate the harvest festival of Sankranti. Once the big table had been laden with bowls and surrounded by the glorious shimmering silks of many of her guests' festive saris, Mridula spoke of the vital importance of gathering together in what her invitation had described as the turbulent times through which we are currently living. It might seem to me, sometimes, that the memories carried back to me by Citrus belong to the temporal and geographic elsewhere of a more hopeful past. In memory, in my 1970s and 1980s, in a time before we really knew about climate change and before the wars that are currently raging, at least some of the goals of struggles including feminism, socialism, anti-racism, and anticolonialism felt achievable. But at Tauhara women's retreat and in Mridula's home, the lineaments of a hoped-for world inspired by past and current struggles feel vividly present. Here at Tauhara, and at Mridula's, and at Citrus, the laughter, warmth, and food make it possible to believe, with Ann Rigney, that suffering might not connect people more than joy, or, I want to add, hope (Rigney 2018a, 377).

Acknowledgements: With heartfelt thanks to the Women Writing Away Retreat, and to the Tauhara Centre, Taupo, Aotearoa/New Zealand.

3 Mediation and Remediation

Alison Landsberg
Mediation and Prosthetic Memory

When I began theorizing what I called "prosthetic memory" (Landsberg 1995; 2004), I was interested both in the way in which the body was implicated in and by memory, and also in the power of film – and audiovisual media more generally – to structure complex forms of engagement with images and narratives about the past. As I continue to explain this genesis, I hope it will be obvious that the production of "prosthetic memory" – emerging as it does at the interface between an individual and a mediated representation of the past – is predicated on the dynamics Ann Rigney and Astrid Erll would call mediation and mediality (Rigney and Erll 2009) and posit as central to any understanding of "cultural memory" (Assmann 1995).

I located the emergence of prosthetic memory at the interface of two simultaneous developments at the turn of the twentieth century: on the one hand, the mass migrations of peoples occasioned by modernity, and on the other, the birth of the cinema. The former ruptured communities, creating the need for new mechanisms for transmitting group memory, and the latter enabled an unprecedented circulation of images and narratives about the past. I was particularly compelled by the latter: film was a form of mass culture with a broad cultural reach, but also a unique and powerful audiovisual medium with a specific phenomenology of its own. Many of its very first theorists attended to the way in which its sensuous mode of address meant that it had the ability to powerfully affect spectators in ways that might have social significance: as early as 1916, Hugo Münsterberg proclaimed of photoplays that "The intensity with which the plays take hold of the audience cannot remain without strong social effects [. . .] The associations become as vivid as realities, because the mind is so completely given up to the moving pictures" (Münsterberg 1970, 95). Early Frankfurt School theorist Walter Benjamin, along with his interlocutor Siegfried Kracauer, also attempted to theorize the implications of the new visual technologies of modernity; of film, Kracauer wrote, it "seizes the human being with skin and hair" (Hansen 1993, 458). It seemed feasible, perhaps even important, to consider cinema *as a* realm of experience, a realm of tactile bodily experience. Even more, with techniques of editing and media-specific forms of narration, film *as a medium* could structure forms of engagement with images and narratives about the past; it could force viewers (through filmic strategies of editing and narration) into subject positions they might not 'naturally' (in terms of ancestry, biology, or other forms of kinship) inhabit. Through point-of view-shots, together with narratives that invited identification with certain characters and scenarios, film had the capacity to bring viewers into proximity with pasts that they did not live and might not otherwise have reason to care about. Moreover, film as a mass medium, and from its outset, offered viewers an intimate and personal engagement with experiences and pasts that were outside of their actual lived experiences.

It was in thinking about the cinema phenomenologically, as a site of experience on the one hand, and culturally, as a place where people came into contact with images and narratives about distant places and pasts on the other, that I developed the theory of prosthetic memory: that through mass cultural engagements with the past, encounters with mediated images and narratives, people could take on memories of a past not properly their own, memories of experiences they did not live. In this way, prosthetic memory resonates with the dimension of cultural memory that Ann Rigney would call "vicarious recollection" (Rigney 2005, 15), and by which she means "recollections" fundamentally "external" to the individual, "the product of representations and not of direct experience" (Rigney 2005, 15). Rigney, too, saw the way that this vicarious recollection worked against the logic of identity politics. Indeed, a key dimension of *Prosthetic Memory* (Landsberg 2004) is that a commodified mass culture has the unintended consequence of de-essentializing, or de-naturalizing memory. In the age of mass culture, memory could no longer be treated as the exclusive property of a single group (ethnic, religious, national, etc.) as memory narratives became much more widely available. For the price of a ticket, one could be brought into an intimate relationship with a past to which one had no ancestral claim, by birth or otherwise. And in the space of a cinema, or at an experiential museum, one might be forced to occupy a subject position one might not otherwise choose to inhabit, to see as if through someone else's eyes.

And yet there are some important differences in emphasis between cultural memory and prosthetic memory: in my account of prosthetic memory the emphasis is less on how mediation and remediation produce memories that circulate publicly, than on the effect those memories have on individuals. For Rigney and Erll, mediation is crucial in the *creation* of cultural memory (as opposed to simply a tool for its retrieval); they emphasize both that "media are more than merely passive and transparent conveyors of information. They play an active role in shaping our understanding of the past" (Rigney and Erll 2009, 3) and also that it is through "specifically medial processes [. . .] [that] memories come into the public arena and *become* collective" (Rigney and Erll 2009, 2). While I, too, suggest that prosthetic memories are created in encounters with mediated representations, my emphasis is on how they interface with and inform individual subjectivities and world views.

Furthermore, the prosthetic memories I have described are not a unified collective memory either: they are not a single memory or memory narrative of a past public event that looks and feels the same to everyone; rather I understand prosthetic memories to work at the level of the individual. Prosthetic memories interface with the individual's own archive of experience and gain meaning in relation to that person's own subject position. Prosthetic memories are privately felt public memories.

The metaphor of the prosthesis is important, too: first of all, that these memories are understood to be prosthetic underscores the point that they are not organic, natural, authentic, or hereditary in any straightforward way, nor are they the product of the individual's lived experience of them, and yet they are powerful, affective, sensuous memories. Second, like an artificial limb, these memories are actually worn on the body; third, their value is measured by their usefulness. Prosthetic memories are useful insofar as they connect the individual to a past that lies outside of their lived or ancestral experience, which might help foster empathy and social responsibility as well as political alliances that transcend race, class, and gender. And finally, even though a prosthesis is worn on the body, and enables actions not otherwise possible, its artificiality never disappears. While one might learn to run with an artificial leg, the leg is always understood to be prosthetic. Similarly, a viewer of a film about enslavement in the US, no matter how affecting the experience might be, does not come away confused about whether or not they lived through the depicted historical episode; but they do come away with an affectively charged feeling of connection to the event, a new sense of its meaningfulness, that might motivate how they think and act in the world. It's an affective experience not *of* the event, but in relation to it.

Because affect is a significant dimension of memory generally, and also a catalyst to action (political and otherwise), it feels important to theorize the affective, intimate, embodied nature of prosthetic memory. When I began work on *Prosthetic Memory* I was drawn to memory as a modality precisely because of its urgency, its tendency to thrust itself upon a person. Unlike history, the other main modality for engaging with the past, which insists on critical distance, memory is powerfully and profoundly intimate and affective. I was drawn to the aliveness of memory, to its complex temporality, to the way in which it lives in the present differently from history. This powerfully affective dimension, it seemed to me, was part of the key to memory's power – its ability to move people, to motivate them to action, to shape subjectivities, to compel individuals into politics, and foster alliances and kinships. Prosthetic memories, in other words, might become the basis for mediated collective identification and the production of potentially counterhegemonic public spheres.

That prosthetic memories are both powerfully affective and fundamentally anti-essentialist means that they open up certain kinds of political potentials. Because anyone might be able to borrow and use someone else's memory – and I do not mean claim it as their own, but rather use it – prosthetic memory has the potential to foster alliances across chasms of difference, to enable empathy for those different from oneself. This in turn might energize new political engagements and commitments. There is obviously a utopian dimension to *Prosthetic Memory* even though it was never meant as a pure or straightforward celebration of this new form of memory. My work has always been, and continues to be, inspired by Walter Benjamin, who despite living against the backdrop of the rise of fascism and amid a broken world, attempted to theorize ways in which the new visual technologies of modernity might enable people to see the world differently and thereby make possible a different future.

With hindsight, it is clear that there was something of a *zeitgeist* in memory studies at the turn of the twenty-first century, of which "prosthetic memory" was a part. Perhaps as a result of the millennial turn, or because we were roughly a generation beyond the Holocaust and at a moment when those who had lived memories of the event were passing away, many of us were thinking about memory transmission, about the mobility or transportability of memory or about how one group's memories might be passed on or taken up by others. Ann Rigney's program at Utrecht University on the "dynamics of cultural remembrance," which led to the seminal work, with Astrid Erll, *Mediation, Remediation, and the Dynamics of Cultural Memory* (2009) along with her groundbreaking work on transnational memory with Chiara De Cesari (2014), was part of this generative moment in memory studies, with critical attention moving away from static forms of memorialization and towards accounts that acknowledge its dynamic and mobile dimension. Around the same time, other seminal theories of memory were emerging, like Marianne Hirsch's idea of "post-memory" (2012), Michael Rothberg's "multidirectional memory" (2009), Anna Reading's "global witnessing" (2009), and Andrew Hoskins conceptualization of the "mediatisation of memory" (2009), most of which attended to the role of media or visual culture in the transmission of cultural memory. Many of us at that moment were compelled by the formative role of media in memory's new mobility across time and space, and the emerging political, cultural, and social implications of these dynamics.

José van Dijck

The Platformization of Scholarly Legacy

1 Introduction

Entering the query "Ann Rigney" on Google Scholar, I receive 14,700 hits – all references to her scholarly work. Doing the same on Google Search, the result pages show an astonishing 943.000 results; I don't even start checking – it's endless. My next probe on Google Image does not yield any quantitative information, but instantly delivers a mixed bag of content: an impressive number of YouTube videos, including an interview with professor Rigney in the series "Thinking Aloud" on BYU broadcasting; a Zoom interview for *Current Issues in Memory Studies*; a podcast in a university-series; a review of one of her books on Goodreads; a recorded lecture for Studium Generale at Utrecht University in 2010; the announcement of a lecture on Cultural Memory in France; a news item about her honorary doctorate from Aarhus University; several featured talks in places such as Frankfurt and Helsinki; pictures of Ann being formally admitted to the Royal Irish Academy; a Wikipedia page; book offerings on Amazon.com; and many, many more.

While scrolling through photos, videos, and texts reflecting Ann Rigney's professional life, you get a fair idea of a scholar at work once you start patching seemingly random pieces together. Born in Ireland, based at Utrecht University, she travels across the world to educate students and inform colleagues about important concepts in memory studies. This online catalogue of professional items constitutes a puzzling object. What (kind of) digital footprints does a renowned scholar leave behind? Can we derive an adequate picture of someone's academic career via online searches? And how is an academic's professional legacy formatted by online platforms?

In this essay, I analyze how online filters shape the academic legacy of scholars, using Ann Rigney as an example. Several decades ago, we deployed the concepts of 'mediation' and 'remediation' as helpful prisms to understand the shaping of memory – collective and individual (van Dijck 2008; Erll and Rigney 2009a); more recently, 'platformization' has been an indispensable concept for understanding how someone's heritage gets formed by online tools (Poell et al. 2019; Helmond 2015; Nieborg and Poell 2018; Van Dijck et al. 2018). And with the recent development of new tools, such as AI-bots, the impact of technology on our ability to make sense of the past may become even bigger.

2 Mediation and remediation

If I had entered Ann Rigney's name in a Google Scholar search in 2009, the result would have been a more modest list of page-ranked results, primarily books and articles. Not just because Ann was younger and had fewer publications to her name, but mostly because of the relative simplicity of technological filters at the time. In their book *Mediation, Remediation, and the Dynamics of Cultural Memory* (2009) editors Astrid Erll and Ann Rigney discussed the growing role of (digital) media in the production and circulation of shared views of the past. The concepts 'mediation,' 'remediation,' and 'intermediality' shed a new light on the rapidly evolving media landscape in the first decade of the twenty-first century. Mediated memories, as I described in my own book (Van Dijck 2008), involved both acts of remembrance and objects of memory; they were dynamic techno-economic and socio-cultural processes that revamped the very concepts of memory and legacy, of individuality and collectivity, unsettling the boundaries between private and public culture.

Looking back on that period, it occurs to me how delightfully simple the digital media landscape was! Concepts like mediation and remediation now evoke nostalgic memories of blogs and personal websites, unadulterated by a complex ecosystem of commercially driven platforms that started to 'mediate' *everything* (Van Dijck 2013). In 2008, Facebook and LinkedIn had just reached the European continent, Wikipedia still looked like a small community project, and Google's search engine was in its infant stages of proliferation. Google Scholar had started to index the full text and metadata of scholarly academic literature in 2004; Google acquired video-sharing platform YouTube in 2006. Much has been written about Google's role in the production and circulation of academic knowledge. Google Scholar was not just an online extension of a catalogue's browser; it was essentially a piece of social software the efficacy of which is rooted in the activity of its users (Van Dijck 2012). Unlike library systems, source retrieval is based on *popularity* rather than truth-value or relevance. Algorithmic ranking mechanisms coupled onto retrieval mechanisms and citation systems gradually enabled a seamless integration of the academic worlds of libraries, scholars, and their outputs with the commercial worlds of publishing, promotion, and advertising.

The term 'googlization,' coined in 2003, signals one tech company's expansion of services to include not just search engines but video-sharing (YouTube), image sharing, web-based mail, online mapping and navigation, news delivery, online advertising, academic referencing, instant messaging, app delivery, and more (Vaidhyanathan 2011). Google's rapid technological and epistemological penetration of online markets rendered the concepts of mediation and remediation virtually obsolete, if not meaningless. Its brand name-turned-into-verb marked the immanent drift towards platformization – a connective culture in which tech companies design and exploit online platforms that powerfully shape human knowledge, activities, memories, and professional lives. These days, a scholar's legacy is inevitably filtered through the technological lenses of platforms that help you navigate a world of scattered digital memory objects. The mediated lives of scholars are increasingly platformized.

3 Platformization of scholarly lives

The 943.000 ranked results that Google Search spits out after entering the query "Ann Rigney" is no proof that her academic visibility or impact has exploded in the past fifteen years. Rather, the explosion of results on Google's search engine divulges how the digital landscape has changed from a collection of single platforms (e.g. search engines) profiling specific personae, to an intricate ecosystem of interconnected platforms exposing a web of networked lives. Social, personal, and professional activities of one academic are interwoven with the social, personal, and professional lives of countless others, while these networks are bound together by a constellation of (mostly commercially driven) platforms.

Despite her notable absence from social media platforms such as Facebook, Twitter, Instagram, or TikTok, Ann Rigney's online presence is inevitably shaped by the dynamics and logics of social media platforms. On LinkedIn (owned by Microsoft since 2016), we find her professional profile linked to 62 followers and 52 connections; judged by its deserted interface, this is most likely a machine-generated profile. On YouTube (owned by Google-Alphabet), dozens of lecture recordings, interviews, and interactive presentations are interlinked and made available. Her university's communication officers have been actively promoting her visibility on Twitter and Instagram. Ann Rigney's Wikipedia page (https://en.wikipedia.org/wiki/Ann_Rigney) reflects a factual overview of her professional achievements, including ten impactful references and one sentence about her personal life.

Platformization has been defined as "the penetration of economic and infrastructural extensions of online platforms into the web, affecting the production, distribution, and circulation of cultural content" (Poell et al. 2019, n.p.). It is the new logic by which people's lives become searchable, observable, and understandable. Platformization renders the assessment of someone's academic achievements and professional life inseparable from the commercial online environment through which it can be accessed in the first place. Scholarly lives, just like knowledge and legacies, get produced on the World Wide Web through an invisible and, to some extent, inscrutable set of mechanisms deployed by tech companies. In this attention economy, data entries are made valuable by inflating the number of connection points. One million hits on Google Search says little about someone's impact or career, but simply reflects the importance of connectivity as a driver for online activity.

So where does that leave our assessment of Ann Rigney's professional life and scholarly legacy? Google's incredible maze of results, braided together by numerous network nodes as part of the platform ecosystem's larger architecture makes it harder, not easier, to construct a coherent picture of someone's professional life. The plenitude of quantitative information, such as the number of links, is no longer a meaningful factor in assessing someone's (academic) legacy. Over the past decade, individuals' academic rankings have notoriously gained ground as official indexes of academic achievements; these indexes are commonly designed to offer academic communities more visibility and exposure – in tune with the commercial incentives for distributing content on the web. However, while accessibility of content has increased dramatically, platformization has facilitated neither a comprehensive review of academic scholarship nor a qualitative assessment.

4 Enter the AI-turn: platformization on steroids

A revolutionary shift was announced in early 2023, when platform companies heralded the emergence of artificial intelligence (AI). The recent acceleration in developing AI-driven chatbots such as ChatGPT (financed by Microsoft) and Bard (developed by Google-Alphabet) has given a tremendous boost to the streamlined processing of online searches. Conversational AI-powered chatbots, built onto Large Language Models (LLMs) that are trained on enormous databases, can very quickly wade through millions of pieces of online content, including Wikipedia entries and academic articles. ChatGPT presents a comprehensive summary of a research topic just seconds after inserting a simple prompt. The tool might be optimized to produce reviews of scholarly lives; built into existing search engines, such as Google Scholar and Search, it fuels the platformization process. One concern about using LLMs for scientific search is that they are unreliable: their output can contain factual errors, biases, and non-existent references. (Roe and Perkins 2023; Ferrari et al. 2023)

So how does this latest tool format Ann Rigney's scholarly legacy? After feeding the prompt "Describe Professor Ann Rigney's scholarly legacy in max 100 words" into ChatGPT3.5, the bot spits out the following summary in milliseconds:

Professor Ann Rigney is an esteemed academic known for her influential contributions to the fields of cultural memory, literary studies, and heritage. Her research delves into the intricate relationship between collective memory, narrative, and identity, often exploring how societies remember and interpret the past. With a strong interdisciplinary approach, Rigney's work has illuminated the dynamics of memory in various contexts, enriching our understanding of cultural continuity and change. Her prolific publications and leadership in academic circles have solidified her reputation as a thought leader in memory studies, inspiring scholars and students alike.

As far as I can tell, there are no obvious mistakes in this digest. However, when I fill out the same prompt the next day, and ask ChatGPT to include sources, I receive a variation on the previous text, embellished by two publications: "The Afterlives of Walter Scott" and "Imperatives of Culture." The second title is obviously a hallucination; when searching for it, I retrieve a book on Korean history and literature. In other words, AI-bots are not reliable instruments to construct a perfect review of one's scholarly legacy (Zuccon et al. 2023).

Evaluating the quality of the bot's summary, though, I must admit the text is remarkably fluent and correct, grammatically as well as rhetorically. ChatGPT's description of Ann Rigney's scholarly legacy is the result of a technological (re) mediation, mining 943.000 potential sources scattered across numerous platforms. The underlying algorithmic dynamics remain a black box, inaccessible to legislators or experts and enigmatic to users. The same prompt fed into ChatGPT yields comparable yet slightly different results each time it is entered; the dynamic system adapts its understanding of someone's legacy at the same time and by the same means as it *shapes* her legacy. Soon, AI-powered chat bots may become the superchargers of platformization.

5 Conclusion: tech power, human judgment

So let's go back to the question of how to assess a scholar's legacy – her career, professional life and academic achievements – using online tools? As I argued before (Van Dijck 2008), we should never completely rely on technologies to evaluate mediated memories; neither should we fully trust digital tools to appraise someone's scholarly legacy. Tech power can only be useful when paired off with human judgment. Scholarly legacies cannot simply be derived from the plenitude of digital traces we encounter on the internet by prompting a predesigned entry. We need to understand how, by what mechanisms and dynamics, they are produced and distributed.

And to guide our understanding of technological systems, we need human judgment that makes sense of what happens outside of these systems. The production of academic knowledge and legacy is first and foremost the outcome of personal interactions and active deliberations, inside and outside of academia. Ann Rigney's scholarly legacy is a case in point: rather than the sum of publications, lectures, and 'output,' her legacy is informed by all these moments in real life where we ("scholars and students alike," according to ChatGPT) have encountered her brilliant mind, unmediated by screens or technology. Intellectual stimulation, sensible engagement, and gracious smiles are the key ingredients for continuous academic inspiration. If scholarly legacy can be automated at all, it should always be anchored in human judgment – the touchstone of all legacies.

Rik Smit
Memory and Platformization

In the introduction to their edited volume *Mediation, Remediation and the Dynam-ics of Cultural Memory* (2009, 2), Astrid Erll and Ann Rigney argue that "the dynam-ics of cultural memory can only be fully understood if we take into account, not just the social factors at work [in remembering], but also the 'medial frameworks' of remembering." This is because media allow us to make sense and give meaning to the world around us, and they mediate between individuals and groups and across time and space. That is, media are active agents in the dynamic construction of memory, whether this concerns autobiographical memory or shared memories of and within groups (e.g., collective, social, or cultural memory). They can enable, shape, and constrain particular memory practices and, related to the construction of cultural memory, engage in the (re)mediation of the past through particular per-formances present in the public arena (Erll and Rigney 2009b, 5). These dynamics are as old as humankind. In fact, cultural memory and our ability to inscribe mean-ing into cultural artefacts that can overcome time and, to various extents, space make us successful as a species. Without this transmission – in some socio-technical manner or medium – of experience and knowledge we simply would not be. We are, in other words, technogenetic creatures (Hayles 2012).

So, what *are* the new medial frameworks of remembering and how do they affect how we remember, and by extension, how we should be doing memory studies related to media? The answer, I contend in this short chapter, lies not so much in media's various capacities and instances of overcoming time and space. This is not to deny that there is more media content than ever, coming from and circulating all over the world and entering our private and public spheres (Rigney 2005). Indeed, we live *in* media (Deuze 2011), in the sense that large parts of our very lives are mediated or stand in relation to media, even if we are not using them (cf. the 'digital detox'). Therefore, critical scholars of memory should be en-gaging more with that which *supports* media content, with those structures that encompass and envelop the 'medial frameworks,' with the very real and material socio-technical assemblages that, to put it as a McLuhanesque pun, *stand under* media today. We should, in short, be talking about platforms, a problematic term I will unpack below. In this chapter, I argue that platforms act as new 'medial frameworks' of memory that support – infrastructurally speaking – and shape new forms, dependencies, and power dynamics when it comes to the keeping and representation of the past (see also: Smit 2023; Smit et al. 2024).

In their introduction Erll and Rigney employ the word 'framework' in a mostly metaphorical sense to extend Halbwachs's notion of the social frameworks of remembering. The word 'framework' denotes a basic conceptual structure related to meaning-making, a mental construct rooted in culture that is the link between individuals and society, a frame of reference. As such, media actively shape our understanding of the past (Erll and Rigney 2009b, 3). But the word framework also has a material meaning that is very closely related to that of the word platform. Merriam Webster's dictionary definition, for example, holds that a framework is "a structure made for admitting, enclosing, or supporting something." A 'medial framework of memory' could therefore not 'just' mean the enabling and shaping of mnemonic meaning-making and mediation, but also the material and infrastructural support of (other) media. This infrastructural meaning is especially important when we scrutinize the relationship between memory and platforms.

The term 'platform,' Tarleton Gillespie (2010, 348) writes in his seminal essay "The Politics of 'Platforms,'" "has emerged recently as an increasingly familiar term in the description of the online services of content intermediaries, both in their self-characterizations and in the broader public discourse of users, the press and commentators." It is a rather vague container term that has, according to Gillespie, (at least) four semantic uses: computational, architectural, figurative, and political. In software developer language, a platform is "an infrastructure that supports the design and use of particular applications, be they computer hardware, operating systems, gaming devices, mobile devices or digital disc formats" (Gillespie 2010, 349). Specifically related to Web development, the term is used to describe "online environments that allow users to design and deploy applications they design or that are offered by third parties" (Gillespie 2010, 349). This meaning relates to an earlier, architectural use of the term as to refer to "human-built or naturally formed physical structures, whether generic or dedicated to a specific use" (Gillespie 2010, 349). In (computer) architecture, then, platform refers to something that allows other structures to be built upon. Importantly, platforms can be stacked, so one platform can be built on top of another.

Figuratively, 'platform' connotes an "opportunity, action and insight" and "we might describe our entry-level job as a 'platform' for climbing the corporate ladder" (Gillespie 2010, 350). Like 'framework,' platform can be used metaphorically. This also holds true for its political meaning as the word might "refer to the issues a political candidate or party endorses" and a phrase often asked to politicians is how they 'stand' on a political issue (Gillespie 2010, 350). The point of Gillespie's semantic and etymological exercise is to show that invoking the word 'platform' is a strategic discursive move. To claim that one's latest ICT product is a platform, for example, "suggests a progressive and egalitarian arrangement, promising to support those who stand upon it" (Gillespie 2010, 351). Importantly, this labeling does political work, in the sense that it "obfuscates as much as it reveals. It obscures how social media and other digital services, labeled as platforms, not just facilitate socioeconomic, cultural, and political interaction, but very much organize and steer this interaction" (Nieborg and Poell 2018, 4276). "Platforms' are 'platforms,'" writes Gillespie (2010, 351), "not necessarily because they allow code to be written or run, but because they afford an opportunity to communicate, interact or sell." By 'offering support' and by 'building infrastructure' in the form of platforms, technology companies are simultaneously making themselves essential while presenting themselves as non-threatening.

A growing body of research in media studies and other fields critically investigates the ongoing 'platformization' of existing markets and fields of cultural production. Helmond (2015, 5) originally defined platformization as "[t]he rise of the platform as the dominant infrastructural and economic model of the social web and the consequences of the expansion of social media platforms into other spaces online." Nieborg and Poell (2018, 4276) take a broader perspective and define the process as "the penetration of economic, governmental, and infrastructural extensions of digital platforms into the web and app ecosystems, fundamentally affecting the operations of the cultural industries." Importantly, these definitions emphasize how platforms create dependence. For example, the music industry is heavily dependent on Spotify and streaming platforms have fundamentally reshaped the film and TV industries, from preproduction to marketing. These and many other examples show that "cultural production is progressively 'contingent on,' that is, *dependent on* a select group of powerful digital platforms" (Nieborg and Poell 2018, 4276).

Dependence, however, is just one meaning of the word contingency. A second important aspect is that "[p]roducts and services offered and circulated via digital platforms are contingent in the sense that they are malleable, modular in design, and informed by datafied user feedback, open to constant revision and recirculation" (Nieborg and Poell 2018, 4276). In other words, through and by platforms, cultural content and consumption are rendered into data that can be analyzed and inform the creation and marketing of new products. Movies, series, and music are now partly produced taking datafied user behavior into account and recommender systems produce lists of cultural content on the basis of 'users like you.' Platforms are meta-media, the media of or for media, because they offer the infrastructure to keep a vast range of mediated cultural content in database form, which can be accessed through smooth interfaces that allow for the seamless consumption and simultaneous tracking of user behavior. They are infrastructural data companies through and through, but also, and perhaps because of that, today, active agents in the workings of memory, whether individual or cultural. Taking the above into account, platforms play at least three roles in the contemporary construction of memory. They are keepers, producers, and selectors of cultural content and user data about consumption of this content. In each of these roles, we see the dual contingency (dependence and constant revision and recirculation) noted by Nieborg and Poell play out. In what follows, I will scrutinize these interrelated roles in the light of platformization and end each discussion with key questions that can be picked up in future research on this topic.

We are increasingly dependent on platforms to keep our cultural content, to produce it, and select and re-present it to us. In a sense this is not so different from our historical dependence on the cultural industries to keep, produce, select, and re-present cultural products. This has been thoroughly critiqued from the Frankfurter Schule onward and may very well be the *raison d'être* of the field of media studies. A difference today, though, might be the sheer scale of what is produced, selected, and re-presented by a relatively small amount of platforms that are built on an even smaller group of server and cloud technology providers, such as Amazon Web Services (AWS). Netflix, for example, uses AWS for almost all its storage and computing needs. This role of keeper of media content does of course not stop at audiovisual and textual material produced by professionals, but also pertains to the huge archive of cultural content produced on social media, ranging from YouTube to Instagram and everything in between (which also holds vast amounts of work created by professionals and influencers). Key critical questions concerning this role might be: what happens when platforms are discontinued? How do copyright laws and regulation affect platforms' archival role? And: how does the (automated) 'cleaning' and moderating of platforms' content impact what *is* or *can* be remembered (Smit et al. 2017)?

Importantly, related to the second meaning of contingent, platforms do not 'see' films, series, music, and books (in the case of Amazon's Kindle) as the rich, meaning-full cultural artefacts that they are, but as data. Cultural-artefact-as-data can be broken apart and analyzed. This can occur on the level of one cultural artefact, but also on a very large scale, using thousands of films or millions of hours of music. In combination with user data (when and where do people consume what; when do people pause or stop; how do they rate and feel about content), predictions can be made about what sort of content (down to the actors, directors, and genre) will be liked by particular consumers at particular times and places. This algorithmic logic drives much cultural production and recommendation today and it is partly made possible by platforms as infrastructural data companies. Concerning memory construction, this logic allows for the selection (from abovementioned archive/database) in the form of recommendations and production of original media content about the past informed by present and datafied audiences interests. As of yet, though, scholars of memory and media have only just started answering the question of how the datafication of cultural artefacts affects the 'working' and circulation of cultural memory.

The purpose of this chapter has been to introduce memory studies scholars to critical scholarship on platforms. Moreover, it argued that the dynamics of cultural memory today cannot be fully understood if we do not take into account platforms, because they are dominant infrastructures for and actors in the keeping, selection, production, and circulation of human experience and knowledge carried in media forms (Smit et al. 2024). These new, material 'frameworks of memory' deserve critical, interdisciplinary scrutiny because present and future memory construction depends on them.

Anna Poletti

Memory and Artificial Intelligence

1 Introduction

What might it mean for Artificial Intelligence to mediate memory? Mediation matters to remembrance because "'media' of all sorts [. . .] provide frameworks for sharing both experience and memory [. . .] in two, interconnected ways: as *instruments* for sense-making, they mediate between the individual and the world; as *agents* of networking, they mediate between individuals and groups" (Erll and Rigney 2009b, 1, emphasis added). As I write this short chapter towards the end of 2023, most areas of human endeavor are predicted to be impacted by Artificial Intelligence.[1] I will reflect on how Rigney's attention to remembrance as an inherently social and collective practice in which the meaning of events or lives is discussed and debated publicly. In particular, I will examine how attention to the role of media in that process might provide a useful framework for considering AI's potential impact on collective remembrance.

Of course, to ask what something might *mean* is, as Rigney has shown, to ask *how is its meaning negotiated, proposed, shared?* To consider the mediation of memory is to consider "the dynamic of remediation whereby collective memories are culturally generated" (Rigney 2021b, 11). Utilizing AI in remembrance involves bringing a computational tool into the process of making meaning about the past. Yet, AI is not (yet) like other media; it is not a tool of prosthetic memory that aids or substitutes the human capacity to store and recall information (Merrill 2023), nor does fit neatly into existing understandings of remediation. AI exemplifies how digital technologies and globalization are destabilizing trust as a bedrock of interpersonal and institutional interactions (Bodó 2021). The question is not if we can trust AI as a mediator in practices of remembrance because, as Balázs Bodó (2021) has argued, trust itself is undergoing reconfiguration in the current era. However, bracketing the direct question of the technology's trustworthiness by acknowledging that it is part of broader developments, does not mean ignoring the very real questions the emerging use of AI in cultural memory raise. AI is arriving, as the material technological requirements for it become a reality. Generations of humans have been thinking about AI through speculative mathematics

---

1 The approach I outline here is partly based on my collaborative research project with David Gauthier, *Voice of Machine Theft*, in which we set about building a sound-based AI from scratch. For more information on the project, see here: https://voice-of-machine-theft.info/ Thanks to David for reading a draft of this essay and providing advice on the descriptions of computing.

and culture. We are fascinated by AI because it emerges from the area of experimental computing dedicated to exploring creativity and autonomy by enabling new degrees of independence in the computational system. Thus, AI is social and cultural. It is social in the sense that the people developing AI today (and those who made it available to be thought through speculative mathematics and culture) are humans living together in communities, and their ideas about the value of intelligence, creativity and autonomy are shaped by their social and historical context. AI is cultural in the sense that it is an expression of the symbolic and material processes we collectively use to generate meaning and assign value to lived experiences.

With this in mind, we can consider how AI functions as an *instrument* and *agent* in the social and cultural practice of remembrance. Such a consideration can only be speculative, given that within the field of cultural memory, AI is still largely an untested participant in the "open dynamic" in which "shared memory and social imaginaries are co-produced" (Rigney 2021b, 13). In light of this, I approach AI as an emerging technology, *and* a cultural phenomenon akin to a wish (Laplanche and Pontalis 1973, 481–483) for an autonomous non-human partner in remembrance.

As a case in point, we can consider the role of AI in the remembrance of an iconic artist of the twentieth century, Andy Warhol (1928–1987). A celebrated and controversial figure during his life, Warhol is canonized within art history as progenitor of the Pop Art Movement, and as one of the most influential artists of his time because of the wide variety of media he used to make his art, and his explicit rejection of the high/low cultural distinction that governed the circulation of cultural, social, and financial capital in the twentieth century. Into this existing understanding of Warhol, in March 2022, the six-part docu-series *The Andy Warhol Diaries*, written and directed by American Andrew Rossi, was released on Netflix (Rossi 2022). The series uses strategies of remediation familiar to documentary; incorporating and reanimating older media forms such as broadcast television, print culture materials, home movie footage, and personal photographs. These materials are intercut with new material made for the documentary in the form of talking-head interviews with people who were close to Warhol during his life, art historians, archivists, and subsequent artists who reflect on Warhol's milieu and legacy. Archival interview footage with important figures from Warhol's life who are no longer living is also used. The innovative element, in terms of AI and remembrance, is the use of a voiceover that imitates the voice of Andy Warhol. The Warhol AI reads extracts from Warhol's diary and is a consistent narrative presence in the docu-series. This voice over was produced using Resemble AI, a commercially available generative sound AI which claims to be able to use relatively small amounts of data from a human speaker to train an AI to read input text in the voice of that speaker.

2 The labor of memory: datafication, training, computation

Upon the release of *The Andy Warhol Diaries*, it was reported that the Warhol AI was trained on a mere 3 minutes and 12 seconds of original audio of Warhol's voice (Resemble AI 2023; Watercutter 2022). That there was merely 3 minutes of usable material available for the AI project demonstrates the extent to which computational approaches to remembrance are dependent on the past being rendered *computable* by the AI. The past must be available as data that a program can read, so that computer can execute the coded process of iterative learning. The process of making usable data out of existing media archives is by no means resource or time neutral: indeed, it requires a significant investment of human labor and material resources to make new datasets that AI can learn from. In my own experience of building an AI in my research collaboration with David Gauthier, I was struck by how the desire to have a non-human intelligent collaborator inverted the traditional relationship between human and machine. In the early stages of AI development, it is clear who is the instrument and who is the agent: many hours of human labor go in to creating, cleaning, and preparing a dataset to train an AI (Resemble AI 2023). AI requires that, at least initially, some humans act in the service of the machine-to-come.

Of course, this idea of humans being enslaved by machines is a dominant trope in the depiction of AI in speculative literature and film, which forms the cultural memory of AI – the archive of our wish for AI that precedes its material arrival. These dystopian views warn against the wish for a non-human collaborator by imagining the threat it poses to our sovereignty in sense-making: think of Hal's dominance in *2001: A Space Odyssey* (dir. Stanley Kubrick, 1968), the cunning of Wintermute in *Neuromancer* (Gibson 1984), or the heartbreak Theodore Twombly experiences in *Her* when his AI lover, Samantha, exceeds his capacities (dir. Spike Jonze, 2013). Yet, Rigney's work shows that we have already surrendered some portion of making meaning about the past to a non-human other (Erll and Rigney 2009a; Rigney 2021b). What might we gain from this surrender in the case of AI?

As an idea and as an emerging technology, AI is appealing because of the potential it has to augment or exceed human perspectives in ways that cannot be predicted. As Gauthier et al. discuss in their short essay on the general process of execution in computing, one of the founding theorists of AI, Alan Turing stated that "machines take me by surprise with great frequency" (Gauthier et al. 2021, 161). In a given process of remembrance, then, the wish for AI might not be a wish for confirmation, but exploration; a desire for "the impossibility of being able to fully predict in advance both the machinations and possibilities of computation and its active executions" (Gauthier et al. 2021, 161). The wish is that AI's capacity to cross-reference multiple sources, analyze (more) data points more quickly and with a unique degree of accuracy and invent interpretations and viewpoints, will tell human users something *new* about the past. To meet this end, it is vital that the AI does not merely *recommend* (as its cousin, the search algorithm, does) but is given the opportunity to *become an agent* (just as Hal, Wintermute, and Samantha do – they use their sovereignty). The AI will not merely execute its code in response to a human query but *interpret the past* through its generative processes: based on what it has learnt from its own previous computations and ever-expanding dataset. It is humans who must labor for AI's sovereignty to be born into a habitable data environment by generating cultural material that is computable, and that labor is in the service of something we cannot know in advance.

But building the Warhol AI shows that iterative learning is a time and resource intensive human process of establishing a computable past. Once the dataset has been made readable and computable by the program, the program must be executed on the relatively rare hardware that has sufficient memory available to support the millions of individual computations (CPU and GPU cycles) that underpin Deep Learning (see Merrill 2023, 178–179). This process involves 1) the program querying the dataset as usable material, 2) the program executing coded instructions on the dataset (computing), 3) the output of that computation being stored, 4) the output being evaluated against programmed rules and through the guidance of human users who identify desirable outputs that should act as a model for future computations. Iterative machine learning involves hundreds or thousands of computational hours, and millions of individual computations, that are augmented by human hours teaching the AI what constitutes useful or interesting engagements with the past (see also Merrill 2023, 179–180). It is in this iterative and materially expensive process that the *agency* of AI is made and encountered. Given the extensive investment AI requires, it seems likely that it will continue to be used for acts of remembrance that can attract (and justify) significant resources, such as Andy Warhol.

3 Mnemonic mimesis

The Andy Warhol Diaries brings together a range of agents to generate a shared understanding of Warhol as a queer artist from Pittsburgh. Rossi frames the contribution of the Warhol AI to this process as "honouring" two elements of Warhol's artistic practice: his stated "desire to be a machine" and his use of techniques of mechanical reproduction (famously screen printing) in his own work (Watercutter 2022). The Warhol AI is a "Warholian portrait" – a means of remembering the artist through a contemporary technology appropriate to his oeuvre and vision (Resemble AI 2023). The Warhol AI reads aloud diary extracts and in so doing remembers how the diary itself was written, for Warhol did not *write* the diary, but *spoke* it. Every morning he phoned his amanuensis Pat Hackett and dictated the diary down the phone to her (Hackett 1991, xix). The Warhol AI is a new kind of digital monument to Warhol that uses AI to re-present how the diary was made. Re-speaking the diary re-enacts Warhol's distinctive practice as an artist interested in collaboration, intimacy, affect, mechanical reproduction, repetition, and scale (Flatley 2017; Wolf 2004).

For viewers unaware of, or not very interested in, the presence of the AI, the Warhol AI still underpins what is new in the remembrance of Warhol in the docu-series. By giving the impression of Warhol's own voice sharing his interiority – his shifting self-perception, desires, feelings, commitments, relationships, and reflections – Warhol appears to speak his interiority in a way he creatively avoided in genres such as the interview (Wolf 2004). The Warhol AI produces an implausibly intimate encounter with an elusive artistic visionary, in collaboration with actor Bill Irwin who added phonemes and modes of expression to the data set (Resemble AI 2023). With its unique focus on Warhol's romantic, sexual, and professional relationships with men, the project addresses what some queer scholars believe is the persistent "de-gaying" of Warhol that is necessitated by his inclusion in the canon of Western Art (Doyle et al. 1996, 1).

In this short piece, I have deliberately bracketed the question of the ethics of using AI in cultural memory. This is not to ignore this vital, and widely discussed, question. Rather, in keeping with Rigney's interest in the productive potential of aesthetics and media, I have focused on why it is we might wish for an AI collaborator in remembrance. *The Andy Warhol Diaries* show us that AI might provoke us to remediate older media in unprecedented ways, and in so doing, remember how mediation has always revealed more than we thought we knew about the past.

Gerardine Meaney

Cultural Memory and Cultural Analytics

> The very concept of cultural memory is itself premised on the idea that memory can only become collective as part of a continuous process whereby memories are shared with the help of symbolic artefacts that mediate between individuals and, in the process, create communality across both space and time. (Erll and Rigney 2009a, 1)

Digital humanities has been creating resources which assist in tracking the processes whereby memory is shared and the temporal and spatial trajectories of its symbolic artefacts for several decades. However, the more recent emergence of cultural analytics offers a different type of opportunity for the analysis of cultural memory. Lev Manovich's influential definition of cultural analytics as "the use of computational and design methods – including data, visualiation, media and interaction, design, statistics, and machine learning – for exploration and analysis of *contemporary* culture at scale" (2020, 90) omits the multiplicity of historical and cultural applications of these methods beyond the contemporary. They offer the potential to develop new methodologies and paradigms to interpret large historical datasets, transmedia memory infrastructures, and the unstable artefacts and communalities they generate. While Manovich's emphasis on scale is typical, cultural analytics is not, at its best, simply a re-orientation of research into culture towards quantitative methods. Andrew Piper admonished readers of the first issue of *Cultural Analytics*: "It would be wrong, and intellectually, limiting, to see this undertaking solely as computer science applied to culture. Cultural analytics requires a whole-scale rethinking of both of these categories" (2016, 2). Such whole-scale rethinking is a work in progress and one which could very much benefit from increased dialogue with the study of cultural memory, not least its emphasis on the complexity of remediation.

There are a number of practical ways in which cultural analytics can extend and support the process of identifying the "continuous processes of memory formation, sharing and change" which is at the heart of so much of Ann Rigney's work on cultural memory. The vast archive of online sources and resources now available for the study of these processes exceeds the capacity of individual or teams of human readers to search and analyze. Machine learning has the capacity to sift and identify sources at unprecedented scale and speed. Methods such as semantic network analysis, used with appropriate sensitivity to cultural and historical context, can illuminate the changing associations of events, histories, and narratives across vast areas of archival space. The question of whether it can change our knowledge of memory is not unrelated. There is real potential for the new perspectives offered by computational methods to assist in the process of "the disruption of old habits in the micropolitics of reading, viewing and reacting, with repeated small movements gradually acquiring larger-scale consequences" (Rigney 2021b, 15), through the excavation of forgotten viewpoints and texts which afford novel perspectives and defamiliarize settled memory cultures. One example of this is the way in which application of machine learning to large textual corpora can subvert inherited practices of classification and prioritization. The historical catalogue classification of the British Library Nineteenth Century corpus, for example, identifies just two "Works on Slavery": machine learning can identify 15,455 references to slavery in the same corpus.[1]

The connective tissue of cultural memory is narrative and stories use data, but they have distinctive characteristics which require a (self-aware, reflexive) "humanities in the loop" (Goodlad 2023). Large data sets and computational methods have value for cultural memory studies precisely because they can map complexity. This potential can only be realized by a dialogic relationship between cultural memory studies and cultural analytics, each putting the other into question and learning from the differences. Graham et al. use the metaphor of "a scientist's workbench, where the investigator moves between different tools for exploring different scales, keeping notes in a lab notebook" (2022, xvi) to describe best practice in "exploring big historical data." Cultural analytics is, despite some claims to the contrary, a means of interpretation not a substitute for it. Cultural data may always resist definitive answers, but the more cultural data we analyze the better we can map the dynamics of cultural continuity and change, the remediation of cultural memory. Rather than distant reading, best practice in cultural analytics is a reflexive and flexible practice of analysis and interpretation, in which results are assessed on both a massive scale (across genres and formats) and on the level of the individual text, site, testimony, or artefact.

The relevance of concepts of remediation in the context of online assemblages of historical memories and the potential for generative AI to curate and personalize memories diffused between user-generated content on social media and the collective archive have raised questions about the continuing relevance of methodologies evolved to analyze more stable media. While change and adaption are definitely required, it is important to remember that these new media and apparatuses have emerged from existing technical and cultural forms. Dialogue between cultural analytics and cultural memory methodologies is crucial for an understanding of the continuity and changes wrought by new infrastructures on much older processes of memory and forgetting. The new 'assemblages' do surface new stories, but they can also obscure the persistence of older and not al-

---

1 https://curatr.ucd.ie, see Leavy et al. 2019.

ways more accurate memory forms in a thicket of media innovation. Conversely, new cultural analytics approaches to detecting 'narrativity' can offer a powerful supplement to the concept of narrative in memory studies, more than useful in an era of fragmentary and multiple micronarratives rapidly reproduced across media. Piper and Bagga's use of predictive modelling to identify key characteristics of narrativity has considerable potential in identifying and extracting data relevant to the understanding of cultural memory from large undifferentiated data sets.[2]

In such a context the ethical and critical frameworks of interpretation implicit in Ann Rigney's analysis of cultural remediation are urgently needed in approaching how the past is and will be constructed in an era where generative AI tools and LLMs will assess the computational probability of competing pasts to produce synthetic memory. There is potential for a highly productive community of purpose between memory studies and cultural analytics, engaging with critical AI studies, integrating analysis of the processes and actors which shape algorithmic memory, maintaining a critical focus on what is being remembered as well as what memories are being produced and how. This requires a collaborative fusion of interpretative tools, combining the ability to use LLLMs knowingly to trace networks of memory, understand and counter algorithmic bias with, crucially, a commitment to create space for the "defamiliarisation constitutive of aesthetic experience [. . .] disrupting our usual habits of identification and understanding of what is memorable" (Rigney 2021b, 13). It is methodologically challenging but absolutely necessary to combine the ability to probe the probabilistic biases of mnemonic structures deploying galaxies of data and simultaneously to ask how can "the artful deployment of a given medium help create new sites of memorability?" (Rigney 2021b, 13).

The challenge of digital transmedia to stable memory formation has generated substantial debate in digital memory studies. Arguing against Andrew Hoskins' (2018) claims that the digital turn implies the end of collective memory, Silvana Mandolessi proposes that: "Instead, digital memory materializes and implements the theoretical claims made by Memory Studies since the field's inception: that collective memory may be conceived of as a process, mediated and remediated by multiple media with the participation of dynamic communities that perform rather than represent the past" (2023, 1514). Contra Hoskins' emphasis on the archive, Mandolessi emphasizes the database and especially the assemblage. In this context, the continuing usefulness of the concept of remediation, understood as tracking memory across multiple media and mediations, is que-

---

2 Their finding that "that temporal distance is far more fundamental than temporal sequence" (2023, 896) in predicting the presence of narrativity is of particular interest.

ried: "the redundancy that defines collective memory, that is, the fact that the meaning we attach to the past does not reside in a particular object or mnemonic site but in a dynamic and contingent multiplicity, can be captured in the digital age with the concept of assemblage, particularly mnemonic assemblage" (Mando-lessi 2023, 1524). While the assemblage has produced some dynamic and fascinating practices, especially of counter memory, there are substantial risks at the present moment in relinquishing theories and paradigms of remediation. The advent of digital platforms as "memory infrastructures" (Makhortykh 2023, 1501) controlled by global companies which act as "crucial gatekeepers of memory" (1503) has already elicited urgent attention from memory studies to the processes of algorithmic memory.[3] The advent of specific tools for the use of generative AI in everyday life should not obscure the extent to which less glamorously titled versions of this technology have been structuring the production of memory for well over a decade:

> Considering that non-human actors are directly responsible for deciding what information about the past is retrievable and in which formats it is delivered to human users, these actors become crucial constituents of human memory practices by shaping what and how is remembered by individuals and societies. At the same time, the lack of transparency of the non-human actors' functionality makes it difficult for human users to assess how AI-driven systems make specific choices. (Makhortykh 2023, 1505)

One of the great challenges for both cultural memory and cultural analytics is creating affordances for counter-memory to prevail against the juggernaut of datafication, probability, and consensus. Probabilistic calculation of a shared narrative does threaten "the agency of particular narratives" in effectuating "small acts of repair" which Rigney identifies as a necessary, even if not sufficient, "condition to change dominant narratives in which many people are already heavily invested" (2021b, 13). Paradoxically, algorithmic memory is a product of incredibly rapid technological change which could potentially obstruct the "slow changes of the social imaginary through creative acts of remembrance that take place at multiple sites and help to shape subjects and publics who are receptive to new voices" (Rigney 2021b, 19). This is not simply a question of bias against difficult truths or manipulation of the past to serve present purposes by commercial operators or political clients. Choices have already been made about the training data from which the most common and commercial generative AI applications have learned and these include the very worst modes of human exploitation and interaction (Birhane et al. 2021). While much of the debate around the use of culture as training data has focused on these extremes and on the violation of intellectual prop-

---

3 See Esposito 2017, *inter alia.*

erty rights, more analysis is needed of the potential flattening of affect and form, generating a simulacrum of human cultural processes which misrepresent its un-predictability and resistance to single interpretations. Such an outcome is not in-evitable. An intriguing example of how Bayesian probability modelling can be used to disrupt this process is offered in Foster and Evans' advocacy of "algorith-mic abduction" to "figure out what data is highly surprising – to predict aesthetic responses or seek out experiments that will rupture or refine our beliefs most ef-fectively" (2024, 383).

Summing up the unease of many scholars with the control of most generative AI and internet platforms by a very small number of large corporations, McGrath et al. point out that, "without scrutiny, technological mediation of culture will al-most certainly heighten existing inequalities and biases [. . .] Generative models of culture are reproducing patterns that have long preoccupied humanists. If our cultural theories have any validity, they ought to be practically useful" (2023, 528). The nature of that usefulness is indicated in a broad ranging article by Katherine Bode and Lauren Goodlad in the inaugural issue of *Critical AI*, where they advo-cate for a "valence-changing dialectics" which critiques "systems [. . .] trained on datasets that reduce tangled relations, multisensory bodies, and complex social situations to available data points" (2023, n.p.). That agenda setting article for the new "critical AI studies" maps the ways in which failings in current data models "disproportionately affect poor people and people of color" and argues for the creation of an alternative data commons. It is striking that alongside Costanza-Chock's aspiration that "generative AI" should "belong to the commons, to all hu-manity, rather than to a handful of powerful for-profit corporations," Bode and Goodlad cite Lesjak's study of the cultural memory of "the commons" and histori-cal resistance to enclosure (of land) as an example of the powerful afterlife of un-appropriated practices and loci of resistance (Chock qtd. in Bode and Goodlad 2023; Lesjak 2021).

The theoretical models developed by cultural memory studies, with their em-phasis on process, change, and collectivity, are potentially among the most useful at our disposal as scholars at the current juncture. Understanding that memory has always been mediated can temper panic that digital memory is an existential threat to human memory. There are real opportunities to benefit from AI tools to excavate lost or marginalized histories and life writings from archives catalogued according to the hierarchies and occlusions of a previous era. Topic modelling large datasets surfaces voices which would otherwise be lost to time – and to the limitations of the human capacity to read beyond the well catalogued and known (Evans and Foster 2024, 379). The black box where the processes of mediation and remediation feed into generative AI's accounts of the past poses a research challenge which can only be met by new collaborations. A strategic alliance and methodological cross-fertilization between cultural memory and cultural analytics is vital to track the role of this new cultural technology in memory remediation, but above all to equip artists and academics for new forms of counter-memory, to generate new possibilities rather than succumb to inherited probabilities.

Laura Basu
The Media Amnesia of Capital Accumulation

1 Introduction

One of Ann Rigney's most important contributions to the field of memory studies is her insistence on understanding cultural memories in terms of their *dynamics*, propelled by processes of constant *mediation and remediation* (Rigney 2005; 2008a; Rigney and Erll 2009). Texts don't do memory work as isolated products but always in dialogue with other texts and in social contexts.

This idea of memory dynamics took on a dramatic resonance during the 2008 global banking collapse and subsequent economic crisis. In September 2008, Lehman Brothers filed the biggest bankruptcy in history. Over the following months, governments around the world bailed out tens of other banks with sums of money the human brain could not compute. This financial catastrophe dominated new cycles across the globe. By Spring 2009, however, something uncanny was happening. Suddenly, the news was all about the inordinate debts that profligate governments had taken on, and how huge cuts to public spending would have to be made to remedy the situation. I remember thinking, "hold on, isn't this supposed to be a financial crisis? I thought you were just telling me it was the 'greedy bankers' and 'casino capitalism' causing all the problems. Why are we now talking about cutting disability benefits and child services?"

With the news coverage of the global financial crisis and its aftermath as my subject, I will develop Rigney's work on the dynamics of cultural memory in five steps: firstly, to see what happens when we look at the dynamics not of the literary texts that are her focus but of a very different medium: journalism; secondly, to investigate the dynamics not of remembering but of forgetting; thirdly, to extend the concept of memory dynamics to encompass the ideological work involved with those dynamics; and fourthly, to bring in the material dynamics that produce the cultural dynamics. To take these steps, I will be making one more move: to put Rigney's ideas about memory dynamics in touch with Marxist critical theory around acceleration and the forgetting involved with capital accumulation.

Compared to the literary texts that are Rigney's domain, news media are sometimes forgotten within cultural memory studies (though see Zelizer and Tenenboim-Weinblatt 2014; Zelizer 2008; Kitch 2008). This may be because they aren't typically seen as mnemonic media but rather as providing the 'first draft of history.' But news media do also engage with the past. Perhaps more importantly, though, in their very capacity as drafters of history, what and how they remember – and forget – is vitally important. It's important because it has ideological outcomes, serving certain social groups and disserving others.

Compared to the countless publications on remembering, forgetting tends to be somewhat forgotten within cultural memory studies as well, especially when it comes to unpacking cultural amnesia's different dynamics (but see Connerton 2009; Plate 2016; Beiner 2018). And there are only a handful of works on news forgetting (but see Pentzold and Lohmeier 2023), even though the amnesiac properties of journalism are regularly noted in passing.

Elsewhere (Basu 2018a) I have offered a typology of news forgetting: the always already forgotten; oblivion; forgotten pasts; rewriting history; and hyper-amnesia. It is the last one – hyper-amnesia – that I will be dealing with here. As we will see, hyper-amnesia has to do with the news media *erasing it's own very recent coverage*. The result of this is that *history is being constantly rewritten as it is happening*. And this is done *in full public view*.

2 Media amnesia: rewriting the economic crisis

In *Media Amnesia* (Basu 2018b), I analyzed news items from five British media outlets from across the political spectrum plus the main broadcaster (*The Guardian*, the *Mirror*, *The Telegraph*, the *Sun*, and the BBC), at different time periods between 2008 and 2016, to see how the coverage of the crisis developed over time. I found that, as the nature of the crisis morphed, from a banking crisis, to a recession, to a public debt crisis, it kept being reframed and and rewritten by the news. This reframing had ideological outcomes, making certain government responses appear as 'common sense' when they might otherwise have seemed absurd.

In 2008 at the time of the banking collapse, the three most frequent explanations cited for the problems were financial misconduct (the 'greedy bankers'), systemic problems with an unregulated financial sector, and the faulty free-market economic model itself. Problems with the economic system were thus in view. This was a crisis of neoliberalism: the form of capitalism we have been living with since the 1980s that espouses deregulation, privatization, low levels of social spending, and low taxes for the rich who are seen as 'wealth creators' (see McNally 2011 for one of the best accounts of the crisis). The news coverage didn't often give this level of analysis, but it did lay the blame on 'casino capitalism' and criticize a modern culture of unrestrained profiteering. These explanations were given across the media spectrum, with even the right-wing *Telegraph* and *Sun* complaining about a lack of regulation. Banking reform was the obvious solution and was advocated across the board.

Fast-forward to April 2009, barely six months after the British government announced a £500 billion bank bailout and similar moves were being made across Europe and the US. A media hysteria was now raging around Britain's deficit. While greedy bankers were still taking some of the blame, the systemic problems in finance and the problems with the free-market economic model had been forgotten. Instead, public profligacy had become the most frequently cited explanation for the deficit. The timeline of the crisis was being erased and rewritten.

Correspondingly, financial and corporate regulation were forgotten as appropriate solutions. Instead, austerity became the star of the show, eclipsing all other possible solutions to the crisis. As a response to the deficit, austerity – cutting public spending and raising taxes on the general population – was mentioned 2.5 as many times as the next most covered policy-response option, which was raising taxes on the wealthy. Austerity was mentioned 18 times more frequently than tackling tax avoidance and evasion (Basu 2018b, 78–79). Although coverage of austerity was polarized, no media outlet rejected it outright, with even the left-leaning press implicitly (and sometimes explicitly) backing a version of 'austerity lite.'

In 2010, the Conservative-Lib Dem coalition government announced £99 billion in spending cuts and £29 billion in tax increases per year by 2014–2015. Having made these 'tough choices,' from 2011 the coalition wanted to focus attention away from austerity and towards economic growth (which was, oops, being stalled by austerity). To do this, they pursued a zealously 'pro-business' agenda, including privatization, deregulation, cutting taxes for the highest earners, and cutting corporation tax.

These measures were a ramped-up version of the kinds of reforms that had produced the crisis in the first place. This fact, however, was forgotten. These 'pro-business' moves were enthusiastically embraced by the media, far more so than austerity. Of the five outlets analyzed, only *The Guardian* rejected them more frequently than endorsing them, and even *The Guardian* coverage was frequently enthusiastic.

When it came to the Eurozone crisis, journalists hardly gave explanations at all. When they did, they most commonly blamed corruption, profligacy, and laziness – of governments and sometimes even of the people themselves. Greedy bankers, systemic problems with the financial system, and the faulty free-market model were forgotten. News items presented the EU and IMF bailouts, with their accompanying deep austerity and privatization, as necessary and inevitable.

These, then, are the dynamics of *hyper-amnesia*, in which it is increasingly difficult to reconstruct timelines and distinguish causes from effects. This media amnesia helped trap us in a kind of neoliberal groundhog day where officials tried to remedy a neoliberal crisis with a form of neoliberalism-on-steroids. This amnesia was no less than an ideological weapon in a class war: the policies it legitimized – austerity, privatization, and tax cuts for the wealthy – transfer wealth and power upwards, from labor to capital.

3 The dynamics behind the dynamics

Between 2015 and 2016 I conducted interviews with journalists and analyzed the sociological and political economic factors driving these dynamics. What causes media amnesia? Make no mistake, sections of the press were actively rewriting and misremembering. Britain's news media, like those of many countries, are largely controlled by media barons. It is in their interests to promote policies that serve the rich. Whether proprietors intervene directly, whether they hire editors whose values reflect their own, or whether journalists censor themselves to fit in with the culture of their title, content will more than likely reflect the interests of proprietors. Politicians intent on bringing in these policies were also doing their best to rewrite events in a way to make them appear remotely logical. The right-wing press and politicians parroted each other's sound bites.

The liberal sections of the press and the broadcasters – who are mandated to be impartial – often reproduced amnesia passively. This was partly because their range of sources was very narrow. Together, politicians and other officials, business and finance accounted for around 70% of all sources quoted. Those responsible for causing the problems were called upon to make sense of them and offer solutions (Basu 2018b, 118). Those who might have had a different perspective – for example campaigners and activists, heterodox economists or trade unions – each accounted for less than 2.5%.

News values also played an important role. A major news value contributing to media amnesia is an obsession with the very latest events at the expense of historical context, explanation, and process. In my sample, 49% of coverage offered no explanation whatsoever for the crisis. In the vacuum created by the absence of other explanations, certain journalists and politicians were able to make the 'public sector profligacy' narrative dominant. This was the key justification for austerity.

All of these factors – media barons, sourcing, and news values – should be contextualized within the neoliberal period itself. Since the 1980s, governments have increasingly deregulated and privatized the cultural sector, as they have other sectors. Within this landscape, media companies stepped up their cost-cutting and revenue-raising practices, including mergers and acquisitions; union busting, job cutting, and forcing down working conditions; and ramping up content production on proliferating platforms (See Davis 2009).

These practices have put enormous pressure on journalists. Unsurprisingly, this has had an effect on the quality of content and has led to problems of inaccuracy, cannibalization, and an unwillingness and lack of time to hold the powerful to account and seek out a range of viewpoints and explanations. Ann Rigney and Astrid Erll (2009, 5) write that "the dynamics of cultural memory has to be studied at the intersection of both social and medial processes." In doing so, we find that the features of neoliberalism that produced the economic crisis were also partly responsible for its amnesiac media coverage.

4 The more things change, the more they stay the same

We can construct a helpful theoretical framework for these dynamics of cultural forgetting. For some critical theorists, forgetting is a key feature of capitalism. Fredric Jameson, in his reading of Karl Marx, describes capital as a "machine constantly breaking down, repairing itself not by solving its local problems, but by mutation onto larger and larger scales, its past always punctually forgotten . . ." (Jameson 2011, 7). One of the ways that capitalism creates amnesia is through one of its other defining features: acceleration. As theorists from Fredric Jameson (2003) to Hartmut Rosa (2013) to Paul Virilio (2006) to David Harvey (1990) have argued, we live in a world of more, more, more; faster, faster, faster.

This goes for all spheres of society, including the cultural sector. The acceleration of media production has created a 'media torrent' and 'information overload.' Although there is now an abundance of information, that does not necessarily mean we can process and remember it – quite the reverse. In their book *No Time to Think*, journalists Howard Rosenberg and Charles S. Feldman (2008) argue that "today's media blitz scrambles the public's perspective in ways that potentially shape how we think, act and react as a global society."

If acceleration causes amnesia, what causes the acceleration? It's the economy, stupid. It is the search for profit – capitalism's driving force – that leads companies to always be looking for ways to produce more and faster. This leads to a speeding up of our experience of time – what David Harvey (1990) has called 'time-space compression.' The neoliberal era, beginning in the 1980s, has taken this acceleration to new velocities, with finance capital's real-time transactions on the one hand and the just-in-time supply chains of transnational corporations on the other. Indeed, it is this dynamic – a new push for profit putting its foot on society's pedal – that produced the 2008 financial crash in the first place.

Profit-driven acceleration leads to cultural amnesia. For Jameson, this amnesia is ideological, allowing capitalism to keep reproducing itself: the more things change, the more they stay the same. Ann Rigney's concept of cultural memory dynamics can help us move from this 'macro' level of a social theory of acceleration and ideological amnesia to the 'meso' level of analyzing how these dynamics of forgetting actually work in practice. Which is what I've just done.

4 Life and Afterlives of Memory

Astrid Erll

Afterlives of Literature: Five Lessons from Odyssean Mnemohistory

1 Introduction

How can we write long-term mnemohistories of literature? How can we trace the complex cultural memory of literary texts and figures such as the *Odyssey* and 'Homer,' *Hamlet* and 'Shakespeare,' or *Waverley* and 'Walter Scott'? With her opus magnum *The Afterlives of Walter Scott*, Ann Rigney (2012a, 12) showed what it means to replace the "methodological textualism" of an older type of literary reception studies that tended to focus on text-text relations only with a rigorous memory studies approach. Rigney made clear that 'afterlives of literature' are not a purely literary phenomenon. Through processes of cultural memory, the literary imagination seeps into everyday life, shapes material culture and public discourse, and engenders all kinds of media products (literary and non-literary, oral and written, analogue and digital) – and all this within dynamic transnational mnemoscapes.

As early as in 2012, Rigney stated that a "long-term perspective on cultural memory in the period since 1800 has been lacking" (Rigney 2012a, 9). Not much has changed since then. Tracing long-term dynamics of memory remains a laborious business. It requires becoming a specialist on different historical epochs, cultural contexts, and media genres. But it is worth our while, because cultural memory *is* a long-term phenomenon: memories building upon, shaping and reshaping earlier memories. Afterlives may be traces of the past in the present, which unfold their own logic (Rigney's book opens with a photograph of "Scott Road" in Cape Town, South Africa), yet they emerge from tightly woven mnemohistories.[1]

In what follows, I will present 'five lessons' from my own work on a *longue durée* literary mnemohistory, that of the *Odyssey*.[2] The afterlives of the *Odyssey* are Odyssean indeed. The narrative has traversed more than 3,000 years, passing through ancient, medieval, and modern memory regimes, and traveled across the globe. The Odysseys we see today (in novels and film, in translation, on Instagram, or in everyday discourse) are the result of a *longue durée* mnemohistory, that is, a history of remembering and forgetting stretching over centuries and millennia.

---

1 The term 'mnemohistory' as the history of memory was introduced by Jan Assmann in *Moses the Egyptian* (1997). See also Tamm 2015.
2 I am grateful to Volkswagen Foundation, who awarded me an Opus Magnum to research the mnemohistory of the *Odyssey*.

This is also a history of remediation (Erll and Rigney 2009a). Like no other cultural memory that is still active today, the *Odyssey* has seen multiple remediations. It started as an oral-performative tradition in ancient Greek, turned into writing on papyri rolls, in handwritten codices, and in printed books, populated the world of analogue media (from silent film to the radio play and to television broadcasts), and has finally arrived in today's digital spheres.

2 Lesson one: Cultural loss is possible!

For scholars who work on the afterlives of hyper-canonical older texts (Virgil, Shakespeare), much-remediated events (the French Revolution, the Holocaust), or on the afterlives of modern authors (Joyce, Proust, Kafka, Brecht), it is something that rarely crosses one's mind: but the complete loss of a cultural memory *is* possible. Sometimes the question is not only *how* something is remembered, but *whether* it can be remembered at all.

The case of the Homeric *Odyssey* in the Middle Ages is such a case of cultural loss. In medieval western Europe, knowledge of the ancient Greek language had more or less disappeared after the fall of the Roman Empire. In fact, "[f]rom the 6th century CE until the 14th, 99 percent of the population of western Europe knew no Greek and thus had no direct access to Homeric epic" (King 2011, 720). 'Homer' had not only become (linguistically) incomprehensible, but also (materially) unavailable. While the manuscripts of certain Greek authors were acquired, kept, and copied within medieval monasteries (such as the Abbey at St. Gall), the Homeric epics were not among them. Young (2003, 71) points out: "There were no bilingual (Greek and Latin) texts of Homer and, in fact, it seems that there were few texts of Homer at all preserved among the ancient manuscripts in medieval monasteries; memory of his works was virtually gone."

As Aleida Assmann (2011 [1999]) has pointed out, written cultures are characterized by their double structure a "functional memory" (canon) and a "storage memory" (archive). Storage memory is a back-up mechanism. Archives and other institutions can keep information that seems irrelevant to present society but that might be useful in the future. In medieval western Europe, however, this storage-mechanism failed with regard to Homeric memory.

3 Lesson two: Transcultural memory can help

Sometimes, cultural memory's back-up mechanism lies not in its own canon/archive architecture, but in the existence of neighboring memory cultures. In 1360, Italian humanist Petrarch wrote in a letter to his friend Boccaccio of a "Homer, who, as far as we are concerned, is a lost author" (Cosenza 1910, 1980). This was true for medieval western Europe. The matter looked differently in the medieval East. In the Byzantine Empire, the Homeric poems were still preserved, studied, and copied. Eventually, Petrarch managed to acquire Byzantine manuscripts of the Homeric epics from Constantinople. But ancient Greek was utterly unreadable to the poet of the Latin West. Together with Boccaccio, Petrarch therefore organized and sponsored the first translation of the Homeric epics into Latin, which was done by the Calabrian Greek Leonzio Pilato in 1366.

This re-entry of Homer to the medieval West was often fashioned as the 're-covery of antiquity' for the project of modernity. What the humanist tradition conveniently forgot – but what becomes visible from today's perspective – is that this recovery was based on an act of transcultural memory.[3] Petrarch and his friends reached across what was felt to be a cultural and religious abyss and took share in traces of the past that others had curated over the centuries. Only with the help of Byzantine memory culture could the European West construct its proud poetic genealogy – from Homer via Virgil to Petrarch and the moderns.

Today, such "lateral dialogues"[4] across cultures are usually discussed when it comes to decentering the classics and including post-colonial voices in the discussion of Homeric memory. The case of Petrarch and Byzantium shows that western Europe, far from being the 'natural center' of Homeric mnemohistory and its afterlives, is indebted to the Byzantine East, from where it appropriated 'Homer' for the construction of its own memory and literary heritage, 'the Western canon.' It is an increasing concern of contemporary scholarship to uncover and better understand the Byzantine elements of the 'Homeric tradition'[5] – an example of how scholarship is an integral part of ongoing transcultural memory work, also across the *longue durée*.

---

3 On traveling and transcultural memory, see Erll 2011a.
4 Hardwick 2020, 27. Lorna Hardwick is one of the most important proponents of the new field of Classical Reception Studies, which shares many concerns with Memory Studies.
5 For an excellent overview, see Mavroudi 2019.

4 Lesson three: Transtemporal translation unfolds mnemonic agency

Emily Wilson's recent translations of the Homeric epics into English (*Odyssey* 2018, *Iliad* 2023) have forcefully brought home that translation history is a form of mnemohistory. Wilson's translations of the Homeric epics are gender-sensitive, antiracist, strongly focused on metrics, and (in a highly reflective way) modernizing. And they are an active intervention into the memory dynamics of translation.

Translation has recently become a major concern in literary memory studies and rightly so, as traveling and transnational memory is unthinkable without interlingual translation.[6] Not only translation across space, but also translation across time – "transtemporal translation" (Bachmann-Medick, 2017) – is a key agent in the memory process. This becomes clear when we look beyond the modern age. Texts in ancient languages such as Latin, Greek, but also Sanskrit were kept alive through their translation into modern vernaculars. Translation moves memory across time. But it is not a neutral transmitter of an 'original language' text. Instead, unfolds agency, co-constructing pasts, co-determining what is remembered, and how.[7]

The history of 'Homer in English' is an interesting example of the transtemporal dynamics and ethical implications of translation. In the Anglophone world, each new Homer-translation appears within the horizon of and is measured against more than a dozen authoritative previous translations – from Chapman to Pope, to Rieu, Fagles, and Lattimore.[8] Translation histories have their own memory logics. In the case of the Homeric *Odyssey*, the rendering of certain untranslatable phrases (such as the epithet *epi oinopa ponton* as "upon the wine-dark sea") has been consolidated over the centuries and now forms a cultural habit-memory. Other untranslatables, such as the epithet *polytropos*, which characterizes Odysseus in the poem's first line, have acquired metamnemonic status: each new translator will try their hand on it in an attempt to re-vision Odysseus – rendering *polytropos* as "much-traveled," "cunning," "resourceful," or (this is Emily Wilson's choice) as "complicated."

In her 2018 translation of the *Odyssey*, Emily Wilson uncovers a modern translation history that has rendered Odysseus's *dmoe* ('female house-slaves')

---

6 See, for example, Laanes 2021, Deane-Cox and Spiessens 2022, Jünke and Schyns 2024, Laanes et al. 2024.

7 On aesthetic agency in the memory process, see Rigney 2021b.

8 In fact, there are hundreds of published English translations of Homer since around 1600 (see Young 2003).

over the centuries euphemistically as 'maids.'[9] This translation practice has concealed the existence of slavery in Homeric society. Even more ethically dubious – and yet fascinating as a memory phenomenon – is the question how to refer to the twelve female slaves in Odysseus's household, who slept with the suitors.[10] For Pope in the eighteenth century, they are "nightly prostitutes to shame." For Fagles in the late twentieth century, they are still "the suitors' whores." However, the Greek text does not suggest any misogynic language. It has Telemachus refer to the women as "these [. . .] who slept beside the suitors." Over the centuries, English translation practice has framed the twelve young women hanged by Telemachus in a way that erases knowledge about their pitiable status as slaves. For readers, their lives are therefore (in Judith Butler's 2009 terms) 'not grievable.' With each new translation that resorted to this framing, such misremembering was further consolidated.

Wilson performs the task of the translator through detaching herself from such (often non-conscious) premediating acts of memory. Reflective transtemporal translation thus becomes an act of counter-memory (and a form of repair), and the translator turns into a memory agent. The 'original Homer' (i.e. the medieval manuscripts on which modern critical editions are based) suddenly appears in a new light, as a text that deals more sensitively with the issue of slavery and the status of enslaved women at Odysseus's court than modern translation history would have suggested. Transtemporal translation is path-dependent and can create problematic afterlives, but translators can break through established ways of remembering, and even change the status of the original for new generations of readers.

5 Lesson four: Mnemonic constellations entangle analogue and digital media

It is quite typical of today's plurimedial memory constellations that Wilson (2018) discusses her decisions not only in the "Translator's Note" prefacing the printed version of her translation, but also on her Twitter/X account. She thus communicates her version of Homeric memory across available media platforms.[11]

---

9 For this and the following arguments, see Wilson 2018.

10 The following refers to the lines spoken by Telemachus in *Odyssey* 22.463–4.

11 On the diachronic dynamics of remediation, see Erll and Rigney 2009a; for definitions of 'premediation' as the preformation of experience through (mediated) schemata and of 'plurimedial constellations' as synchronic memory assemblages, see Erll 2025.

Each medium of Wilson's mnemonic interventions has its own affordances: Arguments that Wilson puts forward in print media in a detailed, nuanced and footnoted manner are transformed on her highly followed Twitter/X account into prose that is characterized by condensation, rich imagery, and the rhythm and rhetoric of what might be called a 'tertiary orality.' In the following tweet, Wilson responds to the press hailing her as the 'first woman to translate Homer' – a problematic statement, which forgets important female translators working with languages other than English (e.g. French and Dutch) and deflects attention from generations of female classicists who have contributed important studies on Homer:

> I don't want to be Smurfette. I don't want to be made to represent THE WOMAN'S PERSPECTIVE, as if there were only one woman in the universe, or even among classicists, or even among Homerists. I don't want to erase other women's work. (@emilyrcwilson, 2. October 2019)[12]

The plurimedial constellation around Wilson's translations also includes the comment function on Twitter/X, which turns the discussion about Homeric memory into a public, nonspecialist, and often highly emotional debate. What needs to be considered, moreover, is the preparation, flanking, and resonance of Wilson's translations, for example through literary texts such as Margaret Atwood's novella *The Penelopiad* (2005), a rewriting of the *Odyssey* that gives the 'maids' a voice and conveys a sense of their grievability, or Pat Barker's *The Silence of the Girls* (2019), a rewriting of the *Iliad*, which reimages the camp of the 'noble Greeks' before Troy as a 'rape camp.' Academic debates, too, feed into the constellation – from the Black Athena debate of the 1980s to its updating in times of Black Lives Matter, and from the development of a gender-sensitive classical philology during the 1980s to more recent publications such as *Homer's Daughters* (Cox and Theodorakopoulos 2019).

Such plurimedial constellations – or mnemonic assemblages – become increasingly complex in the digital age (see Mandolessi 2023, 1514). To imagine literary afterlives as neat 'chains of reception' has always been wrong. But the digital age has heightened the multifariousness of entangled memory mediations. Mnemonic constellations are now constituted by dynamic online and offline polylogues, are shaped by premediation and remediation, and they can turn into temporality-charged switching points, where past presents flow into present pasts and are remade by them.

---

12 This tweet got 1,5K likes. In 2019, Wilson put "NOT the first woman to publish a translation of the Odyssey" on her twitter-bio.

6 Lesson five: Reading backwards – we all do it (but don't tell your professor)

The *modus operandi* of memory studies is 'reading backwards.'[13] But academic training in the humanities often suggests that 'reading forwards' is the 'proper' mode of moving through (literary) history.[14] What tends to be taught at universities are 'original events and texts' in their chronological order. Memory studies switches the temporal perspective around and works with mnemohistorical phenomena as their 'original events and texts.'

These 'mnemonic originals' range from translations, rewritings, and adaptations to archives, political discourse, and commemorative acts. Starting from an early modern translation (such as Mme Dacier's *L'Odyssée*, 1716), a contemporary journalistic use of the Odyssey to frame refugees (such as Patrick Kingsley's *The New Odyssey*, 2016), or a compelling novel about women in Dublin (e.g. Emilie Pine's *Ruth & Pen*, 2022), memory scholars read backwards in time. They try to understand which earlier mediations, strands of remembering and forgetting may have prepared the particular phenomenon at hand, and how the memory object is reshaped and in turn shapes understandings of the present and future.[15]

What distinguishes memory studies approaches to literary afterlives from earlier forms of 'influence studies' is the enormous agency that they assign to the later, the 'secondary,' seemingly 'derivative' work. Acts of memory not only reflect and shape the knowledges, identities, values and norms of their time, but they also co-construct the meaning of the past and its products.

This 'improper' way of reading backwards is arguably the default mode for most nonspecialist readers. They may arrive at the Homeric *Odyssey* through Stanley Kubrick's *2001: A Space Odyssey* (1968) or Derek Walcott's *Omeros* (1990) – or increasingly through content on YouTube or TikTok.

Reading backwards? Approaching texts through their afterlives? We all do it. But don't tell your professor – unless it's Ann Rigney or someone 'doing memory studies with Ann Rigney.'

---

13 On "reading backwards," see Perl 1984.
14 On being an "improper historian," see Rigney 2007.
15 For a discussion of Kingsley's book, see Erll 2018; for a discussion of Pine's *Ruth & Pen* as part of an Odyssean mnemohistory, see Erll 2024.

Rosanne Kennedy

The Afterlives of a National Apology: From Reconciliation to Self-Determination

1 Introduction

Since Australia's National Apology to the Stolen Generations was delivered in 2008, it has generated multiple afterlives. It is remembered in museums, in schools, on plaques and memorials, and in commemorative events, including in Parliament, where it has become an occasion to hold the government to account for its (lack of) progress in 'closing the gap' on Indigenous disadvantage. Rather than focus on official sites of remembrance, I explore the apology's activist afterlives: specifically, its mobilization by a grassroots Indigenous group, Grandmothers Against Removals (GMAR), and in a documentary film, *After the Apology* (2018). In creatively mediating GMAR's activism for future memory, the film goes beyond the "remedial self-determination" (Davis 2019, 78) of the apology – a symbolic offering by the state in the hope of repairing the damage done by its practices and institutions. By contrast, *After the Apology* (2018) remembers and promotes a "strong form" of Indigenous self-determination, which is substantively embedded in institutional arrangements that reflect the collective aspirations of the people being governed – in the case of GMAR, relating to Aboriginal autonomy in developing and providing services for Indigenous children and their families deemed to be at risk (Davis 2019, 79). Remembering and advocating for a strong form of self-determination is vital given the unfinished business of truth-telling and treaty in the Australian settler colonial present.

2 'Sorry' as a figure of memory

In Australia the story of 'sorry,' which has become a "figure of memory" (Assmann 1995, 129), does not start with the National Apology. 'Sorry' became a widely circulated idiom in the 1990s, a decade dedicated to fostering reconciliation between the Australian state and Indigenous peoples. Like other nations confronted with the divisive legacies of colonialism and slavery in the present, settler colonial Australia engaged in a "politics of regret" (Olick 2007). Responding to Indigenous activism that intensified in the 1980s, the Australian government in 1995 commissioned a National Inquiry into the forcible removal, between 1910 and 1970, of Indigenous children from mothers and kin, a practice that exemplifies

https://doi.org/10.1515/9783111439273-023

what Indigenous scholar Aileen Moreton-Robinson calls "the logic of the white possessive" (2015). In 1997, the national inquiry's landmark report, *Bringing Them Home*, controversially found that the transfer of Indigenous children from their cultural group with the intent of forcibly assimilating them into 'white Australia' constituted genocide as defined in international law (Dodson and Wilson 1997). As the first of fifty-four recommendations, the national inquiry recommended that the Federal government issue a national apology to the Stolen Generations.

When presented with the *Bringing Them Home* report at a National Reconciliation convention in May 1997, then Prime Minister John Howard expressed his 'personal regret' for the harm and suffering experienced by the Stolen Generations. But he notoriously refused to offer a parliamentary apology for fear of implicating present generations in guilt, responsibility, and reparations for the past. In response, ordinary citizens engaged in a range of campaigns and events to advocate for an apology, adopting 'sorry' as a rallying cry and contributing to its circulation as an idiom laden with moral and political meaning. For instance, in 1997, a 'Sorry Books' campaign, organized by a grassroots organization, Australians for Native Title and Reconciliation, spread across the nation. Large hardback books, inscribed with an apology on the first page, were available to be signed at commemorative community events, and in churches, schools, universities and other sites. Rather than merely signing, many individuals wrote lengthy personal apologies to the Stolen Generations (Kennedy 2011). 'Sorry' was also inscribed in cultural memory through 'Sorry Day,' first held on 26 May 1998, to commemorate the one-year anniversary of *Bringing Them Home*. In 2000, thousands of Australians marched over the Sydney Harbour bridge and other bridges in support of an apology, with a plane writing 'sorry' in the sky, and 'sorry' became an icon of the movement for apology. But 'sorry' only achieved the status of an official collective memory when newly elected prime minister Kevin Rudd delivered the National Apology to the Stolen Generations – his first act upon opening Parliament on 13 February 2008.

3 Staging the national apology: narrativity and collective memory

National apologies are by now a standard "mnemonic practice" (Rigney 2012b) issued by governments as one of a suite of reconciliation technologies that, by officially acknowledging past injustices, aim to move the nation towards a less divisive future. A staged event, the National Apology to the Stolen Generations was offered as an act of symbolic reparation and a crucial step on the path towards reconciliation. Delivered in front of members of the Stolen Generations and their families at Parliament House, and telecast to the masses assembled there, on the lawns outside, and in parks, workplaces, and schools around the nation, it was designed to be remembered as a formative moment in the nation's history. Delivering the apology, Rudd acknowledged "the uncomfortable truth [. . .] that the parliaments of the nation [. . .] enacted statutes [. . .] that made the forced removal of children on racial grounds fully lawful" (Commonwealth 2008, 169). Figuring Australia's settler colonial history as a 'book,' the government stated its hope that the apology would close "this blemished chapter" and facilitate moving the nation forward to "a new beginning" (Commonwealth 2008). In this figurative language, the national apology shares some of the "unifying force" that Ann Rigney finds in Sir Walter Scott's *Waverly* novels. Specifically, the apology "did much to create a unified public imagination based on the sense that everyone" was hearing the same story "about a past that was becoming collective" (Rigney, 2012a). While Indigenous people responded to the apology in a variety of ways, for many members of the Stolen Generations and their families who were seated in the upper stalls of the Senate chamber, some weeping as Rudd spoke, the long-overdue apology was an affective occasion, mixing relief with hope for the future.

Narratives that deploy the poetic arts of storytelling, with signature characters, may achieve the 'stickiness' that embeds them in memory (Rigney 2012a, 18). The apology did just this by narrating the personal story of a Stolen Generations woman, Nanna Fejo, who suffered a double removal: first removed from her mother as a young child, she was also separated from her siblings and cousins. Years later, when she met the Aboriginal stockman that handed the kids over to authorities, she forgave him. Rudd reminded the audience that hundreds of stories like Nanna Fejo's – stories that voice "the hurt, the humiliation, the degradation and the sheer brutality of [. . .] physically separating a mother from her children" were "graphically told" in *Bringing Them Home* (Commonwealth 2008, 168). Her story was evidently chosen, however, because she embodied the values of resilience and forgiveness that were central to the government's vision for reconciliation. Rudd implored the Stolen Generations and Indigenous peoples: "if the apology [. . .] is accepted in the spirit of reconciliation [. . .] we can today resolve together that there be a new beginning for Australia [. . .] this new page [. . .] can now be written" (Commonwealth 2008, 170). The apology's narrative structure – the past is evil, the evil is past and the future will be grounded in reconciliation rather than division – provides the moral meaning that is a core feature of narrative storytelling (Rigney 2012a, 32).

There is, however, an ambiguity at the heart of the apology. On the one hand, it expresses the government's desire to "close one of the darkest chapters"

(Commonwealth 2008, 168) in Australia's history by asking Indigenous Australians, for the sake of the imagined nation, to move into the future harmoniously, without demanding reparations, sovereignty, treaty, or the return of stolen land. On the other hand, the Parliament's resolution that the "injustices of the past must never, never happen again" (Commonwealth 2008, 168), uttered during the delivery of the apology, keeps it alive through its illocutionary force as a promise. It is this ambiguity that has been exploited, to powerful effect, in the afterlives of the apology in Indigenous activism and documentary.

4 Upstaging the national apology: grandmothers' activism and the afterlives of "Sorry"

Grandmothers Against Removals (GMAR) coalesced as a movement in the state of New South Wales in 2014, when grandmothers whose grandchildren had been suddenly removed from their care, without explanation or reason, discovered that their individual experiences were part of a systemic pattern. They were outraged to discover that, despite the promise of 'never again,' Indigenous children were being transferred out of Indigenous communities at rates higher than before the apology, leading to the possibility of a post-apology Stolen Generation. Between 2014 and 2019, GMAR activists identified and advocated for changes in policy and governance to be implemented urgently. To gain moral and political leverage for their campaign, they mobilized "sorry" in their protest slogan, "sorry means you don't do it again," transmitting their demands with affective force to the public and the government. Whereas the National Apology is remembered by many Australians, and promoted by national institutions, as a proud, iconic moment, GMAR activates the apology as a *broken promise* – an afterlife unanticipated when it was offered. To solicit support for their cause, GMAR held rallies around the nation, often on anniversaries commemorating the Stolen Generations. For example, to mark the tenth anniversary of the National Apology in 2018, GMAR staged a protest in the nation's capital, Canberra, passing the Aboriginal Tent Embassy's living "Sovereignty" memorial, and ending at Parliament House, where the promise of 'never again' was made.

Like many grassroots movements, the GMAR movement is ephemeral – leaving scattered material culture such as posters, t-shirts, photographs, social media posts and video footage that would not typically be archived. The movement, however, is remembered in *After the Apology*, a hybrid documentary directed by Larissa Behrendt, a Euahleyai/Gamillaroi radio broadcaster, filmmaker, novelist, and law professor. In a longer analysis of the film, I take a cue from Ann Rigney's observation that when "the memory of a cause plays into memory with a cause," this may yield a narrative structure with "a complex temporal overlay rather than a linear progression from past to present to future" (Rigney 2018a, 372). In contrast to the National Apology's linear narrative structure, the film shifts between present, past, and future in a recursive mode. After opening with the harrowing sounds of a child being removed in the present (the black screen denying a voyeuristic gaze), the film shows footage of Kevin Rudd delivering the apology. His speech is intercut with historical footage of Stolen Generations children in institutional care, followed by an intertitle stating the escalating numbers of Indigenous children in out of home care in 2016. The film interviews grandmothers whose grandchildren were removed without warning, sometimes in the middle of the night, conveying their shock and anger. Through their activism, however, the film depicts the grandmothers shifting subject positions from being victims of state bureaucracy to becoming active agents in shaping the future.

After the Apology is especially significant in linking GMAR's advocacy "for the cause" of self-determination *in the present* with the memory "of a cause" – the struggle for acknowledgement and redress for the Stolen Generations in the 1990s. A narrative turning point in the film occurs when Wiradjuri woman Linda Burney, then Minister for Indigenous Affairs, states emphatically: "we don't need another National Inquiry into child removal; we need another look at the recommendations of *Bringing Them Home*." If *Bringing Them Home*, published over twenty-five years ago, is remembered at all today outside of Indigenous communities, it is for its affecting testimonies and for the controversy that surrounded its finding of genocide – a symbolic judgment about the Australian settler colonial past with no legal consequences (Kennedy 2001). What is not widely remembered is the final chapter, 'Self-Determination,' which laid out a practical plan for moving forward, with Indigenous people leading governance in their communities. As Indigenous lawyer Megan Davis has observed, *Bringing Them Home* was "drafted during a stronger self-determination period in Australia," which has weakened in the first two decades of the new century (Davis 2019, 84). By returning to *Bringing Them Home*'s recommendations in the present, *After the Apology* engenders an affirmative, Indigenous-centered memory of the struggle for "intimate sovereignty" (Silverstein 2017, 358) in the governance of family matters.

After the Apology re-activates *Bringing Them Home* in two ways. Firstly, an adolescent female actor performs verbatim testimony from the report, mobilizing the memory of the harms of past child removals in and for the present. Secondly, and more significantly, it shifts the focus from the concept of genocide, which emerges from a Eurocentric international law tradition, to focus instead on self-determination – a concept "fundamental to the aspirations of Aboriginal communities" today (Davis 2012, 78), and a fundamental concept in Indigenous international law, enshrined in the United Nations Declaration on the Rights of Indigenous Peoples (UNDRIP) (2007). In their submission to a 2019 inquiry into the high rates of Indigenous children in out of home care, Aunty Glendra Stubbs and Elizabeth Rice assert that self-determination means that "no improved child protection system can meet the needs of Aboriginal and Torres Strait Islander children unless 'it is planned, developed, managed, implemented and reviewed by Aboriginal people themselves'" (Stubbs and Rice cited in Davis 2019, 86). In other words, it means more than mere consultation and participation. To that end, they urge the inquiry, *Family Matters*, to implement *Bringing Them Home's* recommendations regarding self-determination. While the goodwill and moral promise of the apology is shown to be exhausted, *Bringing Them Home* still holds insights that are worth returning to (Davis 2019, 84). In other words, the substantive implementation of Indigenous self-determination, rather than the forgetting imagined by "turning the page on the past," is what must come after the apology. Such an afterlife – embedded in Indigenous governance – would give the apology material as well as symbolic force.

Tashina Blom
The Cultural Memory of Protest Slogans

While they may seem as ephemeral as the cardboard they are written on, some protest slogans have a staying power that can make them survive for decades or even centuries as they travel across countries, contexts, movements, and sometimes even across political divides. As these slogans are adopted and adapted, re-circulated, and remediated, they also travel across surfaces as they become hashtags, materialize on walls, banners, bodies, or badges, and sometimes on mugs, tote bags, and even tea towels. With their long afterlives and their rich re-mediations across an expansive range of media-materialities, these protest slogans can become powerful carriers of the cultural memory of activism.

One of the defining features of protest slogans is their memorability, as short and easy to remember phrases that often use rhyme and rhythm, they are designed to 'catch on' or 'stick,' sometimes quite literally as they become stickers. Yet, there have been few studies to date that focus specifically on what it is exactly that 'catches on.' What memories get attached, conveyed, or reworked when an older protest slogan is used in the present? How do protest slogans with long histories and contemporary afterlives come to accrue memories of past struggles, people, or even tactics? In other words, how do protest slogans become a carrier of cultural memory? And what kind of political purposes can those memories serve for activists? By taking up these questions, I hope to show some of the ways in which protest slogans are ideally suited for analyzing the dynamics of the memory-activism nexus (Rigney 2018a; 2020) since protest slogans highlight the dynamic interplay and feedback loop at stake between the three different elements of this nexus.

The strength of the memory-activism nexus as a conceptual framework lies in its three-pronged approach; when applied to protest slogans, it sheds a valuable light on the various ways in which these cultural objects can become carriers of cultural memory. Protest slogans can become carriers of the *memory of activism*. This can be illustrated with the case of the famous anti-fascist slogan 'No Pasarán,' which gained fame when the Republican fighter Dolores Ibárruri Gomez used it in her 1936 radio speech after Franco's successful coup d'état and has been in use around the world for decades since. When this slogan is used as a book title in a publication about the Spanish Civil War (1936–1939) such as *¡No Pasarán!: Writings from the Spanish Civil War* (Ayrton 2016), the slogan becomes explicitly commemorative of the past that gave rise to it.

This Spanish Civil War memory, then, can also feed into the present when slogans are used politically as *memory in activism*, defined as "how the cultural memory of earlier struggles informs new movements in the present" (Rigney 2018a, 372). Examples abound, for instance when the slogan 'No Pasarán' is used transnationally in anti-racist movements such as during protest actions against the far-right anti-Islam movement Pegida, which originated in Germany but also operated transnationally and had supporters "in the UK, Estonia, Spain, Hungary, Russia, and the United States" (Druxes and Simpson 2016, 2). In this context, the use of the slogan mobilizes the cultural memory of the Spanish Civil War to cast the adversary, Pegida, as a new fascist threat that needs to be resisted. Here, the reference to the past is implicit and the implication is a pattern of framing that casts the addressed party as fascist, or at the very least as being on the wrong side of history. The slogan 'No Pasarán' has also been used in this way by both Ukrainians as well as by pro-Ukrainian foreign volunteers during the Russo-Ukrainian war (Tremlett 2022), thereby casting Putin as "the Franco of today" (Feffer 2022).

Finally, protest slogans can also play a role in *memory activism,* defined as the ways in which "actors struggle to produce cultural memory and to steer future remembrance" (Rigney 2018a, 372). Again taking 'No Pasarán' as an example, this slogan was used in the context of the Spanish anti-austerity movement 15-M which started in 2011 and brought an estimated six to eight million people to the streets, almost 10% of the total population (Servimedia 2011). While 15-M is often framed as an anti-austerity movement, this is too narrow to capture the movement's wide-ranging political claims as it also criticized Spain's two-party political system as well as political corruption, which it framed as the result of a failed transition to democracy. In fact, 15-M contributed to voicing, amplifying, and mainstreaming the idea that the Transition to Democracy was not successful, finished or even adequate (Kornetis 2014; Antenas 2016).

As you can see in Figure 1 below, during a protest in Madrid in May 2012, demonstrators adapted 'No Pasarán' to the longer 'Con Los Recortes y la Represión No Pasarán,' which roughly translates as 'They Shall Not Pass With These Cuts And Repression.' The word 'repression' is a much more historically loaded word in the Spanish context, especially when it is accompanied by the famous slogan 'No Pasarán.' This combination invokes a historical past of brutal political repression and the mass killing of citizens, a period also known as "la Represión Franquista" [Francoist Repression], which refers to the mass executions and rapes perpetrated by Nationalist factions during the Civil War and the Francoist regime. The word 'repressión' is not a neutral term but a semantic carrier of cultural memory, which is activated through its combination with one of the most famous Republican slogans of the Spanish Civil War period.

In this uptake, the slogan was used to highlight structural continuities between the Francoist reign and the present political and judicial structures which

Figure 1: Banner in Madrid featuring the adapted slogan, photo taken on the 23 May 2012. Source: Wikimedia Commons. CC BY-SA 2.0.

were responsible for implementing the austerity measures, criticizing the supposed successfulness of the Spanish transition to democracy as well as the memory politics of the so-called Pact of Forgetting or 'Pacto Del Olvido.' The latter term refers to the unwritten agreement to not deal with the Francoist past and legacy head-on but to instead forget or "dis-remember" that past (Encarnácion 2014). This approach of political forgetting informed the basis for the 1977 Amnesty Law that granted impunity to those who participated in war crimes during the Spanish Civil War and during the Francoist regime and repression. As Paloma Aguilar and Paco Ferrandiz have pointed out in their work on the memory politics of the Spanish Civil War exhumations "the most extreme instances of the ugliest face of the past – received hardly any attention during the transition's first years" (Aguilar and Ferrandiz 2016, 5). Given this background, the protest slogan's use in Spain in 2011 functions to mobilize and amplify the criticism of an until then dominant memory politics of forgetting. This analysis points to the crucial role of the feedback loop between the three different elements of the memory-activism nexus.

Protest slogans with long histories and rich afterlives, such as 'No Pasarán,' but also ones like 'My Body My Choice' or the French 'Ni Dieu Ni Maître,' can start to function as 'portable monuments' (Rigney 2004). Texts are 'portable' monuments, which "can be carried over into new situations" as they "may be recycled among various groups of readers living in different parts of the globe and at different historical moments" (Rigney 2004, 383). While this quote refers to literary works, the same principle holds true for shorter units of language like protest slogans. Rather than providing a full narrative or a visual depiction of the past, protest slogans with long histories can function as shorthand references to the past and, as such, can invoke the memory of the historical period they are thought to belong to, or to the people who have either coined or used the slogan in the past. In fact, the origin stories behind where a slogan comes from or who first used it are often multiple and conflicting, sometimes more mythical than factual. In other words, these stories are produced through the dynamics of cultural memory.

Adaptability, ambiguity, and aesthetic appeal are the three key ingredients that determine whether a protest slogan gains the kind of viscosity that allows it to stick around and become a carrier of cultural memory. Slogans like 'No Pasarán' are ambiguous as to who exactly shall not pass, making it an adaptable sign that mobilizes the memory of the Spanish Civil War to make a political claim which implicates that the adversary is a fascist threat that needs to be resisted. As such, it has been used in a wide range of contexts around the world. Slogans can also be adapted to new forms. In France, for instance, the slogan has even been used as 'No Passaran' during demonstrations against the so-called "pass sanitaire," which was a proof of vaccination required to gain access to bars and shopping centers during the COVID-19 pandemic (De Telegraaf 2021). Its four-syllable concision and punchy meter, that starts and ends with a stressed syllable, aesthetically contributes to its staying power as an easy to remember phrase that packs a rhythmic punch.

This serves as a reminder that there is an agency in the aesthetic appeal of cultural forms, which can help generate memorability (Rigney 2021b, 12). Protest slogans, as much as literary stories, can be seen as examples of the creative use of "cultural forms to generate vibrant (if not always literally true) stories that may then be picked up and reworked in other disciplines" (Rigney 2021b, 12). While the stories and memories that slogans carry might not be reworked in the same way – e.g., a book adapted to become a feature film – slogans do get remediated in a wide range of media materialities. 'No Pasarán,' for instance, is now widely available printed on T-shirts, where its link to Dolores Ibárruri is usually disarticulated since she is not featured or depicted. However, translated to the English 'They Shall Not Pass,' the slogan also features as the title of Dolores Ibárruri's translated memoires (Ibárruri 1966), making it a carrier of her individual memory.

As cultural artifacts that carry the cultural memory of activism, protest slogans are not merely two-dimensional linguistic utterances with certain rhetorical effects, instead they are three-dimensional cultural practices that are embodied by and embedded in political groups. As anthropologist Beatrice Fraenkel has suggested, slogans are simultaneously acts, artifacts, and utterances of writing (Fraenkel 2006). To fully understand slogans, one has to understand them as the triple gestures that they are:

> Common acts, such as those designated by the verbs: copy, record, sign, label, display, etc., have in common the fact that in performing them one engages in three things at the same time: making an artefact (a copy, a record, a label, a signature, a poster), producing an utterance, and performing an act that alters the course of things, both small and large. (Fraenkel 2006, 93, translation mine)

In other words, it matters whether a slogan is chanted in the street, where it can unify a diverse crowd and transform a cacophony of voices into a single speaking subject. It matters whether it is carried on the body as a badge pinned close to the heart, where it travels along with the wearer through both the fabric of literal textiles as well as through the fabric of everyday life. It matters whether they are spray painted onto walls, or – before the invention of the spray can in 1949 – hand-painted onto walls with paint, for those who could afford that, or shoeshine, crayon, or tar, for those who could not (Carle 2020). Not unimportantly, the latter takes longer and thus involves a greater risk to get caught in the act by the authorities.

As these slogans get remediated into a wide array of objects, including even domestic objects such as tea towels like those produced by the London-based Radical Tea Towel company (see Figure 2 below), these ephemera become testaments to what Ann Rigney in reference to Walter Scott's antiquarianism, has called "the materialised presence of the past in the physical environment" (Rigney 2015b, 13). In describing Sir Walter Scott's intricately curated home of Abbotsford as well as its surrounding gardens, Rigney suggests the idea of a memory habitat:

> Unlike a 'site' that was set apart from the everyday, it is better described as a synthetically produced habitat in which everyday life in the modern world could be played out in the continuous presence of testimonial objects and of objects made from memory-saturated materials, including use-objects like pneumatic bells (Rigney 2015, 21).

Whereas Walter Scott's nineteenth-century home featured pneumatic bells, Scottish regalia, and Roman urns, contemporary capitalism has given us slogans printed on every imaginable use object, from tea-towels, tote bags and T-shirts to erasers, key chains and even computer mouse mats. While these are not actual relics from the past imbued with the same affective aura as the ones found in Walter Scott's home, they are representations of the past that function as a kind of late-stage capitalist stand-in for the relic. To paraphrase Walter Benjamin, perhaps these commodity objects can be seen to constitute the relic in the age of its mechanical reproduction (Benjamin 2008).

Figure 2: No Pasarán tea towel by the Radical Tea Towel Company, author's own object and photo made on 5 December 2023.

Importantly, the distinction between activist cultural production and commodity production is not always that clear-cut, given that activist collectives sometimes produce badges, tote bags, and T-shirts with the aim of funding their activist projects. In the case of the Radical Tea Towel company, their mission is to "grow the revolution" by keeping the memory of radical histories alive in the present.[1] As such, they also curate a radical history blog and they have donated part of the proceeds from sales to heritage institutions such as the Manchester People's History Museum. Examples like these show that commodification plays an important role in the memory-activism nexus as it can financially fund movements and heritage institutions that keep the memory of activism alive while also providing us with the commodity-relics that keep those memories in our homes, on our bodies, and in our contemporary memory habitats.

---

1 https://radicalteatowel.co.uk/meet-the-team

Commodity production is an important and sometimes overlooked mode of dissemination for both specific historical protest slogans as well as for protest memories at large. Commodification does not necessarily strip a protest memory of its radical clout or potential. Instead, it is crucial for memory scholars to shed a light on how activist cultural production and commodification, as well as the entanglement between the two, drive and shape the cultural memory of activism.

Kiene Brillenburg Wurth

Musical After/Lives: Cultural Remembrance and Distributed Creativity

1 Living on: coming before coming after

The other day, I heard Louis van Dijk's jazzy version of *The Windmills of Your Mind* (1968).[1] I remember running into this popular Dutch pianist in a pub in Utrecht one night in the early 1990s. Shall we play together? He generously asked. I stammered something about being unable to improvise, but he would have none of it. We did a four-hand flashy version of part of the Schumann piano concerto in A minor, opus 54, and then went for *Les moulins de mon coeur*. At the time, I knew this as a song by the Moroccan French Italian singer Frida Boccara, who had won the Eurovision Song Contest for France in 1969 with *Un jour, un enfant* (a victory shared with the Netherlands, UK, and Spain). We used to play it, along with other *chansons*, in a golden Peugeot 504 on our way to the summer holidays in the 1970s.[2] That night, Van Dijk gave his signature Bach-like swing to *Les moulins*, which made me forget my shame and swept me into the music. Our shared improvisation generated a momentary congruence, a convergence of associations, affects, movements, rhythms, and sound vibrations. A living memory, I would say, of a well-known song, in so far as memories are (re)creative and transformative. It arose, was shared, and ceased, living on in me.

At the start of Ann Rigney's academic career, Jacques Derrida wrote about *survivance* or 'living on' (or 'on living'/'on-living') to mark the mutual implication of life and death, present and past (Derrida 1986 [1979]). 'Living on' is not an afterthought; a memory coming after an event has ceased. Rather, 'living on' is about events marked by the possibility of their disappearance; by what remains to come. *Survivre* defies a linear time frame. It is not a continuation of something given but – peculiarly – what resists continuation as a prolongation or conservation of 'what is.' 'Living on' alludes to what can *transform* the event, what propels its productive cancellation: a potential or excess of meaning that the event cannot yet disclose about itself. For Derrida, therefore, any possible release of this excess cannot be logically said to be coming 'after' the event (just as a translation cannot

---

1 Louis van Dijk. *The windmills of your mind*. 1970. https://www.youtube.com/watch?v=MSmPp6IxtPg
2 Frida Boccara, *Les moulins de mon Coeur*. 1969. https://www.youtube.com/watch?v=8E5EfDsJxAU

strictly be said to be coming after an 'original') (Derrida 1986 [1979]). The return animates or ignites this event and thus, in a way, becomes its predecessor (Weber 2008). Following this anterior logic, I approach 'living on' in this entry as an excess gathered into cultural artifacts; as an openness that haunts or is "after itself" [Nachleben] – that returns, again and again (Weber 2008, 66).

The movement of return – turning back, troubling, re-transforming – has been at the core of cultural memory studies in recent decades. It has been explored in critical trauma studies, translation studies, reception studies or productive aesthetics, and research on cultural continuity (Rigney 2016). In this chapter, I unpack the movement of return through the lens of two popular songs: *The Windmills of Your Mind* and *Les moulins de mon coeur*. I propose approaching the multiple lives of these songs in terms of distributed creativity. In the last decade, this term has been used to understand group processes of creativity and has gained some traction in memory-, sound-, and music studies (Michaelian and Sutton 2016, Glăveanu 2014). Here, however, I tweak the term to attune it to the logic of surplus or 'living on': a dynamic of dissemination and disturbance. I then assess the relevance of distributed creativity to what Rigney calls longevity and cultural remembrance: how the past is made present in media through a shared reservoir of forms and meanings (Rigney 2016). Is mnemonic longevity co-conditioned by distributed creativity, and if so, how?

2 Round like a circle in a spiral

The 1960s. It was a time when *chansons* resonated with classical music – J.S. Bach and Ludwig von Beethoven in Serge Gainsbourg, Wolfgang Amadeus Mozart in Michel Legrand. In 1968, when the Cannes Festival was canceled due to the Paris protests, director Norman Jewison asked Legrand to compose a song for a scene in *The Thomas Crown Affair* (dir. Norman Jewison, 1968), starring Steve McQueen and Faye Dunaway. Lyrics were to be created by songwriters Alan and Marilyn Bergman. Marilyn Bergman recalls how the song was to evoke the state of mind of playboy Thomas Crown – rich, charming, restless – circling in a glider as he contemplates the challenge of a bank heist in a minutes-long shot: "Norman Jewison [. . .] wanted a song that exposed no character, that didn't tell any plot – he just wanted the [. . .] uneasiness of the character underlined" (Songfacts). One of the melodies Legrand proposed stood out. It was a bit odd and strikingly circular. The Bergmans suggested:

Round, like a circle in a spiral
Like a wheel within a wheel
Never ending or beginning
On an ever-spinning reel
Like a snowball down a mountain
Or a carnival balloon
Like a carousel that's burning
Running rings around the moon[3]

Effectively a list of spherical similes evocative of Crown's spinning mind (circle, wheel, reel, snowball, balloon, carousel, rings), the text matched the wave-like movements of Legrand's composition. Thus – repetitive and seemingly unstructured – a popular song was born: *The Windmills of Your Mind*, recorded by Noel Harrison for the movie and soon after (though reluctantly) by Dusty Springfield (Songfacts). Legrand's career would thrive on it, winning him a Golden Globe and an Oscar in 1969 for Best Original Song. A French version was spun that same year as *Les moulins de mon coeur*, with lyrics adapted by Eddie Marnay, first recorded by Marcel Armont in 1969 (Ministru 2021). Not surprisingly, it became a wordy, melancholy song of love lost, of a heart rehearsing a memory in solitude:

Comme une pierre que l'on jette dans l'eau vive d'un ruisseau
Et qui laisse derrière elle des milliers de ronds dans l'eau
Comme un manège de lune avec ses chevaux d'étoiles
Comme un anneau de Saturne, un ballon de carnaval
[. . .]
Et voilà que sur le sable nos pas s'effacent déjà
Et je suis seul à la table qui résonne sous mes doigts[4]

From a bird's eye perspective to an intimate 'I,' from mind to heart, *Windmills* and *Moulins* would go on to lead their separate lives in the English and French-speaking worlds, with over 300 recordings, renditions, and remixes produced in years and decades to come. The song continued its popularity as a chanson, jazz-, choral-, and a cappella work and was adapted into different languages: Dutch, Greek, German, Czech, Croatian, Italian, Japanese, Russian, and so on. Like many

---

3 For the complete lyrics in English, visit Genius: https://genius.com/Noel-harrison-the-wind mills-of-your-mind-lyrics
4 For the complete French lyrics, visit Genius: https://genius.com/Michel-legrand-les-moulins-de-mon-coeur-lyrics. An English translation of these lines reads as follows:
Like a stone thrown into the running water of a stream/ And which leaves behind thousands of circles in the water/ Like a moon carousel with its star horses/ Like a ring of Saturn, a carnival balloon/ . . . And now on the sand our footsteps are already fading/ And I am alone at the table which resonates under my fingers.

other listeners, I had taken *Moulins* for the original version. But even the Oscar-winning *Windmills* wasn't its own resource. Distribution precedes its inception. Thus, Legrand's typical sequencing repeats almost *verbatim* the melody and harmonies of the Andante from Mozart's sinfonia concertante K. 364 (Ministru 2021) – and, I would say, echoes the Andantino from Mozart's piano concerto K. 271.[5] In its turn, the sinfonia concertante dependently arose from the novel musical forms Mozart had heard in Mannheim during his travels – just like the Bergmans, for their part, will have taken their cue from stream-of-consciousness writing in their poetic setting to the melody. Thus, the circling song emerged from (and invigorated) a swirl of past melodies, musical modes, and literary styles. As a creative product, it surfaced from what Vlad Glăveanu calls a "relational space": a space between persons, persons and things, or persons and their cultural stories (Glăveanu 2014, 1).

Did *Windmills* 'live on' so profusely because of an openness that allowed it to transform? What was this openness? Is it the relational space identified by Vlad Glăveanu – a space of creation or generation between persons, persons and things, or persons and cultural stories? Or can such openness be restricted to the agency of persons? Maybe persons and their intentions are no match for it; maybe openness presumes a more radical relational space. I explore this space in the next section. Thinking with Renate Lachmann's notions of intertextuality and surplus value, I imagine creation or creativity as a distributed generative force potentially disseminated *beyond* personal agency. This view of creativity opens our ears and eyes to the life of words and sounds and how they interact and may inadvertently intensify experience.

3 Remembrance as intertextuality: play and openness

I found a picture of Legrand, Van Dijk (at the piano), Rick van der Linden, and Chi Coltrane in the daily *De Telegraaf* (1974).[6] Next to Legrand, each musician

---

5 W.A. Mozart, "Andante" from sinfonia concertante K. 364 for violin, viola, and orchestra in E flat major. See for instance the rendering by Guiliano Carmignola, violin, Antoine Tamestit, viola, Insula Orchestra, under the direction of Laurence Equilbey: https://www.youtube.com/watch?v=jpbYiWbC6PM; W.A. Mozart, "Andantino" from piano concerto K. 271 in E flat major. I recommend the rendering by Artem Belogurov, fortepiano, and Postscript, concertmaster Rachael Beesley: https://www.youtube.com/watch?v=xbG2luqCzoI
6 Cor Berkenbosch, "Zwaar geschut bij Pim" *De Telegraaf* 11 January 1974 https://www.delpher.nl/nl/kranten/view?facets%5Bspatial%5D%5B%5D=Landelijk&query=music±all±in±legrand±chi

would offer their version of *Windmills* in an easy listening show called Music-All-In that night: Rick van der Linden returned the song to J.S. Bach, Chi Coltrane took her cue from Richard Strauss, while pianist-singer Jules de Corte played it à la Franz Schubert. Van Dijk's adaptation, as noted, is also a Baroque-informed piece, just as Legrand had made a Mozart adaptation in his 'original song' . . . *Like a wheel within a wheel/ Never ending or beginning.* Remembrance, as Rigney holds, is remaking (Rigney 2016). But what kind of remaking are we dealing with here?

If re-making defines remembrance, then remembrance is a mode of creativity: a cognitive ability, as social scientists commonly define creativity, to generate things new and useful or meaningful out of whatever is available. The problem with this cognitive frame for creativity is its focus on persons and their abilities rather than material processes: it limits creativity to the mind. As such, it fails to have relevance for remembrance as a *cultural* dynamic (Rigney 2016). Alternatively, a distributed frame sees creativity as a process whereby novelty and meaningfulness emerge from cultural circulations (Glăveanu 2014). As indicated above, Glăveanu stresses that in this frame, creativity circulates not just between groups of people but also between people and things, their environment, their past, their stories, and their (media) environment – an interesting venue for cultural memory studies. Yet, something is missing in this definition of distributed creativity. It does not access the potentially creative tension *between* sounds, rhythms, words, sensations, and associations as I encountered it long ago at the piano with Van Dijk. This is a tension challenging to gauge since it is subtle and evanescent, not a concrete thing to be tracked and traced in quantifiable models for shared, creative production.

In *The Life of Texts*, Rigney recounts how, in the 1960s, semiotics, and more specifically, the concept of intertextuality, took the literary-critical focus away from "individual creativity and more to the collective aspects of culture" (Brillenburg Wurth and Rigney 2019, 91). This new focus was informed by the idea of the conventionality of language as a cultural product and of discursively construed subject positions (Brillenburg Wurth and Rigney 2019, 99). By extension, texts were seen as shared rather than original products: language speaks through subjects, just as culture and textual archives write through individual texts. Still, for theorists like Julia Kristeva, Roland Barthes, Barbara Johnson, and Renate Lachmann, this distributed nature of texts was not about conventionality. It was about play and openness, the uncontrollability of semiosis: the "surplus value" (the 'liv-

---

±coltrane±&coll=ddd&identifier=ddd:011239179:mpeg21:a0185&resultsidentifier=ddd:011239179: mpeg21:a0185&rowid=2

ing on') generated by reverberations between texts (Lachmann 1997, 18). Every text enfolds or rings with its otherness and, thus, generates its longevity. *Comme une pierre que l'on jette [. . .]/ Et qui laisse derrière elle des milliers de ronds dans l'eau . . .*

There is poetic logic to these ideas of play and reverberation. They are about becoming and unbecoming, about carrying over unexpected views and meanings, and perhaps loosening our attachment to established ones. They minimize mastery and maximize accidental interactions between words, sounds, and texts. Intertextuality could thus be seen as a force of interference, a dynamic in the space between texts that shines a light through encrusted sense. It keeps things going as contingent semantic alteration and disordering in a memory space – a space where cultural works re- or overwrite each other.

4 Distributed creativity

In my use of the term, distributed creativity takes its cue from intertextuality as a dynamic of dissemination and disturbance. Dissemination *is* distribution, or scattering, in contrast to creation as a single originating act. It is multiple and ongoing. Creativity is a disturbance to the extent that it interrupts a seemingly consistent state, situation, or relation. Creative work may unsettle the familiar, questioning the given, enlivening perception, and opening different frames of experience. Disturbance has its roots in 'turbid' and the Latin *turbidus*, meaning muddy. Muddy waters tend to clear themselves when left alone; fresh movement gradually emerges from muddy stillness. Carrying the metaphor further, disturbance may thus engender fresh ways of seeing. It implies perspectival change, a transformative process of perception.

As bricolage soundscapes, *Windmills* and *Moulins* may not offer the most exciting or innovative poetic textures. Yet, they exemplify the poetic logic of distributed creativity: an interruption of sedimented sense through an indirect transfer of associations. Both versions consist of similes without a landing, so to speak. They offer a list of tropes that do not integrate but linger in the air to point to a state of mind or heart through comparison.

The more openly words manifest as mere pointers (as they do in both versions of the song), the more robust, perhaps, the transformative potential in language as it leaps from what it establishes. When contexts of meaning cease to work, routes may be opened out of those spinning "circles that you find/ In the windmills of your mind." Discursive logic is then disturbed *by way of language* – a kind of language that encircles rather than coheres. In this light, creativity need not be confined to intentional actions by human agents. Instead, it could be imagined as *survivance* in language: as surplus value that continues to transform or disperse meaning in contexts that, at first sight, merely seemed to hinder or discontinue its possibility.

5 A space of becoming

Leaps, interruptions, and cessations . . . I seem to have moved a far cry from cultural or shared remembrance as a dynamic of continuity. Except that I haven't. As a text, *Windmills* is a typical product of the (post-)psychedelic age. It vibrates with falling – a meaningful contrast, the Bergmans have explained, to the glider in the sky seen on screen in *The Thomas Crown Affair*. Marilyn Bergman recalls how the idea of writing a text with a trance-like quality was triggered by her remembrance of sliding into sedation when she was very young: "When I was seven I had my tonsils out," explains Marilyn. "And as they gave me the ether anaesthetic I remember this circular descent into a sleep state. Alan had had a similar experience. And that's how we got the idea to write for Michel's circular melody."[7] A fragmented textuality recollects half-forgotten experiences.

Remembrance is re-making, as Vanilla Fudge – the famous rock band – illustrates as well in their more experimental take on trance and *Windmills* (1969).[8] What would re-making be without gaps and leaps? More of the same? Affirmation? Words, says poet Jane Hirshfield, have a "breathing aliveness" of their own (Hirshfield 2017, 3). They are not entities but activities that may disturb patterns of perception and heighten experience. Cultural remembrance, Rigney knows, needs a little *ostranenie*, a little estrangement,[9] for meaningful repetition to materialize. Estrangement, alienation from what language establishes, opens a space of becoming. In this space of becoming, distributed creativity propels mnemonic flow.

---

7 No date or author is indicated for the interview in *The Jewish Chronicle*. https://www.thejc.com/life-and-culture/music/happily-married-and-in-a-relationship-with-streisand-l4xhvcqe
8 The rock adaptation, slurring out the circles, can be accessed here: https://www.youtube.com/watch?v=lxthq9AOWoo
9 In *The Life of Texts*, Rigney translates Viktor Shklovksi's formalist concept of *ostranenie* as defamiliarization, to refer to the ability of literary language to effectuate a "de-automatization" of perception in its readers when "expected patterns are broken" (393).

Mads Rosendahl Thomsen

Posthumanist Dreams of Imperfect Memories

1 Memory without limits

As the idea of an eternal self, strongly promoted in Romanticism, has waned, memory has become less and less innocent as its perceived importance for the shape of the self has increased. This has, at times, been a challenge to accept. In the first pages of *Stages on Life's Way* (1845), the Danish philosopher Søren Kierkegaard reflects on what it means to create true recollections that pertain to the individual rather than mere memories of unimportant events:

> Although the difference between memory and recollection is great, they are frequently confused. In human life, this confusion lends itself to studying the depth of the individual. That is, recollection is ideality, but as such it is strenuous and conscientious in a way completely different from indiscriminate memory. (Kierkegaard 1988, 10)

Hopes of eternal life still drove Kierkegaard, but he was skeptical of the conception of the soul as having a nucleus that earthly deeds would not affect. Memory thus becomes an art form that shapes the soul, which may live beyond this world but will be shaped by the ability to form a coherent sum of memories. You are what you remember. That is a great responsibility to put on a human.

Today, the questions of memory, being, and eternity are not so much seen in the light of metaphysics but technology. Visions of the posthuman have been part of literature for a long time, both as a warning of what could be lost and as an alluring promise of things that metaphysics cannot provide (Kurzweil 2005; Bostrom 2014). For a long time, most science fiction seemed so far ahead of the curve that they were comfortably far away, but novelistic visions of profound change are now being read in a dramatically different technological environment (Thomsen 2020, Ferrando 2020).

Written in the late 1960s, Philip K. Dick's short story "The Electric Ant" presents a humanoid robot that has become depressed by discovering that it is not human but merely a robot. It also realizes that a punch card roll in its chest controls its state of mind, which it begins to tamper with fatal consequences. It is striking to compare this (imagined) stage in technological development to the ubiquitous access to all the world's information today through smartphones and other devices that are now also equipped with generative artificial intelligence.

Dreams of a perfect future human would also have to consider the kind of memory such beings would be equipped with. What if we could choose freely how we would recall? The fear of losing memories, in these years amplified by Alzheimer's disease, would intuitively suggest that a perfect human should have a perfect memory. This idea, however, has been elegantly refuted by Jorge Luis Borges in his fiction "Funes the Memorious" (1942) which chronicles the downsides of having a perfect memory as the past becomes overwhelming and rid with insignificant details. Constantly bombarded with images from the past, Ireneo Funes leads an unhappy life with what could otherwise have been described as a blessing of perfect recollection.

That there is a widespread fascination with extraordinary memory is evident as it is central in several films that have used memory as a critical element in their adaptations of works by Philip K. Dick and other writers. *Blade Runner* (dir. Ridley Scott, 1982), *Total Recall* (dir. Paul Verhoeven, 1990), and *Blade Runner 2049* (dir. Denis Villeneuve, 2017) have explored how essential memories are to the individual. Among many ways to show this, the discovery that one's memories are not self-experienced but copied from someone else is among the most shocking moments in *Blade Runner*. *Blade Runner 2049* suggests that even if memories are artificially induced into humanoid robots, Androids, there is still value in creating such memories with a base in authentic human experiences.

2 Better memory for what?

But these stories also remind us of the complexity of memory to the individual. We have our personal memories that are flawed and unreliable and often come back to us involuntarily, but they are ours. At least we think so, but they mingle with mediatized collective memories. If one were to redesign human memory, what would be kept and what would be changed? Is it a blessing that we have more positive than negative memories (Rubin 2003)? Is the ability to make memories that do not correspond perfectly to the events one believes to remember also a suitable mechanism for coping with the world? Would we change the distribution of memories and eliminate the so-called reminiscence bump that makes seniors remember much more from their formative years (Thomsen and Berntsen 2008)? And should we have more or less control over involuntary memories (Berntsen 1996)?

These questions are actually not easy to answer, not least since some unexpected and random memories certainly make up for experiences that we consider to be valuable and human. If we could eliminate all these elements to promote control and predictability that would create a human with a mind that is more like a machine. As I have argued in *The New Human in Literature* (2013), the value of imperfection is a widespread theme in visions of the posthuman that through not least the understanding of the importance of aesthetics to life, including story-telling and memories, goes against the simple idea that life can be perfected (Thomsen 2013, 216).

However, it would also be arrogant to think that we live in the best of all worlds regarding memories. From the haunting effects of trauma to merely useless memories, there should be plenty of ways to think about improvement without losing the human touch. Alan Glynn's novel *The Dark Fields* (2001), later republished as *Limitless* to match the movie version of the original novel, explores a radical enhancement of the human capacity for remembering and reasoning. The protagonist, Edward Spinola, begins to take an experimental drug called MDT-48 and soon becomes aware of his new cognitive powers:

> I went back over to the desk and keyed in some notes on the computer, about ten pages of them, and all from memory. There was a clarity to my thought processes right now that I found exhilarating, and even though all of this was alien to me, at the time it didn't feel in the least bit odd or strange, and in any case I simply couldn't stop – but then I didn't want to stop, because during this last hour or so I had actually done more solid work on my book than I had in the entire previous three months. (Glynn 2011, 30–31)

The drug opens a pathway to success for Spinola as he can outsmart and outperform people, not least by having memory accessible far beyond average human capacity. Being a novel written for entertainment and reflection, not everything turns out well: Spinola's life is in danger as other people want access to MDT-48, and the ups provided by the drug are followed by down periods as the effect ends. In the movie, there is an interesting and unusually optimistic conclusion, namely that Spinola's brain has been rewired and that he is no longer dependent on the drug but has become what one would have to describe as trans- or posthuman.

3 Poetics of prosthetic memory

While the idea of changing the fundamental setup of human memory is fascinating, it is also dangerous territory, better suited for fiction than experiment, even though it is important to remember that there is a long practice of performing psychiatric treatment that influences memories (Lisanby et al. 2000). This is also central in the writer Søren Ulrik Thomsen's memoir on his mother's many treatments with electroconvulsive therapy (*Store Kongensgade 23*). Seemingly more benign, easier to change, but also immensely forceful is the ecosystem of memory technologies and social influences. If robotlike perfect memory would make us less human, it is worth considering how we would think of a world without memory culture and technology to support that. Ann Rigney makes it quite clear how diminished our idea of how life has unfolded would be without what Alison Landsberg has termed "prosthetic memory" (Landsberg 2004):

> Experiential narration is a key element in the making of prosthetic memory. As a result, novelists and film directors have had an important role to play in bringing the past to life for the public at large. If people nowadays share a memory of World War I – the mud, the trenches, the horror – this is thanks to multiple works of historical fiction. (Rigney 2019 [2006], 368)

Three of the great dystopian novels of the twentieth century all revolve around the loss of prosthetic memory and what that would do to the soul. The expulsion of Shakespeare's writing in Aldous Huxley's *Brave New World* (1932), the meticulous manipulation of memory in George Orwell's *Nineteen Eighty-Four* (1949), and the burning of books in Raymond Bradbury's *Fahrenheit 451* (1953), are all examples of the high value of prosthetic memory. What these works also have in common is a rebellion against societies that do not allow the individual to take part in shaping her or his own identity by denying access to a wealth of sources for doing so – to cultural memory, that is.

Rigney also rightly points out that not all memories are created equally or should be treated equally. Novelists, such as Walter Scott, take part in forming collective memories through the power of narratives that will enhance certain memories and leave others to be forgotten:

> [T]he role of novels is not just a matter of recalling, recording, and "stabilizing" but also of selecting certain memories and preparing them for future cultural life as stories. As his work demonstrates, moreover, poetic and narrative forms have an important role to play in this process of "making memorable" and forgetting. (Rigney 2012a, 383)

The thing is, of course, that we now have an abundance of ways to make the past accessible for us with new media, as José van Dijck (2008) has stressed in her work on mediated memory. The problems of Kierkegaard continue to be with us as a desire to have recollections that matter and not just memories that come to us in ever greater and algorithmically controlled streams. The importance of narrative then becomes clear, not least since it is, in essence, the capacity of humans to go outside of the present and to manipulate and bend time to its own will even if we are stuck in mechanical time.

The desire to reach beyond oneself is also a driving force in cultural memory as well as a recurrent theme in posthumanist fiction, which at its best recognizes that individuality cannot be the pinnacle of human existence as we are essentially social beings with a desire to reach beyond ourselves. Or as Alan Glynn puts it in *Limitless:*

In its complexity and ceaseless motion the twenty-four-hour global network of trading systems was nothing less than a template for human consciousness, with the electronic marketplace perhaps forming humanity's first tentative version of a collective nervous system, a global brain. (Glynn 2011, 123)

The fascination in literature and movies of the posthuman is understandable as a fantastic and uncanny figure that both channels our hopes and fears for a different kind of being, not least when it comes to accessing the hidden layers of our minds. However, this fascination should not overshadow how we are already subject to powerful forces of memory technologies that we use and create as they in turn create us.

Claire Connolly

How a Footnote Remembers

1 Introduction

In *The Afterlives of Walter Scott* (2012a, 216), Ann Rigney recounts how, by confining an outsize reputation to "a mere footnote," the influential English literary critic F.R. Leavis placed Scott outside his "great tradition." In doing so, Leavis continued the twentieth-century work of forgetting the great nineteenth-century man of letters. But the involvement of Scott's own writing in this process is central to Rigney's account: just as Scott's novels sought to seal up a contested past, she suggests, so his own reputation suffered from the very "transience" and "obsolescence" proposed in his fictions (Rigney 2012a, 4).

The suggestion that literature might participate in the conditions of its own forgetting is a startling one. In *Imperfect Histories*, Rigney had shown how literary texts persist in time and remain active in culture: they are, in that sense, "'realer' than history" (Rigney 2001, 126). As Hilary Mantel (2017) puts it in *The Guardian*, "if we want to meet the dead looking alive, we turn to art." Read in terms of Rigney's powerful account of the mnemonic agency of literature, its capacity to activate, recall, and repair, the footnote is a medium through which memory moves.

Countless Irish writers of the Romantic period chose to gather information at the foot of the printed page. In national tales, historical novels, and lyric poems, footnotes (along with endnotes and glossaries) routinely offer non-diegetic information about history, manners, and culture. But footnotes do not simply pin Ireland to the page as a strange specimen to be observed, as critics often suggest. Rather, they operate as so many "relay stations" (Rigney 2008a, 350) for an Irish romanticism that responds to a still palpable history of colonial conquest, rebellion, and famine. Footnotes mediate memory for a divided society, bringing print culture into proximity with a palpable and varied community of knowledge (Connolly 2020, 666).

Anthony Grafton's authoritative *The Footnote: A Curious History* (1997) locates footnotes firmly in the arena of fact, enacting, as they do, a positivist belief in a "form of historical research that heaped up citations in the hope of arriving at the truth about the past" (Grafton 1997, 16). For sure, notes can also form part of the texture of creative work, as Grafton acknowledges in a brief discussion of Petrarch, Dante, and T.S. Eliot. But it is difficult to keep footnotes on the side of either truth or fiction. Indeed, they prove excellent vehicles for the kinds of disobedient modes explored by Rigney in "Being an Improper Historian" (2007).

Footnotes break with "illusive immediacy" and express "the power of *visible print*" (Langan 2001, 68); enacting what Rigney (2021b, 14) calls "the defamiliarisation characteristic of aesthetic experience" and prompting critical reflection on acts of remembrance.

But Rigney (2007, 156) also argues that detailed readings, on a "case by case" basis, are needed to track "[t]he actual role of particular fictions in promoting historical consciousness (or in cutting it off)." In what follows, one case, drawn from an Irish Gothic novel whose footnotes press information down to the bottom of the printed page and immerse the reader in a disorienting and uncertain world, brings the disturbing power of literature into view.

2 The work of blood

Charles Robert Maturin's Gothic classic *Melmoth the Wanderer* (1820) introduces readers to an unutterable diabolical bargain made by an Anglo-Irish gentleman, John Melmoth, who seeks out a soul to join him at the brink of damnation. The story begins and ends in Ireland, where Melmoth returns to his ancestral lands, dreams of Hell as an ocean of fire, and disappears into the Irish Sea, leaving only signs of struggle with some terrible being at the edge of the coast.

One of the inset narratives of *Melmoth the Wanderer*, "The Tale of the Spaniard," tells of how a young aristocrat, Alonzo Monçada, born outside marriage and condemned by his parents to a monastic life to expiate their sins, finally escapes the terrors of the monastery with the aid of a fellow monk. But Monçada is betrayed when the former, a man who has killed his own father and who is desperate for a promise of salvation, leads him not to the city but rather to the cells of the Inquisition. When the Inquisition itself burns to the ground and all believe him dead, Monçada makes his way onto the streets of Madrid and forces his way to precarious shelter in the home of a Jewish merchant. From that house, he becomes a horrified witness to the actions of a crowd gathered to pray for the victims of the recent fire. The crowd see the betraying monk, a known parricide, among the religious procession, and surge forward in anger. Monçada lies concealed behind a curtain in the upper floor of the merchant's house, a terrified witness to the "horrible catastrophe" as the crowd drag the parricide through "mud and stones" and finally fling the man, now "a mangled lump of flesh," against the door of the house where his former companion lies hidden (Maturin 2000, 255). The doubled fate of the two men, both reluctant monks, splits violently apart as one, a spectator to "the work of blood," sees the other "trodden in one moment into sanguine and discoloured mud by a thousand feet" (Maturin 2000, 255). The army charges across the square to aid the victim only to find that they too are completing the terrible work of the crowd, for man is now not only in the mud but of it: "The officer who headed the troop dashed his horses' hoofs into a bloody formless mass, and demanded 'Where was the victim?' He was answered 'Beneath your horses feet', and they departed" (Maturin 2000, 256).

The passage describes a scene of popular insurrection that would have resonated with memories of the French Revolution and also, shorn of its Gothic trappings, might anticipate later events discussed by Rigney in her "Differential Memorability and Transnational Activism: Bloody Sunday, 1887–2016" (2016). As if to acknowledge the difficulty of placing the incident in time and space, Maturin offers an authenticating footnote: "This circumstance occurred in Ireland 1797, after the murder of the unfortunate Dr Hamilton. The officer was answered, on inquiring what was that heap of mud at his horses's feet – 'The man you came for'" (Maturin 2000, 284). As the footnote does its authenticating work, mud makes the savage scene actual and we are left with the proposition that men really can dissolve other men into mire and blood.

Via this note, a tale of an "unfortunate" man dragged into the mud on a March evening transmits traceable information of the kind that Rigney (2001, 9) identifies as part of the culture of romantic historicism. Dr William Hamilton (b. 1757), the Protestant rector of Clondavaddg, commonly Fanad, County Donegal, was assassinated by some fifty United Irishmen in March 1797. The killing took place in the house of Dr John Waller at Sharon, near Newtowncunningham, around fifteen miles from Strabane, County Tyrone. As Breandán Mac Suibhne explains, Hamilton was a target because of his "unusually vigorous efforts to disarm United Irishmen in his own parish" (Mac Suibhne 2011, lxiii). Rather than flee to Derry or Dublin or England, as many well-to-do loyalists in Donegal did, Hamilton stood firm in Fanad and with his yeomanry corps, imprisoned several republicans. At the time of his assassination, he had already seen off a United Irish effort to lay siege to his home.

Hamilton was well-connected in Dublin and his assassination resonated at national level and reverberated for decades in the north-west. The violent death of a minister – albeit one who was also a magistrate, a man of law as well as God – precipitated the introduction of martial law in Ulster. Meanwhile his name has a place in the history of earth and climate science. A fellow of Trinity College Dublin and a founding member of the Royal Irish Academy, Hamilton's *Letters Concerning the Northern Coast of the County of Antrim* (1786) showed the volcanic origins of the Giants' Causeway in County Antrim while he also published essays on the temperature of the earth and Ireland's historic climate.

Maturin, in his second year at Trinity College Dublin when the notorious assassination occurred, may have read the news in the press or heard of it in the

College; meanwhile, Rev. Henry Maturin, likely a cousin, succeeded Hamilton as rector of Fanad in 1797. In 1812, when home on holiday, John Gamble, a London-based writer who had been reared in a Presbyterian family in Strabane, met an eyewitness to the events. Gamble heard what had happened when Hamilton tried to hide in Waller's cellar, was "dragged" from there "and thrown out to his murderers, who dispatched him with as many wounds as Caesar was in the capitol" (Gamble 2011, 368). The eyewitness was almost certainly Hamilton's servant Barney McCafferty, who was tried and acquitted for the murder at the Donegal assizes in September 1797 (Mac Suibhne 2011, lxviii).

And the gravestone that now rests on Hamilton in the grounds of St Columb's Cathedral, Derry requires its own footnote, offering as it does a micro-history of memory on the move: the original stone described the "assassination" of a scholar who "fell victim to the brutal fury of an armed Banditti" in 1797; a later one, erected around 1900, replaced the idea of a politically motivated assassination with murder while also getting the date of his death wrong; a brass plaque in the cathedral building repeats the incorrect date (Mac Suibhne 2013, 185). But amidst these changes, "'Hamilton's fate' long remained a byword in north Donegal for a brutal death" (Mac Suibhne 2013, 181). That notion of a "byword," meaning, in its older sense, "a word beside the matter in hand" (OED), might also describe the cultural work performed by Maturin's footnote or Hamilton's gravestone: information is pressed to the bottom of the page, a body is buried beneath a stone, a changing inscription hints at history.

3 Buried memory

The Hamilton case corresponds to what Guy Beiner (2018, 150) calls "the dialectic of preserving and erasing memory" that marked the treatment of the 1798 United Irish rebellion in Ulster in the first half of the nineteenth century. An "inability to openly remember insurgents in public" led to "practices of concealment" (Beiner 2018, 248) among which we might count the placing of the memory of Hamilton's violent death at the foot of the printed page. Patterns of memory and forgetting did not just fasten on singular sites of known insurrection and footnotes can also play a part in the dispersal of the past. In *Melmoth the Wanderer,* the Hamilton material takes its place in a group of three footnotes, a striking paratextual cluster found halfway through the novel, that share a focus on questions of witness and call for a multiscalar response. The first note asserts the reality of a fictional description of multiple human remains buried together, *"their cinders, occupying but a single coffin,"* via an account of "the dreadful fire which consumed sixteen persons in one house, in Stephen's Green, Dublin, 1816." Maturin, who lived close by on York Street, writes in his own person as one who "heard the screams of sufferers whom it was impossible to save" (Maturin, 251). Contemporary newspapers bear out this account. Some pages on, very shortly after the account of Dr Hamilton and appended to the description of the murderous actions of a violent crowd, there follows a longer note that explores the psychological effects of terror. Invoking the authority of an eyewitness, Maturin describes how a Dublin shoemaker came to observe the notorious killing of Arthur Wolfe, Viscount Kilwarden, pulled from his carriage by rebels wielding pikes in the course of Robert Emmet's rebellion in 1803. Watching the crowd, the note asserts, the shoemaker "stood at his window as if nailed to it; and when dragged from it, became – *an idiot for life*" (Maturin, 257). And in the case of William Hamilton too, his servant McCafferty was acquitted by a judge who took into account the man's likely frozen terror.

4 Violence on the page

To return to literature, the scene described and footnoted by Maturin continued to resonate withn Irish romantic fiction. In John and Michael Banim's historical novel, *Crohoore of the Bill-Hook* (1825), a company of mounted British soldiers are ambushed by a group of Kilkenny Whiteboys who stage a mock funeral on the road. The Whiteboy victory is sudden and "electric" (Banim 1826, 238). But the red-coated soldiers, seemingly "unsaddled and unarmed," turn to fire on their assailants with hidden pistols: "Every ball took effect, and fifteen men fell" (Banim 1826, 240). The scene of confrontation is vividly described, as "wretched people" who carry only sticks are trapped between and underneath the army horses. As the Whiteboys are slaughtered by the soldiers, they find themselves "treading and trampling on the bodies of their dead companions." The whole bloody episode, we are told, "was enacted in little over a minute" (Banim 1826, 241) but unfolds in grim detail over several pages.

That contrast between the evanescence of past events and their realization within durable forms of writing resonates with Maturin's footnotes. Such images of ordinary people caught up in destruction suspend and prolong the experience of violence and exploit the affordances of print as living medium. And in the particular case of the footnote, the interconnected acts of recall and forgetting take on a spatial quality that allows memory to be moved around on the page. In *Melmoth the Wanderer* we meet the dead not so much "looking alive" as in the act of being buried alive via the spatializing work of the footnote. The "particular aesthetic and narrative 'staying power'" of literature" (Rigney 2008a, 352) consists not only of its ability to picture conflict or repair history but also its power to inflict damage in the present, as with other forms of media that both represent and suspend violent actions. Analysis of such acts of media suspension can learn something from the role played by footnotes in romantic-era fiction, where dense and effortful representations of violence find succor in the possibilities of page space.

Marek Tamm

A Portable Fatherland: Afterlives of the St. George's Night Uprising (1343) in Estonian Cultural Memory

1 Introduction

From the perspective of cultural memory studies, the key question of historical research is not about the original significance of past events, but, rather, about how these events emerge in specific instances and are then translated over time, and about their everyday actualization and propagation, about their social, if not spectral, energy (Tamm 2015, 4). Or in Ann Rigney's concise wording, "the term 'cultural memory' highlights the extent to which shared memories of the past are the product of mediation, textualization and acts of communication" (Rigney 2005, 14). The historical study of the workings of cultural memory can be called "mnemohistory," to use a concept coined by Jan Assmann (1997, 9). The notion of mnemohistory allows scholars to move beyond the (although still important) question of "what really happened" to questions of how particular ways of construing the past enable later communities to constitute and sustain themselves. From a mnemohistorical point of view, the past as a distinct object of study is by no means a natural given; the distancing of past and present does not simply result from the passing of time but is something that is actively pursued and performed. Mnemohistory focusses on the multilayered dynamics of distance and closeness, presence and absence, anticipation and retrospection, past and present. It argues, in the footsteps of Walter Benjamin (1999, 460), that "historical 'understanding' is to be grasped, in principle, as an afterlife [*Nachleben*] of that which is understood; and what has been recognized in the analysis of the 'afterlife of works,' in the analysis of 'fame,' is, therefore, to be considered the foundation of history in general."

This chapter centers on one of the greatest puzzles of Estonian history: how a historical event – the uprising of local inhabitants against German rule on St. George's Night in 1343 – with very little documentary support, has achieved monumental status in Estonian historical consciousness. The argument posits that the significance of the St. George's Night Uprising owes much to its mediations and remediations in cultural memory, particularly through literature. Foremost is the literary debut of young author Eduard Bornhöhe (1862–1923), with his historical tale *The Avenger* (*Tasuja*, 1880), the first to narrate the St. George's Night Uprising in Estonian. Released in early December 1880, this 147-page work resonated with an extraordinary energy, "something special, grand, and symbolic" (Nirk 1961, 40), as many contemporaneous readers would attest. For example, the schoolteacher Jaan Roos (1888–1965) reflected in early 1930s:

> For me, *The Avenger* evoked a sense of heroism and national sentiment against the people's unjust suppressors [...] Participants in the war against the Baltische Landeswehr [1919] speak of battling with raw fervour and excitement, releasing centuries of pent-up animosity. This deep-seated passion and animus, fomented by historical literature, tipped the scales in favour of defeating the Landeswehr. A compatriot from my home parish, who perished in the battle of Cēsis [June 1919], was found with *The Avenger* in his pocket. (quoted in Palm 1935, 171)

The Avenger has thus become a "portable Fatherland," as Heinrich Heine once characterized language (Rigney 2012a, 20), establishing the groundworks for a foundational narrative revisited and rewritten by successive generations of writers from the national awakening era to the present day.

2 Imitators of *The Avenger*

The profound and varied impact of *The Avenger* remains not fully explored. From 1880 to 1905, over 23,000 copies were distributed, making historical fiction immensely popular in the late nineteenth century. By 1964, *The Avenger* was still the most broadly circulated original Estonian fictional work (Bornhöhe 1964, 339). Its influence soon spread, with Bornhöhe's pioneering success inspiring his followers.

The Struggles of Villu (*Villu võitlused*, 1890), Bornhöhe's follow-up, also tackled the St. George's Night Uprising but did not mirror the debut's impact. The detached narrative stance, with an all-knowing narrator, potentially diluted reader engagement. A few months after *Villu's Struggles* Andres Saal's (1861–1931) historical tale *Hilda* (1890), set against the backdrop of the St. George's Night Uprising, was published. This extensive narrative, spanning almost 300 pages, introduces the uprising's climax in chapter twenty-nine, entitled "The Night of St George's Day." Saal's work is distinct among the imitators of *The Avenger*, with no overt narrative elements borrowed from Bornhöhe. However, the theme of vengeance is palpably manifested, exemplified in Hilda's confrontation with her father's minion Goswin: "Thy bell is full, thou standest before thy avenger, thy terrible guilt condemns thee without mercy" (Saal 1890, 151).

Subsequently, in the latter half of 1892, Jaak Järv's (1852–1920) *Karolus* was released in Tallinn. Järv, once a journalist and exiled in 1888 for disseminating socialist ideologies, on returning to Estonia, rededicated himself to literary pursuits with renewed zeal. *Karolus* echoes *The Avenger* in recounting the tribulations of a valorous Estonian in the prelude to the St. George's Night Uprising. Descended from ancient Estonian nobility, Kahro is estranged from his parents, rechristened Karolus, and groomed as a knight espousing Christian virtues. Yet, the weight of Estonians' subjugation ignites a vengeful yearning within Karolus. He embarks on a quest for Finnish reinforcements for a grand insurrection, only to return to a prematurely commenced uprising. Captured and doomed to torture, Karolus ultimately eludes execution by his own hand.

The Avenger also inspired A. Raha's historical tale *St. George's Night* (*Jüriöö*), published in 1907. In this short 72-page work, the protagonist Tasuja (the Avenger) dominates the narrative from the outset and resurfaces just before the denouement. The principal characters encounter Tasuja in a forest hideout. Here, he spearheads the revolt: "Across Harjumaa, all manors were to be set ablaze in one night, thus the rebellion would simultaneously ignite across the land" (Raha 1907, 17). In Raha's occasionally fantastical tale, Tasuja perishes alongside 3,000 compatriots during Tallinn's siege.

The surge in historical fiction's popularity and its provocative effect did not escape the Russian authorities' scrutiny. In 1892, the Governor of Estonia, Prince Shakhovskoi, articulated concerns to the Russian Ministry of the Interior about historical narratives inciting Estonian resistance against the prevailing power. He recommended a prohibition on all publications recounting Estonians' ancestral resistance to the Germans, which could inflame nationalistic sentiments. His apprehensions were validated in St. Petersburg, placing historical fiction under the censor's stringent scrutiny (Salu 1964, 31–32).

3 The afterlife of St. George's Night in independent Estonia

The resurgence of the St. George's Night narrative during the era of the Estonian Republic (1920–1939) signaled the incorporation of many significant developments into the established tradition. The late 1920s saw a heated debate in the Estonian press about how to commemorate the St. George's Night Uprising. Opinion was split: some regarded the rebellion as a 'day of great defeat,' while others celebrated it as a brave Estonian stand against German domination. The formal recognition of St. George's Night, which began in 1928 with a proposal to make it a national holiday, proved particularly controversial. The events of the past were powerfully linked to the present, elevating the St. George's Night narrative from the literary domain to the arena of public life. For its proponents, the 1343 uprising was a vital precursor to the fight for independence, reaching its zenith in the

War of Independence (Tamm 2008). A 1931 pamphlet by the inter-organizational committee of the St. George's Night celebrations underscored this link: "The shared radiance of St. George's Night's fires symbolizes the true essence of our Great Struggle's Night commemoration – it renews our unity as a nation, ever-ready to persist in our quest for independence" (*Jüriöö. 1343* 1931, 24).

A few years prior to the discussions surrounding the commemoration of St. George's Night, a more focused debate had emerged around Juhan Luiga's (1873–1927) book *The Estonian Freedom Struggle 1343–1345* (1924). Luiga, an amateur historian, sought to recount the events of St. George's Night from an Estonian perspective, positing the uprising as a national fight for liberty. This was thwarted by the Teutonic Order, who provoked the uprising to break out eight days earlier than the leaders of the Estonian freedom movement had intended (Luiga 1924, 45; 75).

The latter half of the 1930s represented the golden era of the historical novel in the Estonian Republic, with no fewer than thirty titles published between 1934 and 1940 (Põldmäe 1973, 342). It was, therefore, a natural progression for the St. George Night Uprising to be reinterpreted within this literary form. Just prior to the conclusion of the era of independence, Enn Kippel's (1901–1942) fourth historical novel, *St. George's Night* (*Jüriöö*, 1939), was published. Kippel's narrative draws inspiration from Luiga's works, portraying Estonians of the period as affluent citizens engaged in international relations and active in urban commerce. As Luiga posited, Kippel permits the meticulously orchestrated uprising to commence prematurely, a full eight days ahead of schedule.

4 The climax of the St Georges Night's Uprising narrative

During the Second World War, coinciding with the 600th anniversary of the St. George's Night Uprising, the established narrative reached its apex. It was promoted with unprecedented vigor, richly reinterpreted across various genres, and extensively depicted in the arts like never before, especially among Estonian soldiers, intellectuals, and artists on the Soviet front and in the rear.

Literary scholar Olev Jõgi recalls, "The figure of Tasuja [the Avenger] energised Estonian soldiers to engage German occupiers, fortifying their combat morale. Tasuja was frequently invoked at political assemblies, and his memory echoed at rallies and in publications" (Jõgi 1962, 290). On 26 September 1942, the Estonian Rifle Division's newspaper was renamed *Tasuja*, proclaiming on 19 April 1945: "The image of Tasuja, our national hero, constantly before us, drives us to eliminate our nation's foes with unwavering precision and resolve." With the impending fall of Berlin, the paper asserted: "United with the formidable divisions of the mighty Red Army, we shall carry Tasuja's legendary quest to a victorious end" (Jõgi 1962, 293). Historian Hans Kruus, in his 1943 pamphlet *The Historical Commandments of the St. George's Night Uprising for Today*, imbued with Old Testament connotations, articulated five commandments, culminating in what he described as "the supreme commandment": "Engage in battle everywhere, both on the front and in the rearguard, to defeat the historic archenemy of your people, obliterating the Hitlerite state and its armies" (Kruus 1943, 23).

The war period's utilization of verse in the St. George's Night narrative merits attention; the wartime poetry – by Johannes Barbarus, Erni Hiir, Aira Kaal, Johannes Semper, Ilmar Sikemäe, among others – is unparalleled. This era also gave birth to Mart Raud's cantata "The Fires of Jüriöö," Jaan Kärner's eponymous poem, and the opera "Flames of Vengeance" by Paul Rummo and Eugen Kapp.

The first Soviet Estonian historical novel, Aristarch Sinkel's (1912–1988) *Under the Black Cross's Yoke* [*Musta risti ikke all*], dates to 1949. This expansive reworking of the St. George's Night narrative was not published until 1956, yet it swiftly captivated readers, its initial run of 14,000 copies sold out in days, and a second edition followed four years later. Sinkel's novel spans from early spring 1342 to May 1343, offering, in an extensive prologue, the social underpinnings of the uprising via the free peasant Vahur. The rebellion erupts unexpectedly on page 292 of the novel with the seizure of a Cistercian monastery, adhering to the precedent set by Luiga and furthered by Kippel, wherein the insurrection's genesis eluded its masterminds' grasp.

5 The emergence of skepticism

The St George's Night narrative has garnered scant popularity among Estonian exile writers, with its sole representation appearing to be a brief chapter in Arvo Mägi's novel *The Nation of the Cross* (*Risti riik*, 1970), penned in Sweden. Nonetheless, within the context of its antecedents, Mägi's work stands as a significant contribution. He deftly weaves his narrative into the fabric of Bornhöhe's *The Struggles of Villu*, drawing a tangible parallel between his character, the blacksmith Tiit, and Bornhöhe's protagonist, Villu. The author elucidates this link towards the chapter's conclusion, stating, "Tiit was not a friend to the Germans, unlike one of his colleagues from Sakala named Villu, who was initially described by an earlier author. Villu eventually started to rebel (although historians claim that such a rebellion never occurred) and ended his days in the dungeon of Viljandi Castle" (Mägi 1970, 136).

A vein of skepticism in Mägi's rendition of the St. George's Night Uprising can be traced to writer and historian Edgar V. Saks (1910–1984), living in Canada, who published the essay "A New Light on the St. George's Night Uprising" in 1971. Saks posits that "the St. George's Night rebellion was a political stratagem, orchestrated by the vassalage to instigate a popular uprising and marshal a militia, intending to align Estonia with the Swedish crown and thus evade the clutches of the German emperor or the Order" (Saks 1971, 32). He attributes the insurrection's failure to the inherent liberty-seeking spirit of the populace, which transmuted a well-orchestrated uprising into a widespread rebellion.

The imperative for a re-evaluation of the St. George's Night events finds a profound voice in the works of theologian and writer Uku Masing (1909–1985), working in internal exile in Estonia. His posthumously published studies, likely composed in the early 1950s, cast fresh perspectives on the 1343 events (Masing 2002). Masing contends that what transpired was not an uprising per se, but rather an episode within a broader campaign to expel the Teutonic Order from Livonia, orchestrated by Estonian vassals of the Danish king in alliance with ecclesiastical powers. This comprehensive scheme, however, was truncated to the St. George's Night uprising instigated by the Order and swiftly quashed by their retributive expedition.

This re-assessment ethos is further explored in Enn Vetemaa's (1936–2017) two-volume novel *The People of the Cross* [*Risti rahvas*], published in the latter half of the 1990s (Vetemaa 1994; 1998). The first volume situates its narrative immediately preceding the St. George's Night events, culminating in the insurrection only in its final passages. The second volume, set against the backdrop of the siege of Tallinn, portrays a colorful tableau of the local populace's activities.

Vetemaa's novel, influenced by the scholarship of Luiga, Masing, and Saks, presents a revisionist backdrop to the uprising narrative. It suggests the St. George's Night Uprising to be a ruse by the Teutonic Knights aimed at seizing Danish territories. Vetemaa intersperses a satirical or conspiratorial reimagining of the uprising's well-known episodes, suffusing his account with vivid depictions of the order's corrupt knights, naïve common folk, and cunning nobility. His picaresque narrative encapsulates the final developmental phase of the St. George's Night narrative tradition, questioning the veracity and importance of the 1343 uprising.

6 Conclusion

The narrative of St. George's Night Uprising, diligently chronicled over more than a century and having undergone numerous interpretive transformations from earnest zeal to critical skepticism, has succeeded in encapsulating over a hundred .

years of Estonian historical experience. It has emerged as one of the foundational narratives of a nascent nation, deriving its historical importance from a plethora of literary and artistic mediations and remediations (Erll and Rigney 2009a). The cultural longevity of "portable monuments" such as Bornhöhe's *The Avenger* illustrates, as Ann Rigney has highlighted, "the importance of a nonlinear approach to the evolution of cultural memory, which would allow for different temporalities and for discontinuities within traditions" (Rigney 2004, 391). By exploring the intricate ways in which the past has an afterlife – is remembered, interpreted, and given significance – mnemohistory challenges the traditional boundaries of historical inquiry. It compels scholars to consider the affective dimensions of history, the emotional investments, and the mnemonic practices that contribute to the making of history.

5 National and Transnational Memory

Chiara De Cesari
Transnational Memory *Reconsidered*

Since it became more widely adopted in memory studies around a decade ago, *transnational memory* has offered a very capacious, plural, malleable analytical category through which to study narratives and uses of the past in the present. What makes this category good to work with is its inclusivity and plasticity. Under its banner, scholars have made space for a diversity of new themes and approaches in memory studies. It has also proven to be "plastic" in Catherine Malabou's (2022) sense of the term, that is, a category open to mutation and transformation and, as such, particularly useful. I think of it as a fluid, elastic space, hospitable and generative, facilitating a coming together, an assembly of diverse projects and trajectories that converge around a set of pressing matters in order to change knowledge production about memory. In what follows, I review key approaches and themes that have dominated the transnational memory agenda in the last decade.

Concepts do not emerge in a vacuum; their ground must be prepared for and nourished. From the late 2000s onwards, several scholars at the forefront of memory theory were thinking along transnational lines. Ann Rigney had created momentum at Utrecht University around her collaborative research on the dynamic mediation of remembrance by bringing together many enthusiastic junior researchers and hosting some of the most interesting theorists of memory (Erll and Rigney 2009a). The forum for rethinking memory that she created was itself transnational as it consisted of a busy local program of events with an international dimension and an active network crisscrossing the world, or at least some parts of it. In 2009 Michael Rothberg published his book on *Multidirectional Memory*; Astrid Erll (2011a) was working on notions of transcultural and travelling memories. Aleida Assmann was also thinking with the transnational at the time. Important points of reference were the South African Truth and Reconciliation Commission dealing with apartheid's crimes and Cape Town's District Six museum as well as the work on post-apartheid heritage by University of Western Cape's historians like Premesh Lalu and Ciraj Rassool (e.g., Lalu 2009). Along with many others, these scholars were frequent guests in Utrecht. There, conversations were intense, deeply enriching, programmatic; participants had a sense of being part of a paradigmatic shift. There was a consensus that the traditional focus on dominant national memories, monuments and other institutionalized sites and practices had exhausted its explanatory potential; or rather, that there was much more beyond them to be investigated – a kind of constitutive outside of national memories made of movements and contestations. It is out of these ideas and conversations, and the vibrant

https://doi.org/10.1515/9783111439273-029

network that sustained them, that the category of transnational memory was crafted (De Cesari and Rigney 2014).

A set of concerns that memory studies had previously neglected came to shape this approach. Scholars in the field were busy exploring the impactful changes of "memory in a global age" (Assmann and Conrad 2010) with a special focus on the Holocaust as spreading cosmopolitan discourse promoting a generalized ethical culture of human rights (Levy and Sznaider 2002). Yet, topics of diaspora and migration remained poorly researched in studies of memory, despite the latter's crucial role in keeping migrant communities together and shaping their identities and social lives across global ethnoscapes. Also, crucial issues of slavery and colonial memory were given little attention – which was surprising especially if one considers the popularity and reach of media and literary phenomena such as the American TV series *Roots* and the work of African-American novelist Toni Morrison, for example. This lack of engagement testified to the truth of Ann Stoler's theory of colonial aphasia (2011), or the idea that the afterlives of colonialism (Hartman 2008) continue to exert a profound influence on the present but are not addressed in both public and scholarly discourse.

Another issue of growing relevance to public life and memory studies was the question of European memory and heritage. Indeed, the European Union had developed a memory-centered narrative defining itself as emerging from the ashes of WWII and the Holocaust – as the latter's radical negation – and in terms of a cosmopolitan identity dissolving the opposition between self and other in an embrace of diversity. This narrative was both at its peak (with the EU being awarded the Nobel Peace prize in 2012) and already in crisis on multiple fronts. It was not only Eurosceptics who were questioning this narrative of the EU as inclusive force for good rooted in a profound awareness of history. There were also scholarly and activist critiques of its fundamental exclusions. Critics exposed a resurging sense of European superiority embedded in this narrative as well as a novel form of moral and epistemic imperialism towards what was and is deemed non-European (perceptible, for example, in the trope of Europe as beacon of human rights). The EU, in essence, was using memory to foster a shared continental identity and legitimate itself in the face of its failures, crises and critics. This involved a politics of regret centered on the Holocaust and, increasingly, also on the crimes committed by communist regimes in Eastern Europe.

Colonialism was largely absent, or only nominally present, in these institutional policies of European memory. As such, these policies continued to reproduce containerized ideas of Europe as separated from the rest of the world and thus, silently but effectively, exclude postcolonial citizens from Europe's (imagined and real) community. Furthermore, European memory policy created a dilemma and discursive split along the East-West axis: by promoting anti-communist memory as articulated by nationalist, right-wing elites in Eastern Europe and beyond, the EU contributed to a form of historical revisionism that rehabilitates anti-communist nationalists who had been Nazi allies during WWII. All these concerns became key topics in transnational memory. But the main goal and achievement of those scholars who mobilized the term was not to add overlooked topics to the memory studies agenda. There was a more foundational drive to this work.

Transnational memory fundamentally took aim at the methodological nationalism and problem of scale in memory studies, that is, at the then largely unquestioned centrality of the nation(-state) as unit and framework of analysis (De Cesari and Rigney 2014; Wüstenberg 2019). Cultural memory was viewed as shaped by and contained within national boundaries. It was viewed as isomorphic with national culture and the national territory. Within these boundaries, the research focus was on canonic sites conveying the national memory narrative, as in the case of Pierre Nora's *lieux de mémoire* approach that long dominated memory studies. Yet, this framework was lacking not only in its poor grasp of obviously transnational phenomena such as migrant and diasporic memory. Another key problem was its limited conceptualization of how national memories and national canons are constituted. Transnational approaches view them as multidirectionally constituted by the agency of an interplay of social, political and symbolic forces beside the nation-state.

In nation-centered analytics, the state is a monolithic entity and the central actor in memory making, barely disturbed by counter-memories pressuring it from below. The relationship between memory actors is viewed as a matter of static, antagonistic opposition. Furthermore, the various scales of memory (local/from below, national, international/global) are conceived as nested containers. If local/grassroots memories are (separated from but) contained within the nation, national memories together combine a kind of mosaic within the larger, world heritage container. For example, the World Heritage List run by UNESCO is organized by country – being essentially made up of national subsets of cultural properties. Many formations of memory, however, do not fit into this neat scheme as they are constituted by and constitutive of complex interplays of cross-scalar phenomena. Between the late 2000s and the early 2010s, then, memory studies was becoming increasingly aware that even the most territorialized national narratives are connected with transnational processes in multiple ways, but these links are obscured. Even memory studies' hallmark case of the French *lieux de mémoire* was shown to be grounded in a constitutive exclusion of the colonial past (Stoler 2011). Ann Stoler further demonstrated that scholars should not conceive contemporary societies' relationship to colonialism in terms of colonial amnesia and forgetting, but illuminate what is rather an occlusion of memory, an inability if not unwillingness to address and take responsibility for colonial duress (2016).

Similarly, Nora's idea that sites of modern, institutional memory had replaced local memories based on community, kinship and intergenerational transmission did not stand the test of a growing body of rich and detailed studies. My own work on Palestinian heritage and memory at the time shed light on the ambivalent contiguity between grassroots counter-memories – already transnationalized by diasporic conditions – and an equally transnational cultural development discourse promoted by local civil societies and NGOs as well as international donors. More generally, across the Global South, (post)coloniality combined with neoliberal policy changes and cultural capitalism had created a fertile ground for new transnational development discourses emphasizing culture and participation, driven by an alliance between international institutions like UNESCO's World Heritage and increasingly NGOized local civil societies. In many contexts, this alliance has sidestepped and taken over functions from states, weakened by neoliberal reforms and budget cuts, and postcolonial failure. Also, EU supranational memory policy, to a certain extent, builds on a similar logic by working via dispersed civil society projects. Yet, this multiplication of actors of governance and memory and the complexification of their relationships did not cause the withering away of the nation-state; to the contrary, ethno-national memories have experienced a resurgence especially in the political imaginary of new right-wing populist movements (De Cesari and Kaya 2020). All these topics continue to be explored by scholars of transnational memory.

What has changed since the early 2010s? Which lines of inquiry are being pursued? What is transnational memory today? Arguably, it continues to offer an open conceptual space fostering diverse inquiries with a commitment to explore memories beyond the nation and analyze matters of transnational agency and power. Yet, three intertwined issues have taken center stage within and beyond this space and memory studies at large: the explosion of colonial memories afforded by digital platforms and memory-related activism (Rigney 2018a; Fridman 2023; De Cesari and Modest forthcoming). Decoloniality, digitality, and memory activism have been articulated with and propelled one another, resulting in a significant shift in tropes and modalities of memory formation. The context now is that of a transnationalized global public sphere becoming more decentralized, polarized, and interconnected in uneven, asymmetric ways. Across this transnationalized space, memory activists' networked initiatives have spread a new sense that the so-called colonial past is not past at all, and that the many "colonial durabilities" that shape the present must be addressed to achieve social justice and peace. Colonialism' invisibilized heritage of racialized inequalities endures, reproducing structural "duress" for a major portion of the world's population (Stoler

2016). Racism is part of this heritage – a kind of "implicit memory" (Erll 2022; De Cesari 2023; see also Wekker 2016) – operating at both the institutional and individual level. Arguably, there is a widespread sense that colonial heritage must be dealt with in order to move forward.

Two major socio-political movements of our times, significantly named after the related hashtags, epitomize the networked production of colonial memory for socio-political change, and the effective mobilization of mnemonic tactics to highlight and fight structural racism: #BlackLivesMatter and #RhodesMustFall. While there are differences between the two, they share key aspects that are particularly relevant for scholars of transnational memory (Jethro and Merrill 2024). They are decentralized, resourceful, creative, consisting of a multitude of loosely connected chapters or simply groups inspiring each other across borders. They mobilize art and memory for a political cause, communicating over social media. Activists use the latter to circulate and magnify highly symbolic, performative physical actions that target sites of celebratory colonial memory, most prominently, statues of major colonial figures across worlds (Rhodes, Colston, etc.). These are attacks on memory sites: statues have been thrown in rivers, or painted over, and feces have been thrown at them (Rigney 2023). Activists perform these attacks in order to expose the violent matrix of the institutions of our social life, which remain imbued with colonialism, all hidden in plain sight. Coloniality not having vanished, the emancipatory work of transnational memory then consists, now, in engaging with this heritage of race.

Since October 2023, memories of the Holocaust are omnipresent in narratives of Gaza and Israel/Palestine – on all political sides – in a kind of asymmetric, antagonistic multidirectionality. Transnational memories are reproduced and transformed while being activated as interpretive lenses to read present events and as affective media through which those events are experienced and acted upon. The memory of the archetypical genocide is being mobilized by the Israeli government to legitimize its Gaza campaign that for many scholars and "plausibly," the International Court of Justice is genocidal (e.g., Goldberg 2024; see also Bartov et al. 2023). The most violent form of racism is perpetrated in the name of a fundamental anti-racism battle, the fight against antisemitism, and a militarized memory. This calls then for a thorough investigation of the specter of race in memory, and of the dangers of uses and abuses of memory and proliferating antagonistic multidirectionalities.

Nicole L. Immler

How (Post) Memory Matters to Justice

1 Introduction

"The anger has been inherited through the generations."[1] This sentence can be heard in many interviews with families who have experienced mass violence and grave injustices. Mass atrocities harm not only individuals, who directly experience violence or loss, but their legacies (can) transcend multiple generations, affecting lives, psyches, mentalities, and narratives at individual, family, and community levels. Wars, genocides, colonization, and decolonization have left many wounds, which time alone has not healed. Rather, the opposite is true: a sequence of new conflicts and tensions reinforce deep-rooted positions in relation to historical grievances. There has been much influential thinking about the transmission of trauma and memory to the (grand)children of victims of historical injustice – what Marianne Hirsch has called *postmemory*, remembering only by means of stories, images, and behaviors, an intergenerational relationship of "identification, imagination and projection" (2008, 114), however, the relationship between postmemory and justice remains hitherto underexplored.

Memory matters to justice. But in which way? This chapter brings expertise from memory studies to the transitional justice field, which explores the mechanisms (such as trials, truth commissions, apologies, reparations, commemoration, education etc.) by which society tries to come to terms with its violent or unjust past (Neumann and Thompson 2015). Those instruments aim to acknowledge and thereby 'repair' the past, though they are often less *transformative* than they claim to be. Specifically, postcolonial scholars argue that many reparation instruments perpetuate the unjust frames in which society operates because the terms of recognition tend "to remain in the possession of those in power" (Coulthard 2007, 449). The *transformative turn* in transitional justice scholarship (Gready and Robins 2018) has sought to better evaluate under which conditions reparations addressing historical injustice make a real difference to the lives of those victim-

---

1 Coen Verbraak, documentary on "Moluccans in the Netherlands," NPO1, 4 parts; 19 May–9 June 2021; https://www.2doc.nl/documentaires/2021/05/Molukkers-in-Nederland.html.

Note: This research was made possible by a Marie Curie Intra European Fellowship, within the 7th European Community Framework Program (No: 626577) and the Dutch Research Council (NWO) within the ASPASIA and VICI scheme (VI.C.191.051/10120). I am also grateful for the precious editorial suggestions.

ized and their descendants, including by engaging with its structural legacies. Instead of focusing on excessive violence by specific agents, the goal is to address the nature of a violent system. Therefore, "radical rethinking of participation" (Gready and Robins 2018) of those victimized and marginalized is seen as crucial, as only they can help to deconstruct the tricky logics of 'who recognizes' and 'who is recognized' so that repair and justice can be undertaken in a more meaningful way instead of reproducing power relations.

I utilize the current debate on Dutch slavery as an exemplary case to elaborate on how intergenerational memory work matters to repair and justice. I argue that the intergenerational perspective – one that embraces multi-voicedness – provides a systemic approach that is an essential element to realizing its transformative potential.

This chapter is written at a moment when the belief in transitional justice has been deeply shaken. Germany's *Wiedergutmachungspolitik* ('the politics to make good again') is widely seen as the model for a successful transition, for rebuilding relationships after mass violence. However, this model shows dramatic shortcomings. Germany's reparations to Israel have contributed to what Ussama Makdisi has called "atonement at the expense of another."[2] In other words, Palestinians, whose perspectives have been excluded and neglected for too long, must become interlocuters in this discussion. The case of Germany's reparations to Israel is today striking example of performing an exclusive logic of victimhood. This suggests an urgent need for a debate that takes into consideration the entangled nature of the histories of the colonial period and the Holocaust.

2 Memory studies and transitional justice

To bring both fields – memory studies and transitional justice – into a more intense dialogue, a decade ago, a Special Issue of *Memory Studies* on "Reconciliation and Memory: Critical Perspectives" (Immler et al. 2012), scrutinized specifically the reconciliation rhetoric dominant in both fields during the 1990s, triggered by the perceived success of the South African Truth and Reconciliation Commission (TRC 1995–1999). The title of Ann Rigney's introduction was "Reconciliation and Remembering: (How) does it work?" While promising transition through truth telling and forgiveness (instead of prosecuting perpetrators), the TRC allowed for

---

2 Ussama Makdisi, http://newfascismsyllabus.com/opinions/the-catechism-debate/atonement-at-the-expense-of-another/.

a state transition, but not for the transformation of lives of those marginalized and impoverished; there was no justice in a social, political and economic sense, nor a redistribution of wealth. While the reconciliation scenario advanced ideas about a clean break with the past, the memory and justice practices hinted instead at the need for a "permanent transition." As Ann Rigney so aptly put it, it was about "continuously re-casting the past" as one of "the most important resources for articulating differences in a pluralistic society" and for "uncovering the transformative potential of historical awareness" (2012b, 254). Her insight that memory work is an ongoing process, a matter of "continuously performing," indicates that reparation is a social act that needs a gesture, a dialogue, and an encounter – a particular type of performance – to be experienced as reparation. This prompted me to study reparation claims as one type of these (intergenerational) performances; and to realize that they are as much about the past as they are about present and future.

The question of how to find the right balance between backward-looking and forward-looking – between identity politics and questions of citizenship and equality (Nobles 2006) – is a major subject of debate in the transitional justice field. An important innovation was incorporating the future more prominently into the analysis of historical wrongs. The call to reach "beyond the traumatic" (Rigney 2018a), beyond the framework of grievance, and to include the "remembering of hope," captures the "transmission of positivity" (2018a, 370) in the commitment to values and ideas. Rigney connects to Andreas Huyssen's earlier demand for integrating more "futurity" into human rights debates. Huyssen stresses the need to reach beyond "righting past wrongs via redress or restitution claims" by instead showing the solid links between past and present forms of injustice as continuities that enable more just futures. This puts emphasis on the broader hope for change inherent in memory and reparation claims. Olúfẹmi O. Táíwò (2022) goes a step further, regarding reparations as not just backward looking but as forward looking too, as a political and aspirational project engaged in building a better social order. In his words, it is a matter of distributing justly the costs of tomorrow's world in light of yesterday's injustice. Identifying reparation claims for past wrongs as an *imaginative process* means seeing reparation claims as ways in which those victimized navigate their social spaces and imagine society otherwise. This became evident when examining the social imaginaries at stake in the civil court cases addressing the mass violence perpetrated by Dutch soldiers in the Indonesian war of independence, revealing an unseen Indonesian diaspora criticizing their felt status as second-class citizens in the Netherlands (Immler and Scagliola 2020). The current debate on Dutch Slavery can also illustrate this process.

3 Dutch slavery reparation

> For centuries, the Dutch State and its representatives facilitated, stimulated, preserved and profited from slavery [. . . .] Human beings were made into commodities, exploited and abused [. . .] Today, on behalf of the Dutch government, I apologize for the past actions of the Dutch State: to enslaved people in the past, everywhere in the world, who suffered as a consequence of those actions, as well as to their daughters and sons, and to all their descendants, up to the present day. [. . .] We are doing this [. . .] so that [. . .] we can find a way forward together. We not only share a past; we share a future too. So with this apology *we are writing not a full stop, but a comma* [emphasis by author].[3]

Recently, we have seen some high-profile apologies in the Netherlands addressing the use of massive violence by the Dutch state in its former colonies and its slavery and slave trade. The apology by Prime Minister Mark Rutte (2022), cited above, was later extended by King Willem Alexander at the annual commemoration on 1 July 2023, marking 150 years since the factual abolition of slavery in the Dutch kingdom in 1863, where he asked for forgiveness "for the obvious lack of action against this crime against humanity" by the House of Orange-Nassau: "What was thought normal in the colonies overseas – practiced on a large-scale and encouraged, in fact – was not allowed here. That is a painful truth [. . .] There's no blueprint for the process of healing, reconciliation and recovery. Together, we are in uncharted territory. So let's support and guide each other".[4]

Ten years earlier, in 2013, the then new King was present at the commemoration for the first time, but stayed silent; he seemed unable to understand or seize the moment. What has happened in the interim? While a National Monument to the Dutch Slavery Past was erected in Amsterdam's Oosterpark as early as 2002 (inaugurated by Queen Beatrix who used the words "deep remorse" on that occasion) as a National Institute for the Study of Dutch Slavery and its Legacies (NiNsee), the annual 1 July Keti Koti commemoration has since evolved from a local event by and for the Surinamese community into a broad public event to be followed on national television. Parallel views on recognition and redress have significantly changed, partly because descendants' voices were more clearly heard

3 https://www.rijksoverheid.nl/documenten/toespraken/2022/12/19/toespraak-minister-president-rutte-over-het-slavernijverleden.
4 https://www.koninklijkhuis.nl/documenten/toespraken/2023/07/01/toespraak-van-koning-willem-alexander-tijdens-de-nationale-herdenking-slavernijverleden-2023.

and public debate demanded more from the government through the activities of dozens of civil society actors.[5]

Those recent speeches – followed by a commemoration year (with events that triggered academic, social and political debate on the multiple legacies of slavery), the establishment not just of a National Slavery Museum but also a Reparation Fund (Figure 1), testify to a radical shift from the so-called 'age of apology,' where the apology is a signifier of transition from authoritarianism to liberal democracy, towards 'the age of reparation,' which is marked by a call from the Global South to seek 'reparatory justice.' This call manifests itself for instance in a 10-point reparation plan,[6] filed by Caribbean countries (CARICOM) against several European governments in 2013. They consider an apology crucial for an awareness process, but not enough in itself: "There needs to be awareness and recognition that there is a problem, before instruments can be offered that are reparatory" (Beckles 2021). Descendants demand reparations in a more fundamental sense "not limited to material repair," but "restoring every aspect of the rights of people of African descent" (Biekman 2014).

Various initiatives supported this shift:[7] the UN Decade of People of African Descent (2014–2024), the Black Lives Matter movement, and the anti-Black Pete (the Black faced helper of Saint Nicholas) movement. Just as important was that increasing numbers of descendants started sharing their complex family histories, showing how the slavery past is not the voice of Black against white, victims against perpetrators, minority-diaspora against majority, revealing postcolonial communities as hybrid, intertwined in myriad ways with Dutch society. It is not about 'their' and 'our' history, but a 'shared' history. Healing thus requires both parties: In communities of descendants, people talk therefore about external and internal repair, distinguishing between "what others owe us and processes of self-repair," arguing that both, enslaved and enslavers, must work to self-repair first, as repair is about getting engaged with oneself before engaging with the other. Exemplary therefore is how the National Slavery Museum was conceptualized as a participatory process from its inception to create connections within as well as beyond the community: "Tell the whole story. About us and with us."

---

5 The Mapping Slavery project, the Keti Koti tables, and the Black Archives were a few of those initiatives that gave the slavery past a prominent place in society.

6 caricomreparations.org/caricom/caricoms-10-point-reparation-plan.

7 A turning point in the US for moving the reparation debate from the periphery to the center was the famous article "The case for reparations" by Ta-Nehisi Coates in *The Atlantic* (2014), showing the devastating effects slavery and centuries of theft and racism have had on the African American community. https://www.theatlantic.com/magazine/archive/2014/06/the-case-for-reparations/361631/.

Figure 1: 01 July 2023 Amsterdam: Protest March "No Healing Without Repair" organized by Zwart Manifest and The Black Archives as part of the annual commemoration and celebration of the abolition of slavery, calling for serious reparation programs in the Netherlands and in the former colonies. The photograph was taken by the author.

With this shift from 'reparations' in terms of monetary compensation to 'restoring rights' the debate has arrived at a crossroads. While the exact definition of "repair" remains a matter of contention, it has become clear that the idea of reparation is less about a specific product than about relation building, about 'social repair' in a much broader sense. I argue (Immler 2021, 13) that the idea of *reparations* and *restoring rights* are quite diametrically opposed. One comes from the idea of harm, the other from a standpoint of justice; one is about individuals, the other about society as a whole; one is about addressing past suffering, the other is about repairing current relations; one is about monetary payments from one group to another, the other is about a more fair and equal society.

4 (Post)memory and justice

While there is a focus in transitional justice literature on state-led actions (seeing the state as the most relevant actor), the crucial role of the family (or the community in a broader sense) for providing recognition and repair has received less attention. As the above case has shown, the intergenerational family perspective is crucial in complexifying the notion of reparation, speaking of internal and external repair, and articulating what transformative justice could look like.

As Holocaust research shows, 'coming to terms with' is also dependent on the way (in)justice is remembered and evaluated within families and communities. While reparation talk is primarily seen as the negotiation of history *between* two opposing parties (victim vs. perpetrator), interviews show that such claims are also about establishing relationships *within* those groups: Many Jewish victims wanted the reparations to acknowledge their suffering as it was witnessed by their children. Many of the children sought reparation in the name of their parents, but also for themselves, as the ones raised by injured parents, creating what Hirsch has called "living connections" between generations. This "performance of anger" constitutes family memory about the Holocaust; it provides moral integrity for descendants, identification and solidarity within families, and empowerment and agency towards the perpetrator state (Immler 2012, 276–278). The term I use is 'Familiengedächtnis' [family memory], which emphasizes the way memory is (re)constructed and instrumentalized. To identify oneself as 'generation' is also a choice, a narrative and performative act "to write oneself into the world" (as Hannah Arendt suggested).

Janna Thompson's concept of *intergenerational responsibility*, defined as lifetime transcending interests, has broadened this familial gaze further, foregrounding the political and institutional dimension of intergenerational relations. "What perpetuates itself is not a family but intergenerational relations of entitlement and obligation, and what is significant about these relationships is that they have no temporal boundaries (but) can be described as a 'generational continuum'" (2009, 151–152). Intergenerational responsibility includes reparations that not just address lived experiences (the suffering) but also the aspirations of the dead (the hope for a more just and equal society).

This connects to current debates about the Dutch colonial past and its legacy, in which *multi-voicedness* has become a catchword, stressing the need to juxtapose different perspectives to do more justice to postcolonial identities than the simplified victim/perpetrator binary that neglects or marginalizes more entangled and transnational experiences. I have utilized the psychological concept of the *dialogical self* (Hermans and Hermans-Konopka in Immler 2022), describing people's inner voices and how those different subject positions interact, to better understand the transnational, entangled, and diasporic experiences of people in postcolonial settings. Just as postcolonial communities are hybrid, multifaceted, and intertwined within Dutch society, personal experiences are far more complex. Acknowledging complex family stories breaks open simplified identities – what Kwame Appiah (2018) so pertinently calls "the lies that bind" – essentialisms and oppositions that polarize debates.

An interesting example of this dynamic are the civil court cases that since 2011 have sought to hold the Dutch state responsible for mass executions, torture, and rape during the Indonesian War of independence (1945–1949). Rather than juxtaposing Indonesian victims and Dutch perpetrators, showing the more 'entangled' experiences of the various actors involved, we (Immler and Scagliola 2020) pushed for a far more complex debate on responsibilities to respond to situated needs.

To reach beyond such simplified perpetrator/victim binaries, Michael Rothberg speaks of *implicated subjects*, those who "occupy positions aligned with power and privilege without being themselves direct agents of harm; they contribute to, inhabit, inherit, or benefit from regimes of domination but do not originate or control those regimes," but "indirect or belated, their actions and inactions help produce and reproduce the positions of victims and perpetrators" (2019, 1). Connecting implicatedness to the notion of the *multi-voiced self,* I draw attention to how these entangled structures are internalized via people's inner voices (Immler 2022) and how this plays out in reparation struggles advocated by diasporic actors. I suggest that the dialogue with oneself (dialogical self) is a precondition for dialogue with others (multi-voicedness); hearing one's own multi-voicedness is the precondition for hearing the multi-voicedness of others. Both processes, I argue, are crucial to reaching 'beyond the traumatic,' beyond a history that holds us captive. This raises larger questions: what are the conditions under which people can hear their own multi-voicedness? How can institutions take responsibility in a way that recognizes such multi-voicedness? How can we imagine reparation beyond the narrow idea that one group of people should be paying financial compensation to another?

As the Dutch slavery case shows: Instead of reproducing racialized legacies of colonialism in a racialized politics of repair, in which colonized subjects become objects of repair, the social relationship as such – its socio-political and socio-economical dimension – needs to be under scrutiny. To 'repair' then means to transform social relationships within affected communities and between these and society. Consequently, reparation is not about the spider (perpetrator) nor the fly (victim), but about the web (society). It is precisely this web a transformative justice approach explores, as it means rejecting the idea of wrongful incidents in an otherwise just system.

Vered Vinitzky-Seroussi

Flags, Hearts, and Stamps: The Transnational Memory of COVID-19

The notion of *transnational memory*, deftly presented and parsed by Ann Rigney (2015c), is first and foremost a dual invitation: to think outside the box – the national box – by acknowledging the lack of research whose unit of analysis either transcends the border of the nation-state or operates on a scale smaller than the nation-state; and to trace and understand cultural productions that traverse nations and oceans, inspiring concatenated representations of the past.[1] In what Rigney dubs *transnational memory studies*, she calls on society to "develop new ways of conceptualizing memory that are better fitted to a world of advanced globalization, regional integration, mass migration, and of new communication technologies that are radically changing traditional calibrations of distance and proximity" (Rigney 2015c, 1).

Writing in 2015, Rigney could not have forecasted the utmost distortion of 'distance and proximity' brought on by the pandemic looming just around the corner, to appear four short years after her publication. In this essay, I wish to delve into the commemoration of COVID-19, which, as a pandemic, is an intrinsically transnational phenomenon: one that embodies, in Rigney's terms, globalization and migration, having leapt across oceans and over nations, ignoring borders, and social and political divisions, in kind.

In addition, COVID-19 has been a point of supply – to borrow again from Rigney – for new communication technologies that have transformed distance and proximity (Fridman and Gensburger 2024), as the distinction between home and work environments has collapsed and as long-distance education, medical care, and much more have become the norm. At the same time, COVID-19 has witnessed the importance of nation-states in an era when many believed these social units to be in decline. While Fridman, Gensburger, and their colleagues chart dimensions of transnational memory *during* the time of COVID-19 (2024), the cross-border collective memory *of* COVID-19 itself remains in question. Will COVID-19, as a transnational phenomenon, necessarily generate transnational memory? That conundrum lies at the heart of this piece.

---

1 I would like to thank the editor, Jenny Wüstenberg, for her insightful comments. I am grateful to Shahar Itzkovitch, Mathias Jalfim Maraschin and Maya Vogel, my devoted research assistants, and to the ISF, grant number 21/759 for funding the research.

Beginning in December 2019, reports from China disclosed that dozens were being hospitalized with a novel and mysterious respiratory illness that seemed highly pathogenic. Initially, many dismissed it as yet another version of 2002 SARS, 2009 Swine Flu (H1N1), or 2012 MERS (not to undermine the suffering they caused), but, in no time, were proven wrong. The start of 2020 saw the first cases of this new disease appear across the globe and the resultant spread of travel bans. In February 2020, the World Health Organization (WHO) named the disease COVID-19 and soon after characterized it as a pandemic. By March, one fifth of all students worldwide were out of school and one third of the world's population was living under various forms of restrictions; Japan postponed the 2020 Summer Olympics, and multiple countries closed their borders. During the first half of that year, a number of nations adopted mask mandates in the public sphere (e.g., public transport, educational settings). By December, the race for vaccines began to yield results, as the earliest versions were approved and administered (succeeded by booster shots in 2021 and 2022). Several of the biomedical companies behind this immense scientific endeavor were national (e.g., the American Moderna) and even state-owned (such as China's Sinopharm), while others were multinational corporations (such as Pfizer). National lockdowns and travel restrictions came and went in 2021 and 2022 in response to new COVID-19 variants (like Omicron). COVID-19 swept the planet, halting most aspects of people's routines and incurring long quarantines, as well as myriad losses in jobs, relationships, and creative and commercial industries, ultimately claiming close to seven million lives. As 2022 progressed, the majority of mask mandates were revoked, remaining only where vulnerable populations were involved (e.g., hospitals). In May 2023, the WHO declared that COVID-19 was no longer a public health emergency of international concern.

Pandemics – and COVID-19 likely will not prove an exception – are scarcely a simple subject for the remembrance pole of collective memory (Vinitzky-Seroussi and Maraschin 2021). Due to the manner in which people die (abruptly, deformed), the failure felt by the medical profession, the lack of human agency as a clear target for blame (contrary to wars), the absence of a corporeal figure to be adored, or a coherent narrative to provide solace and meaning (cf. World War II), pandemics exemplify the concept of "difficult past" (Wagner-Pacifici and Schwartz 1991). Here, the past is "not necessarily more tragic than other commemorated events [or is, as per the Spanish flu]; what constitutes a difficult past is an inherent moral trauma, disputes, tensions . . . conflicts" (Vinitzky-Seroussi 2002, 31) and shame. Thus, major mnemonic projects dedicated to pandemics, in the shape of memorial time or space, are hard to find and rarely central in the public sphere or discourse.

Still, for COVID-19, seeds of transnational commemoration have been sown. Let us address three such mnemonic practices. The first arises with the use of *White Flags*. From 17 September to 3 October 2021 at the National Mall in Washington,

D.C., the art installation *In America: Remember*, created by Suzanne Brennan First-enberg, covered almost ninety thousand square meters of grass with 701,133 small white flags planted in the ground. Each of these white flags, organized in large blocks of perfectly aligned rows and columns, symbolized a life lost to COVID-19 in the United States,[2] as inspired by the architecture and design of Arlington National Cemetery in Arlington, in Northern Virginia. This sizable display was the result of a series of previous projects. When the United States reached 200,000 deaths from COVID-19 on 24 September 2020, the fundraised initiative *COVID Memorial Project* installed 20,000 American flags on the National Mall (echoing the country's long tradition of placing national flags on military gravesites and monuments).[3] While the color white has varied meanings in different cultures, such as purity, marriage, mourning, and surrender, the artist selected it because she "wanted people to be able [to write on them], to dedicate a flag to their loved one who they had lost to COVID-19, and so, white obviously was a blank slate" (NCPCgov 2022, 3:15). From that point on, the idea took off both within the United States as well as abroad. In October 2020, the Spanish organization ANVAC (which stands for National Associa-tion of Victims and Afflicted by Coronavirus) planted 56,000 Spanish flags in Ma-drid and Murcia in tribute to the deceased.[4] On October 15, 2021, a Brazilian activist group positioned 600 white flags in front of their National Congress, with each flag representing one thousand victims.[5] In late 2021, local officials of Los Angeles and San Benito, California also made use of white flags to structure similar displays.

Yellow Hearts constitute a second example of transnational memory. This mnemonic enterprise is anchored in the yellow ribbon practice – itself a form of transnational remembrance. While the history of yellow ribbons evades decisive origins, their customary usage arguably already existed during the American Civil War and in the United Kingdom at that same time. This assumption has as its basis popular songs and paintings citing or depicting the yellow worn by sol-

---

2 https://www.inamericaflags.org/.

3 Lauren M Johnson. "Twenty thousand flags placed on National Mall to memorialize Covid-19 deaths in the US." *CNN*. 24 September 2020.
      https://edition.cnn.com/2020/09/23/us/covid-memorial-flags-on-washington-mall-trnd/index.html. Accessed 01 April 2024.

4 "Más de 50,000 banderines de España en un parque de Madrid en memoria de las víctimas de la covid." *El País*. 27 September 2020. https://elpais.com/espana/madrid/2020-09-27/mas-de-50000-banderines-de-espana-en-un-parque-de-madrid-en-memoria-de-las-victimas-de-la-covid.html. Ac-cessed 1 April 2024.

5 "Grupo coloca bandeiras brancas em frente ao Congresso Nacional em homenagem às mais de 600 mil vítimas de Covid-19." *G1*. 15 October 2021. https://g1.globo.com/df/distrito-federal/noticia/2021/10/15/grupo-coloca-bandeiras-brancas-em-frente-ao-congresso-nacional-em-homenagem-as-mais-de-600-mil-vitimas-de-covid-19.ghtml. Accessed 1 April 2024.

diers either as stripes on their uniforms or as scarves around their necks. The nineteenth-century marching song "Round Her Neck She Wore a Yellow Ribbon," which narrates the tale of a woman awaiting her far-off lover, inspired the eponymously titled 1949 John Ford film. Popularized by the 1973 American hit song "Tie a Yellow Ribbon Round the Ole Oak Tree" and fueled by the 1979 U.S.-Iranian hostage crisis (Santino 1992), fastening yellow ribbons around trees as a tribute to war hostages or welcoming sign for returning soldiers (Crook 2014) became a symbol of solidarity and grief in the United States. This practice traveled back to the United Kingdom finding renewed expression in the time of COVID-19. In April 2020, David Grompetz, a U.K. senior citizen, lost his wife Sheila to the virus. Motivated by the tradition of yellow ribbons but unable to purchase one due to lockdown and supply shortages during the height of the pandemic,[6] he stuck a yellow heart on a window of his home. Following Grompetz's yellow heart, his granddaughter started two commemorative Facebook groups[7] encouraging people to utilize the yellow heart to signal their grief. These online communities quickly grew, and the emblem was adopted and advanced by many others, both on the internet and beyond (e.g., on home windows). The non-profit organization Covid19FamiliesUK, for example, implemented yellow hearts in the temporary memorials it organized across the country.[8] In Wales, in April 2021, a grieving family constructed a yellow heart outdoor memorial out of stones.[9] *Faces of Covid Victims*, a Facebook page where then 15-year-old American Hannah Ernst posted artistic renditions of victims, brought the initiative from the United Kingdom back to the United States (Allen 2020). From August through September 2020, the teenager produced over four hundred silhouettes of victims against a backdrop of a yellow heart.[10] Ernst's work grabbed the attention of a fellow bereaved woman, Rosie Davis, who had lost her mother that same year. From Irving, Texas, Davis organized *The Faces of COVID – Yellow Hearts Memorial* in January 2021. The exhibit shared Hannah Ernst's art and other iterations of the yellow heart to honor the memories and names of the virus' victims.[11] This initiative has since grown into a traveling memorial, appearing in many American cities, including Den-

---

6 https://www.bbc.com/news/av/uk-52589050.
7 "Yellow Hearts to Remember- Covid 19; Private" https://www.facebook.com/groups/669274300301274/ and https://www.facebook.com/groups/262593888277834/ "Yellow Hearts to Remember- Covid 19; Public".
8 https://www.covid19familiesuk.co.uk/.
9 https://www.yellowheartswales.co.uk/.
10 https://www.facebook.com/facesofcovidvictims/.
11 https://www.irvingarchivesandmuseum.com/faces-of-covid-yellow-hearts-memorial.

ver,[12] New York,[13] San Bernadino[14] and others. Inspired by the ubiquitous yellow heart movement, the first permanent COVID-19 national memorial in the United States took root at a New Jersey farm in January 2021: Rami's Heart COVID-19 Memorial showcases eleven yellow hearts filled with stones and shells, representing more than three thousand pandemic victims.[15] The erstwhile ribbon has been transformed; still, the emotions conveyed are consonant, colored by bereavement, yet blanched of the hope Americans once had of their loved ones' safe return. At the close of 2023, as I write this essay, yellow ribbons have migrated yet again, this time to Israel, as the country awaits the homecoming of one hundred twenty-nine hostages still held by Hamas in Gaza.

Our third focus, *Postal Stamps* – despite their inherently transnational dynamics – remain surprisingly understudied as mnemonic objects. Small in size but widely accessible (Brennan 2018), stamps are among the prime vehicles via which national memory is crystalized, built and sustained (Scott 2002). An effective advertising space, they offer a platform to maintain the presence of national assets in the collective consciousness. Concurrently, stamps were and still are highly transnational since, until quite recently, they navigated and comprised "an international system of national images of nationhood" (Simonsen 2013, 4). Moreover, stamps "are also prime examples of transnational dissemination of aesthetic forms through international networks of cultural elites, graphics and stamp designers" (Simonsen 2013, 4) as well as philatelists.

While we live in an era where elaborate stamps largely have been replaced with white sticker price tags or displaced by the pervasive shift to online services and communication, copious amounts of national commemorative stamps were manufactured during the pandemic. Although the methods countries used to combat outbreaks of COVID-19 have proved unique due to political, geographical, demographic, economic, and cultural factors, examination of postal stamps created to commemorate the pandemic reveals their commonality as a mnemonic tack among nation-states and their deep roots in transnational dynamics. In fact, Rigney and De Cesari note the generality that "while each nation proclaimed itself unique, the fact that they did so along remarkably similar lines has tended to be forgotten" (2014, 7). This valence perfectly applies to stamps, which spur and embody the "transnational character of nationalism itself" (De Cesari and Rigney 2014, 7).

---

12 https://kdvr.com/news/local/yellow-heart-memorials-hoping-to-make-day-of-remembrance-for-those-lost-to-covid-19/.

13 https://www.cbsnews.com/newyork/news/covid-19-march-new-york-city-brooklyn-bridge/.

14 https://iecn.com/yellow-heart-memorial-remembers-those-who-passed-from-covid-19/.

15 https://www.ramisheartcovidmemorial.org/.

Indeed, COVID-19 stamps have been discovered in dozens of nations throughout all continents. Pinpointing the causality of COVID-19 commemorative stamps is a challenge, given the inextricable, interrelational impact of specific global periods and cultures. Even so, notably, as soon as national stamps get released, they circulate, and invariably interact with a new "scale," to revisit De Cesari and Rigney (2014, 20), ricocheting through at minimum professional communities such as artists, designers, and the like.

A quick survey of motifs of COVID-19 stamps uncovers two dominant themes. First, there are expressions of gratitude and public recognition for those who filled the ranks in the strenuous fight against the virus. Most typical depictions are of health professionals and other essential workers like cleaners, delivery drivers, and policemen. The earliest such stamp detected dates back to March 2020 and originated in Iran. The Iranian stamp portrays healthcare workers headed by a male doctor, a male soldier wearing a gas mask, and the universal graphic representation of the virus with a green crown of spike proteins. Three short months later, comparable stamps were manufactured in Ukraine. By August 2021, when Singapore imprinted its tribute to the frontline heroes of the pandemic, such designs had become widespread globally. The sentiment borne by these mnemonic devices from nation to nation and across continents is one of pride and homage to the heroism of those who performed their jobs despite fear and the risk of infection or even death.

The second most popular theme among stamps related to COVID-19 regards public policies for coping with the pandemic, such as health protocols or vaccination campaigns. Here, too, while causality remains hard to establish, there are obvious international and intercontinental crossover trends. In October 2020, Austria came out with its version of a "keep your distance" stamp featuring a baby elephant with "= 1 METER" written beside it.[16] The stamp itself was made from toilet paper to reference the panic-buying of the product at the start of the global health crisis. In 2021, Guinea-Bissau highlighted the vaccination effort with its stamp, which shows an elderly woman being inoculated by a medical worker, indicated solely by a pair of hands holding a needle. A whole series of stamps representing COVID-19 responses, such as vaccination, social distancing, hand-washing, and disinfecting, was issued by Central African Republic in 2022. Such mobile memorials have cropped up with the same graphical tropes, albeit with local twists, in nation after nation, continent after continent – very much like the virus itself.

---

16 https://www.dw.com/en/austria-postal-service-prints-coronavirus-themed-stamp-on-toilet-paper/a-55376495.

White flags, yellow hearts and multicolored stamps are three current expressions of transnational memory of COVID-19 following traditions inspired by Rigney's conceptualization. However, in keeping with Rigney (2015c; 2012b), one must ponder some additional questions: Will COVID-19, in itself a transnational phenomenon, result in a lasting memory that transcends national boundaries? And will such transnational memory enhance social solidarity and shared understanding among diverse communities? The verdict is still out. When compared with Rigney's prior work on the *European House of History* (2014), the case of COVID-19 seems a walk in the park, devoid of the conflictual or counter-narratives of the past, which plague major European memories of the twentieth century. On an individual level, there is a profusion of identical stories from around the world, accounts of loneliness, loss, and anxieties during COVID-19 that can be relayed and may co-construct transnational memories of 2020–2023. Alas, for those memories to become transnational, multinational agents of memory wielding political will and substantial resources will be requisite. A first such promising initiative is offered by the *European House of History* and supported by their new platform "COVID Makes History": there, people and institutions (national museums included) from around Europe are invited to share their COVID-19-related experiences, exhibitions, and collections. In this, the transnational project aims at encouraging "solidarity, hope and community building."[17]

Per contra, the memory of COVID-19 – similar to that of the Spanish flu and other pandemics – belongs to the "cold" side of the mnemonic pendulum, in Maier's terms (2002), and thus stands only a small chance of becoming a major symbolic mnemonic force. Instead, what may broaden horizons for humanity hinges primarily not on the remembrance pole of collective memory but, rather, on its knowledge pole (Vinitzky-Seroussi and Maraschin 2021; see also Erll 2020). In this sense, new knowledge generated by challenges raised by COVID-19 (e.g., novel communication technologies respondent to crises in education and medical care) and realized by scientists, educators, engineers, architects, and more, may actually leave us with prospects for a better global future. This is a world that will succeed in solving serious social problems and resolving conflicts – the very world Ann Rigney has sought for so long.

---

17 https://historia-europa.ep.eu/en/covid-makes-history.

Stijn Vervaet
Remembering the Female Partisan: Sanja Iveković's Transnational Memory Work

1 Introduction

In this chapter, I explore photomontages and installations by the Croatian visual and performance artist Sanja Iveković that take the memory of female Yugoslav communist partisans as point of departure for left-wing feminist activism in the present. Why this interest in the figure of the female partisan? In his meticulous analysis of the heyday of Yugoslav socialism and the reasons of its decline, Darko Suvin (2016, 23–33) has rightfully pointed out the antifascist partisan struggle and self-management (rejecting both fascist imperialism and Stalinist totalitarianism) as the two singularities that distinguish Yugoslavia from other socialist state experiments in Eastern Europe, where communism was largely imposed top down. The Yugoslav partisans were the only resistance movement that was open to people from all religious and ethnic backgrounds and that actively recruited women (Batinić 2015, 134–136). Importantly, many female Yugoslav partisan fighters remember(ed) the war "as the high point of their lives, when they acted as historical agents and political subjects in their own right" (Batinić 2015, 16; 164–166). This sense of women's political agency and subjectivity is at the heart of Iveković's work. In what follows, I will test out Gal Kirn's (2020, 25) claim that "partisan ruptures" can be reappropriated in the present for radical feminist, antiracist, and ecological struggles. I aim to demonstrate how Iveković's art transmits and materializes the memory of female Yugoslav antifascists, including its embodied and affective dimensions, and in doing so intervenes against right-wing obliteration in the post-socialist present. Merging the aesthetical, political, and theoretical, Iveković's work also exemplifies what Rigney (2018a, 371–373) called "remembrance with and of a cause": an effective appropriation of the revolutionary energy of women's antifascist struggle for a new, feminist cause in postsocialist times. In doing so, Iveković's work reminds us that the antifascist struggle, just as feminism, was and is an internationalist emancipatory project whose memory not only transcends the national but in complex ways entangles local, national, and transnational scales.

2 "Memory of, and with a Cause": Sanja Iveković's visual interventions into postsocialist memory culture

In their seminal book about transnational memory, Chiara De Cesari and Ann Rigney (2014, 5; 15–16) suggested multiscalarity as an analytical lens to account for the interaction between local, national, regional, transnational, cosmopolitan, and global frameworks of memory. They also highlighted the importance of exploring how narratives about the past are articulated and how through articulation acts of remembrance become part of the constitution of political subjects (De Cesari and Rigney 2014, 15–16). Iveković's memory-related artworks illustrate not only how memory is articulated in the complex crossing and renegotiating of borders between different frameworks of memory. Her work also shows how the (re)making, or (re)imagining, of scale itself plays a role in memory struggles.

Already in the 1990s, in the wake of the Yugoslav wars, Sanja Iveković took up the legacy of female antifascist activists.[1] The photomontage *Gen XX* is one of Iveković's first critical interventions into the postsocialist culture of oblivion. In a move which she calls "the appropriation of authority" (Iveković and Majača 2009, 11), Iveković took photographs of supermodels advertising fashion products, erased the names of the brands, and substituted them with the names of six forgotten female communist partisans: Anka Butorac, Zdenka and Rajka Baković, Nada Dimić, Ljubica Gerovac, and Dragica Končar, alongside the dates of their imprisonment, torture, and death at the hands of the Nazis' local allies (Figure 1). Often doing the dangerous work of partisan couriers in cities, these women were celebrated as national heroines in socialist Yugoslavia; factories (Nada Dimić), schools (Anka Butorac), and streets (the sisters Baković, Dragica Končar) were named after them.

As Susan Gal has argued, "scaling is a relational practice that relies on situated *comparisons* among events, persons, and activities" (2016, 91, original emphasis). In addition, "analogies are often rescaling devices" (Gal 2016, 94), and it is in this sense that Iveković's visual juxtaposition of female antifascist activists and fashion models should be understood. *Gen XX* suggests that the female partisan (as icon) and the beauty model (as icon) share a set of relationships: their internationalist aura and circulation, their appeal as role models for young women, and their link with specific economic models. At the same time, the juxtaposition con-

---

1 Born in 1949, Iveković studied at the Academy of Fine Arts in Zagreb and belongs to the generation of artists emerging after 1968. A good overview of her work is collected in Iveković 2023.

Figure 1: Four photographs from Sanja Iveković's GEN XX-series, reproduced by courtesy of the artist.
Anka Butorac. Charged with anti-fascist activities. Tortured and executed in Kostajnica in 1942. Age at the time of death: 36. **Nera Šafarić.** Charged with anti-fascist activities. Arrested in Crikvenica in 1942 and taken to Auschwitz concentration camp from which she was freed in 1945. Age at the time of arrest: 23. **Dragica Končar.** Charged with anti-fascist activities. Tortured and executed in Zagreb in 1942. Age at the time of death: 27. **Ljubica Gerovac.** Charged with anti-fascist activities. To avoid capture she commited suicide. Age at the time of death: 22.

flates the temporal, political/ideological, and geographical differences between the two.[2] In doing so, Iveković's "juxtaposition makes unexpected, new scalar relations by invoking and then jumping across presumed, conventional scales" (Gal 2016, 94).

Iveković's montage was an explicit response to the *damnatio memoriae* regarding the Yugoslav socialist and antifascist legacy that characterized postwar Croatia and most of the other successor states (see Kirn 2020, 1–15; 211–246). This ban on the socialist past included the destruction of monuments to the antifascist struggle in World War II, the erasure of names of its participants from public space, museums, and history textbooks from which Iveković's daughter's generation learned at school (Iveković and Majača 2009, 10). Initially, Iveković wanted to publish the photographs in women's journals, to offer their young readers alternative models. But the fashion journals rejected them and so the photomontages were published in 1997–1998 in the Croatian underground magazines *Arkzin*, *Kruh & ruže*, and *Zaposlena* (Iveković and Majača 2009, 10). Since the fashion industry is an exemplary case of global capital, the substitution of images of female partisans by photographs of fashion models could also be read as a reference to Yugoslavia's inclusion into the global market. This "transition" was only possible by destroying the Yugoslav model of self-management, which meant an economy of solidarity within the federation and a politics of non-alignment and solidarity with third world countries on the international level (Kirn 2020, 1–14). Indeed, Iveković's *Gen XX* suggests that the revisionist turn of the 1990s and its erasure of the antifascist legacy in Croatia went hand in glove with the replacement of the socialist by the neoliberal market economy.

Importantly, this erasure of the Yugoslav antifascist legacy in post-Yugoslav society corresponded to changes within European memory culture that had been underway since the 1980s. Initially based on remembering the end of World War II as a victory over fascism, attempts after 1989 to define a common European memory increasingly revolved around traumatic memories of the Holocaust and Gulag; communism's crucial role as an ally against Nazism was replaced by the image of Stalinist totalitarianism (Judt 2005, 803–831; Traverso 2016, 2–4). Iveković's montage can thus not only be read as critique of Croatian right-wing revisionism but also as tracing the direction of European memory politics. Noteworthy, one of the photographs in *Gen XX* is not an image of a supermodel but a real photograph of Iveković's mother, Nera Šafarić, who as a communist activist was arrested and sent to Auschwitz at the age of twenty-three (Iveković 2023, 132). Iveković's mother sur-

---

2 To be sure, "a model of some kind is indispensable for guiding comparisons" (Gal 2016, 94); but models "have no *necessary* scale" (Gal 2016, 93; original emphasis). Indeed, "it is the combination of model-plus-situated-invocation that constructs comparison and thus the imagination of scale" (Gal 2016, 94).

vived the camp, but eventually committed suicide in 1988.[3] By including her mother's photograph and biography, Iveković brings in a generational dimension and establishes a postmemorial link, bridging the gap between grandmother and daughter, between the generation of antifascist female activists and the post-socialist one. Iveković's photomontage not only offers alternative memory models to the generation deprived of Yugoslav socialism's transnational memory culture, but also reminds the viewers that Europe's currently victim-centered memory narrative of World War II once had an activist-centered, emancipatory dimension. The insertion of her mother's photograph additionally underlines that the activist and victim-position can overlap and that there runs a direct line from remembering antifascism to remembering Auschwitz.

Iveković uses a similar procedure – juxtaposition through the insertion of documentary material into a fashion advertisement – in her 2007 montage *The Right One. The Pearls of the Revolution (Ona prava. Biseri revolucije)*. The photograph shows a model holding a pearl necklace, clenched in her fist in what is reminiscent of a military salute. The model's left eye is covered by an authentic photograph of two Yugoslav partisan women saluting as if to suggest that the 'true' or 'real' partisan past, caught in a mise en abîme, is looking back at the viewer in what could be seen as an ironic comment on consumer culture and feminine ideals of beauty. In 2010, Iveković recreated the montage together with the photographer Sandra Vitaljić and stand-in model Jana Vukić (otherwise a professor of sociology at the University of Zagreb), which resulted in a series of ten photographs. Replacing the model, Jana Vukić tries to find the "right" gesture which would correspond to the posture of the partisan women from the photograph.[4] The fact that Vukić's own grandmother, the writer Anđelka Martić, was a Yugoslav partisan, adds a transgenerational layer to the reenactment (Iveković 2023, 134; MSU Facebook page).[5] More than just reinserting the partisan past into the postsocialist present, the whole performance also underlines the embodiedness of (post)memory: How does reenacting the partisan gesture feel? As Kirn notes, Didi-Huberman reminds us that gestures are bodily forms and as such related to "forces that make us rise up" and to "'the exclamation of words' which

---

3 In later projects delving into her mother's history, Iveković complicates the heroic dimension of post-war socialist memory culture.
4 In the Croatian title ("Ona prava"), "prava" ("right, correct, just, true, real") is an adjective in the feminine form that hence can be added to a range of feminine nouns, allowing combinations from "the right posture" (prava poza) or "gesture" (prava gesta); to "the right/true past" (prava prošlost), "the right/true value" (prava vrijednost) and, ultimately, "the right woman" (prava žena) or "the right revolution" (prava revolucija).
5 https://www.facebook.com/MSUzagreb/posts/634781588686840/.

carry both conflict in relation to the existing order and an 'indestructible desire' for emancipation" (Didi-Huberman quoted in Kirn 2020, 79–80). Echoing previous revolutionary gestures, the partisan greeting reads as a remediation of the salute of Republican fighters in the Spanish civil war (usually just an upright held clenched fist), one of the first leftist guerilla troops in Europe that prominently included female combatants. This reference is not accidental, since many of the pre-war members of the Communist Party of Yugoslavia had participated in the Spanish civil war, where they had gained organizational and military skills (Batinić 2015, 25). The transnational aspect of the memory of antifascism is here evoked by an iconic bodily gesture.

But who or what are, then, the pearls of the revolution? The female partisans who are looking back at the viewer remind us that the Yugoslav partisan struggle gave an enormous impetus to women's emancipation. Yugoslav women – the majority of whom were young peasant girls – entered the partisan movement as combatants or in other roles through *The Antifascist Front of Women* (AFW; *Antifašistička fronta žena*). Founded on liberated territory in Bosnia in December 1942, the AFW proved very efficient in providing rear support to the partisan army, in eliminating illiteracy, and in raising political consciousness among peasant women. The partisan leadership recognized that they would have never succeeded without the AFW (Batinić 2015, 97–115). But feminist scholars such as anthropologist Lydia Sklevicky, historians Barbara Jancar-Webster and Jelena Batinić have written about the discrimination women often faced within the partisan ranks and pointed out the contradictions at the heart of the communist project of emancipating women from above while denouncing feminism (Batinić 2015, 15; 123). Initially controlled by the Communist Party of Yugoslavia (CPY), the organization grew increasingly autonomous (and in Croatia even relatively financially independent), to the dissatisfaction of the Party. Soon, the AFW was accused of "feminist sectarianism," put under stronger party control, and eventually dissolved in 1953 (Batinić 2015, 115–121), in what Suvin calls "a remarkable example of political blindness" (2016, 25). After World War II, the state-supported memory culture turned partisan women into powerful icons of the revolution. However, together with the decline of socialism, the imagery of female partisans became increasingly sexualized, and from the 1980s onwards trivialized and pushed into oblivion (Batinić 2015, 213–257). Intervening against the degradation and erasure of the legacy of female partisans, Iveković also takes up the question of women's emancipation where the CPY left it when it abolished the AFW and declared the women's question resolved.

The memory of the socialist and feminist struggle is both internationalist in scope and entangled with the national and local memory context, as shown by Iveković's latest sculpture *Pregnant Memory* [*Trudna memorija*] which since June 2023 stands in front of the Museum of Contemporary Art (MSU) in Zagreb. Staging a gilded, pregnant female figure on top of an obelisk, the sculpture is a palimpsest or "translation" (Iveković 2023, 138) of its previous versions: of a counter-memorial created in 2001 in Luxemburg called *Lady Rosa of Luxembourg*, of an unrealized monument for Rosa Luxemburg in Berlin in 2003, as well as of the 2017 *Monument to Revolution*.[6] The obelisk is positioned on a double postament, the upper part listing a mix of gendered allegoric words ("nation, homeland, democracy"), the words "capitalism, kitsch, and culture," and a selection of insulting words for women in Croatian. Both the Luxemburg and the Zagreb installation interrogate not just how national memorial culture includes or excludes women but also remind the viewer how the female figure as an allegory for the nation has spread across the world since the French Revolution and has become an internationally circulating memory template used to articulate a national narrative about the past (see Warner 1985). The reception of Iveković's installations shows that, if artists dare to touch this allegory (e.g. by quoting it with a difference), their work can be perceived as a political attack on the nation – in "Western" and "Eastern" Europe alike (see Pejić 2003).[7]

The lower block showcases the names of women declared national heroines of the Yugoslav National Liberation Struggle. Devoted to women who are victims of domestic violence, the monument reminds us how the legacy of antifascist women activists can be inspiring for emancipative projects today. Within days after its inauguration, the monument was defiled with nationalist graffiti, and then cleaned up by the city's current left-wing government.[8] This last development illlustrates how an intervention into national memory culture is possible by forming an alliance – between artist, museum, and city – below the level of the nation-state, which again casts yet a different light on the interaction between the different scales involved in the articulation and institutionalization of memory. The battle for the memory of antifascism is not yet over.

3 Conclusion

Iveković's work reminds the viewer that the Yugoslav antifascist liberation struggle, transnationalist by definition, was synonym for a politics of hope, the revolution of a struggle *against* fascism and *for* workers,' peasants' and women's emancipation and as such can serve as a powerful mnemonic resource for struggles in the present.

---

6 See https://www.documenta14.de/en/calendar/16469/art-of-the-possible.
7 For the political controversy which Iveković's *Lady Rosa of Luxembourg* caused in Luxembourg, see https://www.moma.org/explore/inside_out/2011/12/01/sanja-ivekovic-lady-rosa-of-luxembourg/.
8 https://www.facebook.com/search/top/?q=sanja%20ivekovic%20monument%20%20.

Through surprising visual interventions, Iveković invites the viewer to rethink the relation between local, national, regional, European, and global memory and, even more so, to interrogate the validity of the scales against which the Yugoslav socialist experience is measured and after which models its memory is being revised. Remediating the figure of the Yugoslav female partisan, she tackles the node of right-wing revisionism and global capitalism, articulates the link between the memory regimes of the new post-Yugoslav nation-states and the rise in violence against women, and hints at the at times uncanny correspondence between post-Yugoslav and wider European memory debates. Proposing new terms of comparison and new analogies, Iveković's work itself functions as an instance of rescaling memory. But in doing so, she does not pretend to occupy a position that is free of ideology. For Iveković, art is a way to intervene into hegemonic discourses and stir up public debate (Iveković and Majača 2009, 11). By re-using pre-existing visual images in a defamiliarizing way Iveković draws attention to the fact that cultural memory is not pre-given or set in stone. While the aesthetic dimension clearly has an important function in creating new social imaginaries and contesting the existing ones, the embodied affect that underpins memory is no less important in Iveković's work. Using guerilla strategies to address postsocialism's blind spots, the left-wing feminist artist proves a true heir to the female antifascist activists from World War II.

Margaret Kelleher
Articulation, Politics and the Aesthetic: Yeats's Nobel Prize, 1923–2023

1 Articulation

Transnational Memory, the 2014 collection of essays edited by Chiara De Cesari and Ann Rigney, is organized in three sections and these section titles – "circulation," "articulation," and "scales" – have become deeply influential concepts in memory studies. Here I wish to focus on one term, "articulation," and to exploit two definitions of the term: "bringing to expression" and "connecting," a doubleness of meaning which the editors identify with keen insight. Cultural memories are "articulated discourses" they observe, but "acts of remembrance" also involve 'articulation' in another sense: they help to link up ('articulate') individuals and groups through their common engagement with those narratives" (De Cesari and Rigney 2014, 15).

By way of connection, three dates are relevant here. In the summer of 1977, as an undergraduate student in English and French at University College Dublin, Ann Rigney attended the Yeats Summer School in Sligo, Ireland; fellow attendees included a Dutch student called Joep Leerssen. At the time of writing this essay, late 2023, Ireland recently celebrated the 100th anniversary of Yeats's Nobel Prize, which was awarded to him in Stockholm on 9 December 1923. More broadly, the status and impact of the Nobel Prize, which will be examined in this essay primarily through the case of Yeats, offers a revealing case of transnational memory wherein, to quote again from De Cesari and Rigney's collection, "'Transnationalism' recognizes the significance of national frameworks alongside the potential of cultural production both to reinforce and to transcend them" (De Cesari and Rigney 2014, 4).

2 1923: bringing to expression

On 14 November 1923, late at night, W.B. Yeats received a telephone call at his Dublin home; the caller was Bertie Smyllie, future editor of the *Irish Times*, bringing the first report that Yeats had won the Nobel Prize in Literature. Ten minutes later a telegram from the Swedish Ambassador confirmed the good news.

While the news was warmly welcomed in Ireland, reactions elsewhere were mixed. Some members of the English press bitterly complained about the passing over of writer Thomas Hardy. In the United States, journalists lamented the continuing absence of American winners (and would continue to do so until 1930 when Sinclair Lewis became the first American to win the award). In the interviews that followed the announcement, and in attempts towards conciliation, Yeats thanked "the English committees" for nominating him, and paid tribute to Thomas Mann as the other leading contender. He was wrong on both fronts. Mann was first nominated in 1924 (he would receive the award in 1929) and Yeats was not nominated by an English committee but instead by a member of the Swedish Academy.

And the most surprising fact of all – also unknown to Yeats – was that the year 1923 did not mark his first nomination but instead his seventh. He was nominated previously in 1922, 1921, 1918, 1915, 1914, and quite amazingly in 1902, at a very early stage of his long writing career. For all of the reputed secrecy concerning the Nobel Prize and its operations, a remarkable amount of information can be gleaned from its own website, nobelprize.org, where one can search its archive by prize and person and find out who was nominated and by whom for every year up to 1971 (a secrecy rule of fifty years applies).

Reports from the Nobel Committee show that Yeats was a very close contender in 1922, losing out to Spanish dramatist Jacinto Benavente, largely on pragmatic grounds. The two writers were found to be of comparable stature in literary worth, with Yeats lauded for his "exceptionally highly developed English poetic culture." The committee feared, however, that the geographic distribution of the Prize looked too limited, and so it went to the Spanish writer (Epsmark 1991, 48–50).

All changed – for Yeats and Ireland – a year later. The Nobel citation for Yeats, read to him in Stockholm on 10 December 1923, praised him "for his always inspired poetry, which in a highly artistic form gives expression to the spirit of a whole nation." Just months before, in September 1923, the fledgling – and fragile – Irish Free State had joined the League of Nations. No longer seen as a writer in the dominant tradition of English, Yeats could now be celebrated by Per Hallström, Chairman of the Nobel Committee of the Swedish Academy, as "the interpreter of his country, a country that had long waited for someone to bestow on it a voice."

As literary historians, we rightly emphasize the role culture has played in the creation of an Irish state, but there's a nice reversal here: in 1923, political independence could enable the global recognition of Irish literature as a distinct tradition, through the awarding of the most famous of prizes. So Yeats's understanding of what had occurred behind the scenes was correct in one dimension, at least: "I consider that this honor has come to me less as an individual than as a representative of Irish literature, it is part of Europe's welcome to the Free State."

"The Irish Dramatic Movement" was the theme of Yeats's Nobel Lecture, delivered to the Swedish Royal Academy on 13 December 1923. From the beginning

Yeats directly names the political background to his work and the influence of recent events: "The modern literature of Ireland, and indeed all that stir of thought which prepared for the Anglo-Irish War, began when Parnell fell from power in 1891" (Yeats 2010, 410). Many times during his lecture, he recounts the challenges facing the theatrical movement including those from Dublin Castle, the center of English Government in Ireland; in his words, "we were from the first a recognised public danger" (Yeats 2010, 415). He claims with pride the continuing influence of that cultural movement – "Indeed the young Ministers and party politicians of the Free State have had, I think, some of their education from our plays" – but also highlights its great precarity: "We are burdened with debt, for we have come through war and civil war and audiences grow thin when there is firing in the street" (Yeats 2010, 418).

Yeats's audience in Stockholm were left in no doubt as to the rawness of current Irish politics: in crediting the importance of his close colleague Lady Augusta Gregory, he reports that "Her own house has been protected by her presence, but the house where she was born was burned down by incendiaries some few months ago, and there has been like disorder over the greater part of Ireland" (Yeats 2010, 411). And in remarks that would prove uncomfortable for a subsequent Irish readership, he observes: "and if in their war with the English auxiliary police they [our people] were shown no mercy, they showed none: murder answered murder. Yet their ignorance and violence can remember the noblest beauty" (Yeats 2010, 411).

In this juncture, the seeds of Yeats's future influence as a poet of decolonization may be glimpsed. One instance of that influence, whose rearticulation is of much relevance to our present, occurs in Edward Said's 1993 work *Culture and Imperialism*, where he writes: "Yeats's prophetic perception that at some point violence cannot be enough and that the strategies of politics and reason must come into play is, to my knowledge, the first important announcement in the context of decolonization of the need to balance violent force with an exigent political and organizational process" (Said 1993, 235).

3 Re-articulation: Heaney, Yeats and the political aesthetic

Reference to Yeats's work and award would appear in a number of other Nobel addresses; for example in 1948, making his presentation speech to T.S. Eliot, Swedish academy member Anders Osterling cited Yeats's award; in 1963 Greek poet Giorgos Seferis began his Nobel lecture by referring to "A poet who is especially dear to me, the Irishman W.B. Yeats" and quoted from Yeats's account of his trip to Stockholm "The Bounty of Sweden" (1924). Most powerful of all is the reference to Yeats by Seamus Heaney in his 1995 Nobel lecture "Crediting Poetry," an extraordinary lecture, many of whose references – including to Russian poet Anna Akhmatova and to the unnamed woman "in the prison queue in Leningrad"– continue to resonate deeply (Heaney 1995).

The Nobel citation for Heaney summarized the grounds of his award as follows: "for works of lyrical beauty and ethical depth, which exalt everyday miracles and the living past." In February 1995, the British and Irish governments published a framework document outlining proposals for a new elected Northern Irish assembly; in May of that year, the representatives of the British government held an official meeting with representatives of Sinn Féin for the first time in twenty-three years.

Speaking in Stockholm, Heaney reminded his listeners that Yeats was, in December 1923, the recent author of the great sequences "Nineteen Hundred and Nineteen" and "Meditations in Time of Civil War." The latter poem, published in *Dial* and the *London Mercury* in January 1923, had at the time of the Nobel award still a limited circulation. But it is impossible now – the anniversary year of the end of the Irish Civil War, and a year that has seen immense global violence – not to connect them together. For Heaney, Yeats's poem achieves a precious doubleness of being "tender-minded" and "tough-minded" (Heaney 1995, 26). In Heaney's articulation, that doubleness of achievement is not only aesthetic in nature but also urgently political: "It [the poem 'Meditations in Time of Civil War'] satisfies the contradictory needs which consciousness experiences at times of extreme crisis, the need on the one hand for a truth telling that will be hard and retributive, and on the other hand, the need not to harden the mind to a point where it denies its own yearnings for sweetness and trust" (Heaney 1995, 26–27). These famous lines from the poem certainly deserve the epithet of 'Ireland's interpreter,' and not ours alone:

> We had fed the heart on fantasies,
> The heart's grown brutal from the fare;
> More substance in our enmities
> Than in our love; O honey-bees,
> Come build in the empty house of the stare.
>   (Yeats 1994, 251)

4 2023: commemorating and connecting

The centenary of Yeats' winning of the Nobel Prize has been marked by a rich variety of events, many of which were organized by the Yeats Society in Sligo. On 9 December 2023, a seminar co-hosted with the National Library, on the topic of "Yeats's Nobel: Then & Now," marked the anniversary of the Stockholm award. That afternoon saw, outside the library and government buildings, a substantial political protest by the Ireland Palestinian Solidarity Campaign, an event already part of the 'memoryscape' of Irish activism – to quote a term from Ann Rigney's landmark work on political protest.[1] The large police presence surrounding the National Library and Irish Parliament that day was due, however, to different events on Dublin streets: the troubling riots that occurred in central Dublin on the evening of 23 November, mobilized around anti-immigrant sentiment and exploited by far-right social media. In the words of poet Paula Meehan at the Yeats seminar, "The streets are loud with shouts and argument. We saw burning trams, we saw burning buses on the streets of Dublin," "scenes on the streets of Dublin that we never would have imagined" (Meehan 2023).

Meehan's powerful address is preserved on the Library's youtube channel and her closing comments eloquently attest to the urgency of our time:

> There is a desperate need to reimagine again what our nation is, to reimagine again what it means to be Irish, and where we can make the journey between nation and home [. . .] We don't have time now for war, for desecration of the very fabric of homes and communities. (Meehan 2023)

As part of that "desperate need" for reimagining, acts of remembrance will be articulated and connected, challenged and renewed, and once again by poets:

> You look to the young poets, you look to the carriers of poetry, which are often in our popular culture the singers of the songs . . . It is poetry's destiny to be able to do that work and to take up that work, and that's the work that poets do. My hopefulness is not overshadowed by what I see on the streets, but I do think we all have a lot of work ahead. (Meehan 2023)

---

1 See Rigney's project Remembering Activism: The Cultural Memory of Protest in Europe (REACT); https://rememberingactivism.eu/. (Accessed 21 May 2024).

Eneken Laanes
Memory Translation and Minor Transnationalism

1 Introduction

On 23 August 2019, the protesters in Hong Kong gathered along the main subway lines of the city to form what they called the Hong Kong Way – the almost 50 km long human chain against the growing influence of China on Hong Kong. This event was one in the series of protests intensifying since March of that year. They were directed against the proposed extradition law and harkened back to the Umbrella movement for universal suffrage in 2014. The name and the date of the 23 August event clearly referred to another human chain – the Baltic Way – which people in Estonia, Latvia, and Lithuania formed thirty years earlier on 23 August 1989, as part of the liberation movement from the non-democratic regime of the Soviet Union.

When Baltic news media reported on the references made by the Hong Kong protesters to the Baltic Way, many locals were surprised that people in a far-away country outside Europe knew about their history and modeled their own political protest on it. The borrowing of this specific form of public protest and the mobilization of the transnational memory of its earlier occurrence(s) offers rich material for understanding the 'genre memory' of social rituals that are simultaneously commemorative practices and public protests. But the case also sheds light on the work of cultural translation that is involved in this process of borrowing and rehearsal.[1] In this contribution, I will draw on Ann Rigney's idea of scarcity of memorial forms and on her work on the memories of hope to explore how hopeful models of political protest and peaceful transformation travel transnationally and are translated so that they contribute to social transformation in the place of destination, but also reorient the (future) memory of the protests in the place of departure.

---

1 On the cultural translation of memories, see Laanes 2021; Radstone and Wilson 2021.

Note: The chapter is part of the project 'Translating Memories: The Eastern European Past in the Global Arena' that has received funding from the European Research Council (ERC) under the European Union's Horizon 2020 research and innovation programme (Grant agreement No 853385). I would like to thank Marju Lauristin and Chun Sing Iverson Ng for their valuable information about the protests in Estonia and Hong Kong.

One of the most fruitful ideas in memory studies in the past two decades has been Rigney's idea of scarcity of memorial forms and templates to articulate historical experiences and their memory (Rigney 2005; see also Laanes and Meretoja 2021). Borrowing from Foucault, Rigney (2005, 21–24) shows that because of the scarcity of these forms, they are often borrowed transnationally and recycled to articulate and remember historical experiences that can be quite different in terms of historical time, location, and the nature of struggles.[2] In relation to commemorative practices as social rituals, in particular, Jeffrey Olick has argued that they are path-dependent, i.e. draw on the 'genre memory' of earlier commemorative practices, and hence depend not only "on the relationship between past and present, but on the accumulation of previous such relationships and their ongoing constitution and reconstruction" (Olick 1999, 382). Another pathbreaking idea in recent years in memory studies has been Rigney's (2018a) call for more serious attention to memories of hope and to memoires of political protests that next to those aiming at atoning past suffering turn our attention to potential hopeful political developments in the future.

2 From Baltic Way to Hong Kong Way: human chain as a form of protest and memory

The Baltic Way has become a symbol of peaceful political protest for democratic state order both in local as well as in the transnational memory of the change of political regimes in Central and Eastern Europe in the 1990s.[3] Although only one of the protest events in the longer process of significant social mobilization that ultimately led to the independence of three Baltic states in 1991, the Baltic Way has had a special place in the post-socialist memory of the transformation because of the large-scale grassroots participation: two of the eight million Baltic people took to busses and private cars across all three countries to drive to the route of the Baltic Way and to stand in the 600 km long human chain for several hours. The demonstration was organized on 23 August 1989, on the 50th anniversary of the Molotov-Ribbentrop Pact between the Soviet Union and Nazi Germany, the secret

---

2 Rigney states that "models of remembrance, like Foucault's utterances, are repeated, transformed and appropriated in new situations with the help of 'mobile' media. This means that one act of remembrance can stimulate comparable acts in other situations and within different social frameworks." (Rigney 2005, 23)

3 On the organizational aspects of Baltic Way, see Christie 2015; on the 20th anniversary of Baltic Way in Latvia, see Eglitis and Ardava 2012.

protocols of which partitioned Central and Eastern Europe between them, relegated Baltic states to the sphere of influence of Soviet Union and paved the way for their annexation in June 1940.[4] So the human chain commemorated a negative past of illegal annexation and loss of independent statehood. But first and foremost, it was a future-oriented protest towards liberation from a non-democratic regime. It is precisely this aspect of large-scale mobilization in the symbolic form of a human chain as a social ritual of political protest and commemoration that was borrowed and translated into the 2019 protests in Hong Kong.

When protesters in Hong Kong picked up the call for a human chain proposed in the Hong Kong forum website LIHKG by an anonymous Hong Kong person based in Estonia, they were drawing on what they understood, despite all historical differences, as the structurally similar positions of Hong Kong and the Baltic states in their relationship to China and Soviet Union respectively. Just as people in Estonia, Latvia, and Lithuania were mobilizing for a free society and for greater autonomy from the Soviet Union in 1989, the Hong Kong protesters have been fighting for universal suffrage and the preservation of human rights throughout the past decade in the contexts of growing control of China after the handover of Hong Kong by the UK in 1997. The call for the Hong Kong Way posted to the LIHKG forum[5] made reference to the Baltic "fight for freedom," to its strong show of a "united stance to the world" and to what the authors of the post understood as the international recognition of the 1989 event though the establishment of 23 August as "a European-wide day to commemorate the victims of totalitarian and authoritarian regimes" in the European Union. Their aim was "to imitate the successful and rational struggle" and "to become a viral video in foreign media."[6]

It is striking how there is something about the content of the form, the 'genre memory' of the human chain as a specific form of protest and memory – the content that this form has acquired over its many reiterative occurrences in different contexts of which the Baltic Way was obviously not the first – that makes it best

---

4 One of the leaders of Estonian Popular Front and the organizers of the Baltic Way in Estonia, Marju Lauristin has explained that the idea for the Baltic Way was born to pressure the Congress of People's Deputies of the Soviet Union founded by Gorbachev in 1989 to recognize the secret protocols of the Molotov-Ribbentrop pact put on the agenda in the first meeting of the congress in May and June 1989. Personal communication, 15 December 2023.
5 https://lihkg.com/thread/1486119/page/1. (Accessed 04 December 2023).
6 The call for the Hong Kong Way rehearses all three guiding principles of the Baltic Way: people's united choice; disciplined self-organization as the basis for democracy; demonstrative non-violence. Lauristin, who was responsible for the communication of the Baltic Way on the side of Estonian Popular Front, explained that their main aim was to reach the Western media threshold and that the form of the human chain was chosen for that purpose. Personal communication, 15 December 2023.

equipped to manifest unity and non-violent struggle and to search for wide international recognition of the cause at hand.[7] To the extent that a large-scale embodied participation and disciplined self-organization is needed to form a human chain and that it is often accompanied by powerful cultural symbolism of songs, slogans, and gestures, it results in a uniting emotional experience for the participants and becomes an impressive show for those who witness it vicariously through the media. These culturally symbolic embodied forms of protest continue to give hope even in the light of recent news of the bounty offered for the Hong Kong protesters residing in Western countries (Ng 2023).

There are many interesting similarities and differences between these two events. Suffice to mention the loosely networked nature of the organizers and participants that drew on the means of communication available at the time – phone and radio in 1989, internet forums and real-time social media channels in 2019 – to organize the events in an extremely short timespan; and the rapidly evolving identity of the protesters and their demands. The Hong Kong protests started in 2014 with the demand for universal suffrage and reignited in 2019 with a campaign against the extradition law. Since the escalation of police violence and the repression of the movement, many protesters have started to demand Hong Kong independence as "the only way out."[8] Similarly, the popular movements in the Baltic states started with the demand for the recognition of historical injustice and the greater political and economic autonomy within Soviet Union. In 1989, at the time of the Baltic Way, only a few dared to dream of independent statehood, which retrospectively has come to define the nature and meaning of the popular movements.

3 Minor transnationalism and reorienting translation

But what are the more general conceptual lessons we can learn from the travel and translation of cultural forms of public protest and memory between the Baltic states in 1989 and Hong Kong in 2019? Firstly, a lot of work on multidirectional transnational encounters of different histories has highlighted the role of majori-

---

7 For the understanding of the content of form in history writing, see Hayden White's ideas about the influence of different plot structures on the nintenteenth-century history writing (White 1973).

8 On the evolving sense of community imagined through artworks and artefacts in 2019 Hong Kong, see Ismangil and Schneider 2023.

tarian memory or more established memorial discourses in offering support for the emergence of minoritarian or silences memories (Rothberg 2009; De Cesari and Rigney 2014). But the afterlife of the Baltic Way in 2019 Hong Kong is a striking example of what Françoise Lionnet and Shu-mei Shih have called minor transnationalism, the travel of memories through the "minor-to-minor networks that circumvent the major" (Lionnet and Shih 2005, 8). Instead of focusing of the vertical relationship with the major and the minor memory cultures, the concept of minor transnationalism foregrounds horizontal networks of minoritized memory cultures instead.[9] The adoption of the Baltic Way in Hong Kong as an example of a horizontal networking of minor memory cultures was surprising for the Baltic people themselves. However, the vertical dynamic between the minor and the major was not entirely absent either, as the Hong Kong protesters aimed to replicate the successful international coverage of the Baltic Way in 1989 and to draw on its canonization in European memory.

Secondly, the Hong Kong cultural translation of the human chain as a form of protest highlights how the forms of protest and memory change in translation not only from the source to the target, but also how translation, a repetition with a difference, changes the 'original,' the source itself, i.e., the understanding and memory of the Baltic Way in its place of 'origin.' To highlight this point, I am borrowing from translation historian Kristin Dickinson (2021) who draws attention to the omnidirectional "dis- and reorienting" potential of translation.[10] In studying the cultural contacts and literary translation histories, she challenges the traditional unidirectional understanding of translation, which treats translations as secondary to an original both by nature as well as in space and time. Instead, she advocates regarding translation as an omnidirectional interplay of language that displaces the configurations of target and source and *reorients* the original itself.[11]

Arguably, the Hong Kong Way not only tried to imitate the Baltic Way in their own way, but has also changed the way the Baltic Way is understood and remembered in the Baltic states in the current political context. In post-socialist times, the memory of the Baltic Way has been appropriated in the Baltic countries by different political forces that emerged from the initially united playing field in 1989 and has retrospectively been rewritten as a nationalist struggle for independent state-

---

9 On minor transnationalism in the context of memory studies, see Lo 2013. My understanding of minor transnationalism is similar to what Andreas Huyssen describes as the South-to-South axis in his recent book on memory art in Global South (2022).

10 Dickinson's use of the term 'omnidirectional' is very close to Rothberg's 'multidirectional memory.'

11 I have developed Dickinson idea of omnidirectional reorienting translation to understand the processes of transnational cultural remembering in Laanes 2024.

hood. Transnationally too, the debates around the establishment of 23 August as the European Day of Remembrance for Victims of Stalinism and Nazism in the European Parliament in 2008 pushed mostly by conservative forces from different Eastern European countries have retrospectively tainted the memory of the Baltic Way as essentially a nationalist struggle at the expense of the fight for freedom in terms of the rule of law and democratic values. The Hong Kong Way, in the way in which it translated the Baltic Way into its own struggles, has reminded the Baltic people that their mobilization thirty years earlier was not only about national independence, but about achieving a free society and liberal values of democracy and human rights. It has also highlighted the value of the Baltic Way as a symbol of a peaceful social and political transformation. These are two very important reminders for the people in the Baltic states, in Europe and in the rest of the world in the context of Russian war of aggression in Ukraine in which the Ukrainian effort to defend the country is framed by the aggressor as a nationalist endeavor, instead of a civic one; an attempt to avoid falling prey to an authoritarian regime without the rule of law, a free press, and freedom of speech.

Liedeke Plate
Remembering Things: The Materiality of Memory and the Memory of Materials

1 Introduction

In an important sense, cultural memory is about things. Souvenirs, monuments, inscriptions, archives, objects of personal memory, memorials materializing a collective memory, places of commemoration, bodies enacting commemorative rituals – ever since Pierre Nora's *lieux de mémoire* (1984–1992) and Jan (and Aleida) Assmann's conception of cultural memory as "objectivized culture" (Assmann 1995, 128), the literature on cultural memory has revolved around things.[1] Although omnipresent and theorized as "the matter and media of memory" (Zirra 2017, 458), things in cultural memory have remained relatively undertheorized *as things*; that is, as animated by liveness and vibrancy of their own and capable of manifesting themselves in unanticipated ways (Brown 2001).[2] Yet, as anthropologists have argued, things have (social) lives and biographies (Appadurai 1986; Kopytoff 1986) and also agency. They "do things to us, and not just the things we want them to do" (Miller 2010, 94). Granting agency to things and recognizing the many complex ways in which human and nonhuman things interact in acts of remembrance requires recalibrating our understanding of the roles and functioning of things in cultural memory and reconsidering the distinction between subject and object of memory.

Noteworthily, Bill Brown introduced his influential "Thing Theory" (2001) in a video on YouTube by stating that we care so much about things today because "our most precious object, the Earth, is dying" (Brown 2010). These words are telling because they ground the material turn in the social sciences and humanities in anthropogenic climate change, which is implicitly linked to extractivist practices of material exhaustion. Herein lies a critical role for memory studies. Precisely because consumer culture is built on the forgetting of how things were made and by whom, including an obliviousness to where the materials they are made of have been retrieved from, how, by whom, and at what (human and nonhuman, environmental) cost, a focus on things and the materials from which they

---

1 Bodies are things, too, which is why they have been added to the list here. However, the brevity of this chapter prevents me from entering into the specificity of the remembering body as *a material thing* in cultural memory.

2 But see Zirra 2017, Rigney 2017, and Munteán, Plate, and Smelik 2017.

are made is a vital counter-amnesiac gesture that recognizes materials as "vibrant matter" (Bennett 2010) with a life of its own, perhaps even rights of its own.[3]

In this chapter, I explain how the new "sense of things" (Brown 2003) that developed in the wake of "Thing Theory" (Brown 2001) and "Stuff Theory" (Boscagli 2014; Miller 2010) transforms the way we think about and study cultural memory. Elaborating on the material turn in memory studies, I build on a body of literature that can be subsumed under "new materialisms" (see Plate 2020) to engage with things as integral to how societies remember, focusing first on the materiality of memory and then delving into the memory of materials. As I maintain, such a perspective decenters humans by recognizing things as (co-)agents of memory and the materials of which they are made – their materiality – to have a memory of their own, which may exceed human memory.

2 Things to remember

The literature on cultural memory is full of all kinds of things.[4] This is not surprising, given the social-constructivist understanding of how we remember. On the one hand, cultural memory is acknowledged as being actively produced and reproduced through material and immaterial culture, "the historical product of cultural mnemotechniques and mnemotechnologies," as Ann Rigney puts it (2004, 366). What we may call "things to remember"[5] are then objects of various kinds serving specific, commemorative and mnemonic, interests. One of the tasks of the cultural memory scholar is thus to unravel those interests and analyze the techniques, technologies, and practices employed to produce, maintain, preserve, and pass on, but also to alter or destroy the memory that the material object is to embody, help endure, transform, or erase.[6] Another is to situate these mnemonic objects historically and (geo)politically and explore the transformation of experience that they entail. One example would be the photo album, a historically and technologically constrained artifact that produces a specific image of the past and a particular way of remembering it. Another would be famous writers' houses, such as Abbotsford

---

3 See "The Universal Declaration of Material Rights" initiated by architects Thomas Rau and Sabine Oberhüber.
4 Although material culture studies distinguish between objects and things, here, I use "thing" both in its general sense as having concrete and real material existence and as synonymous with "object," i.e., as a discrete material thing that can be seen and touched.
5 I owe the phrase to László Munteán. It was the title of a conference on memory and materiality held at Radboud University in 2014.
6 See also Martínez (2022) on neglect as political memory performance.

House, the grand home Walter Scott built in the Scottish Borders to which Ann Rigney (2012a; 2015b) devoted scrupulous scholarly attention.

On the other hand, our encounters with things that make us remember can also seem accidental. These two perspectives come together and, as such, can be illustrated by German artist Gunter Demnig's *Stolpersteine*, "stumbling stones" placed at the last freely chosen place of residency of victims of Nazi extermination or persecution and increasingly found across European cities. Deliberately created and set to be "stumbled across" or "upon," the commemorative brass plates are designed to make unsuspecting passers-by remember the lives of the victims of the National Socialist regime. For those who stumble upon a *Stolperstein*, the effect may indeed be to "evoke the spectre of the expropriation of the Jews: a violent process that may have taken place in our very building, perhaps even in our flat," as Ingrid Scheffer (2008), a journalist in Berlin, observes.

Understanding cultural memory as entangled with things entails a view of memory as "distributed," that is, "as spread over, coupled with, situated among, or incorporating heterogeneous resources beyond the brain" (Michaelian and Sutton 2013, 3). This implies a theory of cognition as embodied, embedded, enacted, and extended – a.k.a. the 4E view of cognition (Rowlands 2010). A distributed memory theory takes Maurice Halbwachs's insight into "the social frameworks of memory" – that it is in society that people acquire, recall, recognize, and localize their memories (1992, 38) – further and couples it with an acknowledgement of the fundamental material dimensions of social life (e.g., Olsen 2010). Indeed, acknowledging the role of things in human social life is crucial to recognizing their role in recollection. Whether understood as assisting memory or preventing forgetting, things to remember are doing delegated memory work. For instance, the Holocaust Memorial in Berlin was designed as a place of remembrance for the murdered Jews of Europe and a warning not to allow history to repeat itself; writers' houses are turned into museums to evoke their lives and work; and statues representing national heroes are placed in public space to remind people of their nation's greatness. However different in form, location, aim, and materials, all these "things" enable (human) remembrance. They express a will to remember and give occasion and shape to individual and collective memory.

3 Things as agents of memory

The view of things as doing their part in memory work allows for a shift in focus away from the individuals or groups who remember and toward the things themselves as agents of memory. Indeed, it is not just that things are enlisted by humans to aid them in remembering what they do not wish to forget. To the extent that they make humans do something (recollect), "triggering and shaping recollection and linking people to each other across generations" (Rigney 2017, 474), things can be said to have *agency*. Thus, the *Stolpersteine* mentioned above require that passers-by bend over if they want to read the inscription and can, therefore, be said to make them bow to the victims. To be sure, these things that the *Stolpersteine* make people do may also be considered part of their design: they are integral to how Demnig designed them. Yet even if the emphasis is put on the human will that created the mnemonic object, there is still no denying that the stone plays a vital role in the act of recollection it enables.

Another view of things as agents of memory emerges from the extended mind thesis, which views the mind and the environment as a "two-way interaction, creating a *coupled system* that can be seen as a cognitive system in its own right" (Clark and Chalmers 1998, 8). In this view, memory is produced in the encounter between the human mind, body, and the material world. A third view posits that memory is not just enacted in the meeting of a preformed mind and material object, but the human mind is also shaped through these encounters. Aligning with insights into the brain's plasticity, this view sees memory as an emergent phenomenon caught in the ongoing dynamic entanglement of the world. Recognizing how things may alter the nature of the cognitive operations involved in remembrance, this view invites inquiry into the things' affordances and how they reconfigure memory itself: its whole social, material, and cognitive ecology and dynamics (Malafouris 2016, 81).

4 Remembering materials

So far, I have presented a relatively stable view of things: as more-or-less demarcated objects, although, since they may be subject to destruction and other processes of decay and ruination, they are not unchangeable and, as such, may affect memory differently over time. Yet, just as the human bodies and minds involved in the act of remembrance are continually changing and subject to all kinds of reconfigurations, so are the other things that constitute the material culture of memory. For instance, if the mnemotechnique of tying a knot in one's handkerchief has fallen into disuse, this has as much to do with the change in media technologies at one's disposal – e.g., the introduction of the smartphone – as with the change in the materials – disposable paper-based tissues for personal hygiene purposes having come to substitute their washable and reusable precursor. Therefore, in this chapter's final section, I plead for paying more attention to materials in the context of cultural memory studies. Countering a view of the world as inert matter to be exploited, such attention is political and links to concerns about memory in the Anthropocene. Indeed, precisely because capitalism revolves around forgetting where things come from, what they are made of, by whom, and at which (human and nonhuman, environmental) costs, it is imperative not to repeat that amnestic gesture and inquire into the materiality of cultural memory.

Materials matter and are an integral constituent of the material, "objectivized" culture of memory. Materials are selected and chosen to last (e.g., a statue made of marble or bronze) or to dissolve and disappear (e.g., Damian and Killian Van Der Velden's WWI soldier sculpted from Passchendaele mud). Their memorial qualities may have effects that are intended or unintended. For instance, many statues commemorating the confederacy in the US were made of zinc, a metal abundantly present in Earth's crust, domestically extracted and smelted into a low-cost material that made it possible for depleted communities to erect the monuments nonetheless. Ironically, the very properties of zinc that enabled the mass production of so-called "white bronze" statues, including their thin wall casting, assisted their spectacular toppling in the wake of the Black Lives Matter movement. By analyzing the role of materials in commemorating the American Civil War, a more complete picture of this memory culture can be obtained; one that acknowledges the role of materials as *actors* and recognizes them as agents that play their role in memory.

Materials, moreover, are not only selected for pragmatic reasons. They may also be chosen because of their symbolic significance, as when the marble of different colors, quarried from various conquered regions of the Roman Empire, served to remind people of the grandeur of their Empire (Stewart 2020). Similarly, Demnig's *Stolpersteine* are made of brass so that those who tread on them make them shine and contribute to keeping the memories alive. Ann Rigney (2015b, 28) gives a telling example of the mnemonic dimension of materials in her discussion of the inauguration of the Stewart Memorial Fountain, reporting: "The steel of the hammer and the drill are made from Scotch iron, the handle of the hammer from a piece of oak, part of the Old Glasgow Bridge, and the box to contain them is made of the oak of the Glasgow Cathedral." Recycled from earlier uses and sites, the iron and wood are doing memory work by metonymically making other histories present.

5 Accidental archives?

Rigney (2015b, 14) coined the term "accidental archive" to refer to the memory of materials: "objects and landscapes can turn out to be an unexpected repository of memory, an 'accidental archive' we might call it, made up of as yet-unarticulated traces rather than verbal records, of potential rather than . . . actualised meanings." And indeed, looked at from a perspective that centers human volition in cultural memory, the memory of materials can be said to be "accidental" and "unexpected," their materiality secreting "more meaning than that which was consciously inscribed in them" (Rigney 2017, 474). Acknowledging the vibrancy and agency of matter, however, new materialisms invite us to move beyond the view of things as "mute materials" (Rigney 2015b, 15) and instead, recognize that far from being "accidental," the materials of memory are archives that may be essential and purposeful, albeit from a more-than-human perspective. As scholars of cultural memory, we need to learn to listen to the stories the materials tell about where they have been and what they have been through; in short, about their memories.

Maria Zirra

Accidental Archives and Diffractive Reading: Gladys Mgudlandlu and the Resistant Periodical Memory Object

1 Introduction

Ann Rigney's exploration of the medial and material uses of literature is rich and encyclopedic ranging from historical imperfections of literary history to the after-lives of hope in cultural activism remembrance.[1] Rigney's seminal work *The After-lives of Walter Scott* (2012a) investigates the medial reception and textual afterlives of Scott's novels as *memory on the move*. It also traces how these texts produce material emanations and become objects of remembrance in their own right. In her 2015 article "Things and the Archive: Scott's Materialist Legacy," she turns from Scott's novels to his collection of "zany and highly original" relics of the past or "ga-bions" (18) to explore the role of objects *in* memory and objects *of* memory. She points out that objects and landscapes can "turn out to be an unexpected repository of memory, or 'accidental archive[s]'" (14). Building on Marianne Hirsch and Leo Spitzer's claim that "objects retrospectively acquire testimonial force" in the "per-ceived incommensurability between 'the meaning of a given object *then* and the one it holds *now*'" (Hirsch and Spitzer cited in Rigney 2015b, 14), Rigney posits that "[o]bjects can thus thicken time: as material sedimentations of past lives whose meaning is delayed, they have a foot both in the present and in the past" (14).

Her account of the vital materiality of Walter Scott's collection of memorial objects, the shifting juxtapositions of meanings they obtain within antiquarianist practices, as well as her mapping of the afterlives of his collecting impetus are inspiring forays into the way objects shape landscapes of remembrance and be-come transferrable across time and across different generations. With nods to-wards scholarship by Jane Bennett, Bruno Latour, Ian Hodder, and Carolyn Steedman, Rigney constructs a framework for a vitalist materialist study of mem-ory, thus participating in a broader movement in the field that seeks to theorize the relationship between materiality and memory (e.g., Munteán et al. 2016; Zirra 2017; Chidgey 2018; Savolainen 2020; Zolkos 2023). "[L]ateral thinking, an eye for

---

1 Research for this piece was made possible by the Swedish Research Council, International Post-doc funding in the project "Reading Artworlds in Small Print: Prismatic Combinations of Litera-ture and Visual Arts in Little Magazines from South Africa, 1960s–1980s," project number 2020-06419. Many thanks to Susanne Knittel for her feedback, patience, and excellent guidance.

telling detail and an imaginative ability to cut across the usual archival categories and thinking outside the box" (2015b, 14), Rigney observes, are skills required to produce a form of memory studies with a materialist slant. I find her focus on the "imaginative ability" required to perform a vitalist reading cognizant of the ecologies of human and nonhuman in the production of memory and especially the notion of the 'accidental archive' particularly inspiring and generative.

In what follows, I attempt an exercise of the kind of lateral thinking that Rigney describes by focusing on South-African literary periodicals. In my current research, I explore how black visual artists are reviewed in literary magazines from the high apartheid period, and conduct my own revisionist readings of these materials as objects of periodical memory accidentally archiving ideas that go counter to mainstream conversations. I suggest that a useful way to approach these periodicals as simultaneous objects of memory and objects in memory can be Karen Barad's feminist new materialist concept of 'diffractive reading' – a manner of understanding differences and different agencies of matter as complex entanglements where humans and nonhumans become mutually intelligible in their intra-activity. In Baradian thought, the concept of intra-action is used instead of 'interaction' to designate the mutual constitution of agencies. Agency is understood here "not as an inherent property of an individual or human to be exercised, but as a dynamism of forces in which all designated 'things' are constantly exchanging and diffracting, influencing and working inseparably" (Stark 2016). Barad posits diffraction as a "useful counterpoint to reflection: both [diffraction and reflection] are optical phenomena, but whereas reflection reflects the theme of mirroring and sameness, diffraction is marked by patterns of difference" (Barad 2007, 71). Barad muses that

> methodology of reflexivity mirrors the geometrical optics of reflection, and that for all of the recent emphasis on reflexivity as a critical method of self-positioning it remains caught up in the geometries of sameness; by contrast, diffractions are attuned to differences – differences that our knowledge-making practices make and the effects they have on the world (2007, 72).

This diffractive way of reading entangled agencies of human (myself, the reader) and matter (archival material) seems apt as I reckon with memory processes that occur in my own brushes with periodical archives.

2 Resistant periodicals and revisionist readings

While mapping what I call the 'prismatic combinations of literature and visual art' in South African literary magazines spanning the early 1960s to the early 1980s in archival collections located in Makhanda at the Amazwi South African Museum of Literature, the Cory Law Library at Rhodes University, and the William Cullen Library at Witwatersrand University in Johannesburg, I found myself transfixed by a series of review columns and art supplements discussing the future of South African art across different 'progressive' anti-apartheid magazines from the 1960s. These reviews are printed in liberal, anti-apartheid periodicals whose reading audience was predominantly white (despite efforts to reach black audiences) and whose limited circulation and ephemerality allowed them to mostly fly under the radar of increasingly strict apartheid censorship (Helgesson 2022). In the 1960s and 1970s, defining South African art as African was a priority shared by the white establishment, the liberal and the radical anti-apartheid thinkers (Van Robbroeck 2006, 128–134; Peffer 2009, 23–26; and Nettleton 2011, 141–143). While official apartheid coverage of black art in glossy magazines and larger newspapers tended to be exoticizing and complicitous with agendas of separate development, small magazines such as *The Classic*, *The New African* and *Contrast* filled a gap in reviewing art from a more racially just perspective (see also Van Robbroeck's assessment of *The Classic*, 2006, 159–163). I was thus hoping to encounter more clear-cut progressives in their pages, yet, to my dismay, liberal reviewers such as Bill Ainslie or Julian Beinart also had numerous blind spots and their own patterns of complicity, much in keeping with Mark Sanders' valuable work on intellectuals under apartheid, or Peter D. McDonald's assessments of the volk avant-garde in *The Literature Police* (Sanders 2002; McDonald 2009).

Moreover, as a memory scholar working with archival material, I felt a certain resistance and opacity to my contemporary perspective 'mounted' by the review material in the magazines. I could understand that the patronizing and prescriptive attitudes of the reviewers fit in perfectly with the political agendas of the day, but I still reeled at the tones. What does it mean then to read periodical objects from the past in the present? What kind of memory objects can periodicals be? Also, can we conceive of the reviews as 'accidental archives'? My focus on tracking discussions about African art in literary periodicals can be considered incidental to the literariness of a literary magazine. This makes the recording of black artists and views on art works of their period 'accidental.' My reading thus offers more importance to the art reviews than an intended reader might.

Furthermore, as illustrated objects – the newspapers and magazines usually reproduce part of the visual works reviewed – and as texts reaching out towards an artistic imaginary of their own age, one can also understand the periodicals as nonhuman entities resisting a type of revisionist reading encompassed by an 'accidental archival' reframing. It can be argued that this resistance happens by virtue of their 'magazineness' – since they are integral pieces of larger conversation networks whose 'organs' are the respective periodicals. This feature resonates with conversations in periodical studies highlighting the materiality of print (Bornstein 2006; Drucker 1996; Bulson 2019).

Moreover, as any periodical scholar can attest, highlighting a particular column for study requires extensive contextualization in the ecology of the magazine itself and magazines around it to justify this selection. Such conversations cannot be easily jettisoned or de-contextualized without ignoring the magazine's social and material dimensions (see also Frank and Podewski 2022). As Rigney has shown, posthumanist materialism

> challenges those studying memory studies from the fields of literature and culture to go beyond methodological textualism. [. . .] It calls for a truly ecological approach that shifts attention away from discrete artifacts towards continuous interactions between humans and non-humans, between medialities and materialities, within particular social and physical environments [. . .] It means taking the multi-sited dynamic interplay of actants as our objects of research and not one privileged site. (Rigney 2017, 475–476)

This multi-sited dynamic interplay of actants can be aided by Barad's emphasis on diffraction in the need to accommodate both perspectives, the contextual reading and the revisionist one.

3 Gladys Mgudlandlu and Bessie Head in *The New African*

I then find myself caught between a desire for revisionist redress where the magazine is an *object of memory* traveling dynamically across time, and a need to affirm the resistance of the magazine column as an object *in memory* while reading Bessie Head's review from *The New African*, 30 November 1963 where she skewers the work of Gladys Mgudlandlu, the most successful black woman artist of her time. Head's negative review of Mgudlandlu's art and politics is instructive in articulating the types of apartheid artworks and lives that could be seen as mattering at the time. The *New African: The Radical Monthly* (1962–1969) edited by Randolph Vigne, James Currey, and Neville Rubin was an anti-communist, non-racial magazine circulating to a mostly white audience of liberal subscribers, with a multiracial cast of contributors from South Africa and from other African countries often publishing communist and decolonizing debates.[2] The magazine's arts column encouraged urban and modernist African art. As a guest arts columnist, Head's vitriol towards Mgudlandlu and her white curators can be explained on account of Head's own precarious position as a mixed-race writer under apartheid, but also by the contemporary drive towards creating African art that was social realist and depicted urban life on the continent. It should also be understood as part of Head's biting critiques of complacency amongst colored[3] and black people in South Africa across her columns in *The New African*.

Gladys Mgudlandlu (1917–1979) born in Peddie, in the Eastern Cape was a Xhosa painter, nurse, and schoolteacher who had limited formal instruction in art (Miles 2002, 14). Together with Marjorie Wallace and Katrine Harries who promoted her, she was associated with the Cape Town New Group. Mgudlandlu lived a precarious life and painted using watercolors and oils after long working days.[4] She was influenced by the Xhosa mural tradition that her mother and grandmother practiced (Miles 2002, 34). Although described as a naïve expressionist painter in the press, she preferred to describe her style as a fusion of expressionism and symbolism which she called *dreamer imaginist* (Miles 2002, 10) – she based her paintings on dreams as well as memories of her rural childhood in the Eastern Cape. Despite Mgudlandlu's warm reception and prolific exhibitions, she gradually disappeared from art histories after she stopped painting in 1971 until the early 2000s when a retrospective recuperative exhibition was mounted in Cape Town and a thin biographical album was put together (Miles 2002). Since 2002, scholarly dissertations have been written about her, two retrospectives have taken place (2012 and 2021), and in 2024, her painting *Two Girls* was shown at the Venice Biennale.

Head's *New African* review has two illustrations – a full-page reproduction opposite the review text, a dynamic line drawing of different animals intertwined in a swirling fashion, and a cassette illustration in the upper right corner interspersed in the columns of the review text depicting two large ducks in the foreground being fed by a black woman wearing a light-colored kerchief. The review

---

2 Caroline Davis points out that after its inception using the Liberal Party's subscriber list, the magazine was funded partly by the CIA who was looking to create a network of non and anti-communist African publications whose priorities would align with an approach to aesthetics rather than politics on the continent. Despite this, there does not appear to be any editorial meddling in the magazine who even published a number of African communists.

3 Colored was an apartheid term for mixed race, Asian and groups of South-Asian populations in South Africa. Though disputed, it is still a term in use today. Head's mother was white, while her father was black putting her in a vulnerable category for the apartheid state policy.

4 The title of the only biographical account of Mgudlandlu written by Elza Miles is *Nomfanekiso who paints at night*. Nomfanekiso is Mgudlandlu's Fingo home name.

opens with a curatorial vignette containing a detailed ekphrastic enumeration of the elements in Mgudlandlu's pictorial universe presented as forming an idealized pastoral existence, at once immobile, timeless, and objectifyingly ethnographic. Head points towards birds reposing 'indifferently' in fields, rural black women gossiping, a 'chief's wife' smoking a corn pipe, as well as fields of dense vegetation and fauna in cheerful colors. Mgudlandlu's anodyne pastoral universe and her adulation by the white public are judged by Head complicit with apartheid and colonialist visual repertoires representing black populations as stuck in a premodern rural state and in need of separate development, craftsmen, rather than artists. Head sees the rural subject matter as escapist and touristic: "In her calm, green valleys through which half-naked tribal women wend their way back home in the late African sunset, one can recline restfully with a cocktail and the past is the future and the present is the past" (Head 1963, 209). She also judges Mgudlandu's technique as lacking, hurried, and unfinished: "she appears to be in such haste to rush after the new burst of inspiration that one is left with the uneasy impression that each picture is slap-dash and incomplete" (Head 1963, 209).

Mgudlandlu's hurried and rural imagery is unflatteringly contrasted with art produced by another urban black painter: "Compared to the clean-cut, sharp and brilliant technique of Johannesburg artist, Ephraim Ngatane, Miss Mgudlandlu indulges in mere childish scrawl" (Head 1963, 209). Ngatane is further praised as being "intense, passionate, controlled, vividly imaginative" with "Township scenes [that] rebound and vibrate with life" (209). Ngatane's realistic approach "highlight-[s] the terrors of township living": extreme poverty, lack of water, and overcrowding. In other words, Ngatane produces the right kind of art for the period – politically responsible, urban, realistic, and exact, but also 'vibrating with life,' in contrast to the timelessness, leisure, and tourism of Mgudlandlu's scenes.

What strikes the contemporary reader is the infantilizing language Head uses in relation to Mgudlandlu. This starts with the title, "The Exuberant Innocent," a running red thread that includes Head's suggestion of artistic immaturity in the vignette, the designation "mere childish scrawl" opposed to Ngatane's maturity, and Head's subtle critique of the painter's complacent religious beliefs. The article's main claim that Mgudlandlu's choices to paint rural secluded scenes are unwittingly drawing attention away from the harsh realities of apartheid detentions and political violence also culminates in infantilization:

> Who can resist her hypnotic call when life and reality mean ninety days detentions and banning orders and bang bang bang? For a few seconds, I could see the attraction in those cool dark clumps of trees, and birds and lilies and elephant trunks! [. . .] and I believe that it is on the appeal of this escape that she so profusely and exuberantly provides, that Miss Mgudlandlu's phenomenal success rests. *Miss Mgudlandlu is too innocent and unaware to have deliberately contrived* this state of affairs. (209, emphasis mine)

Despite her critique being understandable given the embattled political context, Head's language is also itself complicit in apartheid dichotomies where black subjects are infantilized and their agency is systematically stripped. More distressing is the gender dimension of this review, the way a black woman is patronized by another woman of color for her portrayals of leisure and aesthetic choices and unflatteringly compared to a man supposedly technically and politically superior. Ironically, claims of stylistic immaturity also abound in art reviews of urban male black artists such as Durant Sihlali, Dumile Feni, Andrew Motjuadi, or Julian Motau in the press of the 1960s.[5,6]

In hindsight, Head's condemnation of Mgudlandlu's work seems disturbing, but the points she makes about the painter's aesthetic being complicitous with apartheid visual regimes were salient. This is the essence of what Michael Rothberg calls the *implicated subject* – a nuancing of discussions of victim-perpetrator dichotomies, proposing instead a spectrum of implication and responsibility (Rothberg 2019). Mgudlandlu and Head are both placed on this spectrum, and so am I, as a white Eastern European woman reading these apartheid texts and living in post-apartheid South Africa as a guest researcher.

Reading Head's column on Mgudlandlu as part of an 'accidental archive,' as an object of memory with dynamic testimonial force, one also sees the black artist's different potential nowadays. The illustrations and Head's detailed ekphrastic hooks[7] invite reading against the grain. In concert with today's land reclamation movements calling for re-inhabiting ancestral lands and with current publications seeking to present black lives outside the prism of subjection (ka Canham 2023; Phalafala 2024), Mgudlandlu's idiosyncratic paintings depict black leisure and joy that are politically expedient. Her centering of black subjects in intimate conversation, her curious birds, wonderfully vivid colors, and her interest in women lost amongst luxuriating vegetation are valuable idioms post-apartheid. Mgudlandlu can enter different ecologies of knowledge beyond the desire for realism of the 1960s. She can be grouped with later artists hailing from rural environments like Noria Ma-

---

5 What makes this particularly unfair in hindsight is that despite the trend for "Township art" and social realism that developed in the 1960s, Ngatane's generation of urban painters with white benefactors was also later rejected by proponents of Black Consciousness in the late 1970s as voyeuristic poverty porn and formulaic art (see Van Robbroeck 1998, Rankin 2011).

6 Reviewers express a hope for a future of black art where technique is more developed and consistent while bemoaning the lack of art education opportunities or studio space for the artists. See especially Bill Ainslie's "The Living Eye" in *The Classic* 1.4 (1965) and Neville Dubow "Art in Protest" in *Contrast* 1.1 (1960).

7 I use the term ekphrastic hooks elsewhere in my work to define a brief clipped ekphrastic enumeration meant to signal the presence of another medium by creating with memorial implications (Zirra 2019, 24).

basa, Jackson Hlungwane, or Pitika Ntuli whose interests in continuities between woodcarving and mural painting do not oppose tradition to modernity.

A revisionist reading would then activate different post-apartheid contemporary ecologies of ideas, rather than emphasizing the contextual ecologies of magazines as historical conversations. Their very materiality can be said to resist a revisionist reading by means of their embeddedness in large conversation networks. At the same time, as sedimented objects of memory with a foot in the present and one in the past, the magazines have the power to resonate with other 'accidental archives' and with present concerns about a revisionist recuperation of black female artists operating in the extremely rarefied medium of apartheid.

Can one have their methodological cake and eat it? Consider the afterlives of these magazines as periodical objects and still see them as hard to remove and integral parts of these ecologies of the whole? While it is important to outline these resistant magazine caveats, sketching the afterlives of these reviews and helping to create their afterlives as a contemporary criticism remains valuable, I believe.

Barbara Törnquist-Plewa

The Transcultural Mnemonic Agency of "Post-German" Things in Poland

1 Introduction

"Memory sits in the walls" – I heard these words, uttered again and again by my colleague, a Swedish architect, when we strolled through the streets of the former Jewish quarter in Chişinău, the capital of Moldova. It was about ten years ago, and we had both just started a research project on the memory and heritage of people who, due to the Holocaust and forced migrations, had disappeared from many cities in Eastern and Central Europe. At that time, I found his statements rather naïve and a sign of the gap between memory scholars studying narratives, symbols, and social constructions and scholars in heritage studies focusing on material remnants of the past. Material things were for me "inert matter" that could be put in motion only by human mind and action. They were merely objects that could trigger human memories and at best a resource for humans to be used for the production and transfer of memories. Today, however, I would not be so judgmental towards my enthusiastic colleague's belief in the mnemonic power of things. My strong anthropocentrism became challenged when I immersed myself in studies of how places that have almost entirely lost their populations due to ethnic cleansings and the Holocaust deal with the memory and legacy of the vanished others. By observing the important role that material things have played in the mnemonic processes in these places I became inclined to accept, at least to some extent, the ideas of new materialism as formulated by Bruno Latour (2005), Jane Bennett (2010) and others. Agency is distributed and emerges as the effect of the configuration of human and non-human forces. Humans should not be seen as the only possible "actants," to use Latour's term, that is, the only source of action. Material things can also be actants, although mnemonic agency is most likely "distributed" as indicated by Rigney (2015b, 26). It is an agency of an assemblage that includes humans and their social constructions as well as material things that "vibrate" (Bennett 2010), that is, make people feel or act in certain ways. In the following I wish to demonstrate this dynamic interaction between human and nonhuman actants in memory production by using the case of the German material legacy in present-day Poland. This case deserves attention since it deals with the so-called "unwanted heritage" and "difficult memory" of post-war forced migrations.

Following Nazi Germany's defeat in 1945, the victorious allies compelled Germany to cede parts of its eastern territories to Poland as a kind of compensation for the territory that Poland in its turn lost to the USSR. These radical border changes were followed by massive population transfers. Poles living in the lands annexed by the USSR were resettled to the new territories taken from Germany, from which the German population was expelled. These traumatic experiences of war and displacement constitute a challenge to this day and call for memory work that opens up paths for dialogue, reconciliation, and the overcoming of negative stereotypes. While the liberal governments in post-communist Poland have pursued politics of memory along these lines, the Polish nationalist right returned to the anti-German rhetoric of the Communist period by reviving Poland's historical anxieties towards Germany and emphasizing crimes committed by Germany during WWII. However, at the grassroots level, reconciliatory mnemonic activities never ceased, and they have come rather a long way in contemporary Poland. Evidence thereof is to be found in research conducted in Poland in recent years (e.g. Traba and Hahn 2017; Kledzik et al. 2018; Kuszyk 2019; Bukiel et al. 2020; Kurpiel and Maniak 2023) including my own work on the city of Wrocław/Breslau (Törnquist-Plewa and Pietraszewski 2016; 2022). In the following, I will show, on the basis of the material presented in these studies, that the generation of Poles born in the former German lands is at present involved in efforts to create transnational and transcultural memories of this region. Importantly, I will argue that material objects play an active role in these processes by triggering and shaping recollections as well as linking people to each other across generations, nations, and cultures.

2 The destruction of German things and their afterlife

In Communist times, the German lands acquired by Poland in 1945 were called "the Recovered Territories" and the only historical narrative about them that was allowed in the public sphere was that they were quintessentially Polish. The fact that they had for some time in the Middle Ages been ruled by the Polish Piast dynasty was used to cast them as originally Polish, although they had subsequently been seized and controlled for a long time by the Germans and then "rightfully" returned to Poland, not least as compensation for German war crimes. The state authorities ordered the removal of all traces of Germanness from these lands. All German topographic names were replaced by Polish ones, German monuments and cemeteries were destroyed, books and documents burnt. Buildings damaged by bombs were often not repaired, only dismantled and the bricks sent off to re-build Warsaw. The Soviet army, stationed in these territories, contributed to the destruction by dismantling German factories and transporting them to the USSR.

The Polish people that moved to the "Recovered Territories" participated to a large extent in the demolition, since German material traces provoked anger. They reminded them of the oppression, terror and humiliation experienced under German occupation. As one of my interviewees (a former slave laborer) expressed it: "We struck down the German signs with passion, because it was under such signs that we had been beaten, kicked and killed" (Pietraszewski and Törnquist-Plewa 2016, 20).

Many memorial accounts by Polish settlers testify to the dominating feeling of alienation towards the architecture and material culture that they encountered in these areas. Thus, they tried to domesticate the new places by removing things that they called "post-German." However, they had no choice but settle down in "post-German" houses, and since they were destitute through war and migration (they had been allowed to take along just the bare essentials), they had to use the furniture and everyday items found in the post-German homes – pans, cutlery, crockery, linen, or gardening tools. Additionally, prevailing shortages in Communist Poland made them hang on to these things and they learnt to appreciate their robustness.

As a result, children born after the war in the post-German lands grew up surrounded by German material remains. For them it was normal to sleep in a bed with German monograms and see German inscriptions on kitchen utensils. Thus, for the post-war generation of Poles living in these lands, their artefacts and landscape were not alien. They did not see them as German but as their own, as a natural part of their homes and everyday life, a part of their local identity. It happened that they played in the ruined German cemeteries turned into "wild parks" without realizing the character of these places (Kuszyk 2019, 340–345). Neither teachers nor parents spoke to them about the German past of their localities. Until the fall of the Communist regime in 1989 this was an official taboo, and in the privacy of their homes the parents, busy with making ends meet, avoided the subject, not least because they wanted to spare the children their own fears, fostered by Communist propaganda, that the Germans might take back these territories and they would lose their homes.

With the passage of time, however, the children turned into adults who began to discover the German history of their cities, towns, and villages. Not surprisingly, the writers and poets born in these places were the first who started to write about this subject that had been more or less forbidden until the fall of the Communist regime. Novels by Olga Tokarczuk, Stefan Chwin, Joanna Bator, Marek Krajewski, and others contributed significantly to a revival of the memory about the German past. Interestingly, a striking feature of their writings is a fascination with post-German things. The authors see them as signs of an extinct culture which they want to save from oblivion. As Marek Krajewski, the author of a very popular crime novels set in pre-war Wrocław (Breslau) stated:

> German inscriptions on walls, on doors, in tenements and on sewer manholes, trophies such as helmets, badges, caps and bottles, acquired during childhood expeditions into the dark corridors of basements – this shaped my fascination. (Krajewski 2016).

The works by all the authors mentioned above show that "post-German" things triggered questions about the past, searches for answers and storytelling. In novels such as *House of Day, House of Night* by Tokarczuk (1998), *Hannemann* by Chwin (1995), or *Dark, Almost Night* by Bator (2012), they are often the source of "the uncanny" and acquire other meanings than those that were originally inscribed in them.

The material remnants of German culture do not only deliver information about the past but also function as "points of memory" that puncture through the layers of oblivion, interpolating those who seek to know about the past. They expose the unexpected, prick, wound, and grab (Hirsch and Spitzer 2006, 358). For Karolina Kuszyk, the author of the fascinating non-fiction book *Poniemieckie* [Post-German] (2019), such a "point of memory" was a bowl, used for many years during family dinners at her parents' home. One day, a German guest pointed out to her that her favorite bowl had a small swastika on the reverse side. She was shaken by this discovery since she had never noticed it before. Her own home became suddenly "un-heim-lich" as its German past became clearly visible to her. This encounter kindled her will to write about the fate of post-German things in Poland.

Since 1989 there has been an eruption of interest in the German past of western Poland. Local authorities in cities and towns of this region have engaged in uncovering these layers of history, spurred on by local civil society organizations such as Societies for the Beautification of the City in Wrocław and Zielona Góra, or the Historical Foundation of Liegnitz (nowadays Legnica), to name just a few. In this search for memories that might underpin local identities, relieved from the suffocating uniformity of the Communist system, the post-German material legacy turned out to have crucial mnemonic potential. The German relics were reminders of other cultural worlds against the national homogenization implemented in post-war Poland. They fascinated, triggered imagination, offered glimpses of alternative narratives. Thus, even ordinary people, especially those belonging to the second and third post-war generation, began to collect post-German things that at first sight could be seen as rubbish: old utensils, beer mugs, suitcases, prewar German school books and more. It became an obsession to collect postcards showing what a particular locality had looked like before the war. These postcards are often exhibited in local museums, in printed catalogues and on websites. To prepare them for display, the local memory activists made contact with the German expellees or their families. These people were able to tell more about the past and provide old photographs of the places which they or their close ancestors were forced to leave. The old postcards provoke a longing to know more and prompt Germans and Poles to meet and tell each other stories about the localities they come from. Thus, the pictures function as a launching pad for the construction of a shared, transcultural, local memory. This memory is steeped in nostalgia. On the German part it is about the lost home of their parents or grandparents. On the Polish part it is a reminder of the former beauty of the places where they live now, a beauty lost due to war as well as postwar devastation. People participating in this transcultural exchange belong mostly, but not exclusively, to generations born after the war, and they are united in a feeling of emotional connection to the place depicted in the old postcards. They do not engage in discussions about victimhood, guilt, or any historical accusations. In fact, these encounters defy the stereotype of Germans as ever threatening Others, present in Polish nationalist discourse.

The material remnants have given rise not only to private contacts but also to cooperation with German expellee organizations. Remarkably, the Polish mnemonic activists were even willing to lend their collectibles to the ill-famed, revisionist expellee association led by Erika Steinbach when she prepared the exhibition "Forced Paths" in Berlin. What both sides found fascinating and worth exhibiting was a jar of preserved chanterelles, dug out by a Pole in a field together with some German documents from 1945. A preserved food item became "vibrant matter," an "accidental archive" of the kind described by Rigney (2015b, 30) as secreting "more memory that it overtly expressed." It triggered the imagination, but it also created unexpected connections and a transnational exchange of memories.

The passion to collect "post-German" things has resulted, among others, in the creation of a few small, local, private museums. One of them, situated in the village of Pławna Górna, in Silesia, deserves special attention since it is explicitly called the "Museum of Displaced Persons and Expellees" (see figure 1) and it suggests a shared victimhood of Poles and Germans. This kind of narrative is still controversial in Poland, as evidenced by the fact that plans to open the Center against Expulsions in Germany in 2000 caused a temporary crisis in Polish-German relations on a high political level.

However, the website of the museum in Pławna Górna explicitly states: "The museum helps to understand both the pain of the expelled Germans and the fear and uncertainty of the Poles forcibly resettled from the Eastern Borderlands." Additionally, the museum leaflet declares: "You will see how some of them sowed the fields and left in despair, while others, harassed, confused, just as displaced, harvested after them" (my translation). To analyze the museum exhibition is beyond the remit of this short chapter. Suffice it here to point out that the acknowledgement of the similarity of German and Polish fates is more or less done without a curatorial voice. Instead, the museum rooms are filled with mannequins depicting Germans and Poles arranged in a naïve style to present "scenes of local life" and with numerous memorabilia. The latter are old everyday objects, belonging to Germans and Poles, found in attics and cellars and put together in an assemblage that stimulates comparisons, unexpected questions, and multiple interpretations. Thus, the museum truly relies on the mnemonic agency of things.

Figure 1: Signs at the entrance to the Museum of Displaced Persons and Expellees in Pławna Górna, Poland. Photo courtesy of Eleonora Narvselius.

3 Conclusions

As pointed out by Rigney (2015b, 18), the material relics of the past "ensure the enduring presence of former times in the here and now. As sedimentations of earlier experience, they have the power to mobilise memory, provoke storytelling, and cause people to act." The above account of dealings with the German material heritage in Poland illustrates it clearly. "Post-German" things generate affect and action and produce new memories of the past in a network of humans and matter. Most importantly, they not only contribute to memory transfer across generations but also across national borders and cultures. Moreover, they participate in the production of truly transcultural memories, that is, hybrid memories that occur in the crossing of cultural borders and enable the imagining of new communities. Local material heritage of the former German lands connects Poles living in these areas and German expellees and their families. Even trivial commodities such as a jar of mushrooms can become an actant, an "intervener" (Bennett 2010, 9) setting in motion mnemonic dialogue and rapprochement between people separated by a difficult past. What is hard to achieve in politics on the national level, where ghosts of the past are invoked by nationalist politicians, turns out to be possible on a local and individual level. The grassroots or private initiatives create a space for meetings that may have the potential to overcome prejudices and old hostilities. This is precisely where the vitality and mnemonic power of things becomes visible. Their ability to produce transcultural memories deserves further study.

Birgit Meyer
Provocative Objects and the Remaking of Cultural Memory

1 Introduction

Narratives about the past do not fully contain the past. Put together through a process of concomitant remembering and forgetting, they are authorized and shared to sustain a political status quo. But they are also challenged and transformed. "In explaining how collective narratives change," Ann Rigney states poignantly, "it is useful to recall that remembering and forgetting always go hand in glove. Not only because memory needs to be selective to be meaningful, but also because the sense of a shared past and shared present can only be created if people are prepared to paper over historical cracks" (2022, 12). In our time, the cracks that have been covered by conventional narratives through which European societies organize the cultural memory they live by are becoming conspicuously visible. So far neglected and 'forgotten' past occurrences and experiences, those related to legacies of slavery and colonization for instance, are pushed to the fore in the context of calls for more inclusive histories.

Critical work on cultural memory acknowledges not only the extent to which nineteenth-century nationalism and historicism were co-constitutive, yielding a 'cultivation of the past' that naturalizes the nation as given. It also calls "to move memory studies itself beyond methodological nationalism" (De Cesari and Rigney 2014, 1–2), pushing scholars to study collective remembrance from a transnational angle. Doing so, the point is to discern, from the cracks in national narratives, new possibilities for narrating and remembering a past that "is no longer understood as a single story" (Troelenberg et al. 2021, 3). Awareness of the fundamental entanglements of Western and other societies in the wake of colonization, evangelization, trade, and military power opens up a deeper and broader sense of the past that challenges colonial aphasia and makes room for other memories brought forward by people marginalized by dominant national narratives. I see it as an important task for researchers across the humanities to join forces so as to better understand how cultural memory is remade in crucial moments when nation-centered narratives are challenged. As targets of conflicting political-aesthetic meanings, objects, such as statues heroizing perpetrators of colonial violence or – the focus of this essay – items assembled as part of colonial collections in ethnological and other museums, play a key role in this process. For this reason, they offer an apt methodological and conceptual entry point into the study of mnemonic change.

2 Provocative objects

Memory studies pays ample attention to how monuments, memorials, artefacts, and sites are made to operate as the centerpieces through which cultural memories are constructed. Such constructions achieve an aura of factuality by turning material forms into unequivocal signs of a real past. In order to be able to critique how such material signs – be it memory sites or cultural heritage items – are naturalized, the collective narratives that make them meaningful and valuable must be deconstructed. But how far should deconstruction go? After all, objects are not mere targets of human intention and passive vehicles of the significations they are to naturalize. Prompted by new materialism, scholars apprehend objects as actors that influence how their users and beholders relate to them. This view replaces a misguided modernist view of humans as wielding dominance over objects by a relational understanding of humans and objects in networks or assemblages. Working from this angle myself (Meyer 2012), I find it nonetheless important not to exaggerate the agency of objects to such an extent that humans become their passive targets. What is the role of meaning-making narratives, which I see as a practice limited to humans, in such assemblages? How to develop a viable balance between an acknowledgement of the agency of objects *and* of the constructive effects of meaning-making?

In her article "Things and the Archive: Scott's Materialist Legacy" (2015b), Rigney engages explicitly with new materialist thinkers such as Jane Bennett, so as to open up a space for an intellectual appreciation of Scottish writer Walter Scott's "keen awareness of the materialized presence of the past in the physical environment" (2015b, 13). In this remarkable piece, Rigney introduces Scott as a writer *and* collector who, in collecting objects from, for instance, the battlefield of Waterloo, and exhibiting them in his mansion, developed a "fundamentally materialist imagination" (15). Taking objects as "agents with a capacity to trigger emotion and memories in the humans who react to them" (17), Scott prefigured new materialist thought, while also adding a "mnemonic dimension to Bennett's discussion of the vibrancy of matter" (18). Important here is the capacity of objects to "mobilize memory, provoke story-telling, and cause people to act" (18).

This leads Rigney to the insight "that the power of objects to provoke a longing to know more is ultimately dependent on the power of words to release their potential meaning; to set them vibrating" (23). This elegant phrasing presents an integrated perspective on how the powers of objects and of words intersect. I very much like the idea of the object that provokes by signaling a limit of understanding it within a dominant narrative, yet also calls forth a new story that releases a new or dormant meaning. The figure of the provocative object is crucial for identifying the turning points through which collective narratives and mnemonic regimes change. As signs of something that is not yet clearly spelled out through a narrative already told, objects are crucial for the re-making of cultural memory. This methodological insight dovetails with my own approach to religion from a material (rather than mentalistic) angle (Meyer 2012). In order to uncover alternative ways to narrate dimensions of the past that have largely been subdued, as is the case with the memory of colonialism, provocative objects are an apt beginning.

3 Uncomfortable presences

This special power of objects to provoke becomes immediately clear when we consider current calls to remove or destroy contested statues. Cracking mainstream understandings of the past opens up alleys into alternative histories written from a subaltern angle. Rigney aptly calls this memory work "unforgetting" (2022). Next to such conspicuously present provocative objects in public spaces, there are artefacts assembled in the context of colonialism and taken to ethnological and other museums where they are on display or have long been stored away in the depot. Currently, colonial collections are in the limelight of public debate about legacies of colonialism,[1] yielding research on their provenance and claims for restitution to the states in which the descendants of their initial makers and users live. The restitution of looted art such as the much-discussed Benin bronzes and the return of ancestral remains are gaining much attention. Looking at these items from the angle of memory studies with Rigney, the question arises which memories they evoke and, in the process, which narratives they disturb, and possibly enable.

As there is a broad array of items with multiple provenance histories, it is best to address this question through a detailed case. Together with a team of researchers from Ghana, Togo, Germany, and the Netherlands, I am involved in a research project on a collection of about two hundred and fifty items assembled by Protestant missionary Carl Spiess among the Ewe around 1900 in the area currently known as south-eastern Ghana and southern Togo.[2] As a missionary of the

---

[1] See the research program Pressing Matter: Value, Ownership and the Question of Colonial Heritage in Museums in which I co-direct a subproject on missionary collections: https://pressingmatter.nl.

[2] We conducted a pilot study with the team in the Übersee-Museum Bremen in September 2022, for a report see: https://religiousmatters.nl/the-legba-dzoka-project-tracking-and-unpacking-the-collection-carl-spiess-ubersee-museum-bremen/. The project is funded by the Deutsches Zentrum Kulturgutverluste/German Lost Art Foundation.

Norddeutsche Missionsgesellschaft (NMG) Spiess sought to evangelize the Ewe and make them turn away from their spiritual practices. Items such as *dzokawo* ("charms" and "amulets") and *legba*-figures ("idols") were to be discarded and burnt, or taken to what is today the Übersee-Museum Bremen. For our team, this collection (See Fig 1) is a time capsule that can tell us not only about a missionary worldview that took such items as "idolatry" and a colonial-ethnological view that saw them as instances of *Zauberei* (magic). Clearly, the items were taken as evidence of "heathendom" and of a lower stage in the evolution of religion, and thus made to sustain an interrelated, partly overlapping narrative about the primacy of Christian monotheism and about Europe as pinnacle of cultural development, legitimizing missionization and colonization.

Figure 1: Dzokawo, "Collection Spiess", Übersee-Museum Bremen, Photo by the author.

This unpacking is certainly important, especially in a country as Germany where the colonial past has only recently become publicly acknowledged as another uncomfortable national memory next to fascism. Yes, it is clear that the items – I tend to eschew the term "object" for its instrumental slant which affirms the objectifying regime of the museum, yet is not adequate to convey an indigenous Ewe view on items vested with spiritual powers – have more to "say." How could they, to invoke Rigney, "mobilize memory, provoke story-telling, and cause people to act"? Kept in a German museum for more than hundred and twenty years, they are not directly available to the descendants of their initial makers and users, many of whom, in addition, identify as Christians and may look at them with some suspicion. Until recently, the presence of this collection was barely remembered in Germany, let alone in Ghana and Togo. When I told Ewe priest Christopher Voncujovi, who runs the Afrikan Magick Temple in Accra, about this collection he proposed that the spirits inhabiting these artefacts may have pushed me to act as their messenger. While I had conducted extensive research on the activities of the NMG among the Ewe, it was only after I had developed a material approach to religion that I seriously thought about the Übersee-Museum as a crucial node to unpack so far neglected colonial-missionary entanglements of the Ewe people and Germany. Clearly, once one places material forms at the center of attention, entirely new provocative questions arise.

Our team is not only multidisciplinary and transnational, with scholars from Ghana, Germany, the Netherlands, and Togo, but also includes two Ewe priests. Having just embarked on this joint endeavour, it is our wish to bring our respective scholarly knowledge and positionality as well as alternative modes of knowledge production to bear on our research on this amazing and disturbing collection. Doing so as a joint effort will allow us to let these artefacts provoke story-telling about dimensions that are not immediately obvious to secular Western beholders. From the priests' point of view and based on their use of the Ifa-oracle, the collected items are not mere objects, but are alive and hungry, wishing to cause people to act so as to be fed, and possibly returned (Meyer 2024). Further research in Ghana and Togo, where our team will present images of the collection to the local people, may trigger memories of missionization and indigenous powers beyond the usual path, possibly yielding a recognition of these artefacts as cultural assets worth to recognize as Ewe heritage. Time will tell which insights and consequences this collaborative research will yield. What is clear to me already is that the questions posed by Rigney have great value to assess the potential of such a collection of material items to provoke new narratives that change how people, here and there, think and act, remaking cultural memory.

Francisco Ferrándiz

Bones of Contention: *Necrotoxicity* in the Francoist Underworld

Monuments that become toxic, Ann Rigney argues, provide excellent opportunities to evaluate the depth and extent of mnemonic regime changes. Monuments designed to *last* necessarily *outlast* the memory frameworks that created them, and eventually become out-of-sync memorial fossils (Rigney 2022, 21). Based on her study of the demise of the statue of slave owner Edward Colston in Bristol in 2022, Rigney points to the need to understand specific cases in the context of broader memorial processes, well beyond the specific monument under controversy. A given monument or memorial can only be properly understood within ever-mutating *plurimedial* mnemonic networks. She also states that *decommissioning* poisonous or dissonant heritage, or depriving it of its power to unsettle or offend, may involve diverse strategies: *demolition* or, in more reformist counter-memorial patterns, *reframing* (de-contextualization, musealization), or *resignification* (overwriting, juxtaposition). In all cases, emerging counter-memorial narratives and meanings that challenge a monument that has come under fire are necessarily interrelated with the ones they aim to replace (Rigney 2022, 15–20).

In this framework, in what follows I will briefly discuss the case of the Valley of Cuelgamuros (formerly known as Valley of the Fallen or *Valle de los Caídos*), the most conspicuous and astonishingly unresolved Francoist monument in Spain. This massive memorial compound, designed by Franco to last for 'eternity,' is extraordinarily complex. It was conceived to celebrate his military victory in the Spanish Civil War on 1 April 1939, a war triggered by a failed military coup against the democratic Second Republic (1931–1939) on 18 July 1936. This celebratory message was imprinted on every stone, statue, emblem, architectonic feature or iconographic element in the building; a message sealed for history by the very dictator in 1959, in his fiery inaugural speech on the twentieth anniversary of the end of the war.

Surprisingly, its contemporary interpretation continues to be dominated by a narrative of national reconciliation under the loving arms of the huge 150-meter-tall cross topping it, supposedly a universal symbol of peace and forgiveness. The solemn daily mass held for those 'sacrificed' in the war in the underground basilica contributes to this *mise-en-scène*. This deceitful narrative, crafted in late Francoism, has carried over (albeit modulated and somehow blurred with time) into Spanish democracy, and was not seriously challenged until the turn of the century, when the debates around the monument started to heat up in Spanish memorial struggles (Ferrándiz 2022).

Is it possible to decommission, or *de-commemorate* (Gensburger and Wüstenberg 2023), such a gigantic power architecture, still partially controlled by a rightwing religious order and equally by neo-Francoist associations and political groups? To understand the huge memorial challenges of transforming its meaning and memorial use in contemporary Spain, I focus on one specific (if highly delicate and controversial) type of materiality: the massive cemetery surrounding the basilica that was commissioned by Franco in order to bring as many Civil War dead as possible to the Valley.

This underground necropolis hosts almost 34,000 bodies brought from all over the country between 1959 and 1983. Their provenance is very diverse and modulated by time: individual bodies voluntarily sent by relatives who believed in the memorial project, military cemeteries transferred when voluntary transports started to dwindle, victims of religious persecution, and, most controversially, an unknown number from Republican mass graves. In total, more than 20,000 people with names, and more than 12,000 'unknowns.' To make the cemetery even more confusing, the massive body transfer operation was far from clean. Twenty years after the war, for example, the remodeling of cemeteries and the death of the gravediggers responsible for the initial interments complicated the location and unburying of large graves. The non-professional and often hasty unburials also contributed to the confusion.

The arrival of these rank-and-file bodies in the Valley did not occur in a vacuum. Rather, it was part of a higher memorial mission. Over sixteen years, the funerary arrangement in the Valley was presided over by José Antonio Primo de Rivera, the founder of Spain's Mussolini-influenced fascist party, *Falange*, who was buried in a most honorable place directly in front of the main altar in the subterranean basilica in 1959, as part of the inaugural ceremonies. The Valley became the major memorial site for Spanish fascists. As of 1975, José Antonio had to share his funerary prominence when Francisco Franco was buried in a symmetrical position on the other side of the main altar.

A unique temporal coincidence increased their joint memorial potential: both leaders died on the same day (20 November), 39 years apart. José Antonio was executed by Republican authorities in Alicante in 1936, and Franco – his life artificially prolonged in a textbook case of therapeutic cruelty (Preston 2008, 279–306) – in 1975, in a bed in La Paz Hospital in Madrid. This *chronological mnemonic click* consolidated 20 November as the paramount milestone in Francoism's commemorative cycle. With José Antonio and Franco, two formidable political bodies, presiding over the monument, surrounded by tens of thousands of Civil War dead buried in the eight side chapels of the basilica, the place became the undisputed stronghold of Francoist memory: protected by an overwhelming (and unmanageable) pantheon, heavily shielded in political, symbolic, and religious terms, and as such virtually unassailable (Ferrándiz 2019).[1] The unmaking of this memorial site, if ever attempted, would require massive and no doubt costly political, economic, symbolic, and pedagogical efforts. Fifty years after Franco's death, the puzzle is still far from being solved.

To better understand what is at stake in the uncanny burial layout in the Valley, I propose the concept of *necrotoxicity* – a substantial component of the monument's overall toxicity – to describe how certain funerary designs can eventually become a poisonous and divisive memorial legacy. As noted, the noxious burial arrangement in the Valley involves two interconnected death spaces. First, the main altar, in front of which a notorious dictator and a major fascist leader were buried and commemorated in daily masses for decades. The political and memorial tension created by this funerary layout in a post-dictatorial democratic context can be extrapolated, with logical contextual variations, to other cases of perpetrator burial sites around the world (Garibian 2017; Verdery 1999). And second, the crypts, where thousands of bodies of Franco's supporters are mixed up with bodies of Francoist victims brought to the monument without the knowledge or permission of their relatives. Hierarchically, the corpses in the crypts became the funerary entourage of the corpses at the altar. All things considered, in the context of the contemporary memory politics of the Civil War in Spain, this uncanny burial composition was eventually bound to become explosive. With this notion of memorial necrotoxicity in mind, and following Rigney's path, let us broaden our perspective to gain a better understanding of what is at stake in the Valley's funerary profile.

In the last twenty years in Spain, the search for the bodies of Republican civilians executed by Franco's paramilitary during and after the Civil War has set in motion a high-profile memory process known locally as the "recovery of historical memory." This process, a clear example of Rigney's *memory-activism nexus* (2022, 11), was initially propelled by associations of victims and has involved the exhumation of hundreds of mass graves around the country in order to provide the numerous victims of Francoist repression – abandoned to their fate for decades, including in democratic times – with *dignified burials* (Ferrándiz 2019). As a result of this focus on unburials and reburials, the wounded bones exhumed in mass graves – the most obvious manifestation to non-expert onlookers being the

---

1 For more on the political and ideological genealogy of the monument, see the English version of the web page I created for the Secretary of State of Democratic Memory: https://elvalledecuel gamuros.gob.es/en. It contains a twenty-five-minute video with extensive archival material: https://www.rtve.es/play/videos/lab-rtve/cuelgamuros-english-subtitles/6727032/. For an analysis of the history and current controversies around the monument see the *Contested Histories Onsite* Web: https://contestedhistories.org/onsite/.

widespread presence of *coups de grâce* derived from the summary executions – have become the central issue in Spain's contemporary memory politics.

When discussing the materialist legacy of Walter Scott's literary universe, Rigney (2015b) calls our attention to the power of material traces in the configuration of memory regimes and connections, as well as their ability to crystallize or "thicken time," operating as "time capsules" with a marked ability to "trigger reflection and emotion" (2015b, 14–18). As with every memory matter or manifestation, bones are not neutral or stable. They are elaborate material processes, and the technologies deployed to handle them, as well as the meaning attributed to them, are constantly shifting in the framework of broader and often conflicting memory constellations. Furthermore, human bones are a particularly delicate category of materiality. Being, as they are, the remains of particular individuals, they may come to represent different forms of community, from political to ethnic to religious, among many others. As such they are ritualized in many different forms – buried, unburied, reburied, cremated. They may be consecrated – as in relics – or desecrated; exposed, hidden or vandalized; preserved or destroyed. All these actions invest them with changing and often contested meaning, making them powerful memory devices.

In situations where bones become a paramount testimony to mass violence and human right violations, the hegemony of forensic technologies in the search for and dignification of the disappeared has brought about a significant transformation in both the legitimacy of the expert handling of bones and corpses, as well as in the memory cultures emerging in the process. Many authors make sense of these emergent authoritative forms of scientifically modulated social memory, both in Human Rights and Memory Studies, in the context of a broader *forensic turn* affecting many other research areas – forensic architecture, visual forensics, etc.

Particularly interesting is the analysis of popular perceptions of forensics, often conditioned by a so-called *CSI-effect*, attributed to the wide influence of acclaimed streaming TV shows (Ferrándiz 2023; 2021; Dziuban 2017). As a consequence, some authors have predicted a steady epistemic displacement in contemporary memory cultures from the "age of testimony," where survivor-witness narratives were a prestigious entryway to the past, to what may be called the "age of bones," where truth is inscribed in skeletal remains to be interpreted by experts (Keenan and Weizman 2012).

In Spain, the management of the bones of Republican civilians rescued from mass graves has increasingly taken place in a transnational framework dominated by human rights discourses and practices, at first only sketchily, on a high-speed track after Baltasar Garzón's 2008 failed indictment of Francoism. As a consequence, technical exhumations following international protocols for the search of the disappeared multiplied, and archaeologists and forensic doctors became crucial interpreters of the Civil War and post-war repression. These skeletons took central stage in Spanish memorial practices and have been recycled in dynamic mediation and remediation circuits in public and political debates, academic and artistic productions, as well as in the media, including digital media.

The rationale, imagery, and aesthetics of the crime scene associated with the forensic recovery of the bodies in the graves, inserted in global transitional justice parameters, started to take hold at different levels. It increasingly became a highly influential technology of memory making, often overshadowing or marginalizing other alternative narratives of the past. Elsewhere I have used the term *phantom militarism* (Ferrándiz 2019) to evoke this mirror memory process focused on the technical reenactment of the killing scene within the logic of criminology, where life histories or political biographies are often overshadowed by *osteobiographies* derived from the traces of violence – *antemortem, perimortem, postmortem* – forensically interpreted in the bones (Keenan and Weizman 2012).

The Valley was initially in the periphery of the twenty-first century memorial movement in Spain. Given the body-centric nature of the memory process in the country, the monument was swiftly brought to the fore when it was discovered that an unknown number of Republican mass graves had been transferred to its crypts without the knowledge or permission of their relatives. This finding dates back to 2003, although it took some time to seep into public debate. It unveiled one of the many contradictions of the massive body transfers to the Valley. Once the crypts entered the radar of memory activists, some uncomfortable questions started to circulate regarding the memory politics of the war and its aftermath, as manifested in the Valley. How could Republicans assassinated by Franco's paramilitary have been brought to the monument celebrating the advent of a cruel dictatorial regime grounded in widespread repression, incarceration, and execution? How could they have become part of the funerary cortège of the dictator and the founder of Spain's most prominent fascist party? Connected to this: why were the remains of Franco and José Antonio buried in priority locations in such a monument, commemorated by a daily mass? The advocates of the *status quo* at the monument viewed these attacks as nonsensical, mostly expressed in the notion of "let the bodies of the dead rest in peace." The increasingly toxic Valley became first and foremost necrotoxic.

So far (early 2024), except for the name change ("Fallen" or *Caídos*, a term directly referring to Franco's supporters killed in the war, was replaced by the older toponym "Cuelgamuros") and the banning of any political display at the site, the main State-led decommissioning actions in the Valley have been connected to its funerary configuration. That is, to the dismantling of the Francoist underworld installed in the monument. This makes sense to the extent that, as stated, bones are the principal matter – and battlefield – of contemporary memory work in Spain.

The funerary decommissioning of the Valley, a high-risk political and memorial *detox* operation, has two manifestations: the handling of the leading figures buried around the main altar, and the response to demands by the relatives of Republicans buried in the crypts that their bodies be returned to them. Let us now proceed chronologically. In June 2018, the recently sworn-in Socialist Prime Minister Pedro Sánchez announced that one of his new government's priorities was to exhume Franco from the Valley. This announcement ignited a public dispute lasting more than a year. Franco's relatives and their supporters fought in court first to prevent the exhumation, but also to procure the best possible conditions – including military honors and reburial in Madrid's Cathedral – if it were eventually to happen. The details of the ongoing and rapidly moving controversy occupied countless hours in the different media.

Only on 24 October 2019, nineteen months later, was the unburial possible, after a final ruling by the Supreme Court (Ferrándiz 2019, 226–33). Although the actual unburial in the basilica was kept private, the government covered the whole exhumation live on national public television (RTVE), which was broadcast by most Spanish media, and also internationally. The stellar moment was Franco's exit from the church, his deteriorated coffin carried by relatives on their shoulders, and the transport of his remains in a helicopter to the mausoleum where his wife was buried in the cemetery of El Pardo, close to Madrid. The images showing Franco's relatives on their own while exiting the memorial with the dictator's coffin on their shoulders stood in stark contrast to the tens of thousands of supporters and myriad political, judicial, military, and religious authorities who attended his burial in 1975. They were a powerful political statement intended to become a mnemonic turning point in the country: Spain is no longer a comfort zone for dictators – or their remains.

In October 2022, a new *democratic memory* law was passed in Parliament by the Socialist government. The section on the Valley established that no one could be buried in a privileged place in the memorial, with the obvious intention of setting the conditions for José Antonio Primo de Rivera's exit. After the intensity of Franco's exhumation process, the humiliating images of his unburial and reburial, and the legal shield provided by the new law, José Antonio's relatives chose a low-key strategy: they negotiated with the government, and his body was exhumed, cremated, and buried in a family mausoleum in a cemetery in Madrid. The lack of major incidents during the transfer – just a few hundred, albeit enthusiastic, fascist supporters – indicated that his *mnemonic capital*, so overheated during Francoism, was also mostly gone. Stripping the monument of its two most conspicuous corpses was a major necropolitical achievement, crucial in the decommissioning process at the memorial. With their departure, 20 November lost its main monumental anchorage and became a *free-floating* commemoration for Francoist nostalgics.

But beyond Franco and José Antonio, as discussed, the necrotoxicity of the monument also affects the history and arrangement of the tens of thousands of bodies in the crypts. After a long judicial, political, and media struggle, in June of 2023 the exhumations aimed at retrieving the bodies of 160 people – mostly but not only executed Republicans – began. A forensic lab was installed in one of the side chapels. The situation in the crypts is bleak, as many of the boxes have disintegrated due to high humidity, and the place more resembles an immense and labyrinthine ossuary than an organized mausoleum. Nonetheless, the archaeological and forensic team has been able to locate some of the bodies requested by relatives, and a small number of them have already been genetically identified and returned to their places of origin.

Yet the confrontation regarding the fate and custody of the bones in the cemetery persists. Daily mass in memory of the "Fallen" – an uncanny and anachronistic legacy of the Francoist cult installed in the memorial in 1959 – is still being performed. In parallel to the complex ongoing technical intervention, right-wing associations continue to file legal complaints in different courts. One major argument used against the exhumations is the presumed funerary profanation it entails, a claim with more ideological than legal basis. Initially, some of them were successful and, although later overruled, they have been able to hamper the work in progress.

Ann Rigney draws our attention to an understanding of monuments as dynamic material assemblages, stressing their ability to condense narratives, and their potential to elicit counter-narratives (2022, 15–21). Toxic monuments are also privileged grounds for testing the resilience or decadence of well-established hegemonic memory frameworks. In the Valley of Cuelgamuros, a major clash between mnemonic regimes – totalitarian versus democratic – seems to be at stake. A relevant part of it is connected to the management of a very sensitive memory matter: highly-charged bones condensing the tensions of a civil war and the memory politics of the posterior dictatorship. If removing the bodies of Franco and José Antonio sent the monument off-balance, entering the cemetery installed in the crypts is threatening the centerpiece of Francoism's underworld: the collective and chaotic ossuary of a war whose memory remains strikingly unresolved and divisive.

Lucy Bond and Jessica Rapson

Ecologies of the Discarded: Cartographic Collage as Mnemonic Recovery

1 Introduction

Materialist ontologies have impacted recent developments in memory studies (Rigney 2015; Muntean et al. 2016) ushering in "an ecological approach to cultural memory" that foregrounds "the materialised presence of the past in the physical environment" (Rigney 2015b, 13). As a leading voice in this conversation, Ann Rigney contends that "non-human materials [. . .] actively participate in events and [. . .] in an increasingly complex ecology objects, artefacts, machines and the natural environment actually do things to us" (2015, 18). Building on these assertions, this chapter explores the imbrication of human and more-than-human life-forms, environments, artifacts, and objects in the complex "memory habitat" (Rigney 2015, 27) of the 150-mile-long River Road between New Orleans and Baton Rouge, Louisiana. Often referred to as "Cancer Alley," this terrain is testament to a long history of racial capitalism from the plantation past to the petrochemical present.

Over time, official commemorative accounts of the area have invisibilized the racial and environmental violence upon which Louisiana's wealth is founded. This is particularly apparent in the contemporary heritage landscape of the River Road, dominated by antebellum plantation 'big houses' which celebrate nostalgic, white-washed histories of enslavement (Buzinde and Santos 2008; Jackson 2012; Rapson 2018). Many have been transformed into wedding venues or offer boutique hotel accommodation and leisure facilities. Attempts to address the legacy of slavery at these sites have been marginal and frequently operate "within a framework that continues to privilege white ownership" (Adams 2007, 64), not least by physically locating the memory of the enslaved away from the 'big house' within slave quarter exhibits that sanitize, romanticize or otherwise downplay or distort the violent operations and reality of plantation slavery. These are also sites of greenwashing, as local petrochemical corporations who now own much of this land sponsor plantation heritage sites to boost their public image within particular communities. This is a landscape organized according to a logic of forgetting.

In this chapter, we explore how art – in this case selected cartographic collages – can be seen to challenge this forgetting: "thicken time" and space by revealing the "material sedimentation of past lives" (Rigney 2015, 14) in the present. We accordingly examine how Richard Misrach and Kate Orff's artbook-atlas *Pet-*

rochemical America (2014), and Monique Michelle Verdin's collage series "Cancer Alley" (2020) visibilize "ongoing interactions between humans and their material environment, between past and present, verbal stories and mute materials" (Rigney 2015b, 15) along the River Road. In doing so, we argue, these works perform acts of mnemonic recovery, revealing the ecologies of discarded lives and objects exploited and exhausted by racial capitalist industries. In Rigney's terms, these representations transform an "accidental archive" of "as-yet-unarticulated meaning" (2015, 14) into a critical history of "slow violence" (Nixon 2011).

2 Racial capitalism and environmental racism on the River Road

Structures of racial capitalism have determined the conditions of life on the River Road since the arrival of the first European colonialists and the African men, women, and children they enslaved and brutalized. The concept of racial capitalism highlights the central ideological role that racism has played in capital expansion since colonialism and enslavement (Robinson 2000). The first iteration of racial capitalism to define the River Road was the plantation economy, which transformed the area socially and ecologically in the eighteenth and nineteenth centuries. European colonists coerced enslaved laborers to raze the native environment, preparing the land for the cultivation of alien plant species such as sugar, indigo, cotton, rice, and tobacco. These cash crops formed the major source of the region's wealth until the early twentieth century, when the discovery of oil reserves throughout the Deep South saw agrarian industry superseded by petrochemical production. Leading sugar producers diversified into oil and natural gas throughout the early 1900s, and in the 1950s and 60s, Louisiana's Governor, Edwin Edwards, led a push to sell former sugar plantations on the River Road to petrochemical companies who constructed increasingly large and complex refineries and processing plants. In the twenty-first century, the River Road landscape accommodates an unsettling "juxtaposition of the architectural legacy of the wealthy eighteenth-century sugar planters with petrochemical plants and poverty-stricken settlements" (Rapson 2018, 755), as past and present materialities coincide and overlap.

The communities along the River Road today are majority African American, many living on the land their ancestors acquired at Emancipation. They tend to be low income and high in unemployment, with most residents not possessing a college education. In this area, "more than one hundred firms manufacture sulfuric acid, ethylene, fertilizers, petrochemicals, and vinyl chloride" (Markowitz and Rosner 2013, 264), causing high rates of cancer among local residents, who are often deprived of the political and economic capital to contest their circumstances. The history of the River Road thus underscores the connection between the historic operations of racial capitalism and contemporary forms of environmental racism – a term defined by the United Church of Christ's Commission for Racial Justice in 1987 as "racial discrimination in environmental policy making and the enforcement of regulations and laws, the deliberate targeting of people of colour communities for toxic waste facilities, the official sanctioning of the life-threatening presence of poison and pollutants in our communities, and the history of excluding people of colour from leadership in the environmental movement" (cited in Zimring 2015, 1–2). As Beverley Wright acknowledges, "[a] history of human slavery spawned environmental racism," which is "also a by-product of the racial segregation and discrimination" (2005, 87). As forms of discrimination premised upon structural injustice, enslavement and environmental racism may be identified as examples of slow violence, which Rob Nixon defines as "violence that is neither spectacular nor instantaneous, but rather incremental and accretive, its calamitous repercussions playing out across a range of temporal scales" (2011, 2). As Nixon notes, slow violence is resistant to the dominant frames of representation utilized in contemporary media and political discourse. In the Deep South, it has also been deliberately occluded in a heritage landscape that whitewashes the plantation past and greenwashes the petrochemical present.

3 Commemoration and cartography along the River Road

While official heritage activity has tended to marginalize the human horror of chattel slavery, official cartographic practices have minimalized the slow violence of extractive environmental processes. A widely circulated map of 1858 documents plantation sites along River Road before the Civil War. This attractively illustrated document, which is today sold as a souvenir in the gift shops of plantation museums, elides the racial and environmental violence that drove colonial expansion and fueled enslavement. Through its fixity in time and space, the plantation economy is naturalized and its horror neutralized. A similar process of cartographic abstraction is used to mask the damaging social and ecological effects of the contemporary petrochemical economy. Tourist maps of the area occlude the massive infrastructure of pipes and refineries that have imperiled Louisiana's wetlands, eroded its coastline, and polluted air and water supplies, causing damage and significant loss of life to the region's human and more-than-human inhabitants.

Since the beginnings of European settler-colonialism, mapping has functioned as a powerful hegemonic tool, stratifying land and segregating society. Cartographic practices enshrined violent and inequitable hierarchies along spatial and racial lines, naturalizing processes of enslavement and exploitation, while invisibilizing their attendant violence. Maps submit (material and social) environments to violent abstraction – reducing diverse ecosystems and communities to a series of lines, spaces, and symbols. Maps reify space, creating "a world apart from life" (Ingold 2000, 44). They also have a distorting effect on time; "mainstream cartography envelops the earth in a single uniform temporality" (Ferdinand 2019, 10), a frozen moment that is antithetical to change and forgets more than it preserves. Maps, then, seem impervious to both the lived dynamics of space and the memorative dimensions of time. The petrified space-time of hegemonic cartography engenders a "God's-Eye" perspective: a "masculinist construction of a disembodied and disinterred visuality [that presents] the whole earth as a passive body for that domineering gaze to conquer, engineer, and control" (Ferdinand 2019, 55).

However, creative practice has the potential to undermine the 'domineering gaze' of mainstream cartography. Produced by photographer Richard Misrach and landscape architect Kate Orff, *Petrochemical America* charts the social and ecological impact the extractive industries have had on the River Road and its environs. The book is divided into two interconnected sections: Part 1 documents Misrach's photographic tour of "Cancer Alley"; Part 2 comprises Orff's "Ecological Atlas" of the area. As the introduction asserts, the text creates "a collaborative ecology of seeing [and] analyzing [. . .] the constructed landscapes that characterize" (Misrach and Orff 2014, 17) the area. Orff's work adds "layers of maps, graphs, and illustrations" (17) to Misrach's images, creating a "visual narrative" comprised by "throughlines" (17), which allow the reader to cross-reference elements of the text, generating causal and imaginative connections between landscapes and lives across time and space. Human and more-than-human suffering are placed in a horizontal relationship to each other (178–179; 154) as Misrach and Orff expose the effects of toxic waste on different transcorporeal assemblages.

Petrochemical America undermines the categorizing principles of conventional cartography, opening up the spatial and temporal frames of the map. As Orff explains, "To understand Cancer Alley, we researched the regional, national, and global dynamics that transformed the lower Mississippi from lush fishing grounds for Native Americans to thriving indigo and sugarcane plantations worked by African slaves, to a startling conflation of petrochemical factories and small towns" (Misrach and Orff 2014, 115). The text emphasizes the insidious stranglehold the petrochemical industry exerts on economies and ecologies around the world. As Orff comments, today "global corporations, primarily petroleum and financial-services based, have outstripped the sovereignty of many nation-states and US-states," generating "invisible and profound changes in our geography and ecology. Atmospheric emissions from the combustion of coal and oil are transforming the globe's physical landscape, flora, and fauna in ways that exceed the resilient capacities of those ecosystems" (Misrach and Orff 2014, 119). These environmental changes are mapped in a series of illustrations that demonstrate the toxic effects of Cancer Alleys at local and global levels (151 and 166). Misrach and Orff highlight the historical reach of this economy. The ecological atlas operates across a number of timescales, from the deep time of Louisiana's Pleistocene era geology (120–121) to the construction of petrochemical plants since the early twentieth century (124–125).

A similar mapping of invisibilized racial capitalism emerges from interdisciplinary artist Monique Michelle Verdin's River Road collage series (disseminated in digital form in *Southern Cultures*, 2020). Verdin juxtaposes public records with her own photography, providing a re-constructed vision of the area through the 'manipulation' of US Geological Survey (USGS) maps. Verdin thus reveals how sites (and histories) along the road "are variously represented or simply erased, and how the challenges of today are founded in colonialism" (Verdin 2020). These collages visualize the interpenetration of human and non-human lifeworlds. *Istrouma: Baton Rouge,* for example, presents a 1939 USGS map of Baton Rouge upon which Verdin has circled 'Indian Mound' in red, highlighting a sacred site for the indigenous population, who are themselves literally inserted back into the landscape as pasted figures 'Bringing the Peace Pipe,' reproduced from an illustrated *History of Louisiana.* At the bottom-left corner of the collage Verdin introduces a photograph labelled "Runaway Mississippi Slave," or "The Scourged Back," 1863. This highly circulated nineteenth-century photograph shows a formerly enslaved man with a heavily scarred back, often referred to as 'Whipped Peter' and seen to represent the brutality of slavery. These figures appear against a backdrop of an Exxon-Mobil refinery which stands alongside a pasted image of the Baton Rouge Capitol Building, the regional seat of political power. In this way Verdin marks how, supported by elite politicians, "commercial industries disrespected and disconnected Native settlements and ceremonial grounds, corrupting historical and cultural ties to ancestral lands" (2020) – a structural violence concomitant with the legacy of plantation slavery represented by 'Whipped Peter.'

Verdin's collages present a nexus of human and non-human-human exploitation that has characterized the colonial "extraction of land, labor, and lives" (Verdin 2020) across the locations mapped along the River Road. Alongside human bodies appear those of the animals – from buffalo to beavers – that have been historically hunted and processed into products for human consumption (some to the point of near extinction). The infrastructure of extraction and trade – a Navios oil Supertanker, an industrial spillway, a mural of an oil refinery – is integrated via Verdin's contemporary photographic works, alongside plantation-era images of enslaved field workers. Within Verdin's collages, objects, people and animals hold their own historical referents, but, are most productively interpreted within the past-present ecology they create – in their relation to one another. In this sense, Verdin's collages perform a similar function to those of Misrach and Orff: human and more-than-human suffering are placed in a horizontal relationship, highlighting cartographic ecologies of the discarded. This leads us to finally consider the mnemonic potential of cartographic collage for the representation of slow violence.

4 Cartographic collage as mnemonic praxis

Collage has much in common with the literary form of allegory which, in Walter Benjamin's (1977) reading both thematizes the violence of history and, in its fragmented narrative form, reflects it. As a mnemonic device, this fragmentation is highly generative. As David Michalski argues:

> As a memory technology [. . .] collage serves as both a launching point and crossroads. From the ordered juxtaposition of distinct pieces, stories extend like mathematical singularities outward, while simultaneously pulling distinct forms onto its imaginary stage. The dual character of collage [. . .] a zone where objects exist alternatively as objects and referents, provides a way of understanding how memory plays off of our physical and social environments. (Michalski 2002, 107)

While the aforementioned case studies represent different forms of cartographic collage, by refusing the "God's Eye" perspective outlined above, they each demand that the cartographic gaze reengage in lived entanglements with the Earth, emphasizing the interpenetration of social and ecological lifeworlds while acknowledging the necessary incompleteness of all processes of memory and mapping. In so doing, they share a common purpose, which clearly resonates with Rigney's ecological approach to cultural memory. By directly foregrounding the "virtual dumping ground of things" that official commemorative and cartographic processes have deemed "too dangerous to be remembered" (Rigney 2015b, 13), they reveal the River Road as a memory habitat which is thick with the traces of past and present forms of slow violence.

In mapping these ecologies of the discarded (however partially or imperfectly), cartographic collages have the potential to act as a kind of "restitutional assemblage." As conceptualized by Anna Reading, restitutional assemblages comprise "material and non-material practices across multiple domains (material, economic, emotional, spiritual, affective) operating in a non-linear fashion across spatialized temporalities to transform broader and ongoing structures of oppression" (2019, 235). In Rigney's terms, as semiotic "sedimentations of [. . .] experience" that reveal the "enduring presence of former times in the here and now," cartographic collages "have the power to mobilise memory, provoke story-telling, and cause people to act." (2015b, 17–18) By gesturing to that which has been violently othered and discarded, both human and more-than-human, we suggest that they might just provide a way of translating the accidental archive of racial capitalism into a critical history of slow violence.

Richard Crownshaw
Who and What Matters in Literary Memory

The relatively recent emergence of environmental memory studies, characterizing the interests of our current fourth wave of cultural memory studies, is usually focused on one aspect or other of what has been described as our new geological epoch, the Anthropocene (but about which there is yet to be scientific consensus) (Olick et al. 2023). The Anthropocene can be defined in terms of the primacy of the human species in (catastrophically) shaping the planet – a non-uniform collective agency, the transformative inscriptions of which can be measured in the Earth's strata and atmosphere. In short, environmental memory studies analyzes and theorizes how the causes and effects of environmental change are culturally represented and remembered (and forgotten). The disposition of this subfield has to be ecological in that it elicits the remembrance of events in the nonhuman and human world, or, rather, of the relationship and entanglement between the (synthetic, organic, and inorganic) nonhuman and the human world. That disposition also entails an understanding that these events are engendered by assemblages of, as Bruno Latour (2005) and then Jane Bennett (2010) would put it, human and/or nonhuman actants, assemblages in which the nonhuman is potentially agential. Environmental memory studies, then, maps the entities (human and nonhuman), matter and things that assemble and become eventful across multiple and often inhuman temporal and spatial scales and finds ecological common ground between the cultural forms that remembrance takes and the assemblage remembered.

While the fourth wave of memory studies has been busily de-centering the human, activating the nonhuman, and recalibrating the scales of remembrance, a review of Ann Rigney's work finds in it a prescient exploration of the possibilities of such new materialist and posthumanist thought for cultural memory studies. Rigney's engagement with the nonhuman has anticipated cultural memory studies' recent direction. Crucially, for the purposes of this short essay, Rigney's subtle emphasis on the role of the human in the assemblages of remembrance is something cultural memory studies should remember as it begins to adopt redistributive models of agency and recalibrations of scale.

Why should the human be remembered in and by environmental memory studies, or more particularly, why should the agency and purview of humans be not entirely decentered? Bennett argues that the "locus of agency is always a human-nonhuman working group," and so an effect of an "assemblage" of "actants" that emerges temporarily and contingently, depending on particular circumstances and contexts, but with "the capacity of things [. . .] to act as quasi agents or forces with trajectories, propensities, or tendencies of their own" (Ben-

nett 2010, ix). Agency is not an inherent or immanent property of a particular actant or thing or the matter from which they derive but is effected by the relation
and configuration of things and matter. However, the problem is that everything
has the potential to make a difference – "everything is, in a sense, alive" (Bennett
2010, 117) – because of its potential to be an actant in an assemblage. That means
it becomes increasingly difficult to tell what makes the most difference and
where differentiation originated. As David Farrier puts it, Bennett's theory delivers a "totally flat field of experience and potential" (2019, 17). If the potential for
agency extends as far as any thing, because any thing in an assemblage has, theo-
retically, the potential to effect material change, then, for Andreas Malm, this is
an unwelcome universalization of agency because it blurs the anthropogenesis of
environmental catastrophe (Malm 2018). And, in terms of scale, as environmental
memory studies adopts ecocritical demands for scalar flexibility – to remember
and theorize the remembrance of events across human and inhuman temporal
and spatial scales – such recalibrations risk abstractness. The inhuman scales of
the Anthropocene's processes need to be apprehended through localized cultural
and social specificity to become meaningful, in other words, through very human
experiences (Clark 2015; McGurl 2021). That said, grounding memory in localized
"human experiences" must entail the further particularization of those experiences, to prevent the homogenization of contributions to and the impacts of the
Anthropocene.

Rigney's salutary reminders of the conceptual limits of nonhuman agency
can be found foremost in her identification of an "ecological approach to cultural
memory in Walter Scott's work," particularly in works such as *The Antiquary*
(1816), that stage "intense entanglements between people and the material environments in which they conduct their lives" (2015b, 13–15). Scott, like Rigney, is
interested in the material, objectified traces of past happenings – objects that are
not necessarily and mostly not archived in any official way – that can trigger historical memories in the present when accidentally or deliberately encountered
(Rigney 2015b, 14). In theorizing the resonance of such objects and the material
environment generally, Rigney draws on Bennett's "vibrant materialism," which
she summarizes as the way in which "in an increasingly complex ecology, objects,
artefacts, machines and the natural environment actually do things to us: they
fascinate us, offer resources, support our actions, demand our investment, call
for maintenance and [. . .] our constant attention" (2015b, 18).

In Rigney's application of new materialist ideas it is not just the events remembered but the act of recollection itself that is assembled and ecological:

> many of the objects in *The Antiquary* activate not just emotions in the present but also mem-
> ories of times past. As relics of the past, they ensure the enduring presence of former times

in the here and now. As sedimentations of earlier experience, they have the power to mobilise memory, provoke story-telling, and cause people to act. (2015b, 18)

It is not just the inorganic and synthetic that resonates with memory and contributes to acts of recollection in Scott's work but also the so-called natural landscape. For example, in the novel *Waverley* (1814), the state and growth of forestry mnemonically marks the integration of environmental and human histories and registers the impact of war (the Napoleonic Wars) and the natural resources needed to fuel warfare.

However, if, for Rigney, "Scott's historical imagination was profoundly attuned to materiality" showing an awareness of "the mnemonic power of 'things'" that "continuously exceeds verbalization," the force of matter also feeds "back into the desire to tell new stories" to "provoke a longing to know more [that] is ultimately dependent on the power of words to release their potential meaning; to set them vibrating" (Rigney 2015b, 18–21). That the "mnemonic power of things" feeds "back into the desire to tell new stories" reminds us that those things, no matter how lively, do not speak for themselves. While, of course, language and discourse may be unreliable, uncontrollable, and meaningful in unintended ways, in Rigney's theorization of Scott's literature, memory is ultimately anthropogenic – the product of human cultural intentions contingent on the material world. In other words, a critical humanism is intimated that keeps in check the conceptualization of nonhuman agency.

As ecocriticism reminds us, the novel is not just a representation of the world but part of it. As I have co-written elsewhere, the novel is not just assembled ideationally and discursively but also materially (Craps and Crownshaw 2018). "As a social and cultural formation, the novel has always been enabled by economic and industrial systems of modernity and their resources, from its origins to the present day [. . .] The product of energy regimes as much as intellectual labor, the novel is the materialization" of environmental histories that inform the subject matter represented in the novel's pages (Craps and Crownshaw 2018, 2). So "[a] nimated by the energy regimes that brought it into being" as well as by the cultural work it does and its "usage as a cultural object [. . .] the novel bodies forth (implicitly and explicitly) entangled human and nonhuman dramas of people and things," life and matter, structures, systems and processes, mediating ideas and belief systems, and the way they combine to shape the planet – combinations found "within its pages" and "in the material emergence of those pages" (Craps and Crownshaw 2018, 2; see also Trexler 2015; Taylor 2016). By tracking human agency, among other things, in the literary production of memory, Rigney models the importance of human agency in the events remembered, given the ecological interconnections between text and world.

The insistence on the human can also be seen in the issues of scale that have also come to the fore in Rigney's more recent work that explores "what it takes for inert or occluded aspects of the past to become memorable again" (2021b, 12). As social imaginaries change to accommodate changing social formations – for example, because national communities once imagined no longer convincingly correspond to new realities – frameworks are created for the remembrance of different societally shared pasts (Rigney 2021b, 13). It is not just changing social frameworks that make the past memorable and relevant again with sufficient cultural and social value to be reconstituted *as* memory, but the mediation of the past: its translation "into transmissible experience [. . .] using available media and calling on a repertoire of cultural forms (memoirs, monuments, documentaries, exhibitions and so on) which act as carriers of memory and structure information in a meaningful way" (Rigney 2021b, 13). As "media technologies," "cultural forms" and familiar generic patterns combine to transmit the past and to make it resonant and memorable, it is often the production of unfamiliar and unsettling aesthetic experiences that drives memorability. An affective departure from the generically familiar contributes to what Rigney, borrowing from Derek Attridge, describes as the "singularity" of a cultural carrier of memory. For Rigney, literature's, and more generally art's, affect makes it agential, and more than a "passive transmitter of stories in people's heads" (2021b, 13–14). In other words, and following "Latour's theory of actor networks, the arts can be seen as actants in a network that involves both human and non-human agents: particular constellations of words, images and sounds have the power to command our attention and to generate affect and interest in the lives of others" (Rigney 2021b, 14). However, "the role of the arts in the remaking of memory [. . .] derives from their power to enchant; specifically, to capture our attention through mastery of a given medium," in other words, from human creative agency in the formation of cultural memory (2021b, 15). What is more, it is the aggregation of micro acts of literary production and consumption – acts of authorship and reading – that reconstitutes memory at the collective (collected) level (enabled, that is, by the necessary cultural, social, political and ideological conditions, institutions, systems and processes) (Rigney 2021b, 14). So, while the fourth wave of memory studies scales up and down to track the unfolding of events previously beyond the field's remit, the past only becomes meaningful, and cultural memory only achieves critical mass, through locally specific acts of remembrance, or, in this case, very human literary engagements.

The last section of this essay will briefly discuss a literary text that is a far cry from Rigney's usual subject matter but which demonstrates the valence and reach of her theories of memory while fleshing out some of this essay's concerns over scale and agency. Like much climate change fiction, Claire Vaye Watkins' novel *Gold Fame Citrus* (2015) speculates on the climate-changed near future, in this case a drought-ravaged and desertified American Southwest which is being engulfed by the Amargosa, a gigantic moving dune sea. So, typical of literary speculations on the environmental future, this novel imagines a more fully realized Anthropocene – a future from which our geological epoch's aetiology is remembered. The novel deploys well-trodden themes, settings, and motifs of climate change fiction – desertification and extreme weather, toxic landscapes, uncontrollable environments, socio-economic and ecological collapse, the disposability of life, the prospect of extinction, and an imperiled future – that have been the subject of much ecocritical theorization. Arguably, the novel anticipates its own paradigmatic theorization and so affords opportunities to reflect critically on the limits and possibilities of the theory and practice of climate change fiction. What the novel foregrounds in particular are issues of scale and agency.

For example, given its growing size, and inexorable momentum, the Amargosa, and the process of desertification that engenders the dune sea, appears to be autopoietic, or at least that is the widely held belief in the world of the novel. This fetishization of an apparently animated dune sea is compounded by the desert's materialization of the deep time of geological processes that are seemingly beyond the human horizons of current historical memory. As the narrator points out, the moving dune sea subsumes the topography of human settlement of the Southwest, enfolding the human landscape into sand and rock and creating what is in effect a geological layer bearing the signature of human activity. These environmental conditions of the future compress geological processes – not just desertification and the generation of a massive dune sea, but the reduction of human history to a seam in the Earth's strata – that would otherwise take "five hundred thousand years" into "fifty" (Watkins 2016, 114–117). In other words, while human history can and will be read in the rocks, and the anthropogenesis of environmental catastrophe and planetary change understood, the society of the novel's present is overwhelmed by what it perceives as the sublime temporal and spatial scales of the Amargosa. Unable to historicize its climatic conditions, the society of the present attributes its demise to an insurrectionary and agentic nonhuman word. It is the narrator's description of the animated dune sea, focalizing popular beliefs and various characters, that tempts and provokes ecocritical readings overly focused on nonhuman agency, but which Watkins anticipates and counters through the narrator's histories of ecologically unsound Western settlement and its hydrological ramifications (ideologically underwritten by the legacies of Manifest Destiny) (Watkins 2016, 120). Watkins also demonstrates the ways that the reader's, critic's, and novel's society's transferal of power to things screens the powerful biopolitical operations of that society. Ranging across the wastelands of the Southwest, the narrator reveals secret detention centers that have incarcerated those deemed un-American, but it is the power of the Armagosa that remains the focus of public attention and not the power of the state (252).

If Watkins' novel is, as Rigney might put it, a "textual monument" (2004, 372) to the future's past, then what it recalls are the implications of ecocritical theories that extend the distribution of agency too far. While this chapter has argued that Rigney in effect provides a humanist lens through which to view the ecology of memory and the memory of ecology – the inter- and intra-actions of human and nonhuman in the act of remembrance and what is remembered – it does not mean to suggest that matter does not matter at all. Doing memory work with Rigney means taking materiality seriously, but it also means not forgetting human causality, whether that be in the eighteenth-century Scottish setting of Scott's novels and its nineteenth-century inscription, or in writing about a near-future climate-changed California of the twenty-first century. That said, given the changing nature of actants as they ceaselessly and contingently recombine in acts of remembrance, Rigney would also remind us that literary speculations on the environmental future can only ever be impermanent monuments to the "anticipatory memory" of who and what matters (Craps 2017), for their memorative agency is dependent on who and what they assemble with and in which enabling cultural and social contexts. The future of memory may be written, but it is not set in stone.

7 The Agency of the Aesthetic

Michael Rothberg
Multidirectional Memory and the Agency of the Aesthetic

1 Differential memorability, aesthetic agency, and multidirectional memory

Our world is full of traces – material markers of the presence of the past – but not all of those traces come to constitute sites of memory. Why are some traces of the past overlooked while others come to occupy a prominent place in public memory? How do traces of the past move from the archive to the canon, from passive to active cultural memory, to borrow Aleida Assmann's terms (2008a)? Ann Rigney takes up this question throughout her oeuvre: her concept of "differential memorability" names the problem of the disparities that mark which histories and experiences are remembered and which fall into oblivion; and her work, both alone and with Astrid Erll, on the dynamics of mediation and remediation provides a powerful account of how sites become memorable through repeated, transmedial evocations and translations (cf. Rigney 2005; 2012a; 2016; and Erll and Rigney 2009a). Within the plurimedial networks that Rigney explores in addressing the question of differential memorability, the aesthetic realm occupies a privileged position. The affordances of the aesthetic – including its capacity to create affective experiences through both immersive and defamiliarizing forms – provide art with the potential to enact a powerful mnemonic force.

In her 2021 essay "Remaking Memory and the Agency of the Aesthetic," Rigney addresses this central question of mnemonic agency in considering the memorability of colonial soldiers who fought for Europe in the First World War. Millions of troops from the colonies took part in the war, and memorials and graves can be found in European cities like Mainz (Rigney's opening example) as well as in formerly colonized countries. Yet, despite the "existence of archival evidence and the personal recollections of the combatants, the memory of the colonial soldiers became 'inert'" (Rigney 2021b, 11); it largely fell out of the canon of remembrance for decades. This "forgetting" of the colonial presence in a "European" world war, Rigney suggests, "can be taken as symptomatic of a long-standing failure across the continent to link the memory of World War One to the memory of European colonialism" (2021b, 11). Only recently, with the centenary of the war, did the presence of colonial soldiers in this truly global conflict start to become a topic of wider public concern and commemoration. Adopting a "multiscalar" approach (2021b, 12; see also De Cesari and Rigney 2014), Rigney outlines the way that changing social frameworks, familiar narrative templates, and the defamiliarizing powers of the aesthetic have combined to render the histories of colonial subjects more memorable in recent years, in both post-imperial European and postcolonial spaces. Among the drivers of this newfound interest over the last decade have been particular films, novels, and performances. A work of art, Rigney tells us, drawing on Derek Attridge, possesses a "singularity" that "makes it stick in memory and, in the process, enhances the memorability of its subject matter" (2021b, 14). Art's agency derives from its capacity to produce "particular constellations of words, images and sounds [that] have the power to command our attention and to generate affect and interest in the lives of others" (Rigney 2021b, 14). Such affective power can challenge the contours of our usually narrow imagined communities by "help[ing] to shift, or at least temporarily suspend, the imagined boundary between 'us' and the 'other'" (Rigney 2021b, 15).

In my own work, that process of crossing boundaries between imagined communities usually considered discrete – or even antagonistic – involves what I call "multidirectional memory": the productive and dialogic interaction of mnemonic materials from ostensibly different historical traditions (Rothberg 2009). Rigney recognizes in "Remaking Memory" that among the factors contributing to the dynamics of memorability are those we can call multidirectional (2021b, 13–14). This multidirectionality involves bringing into a shared mnemonic space the history of European colonialism and the history of World War I – after all, how could one explain the presence of four million soldiers from the colonies in the European theater of war without such a lens? In the case of my book *Multidirectional Memory*, the mnemonic constellation involved World War II – and in particular the Holocaust – and its intersections with the history and memory of European colonialism, transatlantic slavery, and anti-Black racism. While the archives of the Second World War and Holocaust, like the First World War, contain entangled European and non-European histories – including colonial soldiers held in Nazi concentration camps and many more who contributed to the liberation of Europe from fascism – acts of multidirectional remembrance do not only derive from such material entanglements, but also from the kinds of imaginative investments, narrative patterns, and social frameworks that feed and accompany the agency of the aesthetic. Historical experiences such as camps, torture, deportations, and ghettos and aesthetic genres such as testimony and documentary were reimagined and reworked in various cultural texts and thus became sites of memory where Jewish, Black, and colonial histories intersected in acts of public remembrance.

While conventional wisdom has long held that the confrontation between different memories in public space leads necessarily to the sidelining of one memory to the advantage of another – what I called the competitive logic of the zero-sum game – the multidirectional approach foregrounds the productive dynamic in which different memories draw on each other's tropes and narratives in their own articulation. And yet, the problem of differential memorability remains; despite the multidirectionality of memory, not all significant histories are equally – or, better, *adequately* – present in any given memory culture. The problem, however, is not zero-sum logic but rather the fading or active repression of mnemonic linkages. How – to reframe our opening question – can we move from a passive and unacknowledged multidirectionality to an active and effective recognition of the ongoing claims of multiple pasts? Again, the answer may lie in the realm of the aesthetic.

2 *Aşît* and the agency of the aesthetic

In the remainder of this essay, I turn to a work of art composed of a multidirectional network of references and traces that also addresses the problem of submerged and repressed memories of political violence. In such cases of forced forgetting, the agency of the aesthetic may consist in reactivating links that have gone dormant, but that persist as unremarked traces in landscapes, languages, and individual memories. While the aesthetic holds a central place in Rigney's theory of the dynamics of memory, she is also rightly skeptical about the agency of singular works to transform memory culture by themselves: the dynamics of memory require remediation and convergence (Rigney 2005) to create meaningful sites of memory. For reasons of space, I focus here on a specific work, Pınar Öğrenci's 2022 film *Aşît* [The Avalanche], but this work itself already condenses multiple other texts: it is itself, in other words, a site of dynamic convergence and its aesthetic power derives in part from that convergence. A sixty-minute essay-film screened first at the 2022 *documenta 15* exhibition in Kassel, Germany, *Aşît* was subsequently shown at the Berlinische Gallerie, where I had the opportunity to see it in 2023.

Öğrenci's film addresses head-on the differential memorability and unequal grievability of Armenian and Kurdish lives in a twentieth- and twenty-first-century Turkey that has sought to produce demographic homogeneity through genocide and ongoing political violence against ethnic and religious minorities. *Aşît* is a work created partly in political exile, and the fact of exile influences both the form and the content of the work. A Kurdish artist and activist from Van, Turkey, Öğrenci fled the country of her birth in 2018 for Germany after being threatened with prison because of her involvement in the Kurdish cause. Settled in Germany for several years, she has created a series of works that address transnational histories of migration and persecution. In *Aşît*, she returns to her father's native village of Müküs [Turkish: Bahçesaray], a remote town in the eastern Turkish province of Van, close to the Armenian and Iranian borders, in order to excavate entangled, highly local histories that also intersect with transnational movements of exile. In taking up the Armenian genocide, a history that has been actively suppressed by the Turkish state, and placing it in relation to the ongoing military repression of Kurds as well as the Holocaust, Öğrenci's film deliberately counters forgetting, but it also acknowledges the limits of its own attempts at reclamation. *Aşît* thus confronts both the dilemmas of differential memorability and problems of the singular aesthetic work, with its necessary but insufficient agency.

Aşît is a work that searches for traces of the past against the forces of violence in the present and in the face of blocked access to that past. Although the filmmaker remains outside the film – visually and sonically – she frames *Aşît* through a personal, textual narrative rendered in English. Early on, we look down into a valley surrounded by imposing, snow-covered mountains that are shrouded in clouds. At the top right corner of the screen, a series of three narrative subtitles announces: "My father wanted to see Müküs, the hometown that he left when he was 10, one last time before he passed away./ But because the roads to Müküs are closed during winter and dangerous during summer, he was unable to go./ When the first asphalt road was laid in 2013, my father had already passed away." The film, then, takes up an intergenerational quest that has been frustrated by blocked paths and death. Yet, while a return to Müküs was impossible for the narrator's father, the film itself constitutes evidence of the narrator's return to this site; it is thus a work of postmemory, but one that, after the initial reference to the father, focuses solely on multiple communal (as opposed to familial) histories. The tension between blockage and access and the question of who gets to speak and in which language – a question raised by the silent English narrative and explored over the course of the film's sixty minutes – comprise two of the film's key motifs.

Those motifs appear in a pair of sequences from the final section of the film. The question of language and of differential memorability of traces of the past emerges in an unlikely place: the names of sheep. Sheep are a recurring motif in *Aşît*. In the earliest scenes, where a close-up evokes the tactile nature of their wool and then shows a Kurdish shepherd leading them away, sheep appear in harmony with the landscape and with traditional village lifeways. Eventually, as the film returns to them again and again, we see how this particular way of life is being eroded by anti-Kurdish state violence and climate change, which have forced many peasants to abandon their land and livestock and to migrate into the city or further afield. A key scene supplements these present-tense forms of forced displacement with an additional association: the sheep also call up the forgotten traces of eradicated Armenian culture. In a late sequence, a herd of sheep grazes by a rushing river and across from an imposing digger, itself symptomatic of the destruction of the landscape; the camera then moves into the animals' hut. As the camera pans over the sheep, staying close to them and positioned just below their eye level, a Kurdish narrator – one of several off-screen interviewees whose voices Öğrenci includes in the film – begins to describe the different animals: "The ones with the horns are known as Keels. Those with no horns and with small ears are Kurrs." The interviewee proceeds to name fifteen different kinds of sheep, all of which are distinguished by physical features such as the presence or absence of horns and the color of their mouths and eyes. He then clarifies: "These names have entered our culture from Persian or Armenian. Because many words have no equivalent in Kurdish we do not know the meanings of these names." The names constitute a trace of cultural difference that lives on despite the forces of homogenizing violence that have sought to eliminate non-Turkish language, culture, and, often enough, people. Conveyed in a Kurdish-language narrative, the names of the sheep transmit that trace of difference but also reveal the genocidal loss that haunts cultural transmission: the memory of the Armenian (and Persian) past survives in Müküs as non-signifying sounds whose meaning is withheld from those who voice them. The film includes other instances of this paradoxical (non-)transmission, such as its frequent lingering over chiseled stones in ruined or still-standing houses that bear decorative patterns and Armenian script – signifiers that for most viewers and the local inhabitants of Müküs will be illegible. In drawing our attention to this peculiar form of transmission without meaning, and contextualizing it within a narrative that explicitly names genocide and state violence as the forces behind the process of designification, the film remediates the lost memory: not to bring it to fullness, but to suggest the fullness that has been lost. It foregrounds differential memorability, while turning viewers into sensitive detectives of marginalized traces, as the film's final sequence also suggests.

The film is accompanied by three songs collected and recorded by Hayrik Muradyan, a child survivor of the Armenian genocide from a neighboring town who made it his life's work in exile to collect and record Armenian songs from his childhood. *Aşît* "returns" Muradyan's voice to the landscape that once held a thriving Armenian community, but it does so self-consciously through montage: through the filmmaker's ability to edit together sounds and images that are not synchronous. Nor is there anything cathartic or redemptive about the direction in which the film moves: from its initial stunning shots of the town's natural setting, the film builds toward a recognition that "The catastrophe of 1915 was a turning point" in the erasure of Armenians from the town, as one of the last English subtitles reads. This recognition of the town as the site of a catastrophe – really, multiple catastrophes, as the film has shown us – also inspires multidirectional remembrance. Earlier, the film associates chess – played constantly in the cafes of Müküs – with the Austrian-Jewish writer Stefan Zweig's *Schachnovelle*, the final work he wrote in exile from the Nazis before his suicide. Now, immediately following the reference to the 1915 genocide, a series of subtitles (the final three of the film) evokes the Holocaust survivor and psychoanalyst Dori Laub and links his theory of trauma and testimony to Hayrik Muradyan. Set against a dark cave and the sound of dripping water, we read: "Dori Laub says that communities that have experienced major traumas like genocide need to be listened to gently: "Ears appropriate for listening./ The voice of Mouradyan, who could never return to his homeland, was one of these voices for me./ The voice of trauma and the unspeakable." After a brief pause, we hear the elegiac voice of Mouradyan singing "I Am a Deer of the Highlands," the third and final song included in *Aşît*. After a few seconds, the song continues and the image-track shifts to an ordinary Müküs street scene: the camera appears to be mounted on the back of a truck and a continuous shot documents the filmmaker leaving town. We pass police cars and military barricades – metonymies of anti-Kurdish violence – waiting to be deployed by the side of the road. As the camera moves over a bridge, an older man half turns around and waves, and then the camera moves out into the countryside; the screen fades to black and the credits roll, accompanied by Muradyan's untranslated song.

This final sequence encapsulates much about the agency of the aesthetic in *Aşît*, all of which is illuminated by what Ann Rigney has taught us about the dynamics and differential resonance of memory. The film creates a multidirectional constellation of histories through a careful montage of image and sound. This montage brings together different histories of violence, but at the same time, through its dislocation of sound and image, reveals the limits of mnemonic reparation in the face of denial, trauma, and ongoing military occupation. An exiled Armenian voice; English-language subtitles evoking the Holocaust; barely glimpsed scenes of military repression in a remote town: these cinematic materials are invested with forms of historical content that resonate with each other but – in their formal distinctness – are deliberately prevented from melding. Grasping both their connection and their unredeemable separation requires a particular form of perception that *Aşît* also seeks to supply. The film has, indeed, taught us to "listen gently" to multiple traumas – a training that its quiet early scenes of nature began to impart to us before we even knew the violent content buried in the landscape and visible in the texture of contemporary everyday life in the Kurdish regions.

Through its aesthetic agency – both its form and its content – Öğrenci's film contests a particular shape of differential memorability that devalues Armenian and Kurdish voices, while refusing to pretend that it can singlehandedly overcome the lacunae of state-enforced memory and forgetting. Its last gesture combines melancholia and mourning: it leaves the town unchanged but preserves the voice of Muradyan. Its intertextual and intermedial dynamics create a new, multidirectional memory in the aesthetic space of the film, but that memory remains in exile from the landscape where its traces persist. In other words, the film responds to the paradox of traces that persist but do not constitute sites of memory by remediating those traces and creating a virtual *lieu de mémoire*. The virtuality of this space embodies the agency of the aesthetic – and its limits.

Susanne Knittel

Scales of Memory: Family Chronicles and the Agency of the Aesthetic

1 Scales of memory and the family chronicle

In her article "Remaking Memory and the Agency of the Aesthetic" (2021b), Ann Rigney explores the role of cultural forms in bringing "inert or occluded aspects of the past" (12) back into circulation and making them memorable. Cultural forms generate memorability either by "representing less familiar events through the lens of more familiar ones" (13), or by defamiliarizing and unsettling established narratives about the past bringing to the fore repressed or unacknowledged aspects of that same past. Broadly speaking, the former corresponds to what Michael Rothberg (2009) has theorized as multidirectionality, the latter resonates with what I have called the historical uncanny (Knittel 2014). In both cases, Rigney argues, it is the affective qualities of cultural forms that imbue them with agency. Taking the "(un)forgetting" (10) of colonial soldiers in European armies during World War I as her case study, Rigney argues that aesthetic forms can contribute to reshaping imagined communities by capturing individual attention and fostering openness to the memories of strangers. Importantly, she argues that memory studies should adopt a multi-scalar approach, considering how individual, micro-level acts of writing, reading, or viewing can reconstitute memory also at a collective and macro level.

The question of scale has recently come to occupy a central position in the humanities in the context of the Anthropocene. The Anthropocene has destabilized traditional understandings of scales and scalability and disrupted our conception of individual agency (Ghosh 2016; Clarke and Wittenberg 2017). The sum of individual actions, insignificant in themselves, has come to affect the planet as a whole – but not in a linear way, as agency is distributed across humans, non-humans, and technology, as well as time and space. Different things come to matter differently at different scales. Thinking about different scales in the Anthropocene context means thinking in terms of discontinuity or incommensurability rather than in terms of a smooth, linear zooming in and out between the small and the large. The influence of the Anthropocene discourse can be felt in memory studies in discussions about the scope and temporality of memory and has led to conceptualizations of memory as "planetary" (Bond et al. 2017; Craps et al. 2018) or "anticipatory" (Craps 2017), among others. These terms attempt to give form to the complex interrelations between human and non-human life worlds, between local, national, and global concerns, but also, and importantly, between historical and geological pasts, presents, and futures.

Implicitly or explicitly, however, scale has of course always been at the heart of the field, starting with the relationship between individual and collective memory (Assmann 2006), national and transnational memory (De Cesari and Rigney 2014; Kennedy and Nugent 2016), theorizations of individual or collective trauma (Bond and Craps 2020) and the vexed problem of individual or collective guilt and responsibility. Recent conceptualizations of complicity (Sanders 2002; Sanyal 2015; Mandel 2019; Mihai 2019) and implication (Rothberg 2019; 2023) describe scalar relations between individual agency and structures and histories of violence and injustice such as genocide or colonialism. The question of scale pertains both to the object of study and to the activity of studying it. Scales are conceptual or representational devices for describing relational arrangements between different-sized phenomena, between the local and the global, between the micro and the macro (Zylinska 2014). Cultural forms – novels, films, poems, etc. – can make visible scalar relations and perform scaling operations through their depiction of individuals and their relations to larger structures and processes.

Literary critics have theorized scale as both a writerly and a readerly enterprise, focusing on the one hand on scaling as a textual performance, with literary texts acting as "scaling devices" (Dimock 2013; McGurl 2013) that depict the spatiotemporal relationships between individuals and larger events, processes, and structures. A novel, for example, may focus on minute details of a person's life only then, apparently seamlessly to zoom out to reflect on world historical events, and vice versa. Scaling as a readerly performance, on the other hand, means to take into account multiple different and often incommensurable scales in the process of interpretation (Clark 2015). Timothy Clark distinguishes between three spatiotemporal scales of reading: first, the individual, psychological scale (thoughts and relations between characters), second, the (trans)national, (multi)generational, and historical scale (e.g. focusing on a particular historical period), and third, the planetary scale, which moves beyond the usual scope of literary analysis to consider an environmental history that unfolds over a much longer time frame. This has significant implications for how we approach the scales of memory in cultural representations. In what follows I will focus on one of the paradigmatic forms for the representation of scalar relationships and individual and collective memory: the multigenerational family novel or family chronicle. After a brief discussion of the affordances of the form itself, I will, with the help of two recent examples, sketch some elements of the writerly and the readerly practice of scaling as it relates to the question of implication in large-scale histories of violence against humans and the natural world.

Long a popular genre of world literature, over the past two decades the family chronicle has emerged as a powerful site, across languages and cultures, of the construction of the cultural memory of genocide – most notably the Holocaust – and other histories of violence. Emblematic of the "era of generational discourse" (Weigel 2006, 87), in which the category of the generation becomes a key to the cultural, public, and scholarly understanding of the experience and transmission of history and memory, these chronicles take as their central conceit the family tree, featuring often semi-autobiographical narrators who confront their parents', grandparents', and great-grandparents' entanglements in the violent histories of the past century and beyond, and their own implication in those histories.[1] Situated at the intersection of microhistorical and macrohistorical scales, the family chronicle explores how ordinary people become involved in violent regimes and how they make sense of this involvement after the fact. As such, it can make unfamiliar histories legible and memorable within a familiar form: the generational structure. Furthermore, the genre lends itself to the critical interrogation of overly schematic conceptions of perpetrators versus victims and instead allows for an exploration of complex – multidirectional – forms of complicity and implication, both synchronic (present-day) and diachronic (historical), as theorized by Rothberg (2019). Focusing on the trials and tribulations of different generations of a single family allows authors to place different, seemingly unrelated histories of violence side by side, without equating them. In so doing, the form makes visible connections between structures and histories of violence that in public discourse are often regarded as separate, defamiliarizing well-known histories.[2]

---

1 The list of potential examples is long, but some recent family chronicles that deal with questions of perpetration and implication include Per Leo's *Flut und Boden* (2015), a reckoning with the difficult legacy of Nazi crimes; Francesca Melandri's *Sangue Giusto* (2017), which revolves around Italian fascist colonial crimes in Ethiopia; Maria Stepanova's *In Memory of Memory* (2021), which focuses on the legacies of Soviet repression and displacement; or Gabriela Wiener's *Huaco retrato* (2021), which deals with the long shadow of colonialism in Peru.
2 Recent examples of multidirectional family chronicles include Honorée Fannone Jeffers' *The Love Songs of W.E.B. Du Bois* (2021), which interweaves the histories of violence against Indigenous and enslaved people in the United States and Anouar Benmalek's *Fils du Shéol* (2015), which triangulates North African history with the Holocaust and German colonial violence in Namibia.

2 The Anthropocene and the Dendro-Chronicle: *Barkskins* (2016)

The Anthropocene discourse brings with it also a recalibration of the temporal and geographic scales of violence, making visible environmental degradation *as violence* against both humans and non-humans, and forcing us to rethink questions of responsibility (Knittel 2023). This "derangement" (Ghosh 2016) of scalar relations has left its mark on contemporary cultural forms – including, of course, the family chronicle. Indeed, the resurgence of this genre over the past two decades must also be seen in the context of the unfolding environmental crisis. Authors have re-imagined the genre to explicitly incorporate non-human presences and timescales. One particularly salient type in this respect is what one might call the dendro-chronicle, i.e. novels that take the conceit of the family tree literally by interweaving (fictional) family histories with the lives of trees and forests – and the *longue durée* history of deforestation. Annie Proulx's *Barkskins* (2016), Michael Christie's *Greenwood* (2019) or Ash Davidson's *Damnation Spring* (2021) for example, focus on the family histories of North American logging dynasties, charting the interactions between humans and trees across hundreds of years, a timeframe that corresponds to multiple generations in human terms, but a single lifetime for a tree.

Barkskins, for example, begins in the late seventeenth century with the arrival in Canada of two loggers from Paris and traces the story of their descendants up to the present day. It chronicles in detail the establishment of the global timber trading industry and its long-term impact on indigenous peoples and the environment, and in so doing shows how settler colonialism and global capitalist expansion have gone hand in hand with the destruction of indigenous lifeways and native ecosystems. It thus reveals – and makes memorable – the persecution and oppression of humans as historically and structurally bound up with the exploitation of non-humans. The novel features a large cast of more than 100 human characters who represent the myriad different ways in which humans participate in these interconnected histories of violence. Making visible the implications of individual actions on a larger scale, the novel raises the difficult question of human culpability and the "diffusion of agency in structural injustices" (Rothberg 2019, 51). At the same time, *Barkskins* gestures toward a wide perspective that is, in a way, more-than-human: because the human characters pass by quickly, the focus remains primarily on the natural world, and specifically the forests, which may change but are always present.

In its portrayal of generations upon generations devising ever more efficient ways of cutting down trees, *Barkskins* illustrates not only the crushing accumulation over centuries of human destruction of forests and ecosystems but also a more general ability of humans to accelerate processes that would normally take much longer to complete. It does so by way of temporal scaling operations. The novel covers 320 years (1693–2013), but speeds up in the nineteenth century, and then again in the 1960s. Through this acceleration in narrated time, the structure of the novel also reflects two proposed starting points for the Anthropocene, which hold different implications for the responsibility of humans in the destruction of the planet: on the one hand, the industrial revolution (the beginning of capitalist expansion in the late eighteenth century), and on the other hand, the so-called "Great Acceleration" after the Second World War (the beginning of global consumer capitalism). *Barkskins* represents this acceleration of human impact on nature by ramping up the speed of the narrative over the course of the novel. The bulk of the novel takes place *before* the Great Acceleration, and this slow build up reenacts the temporal scale of the devastation. Moreover, by dwelling on the pre-industrial history of deforestation, the novel also alludes to a third possible starting point for the Anthropocene, namely the early seventeenth century, the point at which atmospheric carbon dioxide was at its lowest, owing to the colonial genocide of the Indigenous population of the Americas, which resulted in widespread *re*forestation (see Luciano 2015). Thus, the history of the Anthropocene is the history of European colonization and the trees bear witness to that history.

Barkskins and the other dendro-chronicles are thus explicitly concerned with the ecological dimension and seek to re-imagine the familiar literary form in more-than-human terms. While they may not necessarily bear all the hallmarks of cultural memory narratives (e.g. self-reflexive and/or unreliable narration, meta-commentary on remembrance and representation, etc.), I argue that they do important memory work in that they render the history of deforestation memorable and legible *as violence*, and in so doing they also challenge and make strange or uncanny the narrative of "manifest destiny," of the heroic and pioneering discovery and settlement of North America.

3 Reading for scale in the multidirectional family chronicle: *Ein unsichtbares Land* (2003)

The popularity of the family chronicle as a genre in recent decades speaks to a desire to understand how we as individuals are implicated in larger historical processes. In the German-speaking world, the family chronicle has been an important site of Holocaust memory, and more recently has also provided a space to recover the forgotten or repressed history of German colonialism and to link it to other histories of violence. By and large, however, given that these family novels are primarily conceived as interventions into cultural memory – i.e. focusing on genocidal histories in a self-reflexive, metafictional mode – they tend not to be explicitly concerned with ecological violence.[3] Nevertheless, a reader attuned to the more-than-human scales of the Anthropocene will encounter an "ecological uncanny" even here, which has the potential to transform our understanding of these histories of violence. And here, too, the formal affordances of the family chronicle invite the reader to perform scaling operations, even beyond the explicit intention of the narrative itself.

This can be illustrated with reference to one of the best-known examples of a multidirectional German family chronicle, Stephan Wackwitz's *Ein unsichtbares Land* (2003, transl. *An Invisible Country*, 2005). The novel explores the links between the author's own family and the main traumatic events of twentieth century German history, in particular the Herero genocide in Namibia, WWI and II, and the Holocaust. A prime example of a post-memorial metahistorical family chronicle, it is constructed around material objects such as family photographs and the unpublished memoirs of the author's grandfather, as well as material objects and family heirlooms. Having survived both the Eastern and the Western Front during WWI, in 1921, Wackwitz's grandfather became a pastor in the German town of Anhalt in Poland, which is situated in close proximity to Oświęcim (Auschwitz). In 1933, the family emigrated to South-West Africa where they stayed until 1939. On the way back to Bremerhaven their steamer was intercepted and sunk by the British army, the family were interned in Canada and only returned to Germany after the end of WWII. Purely by coincidence, thus, the Wackwitz family "missed" WWII and the Holocaust (and of course the Herero genocide, since they moved to South-West Africa two decades after its occurrence). Nevertheless, the family history unfolds in close proximity to these events, both through geographical nearness and through ideological implication. This is precisely what the novel is preoccupied with mapping.

The novel as a whole can be seen as a masterful exercise in the historical uncanny, chronicling the incessant intrusion of repressed or silenced aspects of the past into the present. What contributes to this uncanny effect on a formal level is the constant juxtaposition of different temporal and geographic scales, and a collage technique of integrating passages from the grandfather's memoirs and other historical and literary sources, including photographs.

---

[3] A notable exception in this regard is Christof Hamann's *Usambara* (2007), which I explore in greater detail elsewhere (Knittel and Forchieri 2024).

This juxtaposition of different temporalities serves as a productive tool for exploring complex scalar relations and unexpected connections between disparate times and places. The novel's narrated time spans from the Middle Ages to the early 2000s, it connects the local, the national, and the global, and carefully and self-reflexively places the histories of colonialism and the Holocaust as well as other traumatic histories of the twentieth century within a multidirectional constellation.

Throughout, the novel is concerned with the question of implication, particularly with regard to racist and imperialist ideology, which finds expression in the grandfather's autobiography, which Wackwitz quotes at length. While he is heavily critical of the latent racism in these passages, he nevertheless emphasizes the similarities between his grandfather's life and his own and betrays a fascination with and even admiration for his grandfather's adventures in South-West Africa. This highly ambivalent mix of disgust and pride comes to the fore especially in passages that deal with his grandfather's hunting exploits. An avid hunter, the grandfather kept notes on the animals he shot (even as a soldier during WWI), and his memoirs include detailed accounts of his safari-type excursions in Africa.

Wackwitz quotes several of these, notably the gruesome account of shooting a leopard, whose taxidermied skin and head he remembers seeing in his grandfather's study, as well as a story about how his grandfather killed a cobra that was sunning itself on a grave in one of the *Schutztruppen* cemeteries in Namibia, where the perpetrators of the Herero genocide lie buried. The latter episode is heavily overdetermined, as the narrator acknowledges: his grandfather, who had been elsewhere during the genocide visits the graves of the perpetrators, accompanied by a "Herero boy," a descendant of the victims, and unconsciously re-enacts the violence, killing this unsuspecting but highly symbolic creature. The narrator offers an array of symbolic interpretations of this incident, but at no point does he entertain the possibility of reading it literally, as an act of violence against nonhuman nature, and to connect it to the staggering number of dead animals that haunt the novel, including the leopard in the grandfather's study. Nevertheless, the preponderance of these nonhuman presences demands attention and resists purely allegorical or metaphorical interpretation. While the novel does not explicitly reflect on issues of ecology or extinction, its inherent multidirectionality invites an ecological reading that reflects on the direct and indirect connections between colonialism, genocide, and the large-scale devastation of the natural world. Such a reading, moreover, requires a relational approach across scales that significantly complicates our understanding of implication.

My aim in this chapter has been to sketch the affordances of the family chronicle for making visible the multidirectional links between different histories of violence across multiple scales. Reading at the planetary scale is not so much a question of reframing historical atrocities so that they would lose their historical and ethical significance, which would open the door to problematic relativizations. Rather, it is a question of what Clark calls "unframing" our more traditional scales of interpretation in such a way that our implicit assumptions are called productively into question. Such a reading can open up a space in which phenomena belonging to different scales, places, and temporalities can coexist, making strange our habits of remembering.

Stef Craps

Remembering Earth: Countering Planetary Amnesia through the Creative Arts

1 Introduction

This chapter explores the problem of society's environmental memory loss and the potential for literary and other artistic works to counteract it.[1] The psychologist Peter Kahn has coined the term "environmental generational amnesia" to refer to the idea that each generation's perception of what is "normal" in nature is shaped by their own experience rather than an objective standard. As a result, Kahn notes, we forget what we have lost and do not realize the full extent of environmental degradation that has occurred over time. This phenomenon is closely related to the notion of "shifting baseline syndrome," introduced by the marine biologist Daniel Pauly, which describes how people's baseline expectations of the state of the environment are constantly being reset to a lower level as they are born into a world with fewer resources and a more degraded environment than the generation before. Drawing on the work of Ann Rigney and the political theorist Mihaela Mihai, I argue that creative works can play a vital role in reversing these trends and curing our planetary amnesia.

2 Environmental generational amnesia

Each generation is handed a world shaped by their forebears, but seemingly forgets that fact. This kind of generational amnesia was observed in the mid-1990s, independently of one another, by Pauly and Kahn. In a short article published in 1995, the former proposed the term "shifting baseline syndrome" to describe the invisible long-term decline in fish stocks (Pauly 1995). As a fisheries scientist, Pauly noticed that, despite evidence of a sustained reduction in the numbers of certain fish populations, each new generation of scientists appeared to be using the lower levels of abundance and diversity they studied as the new standard. According to Pauly, fisheries scientists do not tend to pay any serious attention to accounts by previous generations that reported seeing marine life in significantly different conditions. As a result of this blind spot, each new generation accepts

---

1 This chapter is a heavily condensed and revised version of Craps 2024.

the diminished world it inherits as normal. Pauly discussed shifting baseline syndrome as an effect afflicting researchers studying fish, but the phenomenon has since been observed in many areas of society beyond the fisheries community.

While shifting baseline syndrome is a concept developed and used in conservation biology, it has an important psychological dimension, which is the focus of Kahn's research. Around the same time as Pauly, Kahn described a similar effect in a very different context. In a psychological study conducted together with his colleague Batya Friedman, he had interviewed inner-city African American children in Houston, Texas – one of the most heavily polluted cities in the US – about their environmental views (Kahn and Friedman 1995). To their surprise, they found that while two thirds of the children understood ideas of air and water pollution in general, only one third believed their own city to be affected. "How could this be?" they wondered. "How could children who know about pollution in general, and live in a polluted city, be unaware of their own city's pollution?" (Kahn and Friedman 1995, 1414). The answer they came up with was that

> to understand the idea of pollution one needs to compare existing polluted states to those that are less polluted. In other words, if one's only experience is with a certain amount of pollution, then that amount becomes not pollution, but the norm against which more polluted states are measured. (Kahn and Friedman 1995, 1414)

Kahn and Friedman went on to suggest that the psychological phenomenon they had observed in these Houston children was not unusual: it could occur whenever individuals lack an experiential baseline by which to judge the health or integrity of nature. Indeed, they ventured, it affects us all from generation to generation (Kahn and Friedman 1995, 1414–1415).

Kahn elaborates on these ideas in a series of later publications. Among other things, he points out that there are both upsides and downsides to environmental generational amnesia. The positive aspect is that "each generation starts afresh, unencumbered mentally by the environmental mistakes and misdeeds of previous generations" (Kahn 2007, 204). The drawback, though, is enormous as we fail to fully comprehend that the nature we experienced during childhood is not the norm but already degraded: "Thus we're constructing our environmental ethic, and structuring our relationship with nature, based on incomplete and partly inaccurate perceptions and understandings" (Kahn 2007, 204). As a result, the sense of urgency required to tackle major environmental issues is diminished. In an article co-authored with Thea Weiss, Kahn identifies environmental generational amnesia as "one of the most pressing psychological problems of our lifetime," whose "insidiousness" makes it particularly challenging to address (Kahn and Weiss 2017, 20).

While he can see "no easy answer" to the question of how to solve the problem of environmental generational amnesia, Kahn does offer some suggestions, which revolve around childhood, as that is where it has its genesis (2002, 110). He recommends "engag[ing] in dialogue with children about what has been lost" and "us[ing] such dialogue to help shape the future" (2002, 111). Such dialogues "provide a means for children to gain information (otherwise unavailable in a direct experiential way) from which they can construct more veridical understandings of the natural world" (2002, 111). Other solutions he proposes besides intergenerational communication include teachers "us[ing] historical diaries and historical novels to convey a sense of the landscape of years past" and setting writing assignments asking students to compare the landscapes described in these texts with their contemporary environments. Moreover, Khan recommends "help[ing] children experience more pristine nature" that can "provide the baseline of ecological health from which children (and societies at large) can construct notions of ecological disease" (2002, 112). However, the tricky question of just how far back one is supposed to go – how "pristine" a state of nature one should aim for – remains unaddressed, as does the equally thorny issue of whether a yearning for a comparatively "unspoiled" past could not be politically suspect or lead to a sense of despair, given the practical impossibility of returning to an assumed pre-industrial Eden.

3 The agency of the aesthetic

But for a passing reference to historical novels (by which Kahn seems to mean novels both from and set in an earlier era), the role the creative arts can play in countering environmental generational amnesia appears to be of little interest to both Khan and Pauly. I will draw on recent research by Rigney and Mihai to argue that literature and the other arts do in fact have a major contribution to make to the project of unforgetting lost environmental knowledge, which not only has a cognitive dimension but is also affective and embodied. In an essay titled "Remaking Memory and the Agency of the Aesthetic," Rigney theorizes the role of artworks in bringing about mnemonic change. In order to find out how histories can change from "inert" or "disabled" to active, from overlooked to not forgotten, she focuses on the ways in which cultural forms contribute to generating memorability (Rigney 2021b, 12). She posits that the creative arts can be seen as "catalysts in creating new memories, supplementing what has been documented with imaginative power and creatively using cultural forms to generate vibrant (if not always literally true) stories that may then be picked up and reworked in other disciplines" (2021b, 12). Rigney insists on the importance of studying what happens in "the intimacy of reading and viewing," which, she maintains, is as crucial as "larger-scale social and cultural developments" (2021b, 12). Taking her cue from Rita Felski, she argues that the artful deployment of media can help create new sites of memorability by enchanting the reader or viewer: "the role of the arts in the remaking of memory [. . .] derives from their power to enchant; specifically, to capture our attention through mastery of a given medium" (2021b, 15). The use of complex forms that disrupt habits of memory can provide an opportunity for unfamiliar experiences to register as memorable: "Remaking collective memory begins with the disruption of old habits in the micropolitics of reading, viewing and reacting, with repeated small movements gradually acquiring larger-scale consequences" (2021b, 18).

Rigney's emphasis on the enchantment of artworks that seduces people into stepping beyond the comfort of habitual patterns of perception as a starting point for transformations in collective memory resonates strongly with the conceptual apparatus Mihai employs in her book *Political Memory and the Aesthetics of Care: The Art of Complicity and Resistance* (2022) to account for the ways in which certain artworks can open up a space for remembering and imagining differently. Mihai contends that literature, cinema, and other artforms can *"seductively sabotage* our attachments to dominant – comfortable and reductive – narratives about the past" (2022, 9). Thanks to their capacity to provide a powerful prosthetic experience and to pleasurably sabotage reductive discourses, certain artworks have the potential to create "'epistemic friction' between shared, entrenched, exclusionary mnemonic habits, on the one hand, and alternative visions of historical temporality, on the other" (2022, 9). Mihai reads these artists' work of seductive sabotage as "a work of *mnemonic care* for the health of the hermeneutical space of memory – one that is delivered aesthetically" (2022, 9). She refers to the artists in question as "caring refuseniks," that is, dissenting memory agents who reject reductive narratives and who nurture a plural space of memory-making (2022, 62).

The case studies Rigney and Mihai consider in their respective publications have little to do with the phenomenon that concerns us here: the former investigates the (un)forgetting of colonial soldiers in European armies during the First World War; the latter (challenges to) the double erasure of the realities of pervasive complicity and impure resistance in the aftermath of political violence in France, Romania, and South Africa. Even so, the theoretical frameworks they advance can also illuminate other cases, including, it seems to me, the problem of environmental generational amnesia. Like the artworks Rigney and Mihai look at, artistic engagements with this intractable psychological phenomenon such as Robert Macfarlane and Jackie Morris's illustrated poetry collections *The Lost Words: A Spell Book* (2017) and *The Lost Spells* (2020) and Maya Lin's ongoing multi-platform memorial project *What Is Missing?* (2010–) can be seen to perform vital mnemonic care-work, "the work of caring refusal" (Mihai 2022, 238), in identifying and rejecting shifting baselines of ecological health and recovering forgotten (or about to be forgotten) cognitive, affective, and sensory knowledge of past environmental conditions.[2] By engaging the intellect, the emotions, and the body, they subvert the public's investment in its own ignorance about the true state of the world, destabilize hegemonic memory regimes, and hold out hopes for a liveable future.

The Lost Words and its sequel *The Lost Spells* came about as an attempt to restore nature words to the vocabulary of British children after the *Oxford Junior Dictionary* decided to drop a number of such words from its pages, in a clear example of shifting baseline syndrome in action. Macfarlane and Morris responded by evoking the wonders of nature through enchanting verse and beautiful illustrations that together seek to conjure lost, or nearly lost, words and species back into our everyday lives. By insisting on the importance of naming and knowing nature, both books appeal to the reader to engage more fully with their environment. They allow children and adults alike to see the world anew and remind them of wat they lose when they let it slip away. Selling hundreds of thousands of copies worldwide, *The Lost Words* and *The Lost Spells* have effectively begun a grassroots movement to re-enchant the world and re-wild the lives of both children and adults. An eloquent protest at the loss of the natural world around us, they have managed to make the very words that were not being used enough anymore to merit inclusion in a children's dictionary central to the cultural conversation once again. In a powerful demonstration of the role of the creative arts in effecting mnemonic change – or rather, counteracting it – through enchantment, the books' runaway success has helped shift the baseline for what is considered normal in nature across the UK and far beyond back upwards, if only ever so slightly.

What Is Missing? makes a no less determined attempt in this direction. Its creator is best known for designing Washington, DC's Vietnam Veterans Memorial, which honours all members of the US armed forces who died as a result of their service in the Vietnam War. More recently, though, Lin has turned her attention to more-than-human losses. In 2010 she launched a website called *What Is Missing?*, which serves as a global memorial to the planet. Its home page features a map covered in colourful dots, many of which represent endangered or extinct species. Clicking on these dots leads the visitor to images or videos of, and stories

---

2 For a more in-depth analysis of these and other works as creative responses to our amnesiac condition, see Craps 2024.

about, those species. There is also an interactive page allowing people to add their own memories to the map, or stories they were told by their parents or grandparents about *their* memories of the way it used to be: something they have personally witnessed diminish or disappear from the natural world. The project's goal, which is made explicit on the "about" page, is to create "a collective memory of the planet" that can help wake people up to environmental generational amnesia (Lin 2010). Engaging with Lin's interactive archive documenting extinct and endangered life forms and ruined environments is a powerful experience for visitors. However, *What Is Missing?* seeks not so much to overwhelm the visitor with grief for what has been lost as to spur the transition to a more sustainable world by offering them "steps each one of us can take in our own lives to help make a difference" (Lin 2010). While grief is an unavoidable part of Lin's memorial project, so too are hope, advocacy, and action. Beyond lamenting environmental destruction, *What Is Missing?* includes conservation and restoration success stories as well as a comprehensive set of solutions, a "Greenprint" showing how we could yet forge a different path and envisage a viable alternative future.

4 Conclusion

To avoid sleepwalking into environmental collapse, we have to confront the problem of environmental generational amnesia, which can be seen to sustain the Anthropocene. It is vital that society at large wake up to the ramifications of our impaired vision. Zoomed in too tightly to see things for what they really are, we need to ensure that memories of past environmental conditions are kept alive in the social fabric, while remaining vigilant not to succumb to a politically dubious and debilitating nostalgia. Acknowledgement of nature's past abundance and diversity has to go beyond mere cognition and into the realms of affect and embodied experience for it to be effective. This is where literature and art come in: they can make present and felt what is absent, with stories, images, and sounds that are corporally sensed and that openly engage emotions. Works such as Macfarlane and Morris's books and Lin's memorial project can be interpreted as instances of environmental mnemonic care-work that enchant the public, seducing it away from its habitual ways of seeing, thinking, and feeling to remember and imagine differently. Through their aesthetic agency, they help shatter our environmental generational amnesia with a view to halting the creeping destruction of the natural environment and safeguarding the habitability of the planet for future generations.

Jesseka Batteau

Post-Religious Memory and the Agency of the Aesthetic: 'Small acts of repair' in Lucas Rijneveld's *The Discomfort of Evening*

1 Introduction

In 2020, Lucas Rijneveld (formerly Marieke Lucas Rijneveld) made headlines by being not only the first Dutch author, but also the youngest author ever to win the International Booker Prize. Rijneveld's debut novel, *The Discomfort of Evening* (2020 [2018]) – translated into English by Michele Hutchison – follows Jas, a ten-year-old girl growing up in an orthodox Protestant farming family, whose brother Matthies drowns in a skating accident. Overwhelmed by grief, the family slowly falls apart. The parents, emotionally stunted and unable to provide the solace and comfort needed by their children, leave Jas and her siblings to fend for them-selves. The children drift off into ever more dangerous rituals in an attempt to soothe their pain and to understand the finality of death. Through the eyes of Jas, the reader is presented with the stark realities of an orthodox religious upbring-ing and life on a dairy farm; emotional and physical neglect, cruelty and violence, and the repeated transgression of bodily and sexual boundaries of not only the human protagonists, but also those of the more-than-human (hamsters, toads, crickets, rabbits, chickens and cows) make for difficult, yet memorable reading.

Rijneveld, who identifies as non-binary, wrote his autobiographical novel in richly poetic language described by national and international reviewers as in-credibly powerful and truly transformative. His language is described as "fero-ciously foaming" (*NRC Handelsblad*), as "electric" (*The Times*), "exhilarating" (*The Independent*), "intensely raw, shockingly graphic, and memorable" (*Financial Times*) and as "shudderingly vivid" (*Literary Review*). In an interview in *The Guardian*, Ted Hodgkinson, chair of the International Booker Prize jury, noted that the novel "absolutely arrests the attention":

> there's something about the inquisitive gaze, that poetic perspective [. . .], the ability to see in the everyday something remarkable, extraordinary. Even though it is a book that takes you through some difficult and unsettling cases, it has that ability to make the world new. (Flood 2020)

To make the world anew. What is this mysterious faculty of literature that enables readers to see things, whether past, present, or future, in a completely new light? Following Felski (2008), Ann Rigney coins the term "enchantment" which helps to explain the unique role of the arts to captivate and help us to identify with others, with other pasts (Rigney 2021b, 17). Rigney points out that cultural carriers such as literary texts indeed have the power to move and transport the reader through a combination of distinctive characteristics connected to form, style, and content. For Rigney, this distinctiveness, the arresting qualities of literature, can be associated with its "writability," that is to say, the way particular textual constellations have the potential to unsettle readers and take them into unfamiliar territory (Rigney 2021b, 14).

This seems to be precisely what is at hand in the case of Rijneveld's remarkable debut. A story of a traumatized religious past, set in a marginal religious environment few are familiar with nowadays, was able to not only traverse Dutch cultural and social boundaries, but also capture the attention of international audiences near and far. What is at play here? In what follows, I investigate the beginnings of an answer, arguing that the unique poetic force of Rijneveld's novel, that is to say, its 'singularity as cultural carrier' (Rigney 2021b, 14), has the potential to subtly shift the narrative of secular liberation and make visible lives previously unseen.

2 Memorable readings: bovine metaphors and religious dogma

The combination of hard-to-bear scenes, the exceptionally poetic language, and the vulnerability of Jas, a child systematically denied human care and warmth, is perhaps where the arresting features of this novel lie. Jas' narration is rich with metaphors, but as the reviewer of the *New York Times* points out, most are bovine: "she cannot tether herself to anything human" (Sehgal 2020). Jas can only find corollaries in the non-human, and I would say in the deeply *inhumane*, world of dairy farming. This is underlined by the way the parents treat their children; having no language for human emotions and affection, the children are handled and spoken to as if they were livestock. A good example is the opening scene of the novel in which Jas' neglect is artfully connected to the 'bovine':

> That morning, Mum covered us one by one in udder ointment to protect us from the cold. It came out of a yellow Bogena tin and was normally used to prevent dairy cows' teats from getting cracks, calluses and cauliflower-like lumps. [. . .] It smelled of stewed udder, the

thick slices I'd sometimes find cooking in a pan of stock on our stove, sprinkled with salt and pepper. They filled me with horror, just like the reeking ointment on my skin. Mum pressed her fat fingers into our faces like the round cheeses she patted to check whether the rind was ripening. (Rijneveld 2020, 3)

Here, the application of udder ointment becomes an entryway into the force field of neglect and violence, finding affective expression in the disruptive complexity of the bovine metaphor. The ointment itself is meant for dairy cows whose udders are often swollen and infected due to intensive milking, but this is applied to the *faces* of the children. The smell horrifies Jas, reminding her of the udders – severed, meaty body parts – cooked and eaten by her family. In this way, Jas' suffering is directly connected to the violent existence and deaths of dairy cows (who only lactate when they give birth to a calf). The quotation ends with the children becoming dairy produce themselves: the round cheeses that form the core of the family business. This powerful and disruptive technique, revealing human and non-human suffering as part of the same structures of violence, returns in many forms in Rijneveld's novel: from the way Jas' father treats her constipation, to the cruel sexual game played by the siblings on an insemination machine, and the brutal slaughter of all the dairy cows because of the outbreak of foot-and-mouth disease.

The fact that many of Jas' thoughts and deeds are informed by the alienating dogma of orthodox religion is another feature that makes this novel stand out. The Biblical language innocently reproduced by Jas has a defamiliarizing effect on the reader, and her childish attempts to comprehend and apply Bible texts and religious customs in her life are heartbreaking. For example, during a silent family visit to the grave of her brother Matthies, Jas reminds herself that, as the Bible says, one day all graves will break open, and the dead will return:

I'd always found that a scary thought: I pictured all the bodies coming out of the earth and marching through the village like a procession of biology models, with chattering teeth and hollow eyes. [. . .] I remember the lines from Corinthians that Granny once read to me when I was worried we'd no longer recognise Matthies: 'How foolish! What you sow does not come to life unless it dies.' [. . .] I didn't understand why we'd had to plant Matthies in the ground like a seed if above the earth he'd have been able to blossom into something wonderful." (Rijneveld 2020, 215)

Focalized through Jas, the reader sees the world in the cold and ruthless light of orthodox Protestantism which offers no solace for those mourning the passing of their loved ones.

3 Mnemonic grafting

For Dutch readers, the literary ingredients of Rijneveld's novel ring some iconic post-religious memory bells. The epigraph of the novel is a poem by one of the most celebrated Dutch writers of the twentieth century, Jan Wolkers, whose oeuvre and media persona played a major role in the construction and mediation of the remembrance of the religious past in the Netherlands (Batteau 2022). Born in the 1920s, Wolkers rose to fame in the 1960s and 1970s with his many autobiographical stories and novels about a repressive Protestant childhood. His shockingly straightforward literary style and his preoccupation with sex, death, cruelty, and violence made for memorable reading for generations of Dutch readers, offering a shared narrative framework for processing and understanding the rapid process of secularization taking place in Dutch society. This narrative can be summarized in the following manner: a young boy grows up in a repressive orthodox protestant environment and comes to resist his religious background through the denouncement of religious dogma and the ridicule of the father (who stands for religious authority). As an adult, the post-religious male individual celebrates and expresses his liberated status through uninhibited (hetero)sexuality and artistic success. It has become an iconic narrative for the Dutch, or as I have argued following Diana Taylor (2003), a key *cultural scenario*, that is, a culturally specific imaginary offering a fixed set of possibilities for dealing with recurring conflicts or crises that can be represented and acted out again and again in different medial contexts (Batteau 2022). The cultural scenario carries resemblances to other concepts coined by cultural memory scholars such as "schemata" (Erll 2011b) or "narrative templates" (Wertsch 2002) all pointing toward a basic mnemonic dynamic by which particular stories are subsumed into more generic patterns (Rigney 2021b, 13).

Rijneveld's debut is strongly grafted upon the Dutch post-religious scenario represented by Wolkers. The connection can be found not only in paratextual signals such as the epigraph, but also in many scenes and topoi evoked in the novel itself. A central example can be found in the references made to the slaughter of Jas' rabbit, and her fear that her father will not only kill her beloved pet but is also planning to sacrifice his children. This theme of violence perpetrated by the father strongly evokes a well-known story of Wolkers, "De achtste plaag" [The eighth plague] in which the young protagonist, suffering under the tyranny of his orthodox Protestant father, discovers that his pet rabbit has been killed and will be served for Easter dinner. He finds the pelt of the rabbit in the shed:

> Against the wall hung the rabbit skin on a nail, inside out. [. . .] There were holes in the head where the eyes had been. The skin was frayed at the muzzle, and black hair was pro-

truding. It must have been forcibly torn off the head. My teeth suddenly felt very large and awkward behind my upper lip. (Wolkers 1964, 13, my translation)

In Rijneveld's novel, this motif of rabbit slaughter returns many times. In the first chapter, Jas notices her father is feeding her rabbit more food than usual, and a rope with a noose has recently appeared in the attic. She fears her rabbit may be being fattened for Christmas dinner: "Maybe, I thought, Dad wanted us to watch: maybe it would happen if we sinned. I briefly pictured my rabbit hanging broken-necked from the rope in the attic, behind Matthies' bed, so that our father could skin it more easily" (Rijneveld 2020, 13). When the family vet brings the news of Matthies death, Jas and her sister are being bathed, and the mother forgets her daughters as they get out of bath. Jas makes sure they dry themselves off thoroughly, thinking of her father's joke: "Dad sometimes joked that our skin would come loose if we stayed in the bath for too long and that he'd nail it to the wooden wall of the shed, next to the pelts of the skinned rabbits" (Rijneveld 2020, 21).

The many sexually explicit, often cruel, scenes between the siblings and with animals also echo episodes from Wolkers' work. Through clear para- and intertextual signals, Rijneveld's debut firmly positions itself in an already existing post-religious narrative, thus allowing itself to be heard and interpreted as socially relevant. However, the grafting of a story upon an existing cultural scenario works *two ways*. It allows for visibility, for the story to be heard and find an audience, but on the other hand, it also constitutes a stage or platform where the *deviation* from this iconic narrative can be performed to maximum effect. In other words, Rijneveld takes familiar literary post-religious ingredients and then proceeds to tell a different story.

4 Loss, vulnerability and the micropolitics of reading

Wolkers' oeuvre is very much a victorious narrative, one narrating the secular refutation of religion and the emergence of the sexually liberated (male) individual (Batteau 2022, 232–233, 316). The ingredients of this heroic story are already visible in the furiously defiant stance of the protagonist in "The eighth plague," who takes revenge on the father. In contrast, in Rijneveld's novel, a young girl is crushed by her orthodox Protestant environment: Jas does not survive the ordeal. This narrative of loss has something to say about the visibility and agency of vulnerable persons within orthodox religious communities of past and present.

Up until now, the post-religious narrative of liberation in the Netherlands has been written and performed by men. Post-religious female perspectives are absent in the Dutch novels and stories of the 1960s and 1970s – women have only subordinate roles to play as by-figures. In Rijneveld's novel, we suddenly see the world through the eyes of one of these disregarded sisters. In contrast to the usual voices of defiant male protagonists, we hear the tender, compassionate voice of Jas, who is seeking to love and be loved. What is perhaps most poignant is her small, futile attempts at soothing her pain and suffering, and 'healing' her family through small compulsive rituals: the toads she keeps hidden under her desk whom she urges to copulate to rekindle her parents' affection for each other, the thumb tack she inserts into her navel to remind herself that "I don't want to go to God, but to myself" (Rijneveld 2020, 93); her fantasies shared with her younger sister of being rescued and escaping to the 'other side'; her self-induced constipation and her refusal to take off her coat. Where Wolkers' stories fit into a pattern of heroic refutation of institutional religion, Rijneveld brings a different post-religious discursive register to the table, namely one of loss and vulnerability. Loss reveals who we truly are, according to Jas. In a harrowing chapter describing the horrific mass killing of the cows and calves due to an outbreak of foot-and-mouth disease (which indeed took place in the 90s in the Netherlands), Jas is overwhelmed by grief: "We find ourselves in loss and we are who we are – vulnerable beings, like stripped starling chicks that fall naked from their nests and hope they'll be picked up again. I cry for the cows, I cry for the three kings [i.e., the three siblings, a reference to the three wise men from the east who paid tribute to the infant Jesus, JB]" (Rijneveld 2020, 198–199).

The question arises if and how such a narrative of painful vulnerability may alter a firmly entrenched post-religious cultural scenario. A beginning of an answer can be found in Ann Rigney's reflections on the multiscalar nature of memory. Rigney points out that "small, qualitative changes occurring at the intimate scale of reading" have a strong transformational potential once they start to circulate and resonate in other sites and media (Rigney 2021b, 18). In reference to Hirsch and Spitzer's "small acts of repair" (2015) and Goldfarb's "politics of small things" (2012), Rigney underlines the importance of the small-scale: "[r]emaking collective memory begins with the disruption of old habits in the micropolitics of reading, viewing and reacting, with repeated small movements gradually acquiring larger-scale consequences" (Rigney 2021b, 18).

Jas' "small acts of repair," seemingly futile within the setting of the story, might indeed, through the micropolitics of reading, contribute to a new shading of the dominant narrative of secular liberation. At the very least, they open our eyes to a more subtle and complex understanding of our relation to the religious past, one in which we come to see that the 'struggle against institutional religion' is non-linear and subject to gendered inequalities. We are made aware that those in positions of vulnerability – most often women and children – are not only at risk of being forgotten but are also denied the emancipation reserved for their male counterparts. Whether or not Rijneveld's story will be able to resonate as part of more inclusive post-religious narratives is of course dependent on the societal and medial configurations in which his book is read and circulated, a question that certainly deserves more investigation. The great (inter)national success of the novel suggests that its aesthetic and emotional power does indeed have the potential to change our understanding of the religious past and in so doing, gently make the world anew.

Ann Dooley
Writing for the Birds: Early Irish Lyrics and the Unravelling of Cultural Memory

My aim in this chapter is to think about the status of literary genres in memory studies. I place my sample genre, early Irish 'nature' lyric, in a continuum of influence – as an archive that has been made to resurface and to enter a contemporary Irish frame, both in elite literary form, but also, and more importantly for the context of memory studies, as an instrument in a popularizing social movement. I suggest ways in which one might counter the 'solitary speaker' limitations of lyric address. One can acknowledge what it has now become – a banner, a cultural splint, or, more harshly, an excuse for a green nation identity – and then play it backwards to its beginnings, to expose deeply conflicted group identities poised in social time between writing and oral expression. I see this back-walking as a corrective to presentist bias in memory studies.

> "The scribe in the woods."
> *Dom-fharcai fidbaide fál*
> *fom-chain loíd loin, lúad nád cél;*
> *húas mo lebrán, in línech,*
> *fom-chain trírech inna n-én.*
>
> *Fomm-chain cói menn, medar mass,*
> *hi mbrot glass de dingnaib doss.*
> *Debrath! nom-Choimmdiu-coíma:*
> *caín-scribaimm fo roída ross.*
> (Murphy 1956, 4, 172)[1]

[A wall of trees surrounds me, a blackbird's song serenades me; above my lined booklet, the bird-chorus sings for me.

A fine cuckoo sings for me in joyful loveliness from the green shelter of the bushes. By the God I swear by, the Lord protects me! beautifully I write under the forest cover.]

The Third Policeman
A bird sang a solo from nearby, a cunning blackbird in a dark hedge giving thanks in his native language. I listened and agreed with him completely. (Flann O'Brien 156)

---

1 The poem is found in the margin of a mid-ninth-century manuscript, St. Gallen MS 904, a copy of Priscian's Latin Grammar; with its numerous glosses in Latin and Irish it is a schoolroom teaching text (Ó Corráin 2017, 1040–1041)

These brief examples of Irish writing obviously echo each other but are widely different in time, one a ninth-century lyric, the other a mid-twentieth satire. Early monastic lyrics attesting to a love of the natural world have had many subsequent admirers and speak powerfully to a contemporary audience. A cloud of 'Celtic New Age' witnesses now invokes the genre as an essential Irish cultural-action environmental charter.[2] Transformation and mediation of cultural artifacts over time are, of course, only to be expected. Cultural memory studies often trace a line of communication that is presentist and of necessity future-oriented: as events and their frames constantly mutate as they move forward, often by small steps, a critical threshold is reached where it may seem irrelevant to examine their point of departure. A medievalist might worry if it is at all legitimate to use the terms of cultural memory to excavate a richer social context for an early Irish poem. Do such poems belong in "accidental archives" – too small, too discrete, or too past and gone to matter – or are they "vibrant/vibrating objects"?[3] In a memory studies frame foregrounding thinking collectively it should be possible to explore all temporal cultural interactions. Walking backward can reveal crucial fissures in cultural time in the social moment of a cultural text's genesis.

Rigney's rich memory studies dossier has delimited (2017, 2021b) a place for aesthetics in activating collective memories. Exposing literary studies to the socially significant body of critical memory work, however, runs a serious risk of dissipating its impact and critical integrity. Rigney questions liaisons with lyric poetry – one of the most difficult genres to associate with collective memory enterprises since the "romantic turn" makes the reading of any ego-based poetry inwardly referential, hence less amenable to a future collective use.[4] Irish cultural contexts, however, may offer an easement into poetry whether in Irish or in English in its retention of a shared oral performative role, for both pleasure and meaning.[5]

It is easy enough to place Flann O'Brien's novel's evocation of the older blackbird. A scholar of early Irish language himself, Ó Núalláin's love for that language and literature was deep-seated, even if his mockery scalded ineffectual efforts by

---

2 Paidrigín Ni Uallacháin's recording, 'Songs of the Scribe' (2011), to list a scholarly/popular example, adapts the Seamus Heaney version of our poem in this environment. She also uses St. Brigit as a goddess meme (2023). Imogen Stuart's sculpture of the monk's cat, Pangur Ban, was the first representation of a figure who has achieved quasi-cult status in numerous re-imaginings in children's park settings.
3 I use here terms deployed by Rigney and Zirra in Rigney's robust response to Zirra's bold justification of lyric as linking the human and materialities (Zirra 2017, Rigney 2017).
4 Assmann's (2011) linkage of the past as narrative form allows little space for lyric.
5 In my childhood, most rural Irish families made ample use of broadsheet ballads and anthologies for communal entertainment.

the political class of the thirties to restore the Irish language as the major unifying ideal of the nation. The joke is on all participants: the blackbird is preposterously concert-performing in Irish: but what he is really articulating is known only to his avian self, even as he is too confidently appropriated by the condemned hero as a symbol for hope. We may think we know what the subaltern speaking 'other' says but often we don't or can't: the citizen-hero pays lip service to 'native language' but hides his non-comprehension by simply paying clichéd tribute to it.

Easy too to locate the blackbirds that follow on in modern Irish literature: Heaney, for example, celebrates these singers as uninhibited freedom speakers in a lyric free space of nature: southern Irish blackbirds channel the monastic blackbirds of his native north and offer an access to the grounds of a deepest self;[6] they link back to a stable cultural world at the bottom of the confused historical palimpsest, to a ground that seems "naturally Irish" in more ways than the present one. On the level of a sustaining cultural memory, Heaney's allegiance to an early Irish monastic world view assumes a precious importance as he moves to the end of his life.

The timespan O'Brien (Ó Núalláin) to Heaney is short but, nevertheless, it is instructive to note the speed with which new Irish systems of relevance emerge – from social language policy to post-Christian and neo-pagan identity coding – even in this short period. In these examples a mediating energy imbues the old Irish blackbird with vatic force.[7] His voice has travelled a long way but leads back to my original question: are we not equally obliged to unravel change from the beginning to better place the old Irish poet in his world?

Most powerfully impressed in our poem is the extreme emphasis on the speaker's individual consciousness. It aggressively pushes away all human communication to emphasize that all remaining flows are vertical: ear up to birds, the tree-tops, God. A flow is first forced between birds and man by the farcing of verbs with ego-infixes (*dom-fharcai* etc) and the poem ends split open (*Debrath*) in truth-assertion and recognition that God has indeed gifted him with that skill that transforms utterance, the far-reaching technology of writing. But on the cleared ground there is not even a writing shed in sight to give a sense that the speaker is part of any community.[8]

---

6 Heaney's translation of the poem is in *Human Chain* (2011). His many other blackbirds are found throughout his works.
7 "The Blackbird of Glanmore" in *Human Chain* assumes a dark vaticination, however.
8 Spring/Summer poems abound in early Irish. In an earlier one in native Irish metre, "Cetamon," an overflowing riot of summer effects integrates the human casually into the general happiness. Some effects here indicate a courtly setting rather than a monastic one.

However, in the glossed manuscript itself and in its wealth of *marginalia* a lively support group springs to life (Strachan and Stokes 1910, xii; Ó Corráin 2017, 1041): Fergus, Ruaidri, Finguine, Donngus, Cobtach, Mail Gaimrid, Mailecáin and Mochoe appear. The scriptorium master would seem to be a Mael Brigte. Some proudly localize themselves: Mochoe of Nendruim, Coirbre and his friend (*d' inis Maddoc dund .i. meisse & Coirbre*).[9] On the bottom of p. 202 (the page before our poem) a scribe prays to St Patrick and Brigit '*. . . thas ar Mael Brigte namba olcc a menma frim arin scribund roscribad in dul so'* (. . . on Mael Brigte that he may not be angry with me for the writing written this session).[10] Is he having regrets for adding the verse on the overleaf, or is the wrath of the master directed at another suggestive metrical line to Maelecáin on p. 203: '*Maraith serc céin mardda aithne a Maelecáin* (O Maelecáin, love lasts as long as knowledge)? In p. 203 itself the scribe has written four separate invocations to St. Brigit as if to further assuage the wrath of Brigit's stern devotee. She is invoked sixteen times in all, far exceeding other Irish saints like Patrick. A cluster of three invocations to a St. Diormitius may indicate provenance from the monastery of Castledermot (some ten miles from Brigit's great abbey) in Kildare and all this suggest the locality in which the manuscript was used before its journey to St. Gallen.

The solitude invoked, then, is unreal and speaks to an aspirational ascetic model of awareness, a drawing apart from society basic to a monastic calling and manifest most dramatically to the world of the early Middle Ages in the Irish love of peregrination. The chattiness of the manuscript's *marginalia* notwithstanding, Irish monasticism maintained a strong attraction to eremetic separation: grammatically and spatially the poem describes an act of enclosure. Separation is linked with the cuckoo as in a clichéd trait about the Irish in a list found in several Carolingian manuscripts:[11] *cuculus cantando scottos iter ire perurget* [the cuckoo in its song urges the Irish to go on a journey.]

The whole written poetic scene describes a classical *locus amoenus* assemblage constituted by the enclosed forest space and the bird song. Nagy has outlined the long persistence of the triad, trees in springtime leaf, bird song and poetry, stressing its deep continuity by placing side by side examples from the *Odyssey* and later medieval Provencal song (Nagy 1996). Pastoral frames act as the pre-conditions or even the movers of the poet's utterance/performance.

Inherent in this tradition is the idea of movement, of inspiration, composition, and transmission in which the crafted human song is embedded. From Pe-

---

9 Inis Mochta, in Co. Louth, by this time an Armagh-related monastery (Ó Riain, 300).
10 Note the little literary flourish of a *figura etymologica, scribund roscribad,* in his *mea culpa.*
11 Paris BN, MS 8069, St. Gallen MS 644, Weissenborn MS 103. (Buecheler and Riese 1869, 288; Warren 2019).

nelope to Chaucer's pilgrim our poet's blackbird joins this group. In all, the Spring trope links human and natural utterance in a riot of communication. Armed with his little book (*lebrán*), his monastic badge of cultural identity, he not just voices but actively memorializes this joint praise. A case can be made that the *lebrán* is not a psalter, or a grammatical treatise or any more familiar Irish writing product. It is probably the *libellus* which Alcuin describes as an essential part of a student's educational program. First, he learns the fundamentals of Latin grammar, then he studies composition, *epistolae* and *libelli*, short texts composed by the student himself on given topics; only then does he turn to the study of Scripture.[12]

The community in which the poet operates is a multi-stratum language community, a knowledge world sturdily in line with other continental learning sites in being based on a learned Latin background. Notker reports of Charlemagne that his custom was, on visiting the school of Clement, the Irish scholar *peregrinus*, to summon the pupils to him that they might show him their own *epistolas* and *carmina* out of their *libelli*.[13]

But more specifically, Irish blackbirds are in Irish books because Irish monks inherited and made their own a long line of scientific enquiry into natural history, a tradition beginning in Herodotus and the pre-Socratics, thence to the Christian west via Pliny's *Natural History*, Virgil's *Georgics*, and, finally, through Isidore of Seville's *Etymologiae* into Ireland. This is Isidore on the blackbird: *Merula antiquitus medula vocabantur, eo quod modulet. Alii merulam aiunt vocatum quia sola volat, quasi mera volans* (XII. 7, 69). [The blackbird was once called *medula* because it sings. Others called it *merula*, because it flies alone.][14] This same gloss is offered in the late ninth-century Irish *Cormac's Glossary* (*Cormac*, no. 890).

For the early Irish monk-poet then, there is no 'natural' world. There are birds and men that are already subsumed into the discourse of a Christian Latin environment of learning. He may write flawlessly in his own language, but he must use a new Latin-derived metre to express himself. Like all of us, learning has already de-cultured him out of himself.

---

12 *eMGH*, Epistola,161, 259–260. One Irish example of this kind of monastic composition on a bird is the Hisperic Latin 'Rubisca,' (Herren 1987, 79–87).
13 Haefele 1959, Ch. 3.
14 Isidore *Etymologiae* XII, 7, 69. The latter explanation occurs in Varro (*Linguistica* 5.76); Isidore likely got it from Quintilian (*Institutiones* I, 6, 38).

Emilie Pine

Affiliation and Mediation: Memory in Performance in *An Old Song Half Forgotten* by Deirdre Kinahan

This essay considers what theatre offers our understanding of the processes of memory, both individual and cultural, and what in turn the subject and forms of memory offer to theatre makers and audiences. Theatrical performances are not just a leap of faith, but a feat of memory as actors remember lines, cues, accents, character, when to pause for laughter, and when to pause for tears. There are other ways, too, that theatre and memory overlap, not least in the inbuilt repetition of theatrical and memory performances and the roles of mediation and affiliation in both. As Marvin Carlson argues

> theatre, as a simulacrum of the cultural and historical process itself [. . .] has always provided society with the most tangible records of its attempts to understand its own operations. It is the repository of cultural memory, but, like the memory of each individual, it is also subject to continual adjustment and modification as the memory is recalled in new circumstances and contexts. (Carlson 2004, 2)

As I will argue, these continual adjustments enable theatrical work not just to rehearse the past, but to build new cultural memory through staging personal stories and including the audience in the co-production of meaning and remembrance. As Ann Rigney puts it, "aesthetically crafted works help to shift, or at least temporarily suspend, the imagined boundary between 'us' and the 'other'" (Rigney 2021b, 15) enabling a new space of possibility.

*

My friend Alan is a theatre reviewer and one rainy spring evening he texts me to say he has a free ticket to see a new play, *An Old Song Half Forgotten* by Deirdre Kinahan, do I want to come? And so I meet him at the Peacock, the studio space of Ireland's National Theatre, and as we take our seats and the lights go down I think, as I have thought so many times before, that I have no idea what is about to happen.

When the lights come up, we are met with a simple set – a long bench and an archway. There are two actors onstage, and a musician. One of the actors is older, Bryan Murray, a well-known face from Irish stage and television. He begins to speak as the character James, recalling memories of his childhood and early adulthood, viewed from the perspective of a man towards the end of his life. Mediating these memories, the second actor, Matthew Malone, acts out multiple roles: confidant, James's younger self, his friends, and his mother.

> JAMES: Front door. Front door. Big Blue Front Door.
>
> BOTH: I can remember.
>
> JAMES: I can remember way back. I can remember the Alley. I can remember Danny. But yesterday? No. Yesterday is all a fog. Yesterday is empty. Yesterday is gone.
>
> YOUNG JAMES: I am your yesterday. I am my yesterday when we write it all down.
>
> JAMES: Write it. Keep it. Keep my life. (Kinahan 2023, 162)

James seeks to create a permanent written record that can stand against the 'fog' of waning memory. What Kinahan demonstrates, however, for both personal and cultural memory, is that memory can't be *kept*, but only performed and re-performed. That is, theatre shows us that memory is an act, not an object. The commitment to bringing memory to life is central to many memory plays, which can be defined as having both "thematic attention to remembered (or repressed) pasts [. . . and a] memoried structure: repetition [. . .] echoing, overlap & simultaneity" (Malkin 1999, 1).[1] When James confesses to emptiness, he highlights the fragility of personal memory. Theatre, however, has the ability to resist that fragility, in this instance through using a dialogic structure. As James and Young James together reconstruct childhood, we see memory embodied as "a dynamic process, striving to establish continuity between past and present selves" (Favorini 2008, 9). This striving is an effort – of actors, production team, and audience – in co-imagining the past and, when Young James says "I am your yesterday", Kinahan shows how this effort can lead to a successful memory performance. There are, however, inevitable moments of failure. Theatre is, as Favorini argues, only "a placeholder for memory" (2008, 7).

∗

We are about ten minutes into the play when Murray stumbles over a line. Because it is opening night, I think perhaps he hasn't quite settled into the show yet. Then he stumbles over another line and, after a miniscule pause, Malone corrects him. Perhaps 'corrects' isn't quite the right word – Malone helps Murray get to the right phrase. Murray nods, and then Malone carries the story on.

---

1 'Memory play' was adopted by theatre scholars following Tennessee Williams' description of the autobiographical work, *The Glass Menagerie*, as "my memory play." For further definition and discussion of memory plays see Favorini 2007 and Jacobs 2002.

I watch as Malone watches Murray. I see him take Murray's arm and guide him to a chair. I see Malone set up cues for Murray's next lines. I see Malone supply missing words and lines. I slowly realize that this play is not just about a character who has a hazy recollection of the past. This play is about this actor, it is about Bryan Murray, it is built for him, because he is living with early-stage Alzheimer's.[2]

∗

Favorini, in *Memory in Play*, argues that sitting in a theatre space and watching a live performance, "organize[s] us into a group of rememberers" (Favorini 2008, 133). This statement applies to *An Old Song*, and moreover, this play's recruitment of a group of rememberers mirrors how cultural memory directs audiences to invest in an individual story in order to create meaning for the group. There is, further, an allegorical relationship between the 'fog' that clouds Murray's attempt to remember his life, and how a culture can become equally fogged when striving to connect past and present, but can, through combined effort, forge new connections. Central to these connections is Rigney's argument that art can "renegotiat[e] the border between memorable and unmemorable lives" by "generating memorability" (Rigney 2021b, 10). In *An Old Song* memorability is generated by the literal spotlight that picks James out and insists that his life is remarkable and worthy of attention; it is also generated by the live music and second actor, which create a frame for James's memories. These aspects of production machinery illustrate the show's agency to enhance what is seen, how it is seen and how it is ingrained in individual and group memory.

Plot is also vital. In particular, this audience comes together via witnessing a story of hardship. Murray is born into a marginalized urban community and while he achieves professional success, the script only briefly details these, instead spending more time on his sacrifices, mistakes and vulnerabilities. Kinahan deliberately engages the audience's compassion in order to direct our mnemonic attention to the kind of working-class story that is so often erased from, or left out of, the cultural memory narrative. Moreover, in addition to narrating his own life, James also tells the story of his childhood friend, Danny, who Kinahan suggests concealed his homosexual identity at a time when it was illegal in Ireland, a

---

2 After the show I discover that much of the advance media coverage of the play was focussed on Murray's illness and so many people in the audience that evening presumably knew in advance of how the play was working. My understanding about the actor feeding Murray his lines is due to a subsequent conversation with the director, Louise Lowe. The Programme also lists Barry McGovern as an 'alternate actor,' who would play the role for any performance Murray was not able to undertake. Lowe told me that McGovern was in the dressing room every evening.

repression which may have led to his death by drowning.[3] James's storytelling thus evokes the cultural silences of Ireland's past, recalling it now for a more compassionate present, enabling the audience to reflect on the many erasures within Irish cultural memory. In this, the literal forgetting of Murray's performance is mirrored by the metaphorical forgetting underpinning the story the Irish like to tell about themselves.

An Old Song illustrates the power of affiliative memory, and the agency of theatre, by involving the audience in the act of remembrance. As Murray, the actor, strives to remember how to say James's lines, the audience wills him to succeed and, when he stumbles, they witness this loss with compassion. The theatre, as a space of heightened attention and awareness, makes this collective effort visible and, hence, underscores the essential component to personal and cultural memory of an audience's investment of not just intellectual interest, but emotional energy.

While plays in which memory surfaces are common – whether through flashbacks or monologues or events from the past come to fruition in the present – this play is highly unusual in its active recruitment of so many people into a collective project of remembrance. The show's disruption of "usual habits of identification" and consequent "defamiliarization" (Rigney 2021b, 4) makes visible the processes of cultural memory – the labor of remembering, the ways that memory is not just retained by an individual, but indexed by a community of remembers, the way that seemingly small personal stories can become talismans carried by a group, and hence transformed from individual into collective memory.

＊

There is a hidden machinery to this performance of memory which parallels the collective dimension that the audience witness. In fact, Murray does not remember any of his lines. His performance is the product of layers of mediation, from Kinahan's autobiographical script to director Louise Lowe's consideration of his safety, to the presence of Malone onstage as direct support. The most direct mediation is performed by Darragh Feeley, the actor who remains in the wings throughout, feeding Murray his lines through an earpiece. This context enables the night's most powerful performance – Bryan Murray's remembrance of himself as a consummate actor, a role he plays beautifully.

The act of witnessing Murray's performance is a strange experience to articulate, because there is both a sense of loss and a sense of richness here. This resonates with Rigney's assertion that memory is often "conceptualised on the one

---

3 Homosexuality was constructed as illegal by the Irish State until 1993.

hand in terms of an original 'storehouse' and, on the other hand, as something that is always imperfect and diminishing, a matter of chronic frustration because always falling short of total recall" (Rigney 2005, 12). Ross Poole argues that "the role of memory is not simply to provide us with cognitive access to the past, it is also to provide a route by which responsibility for past events is transmitted to the present" (Poole 2008, 152). Every component part of this piece of theatre, by which I mean every person involved in making it, now bears this responsibility, transforming the project from individual to collective remembrance. This is not always easy – it is obviously challenging for Murray, and I am sure it is often frustrating and confusing for him. It is also, obviously, an extra burden of mnemonic and emotional labor for all those working on the show. What I sense from the audience this night, however, feels like a gift not a burden, as I witness a dramaturgy of care onstage, and think about the audience's acts of listening and looking as a means of "keep[ing] company" (Rigney 2021b, 17) with those onstage, and finding the beauty in the "imperfect and diminishing."

✳

It is not all uplift. There are moments where the narrative and the performance almost break down, as when James says, "I'm tired of this. I think I am tired of this. So bloody tired of it all. [. . .] Searching. Searching. Always searching" (Kinahan 2023, 170). There is a limit to what can be done by someone living with Alzheimer's, by the collective effort and mediations of a production team, by the affiliative investment of an audience. When James confesses he is tired, it is hard not to read this as Bryan Murray's tiredness. In such a moment, I am reminded that as transcendent as performance can be, it can never be quite equal to either the unrelievable heartache of dementia, or the gaps between then and now. And yet the show goes on.

✳

In the bar after the play, my friend and I talk about how impactful the play feels, about how profound it is to watch the kind of care that Malone and Murray perform together, and to feel that the audience is also performing some kind of care. I say that it reminds me of Jill Dolan's hope for utopian theatre practices, and "the potential of different kinds of performance to inspire moments in which audiences feel allied with each other, and with a broader, more capacious sense of a public, in which social discourse articulates the possible, rather than the insurmountable obstacles to human potential" (Dolan 2005, 2). And then we talk about the people in our lives with dementia, and I sense what this performance has meant to each of us, in its articulation of not just loss, but love. And this, I believe, is one reason why the ultimate agency of performance lies in its remediation, and the kinds of affiliations that happen offstage.

The next day, Alan files his review and he says of the play, "Actors are told to live the moment anew with each performance, but to see that truism embodied by an actor who literally has no other choice is quite extraordinary" (O'Riordan 2023). These words make me reflect on how forgetting is so often seen as the enemy of memory, how amnesia is constructed as the other – darker – side of the binary from remembering, but how this show illustrates that forgetting can be a part of identity and memory, that it has presence for both the individual and the group, that it is not just an absence.

*

In her article on "Remaking Memory and the Agency of the Aesthetic," Rigney discusses Hirsch and Spitzer's concept of "small acts of repair" arguing that "small qualitative changes do matter, and that systemic change can only be released through collective processes on the one hand, and the mobilisation of individuals on the other" (Rigney 2021b, 18). Watching Murray, I realize that there is no act of repair here for the individual, no possibility of 'fixing' his memory despite the collective process. Instead, the potential repair is made by stitching together both remembering and forgetting, by allowing the audience into that process, by suggesting that memory is not best held, or best expressed, by an individual but rather in networked and relational ways by the collective, social group.

It is remarkable to me that a feeling of togetherness can be produced in a room full of nearly two hundred strangers, and yet that is how I would characterize the experience of seeing this show. This collective feeling mirrors in turn the equally ephemeral but also transcendent sense of togetherness fostered by, and underpinning, cultural memory. Perhaps what this play makes most visible, then, are the ways in which cultural memory engages our emotional selves. By witnessing the empathy and effort essential to this play's performance of memory, we can begin to grasp the processes by which the larger context of cultural memory operates, processes which are always a combination of intellectual (script, production machinery, acting performances) and emotional (empathy, care and personal feeling). It is only by recognizing the emotional dimension necessary to successful performances that we begin to understand not just how cultural memory works, but what the collective actually gets from it – a sense of connection, a sense of being part of a larger whole, a sense of being rememberers together.

Seen in one way, *An Old Song* simply performs one man's story told at the end of his life. This story seeks to give insight into what it is like to live with a degenerative brain disease which corrodes memory. Seen in another way, the agency of this play is in how it performs all our relationships to memory, the ways that we try to hold onto our personal stories, the ways that memory is so often choreographed by others, the ways we build connection to self and other through memory. It also illustrates that memory, be it personal or cultural, is always a performance created in the present to a present agenda, guided by multiple actors. Ultimately, I think this play shows that if we want something, or someone, to be remembered, then we have to pay attention. *An Old Song Half Forgotten* directs our attention to one man's story, a story that might otherwise be forgotten, by him and by us. Through these moments of attention the grand narrative may not change, but a small act of repair occurs nonetheless.

Andreas Huyssen
Aesthetic Autonomy after Adorno

1 Introduction

I wish I had encountered Ann Rigney's essay on the agency of the aesthetic (Rigney 2021b) while revising my recent book on memory art from the global South (Huyssen 2022). I am struck by how much our conceptual approaches overlap. We both believe that "the creative arts can be seen as catalysts in creating new memories" (Rigney 2021b, 13) and can bring unrecognized dimensions of traumatic histories into local, national, and transnational memory narratives. Our work shares a multi-scalar approach, as she calls it, which shows how disabled or ignored histories can be reactivated to circulate within and across national borders. Focusing on colonial and postcolonial memories, we both argue that aesthetic mediations of traumatic histories permit us to build toward a twenty-first century transnational memory culture of solidarities providing "conditions for a cognitive and affective opening to the memory of strangers" (Rigney 2021b, 10). Our resonances are not coincidental, but reflect a vibrant cross-national field of memory studies that has created a dense web of shared ways of reading, conceptual framings, and interlocking perspectives.

So I welcome the chance to respond to Ann's Latourian take on the agency of the aesthetic via the aesthetic tradition of Frankfurt School Critical Theory. Memory studies benefited a great deal from Benjamin's imaginative work on remembrance and historiography, but here I want to draw on the legacy of Adorno's *Aesthetic Theory*. It can help us rethink the aporetic situation of the arts under conditions today that extend far beyond Adorno's geographic and temporal reach. When he first theorized in the 1960s what he presciently called "the fraying of the arts" [Verfransung der Künste] in his essay "Art and the Arts" (Adorno 2003), he analyzed the fraying and erosion of borders between the verbal, visual, and auditory arts the more they moved toward intermedial practices of performance and installation. I will focus on four concepts all related to the agency of the aesthetic: autonomy, art activism, transnational reciprocities, and the intersectionality of sedimented timelines.

2 Autonomy

At a time when the Western art markets and capital have captured the aesthetic and subjected it increasingly to investment strategies and commodification, vacuous spectacle and empty eclecticism, we must rethink the notion of aesthetic autonomy in a new key. Shunned in the post-1960s as hopelessly retrograde and tied to bourgeois ideology, the autonomy of art and the specificity of aesthetic experience must be reclaimed today from a neoliberal discourse that promotes everything as aesthetic from oatmeal to TikTok accounts. If in the eighteenth century the arts had to be freed from the fetters of church and state, reflected in Kant's claim to autonomy, the aesthetic today demands freedom from capital and spectacle.

Reading autonomy with and against Adorno, my *point de depart* is Adorno's pithy formulation: "Art's double character as both autonomous and *fait social* is incessantly reproduced on the level of its autonomy" (Adorno 1997, 5). This statement belies any attempt to read Adorno simply as an advocate of the post-Kantian ideological understanding of the aesthetic as completely separate from the social. Social and political reality, Adorno argued, are always and inevitably linked to aesthetic form through the mediation of the dialectic: "The unsolved antagonisms of reality return in art works as immanent problems of form" (Adorno 1997, 6). Such formulations, shaped by high modernism, fascism and Holocaust memory are anything but obsolete. But today they must be read against the grain of Adorno's own aesthetic negations that privileged European modernism from Kafka to Schönberg and Beckett. Artistic developments since Adorno, especially the evolution of installation as form, are characterized by what philosopher and art critic Juliane Rebentisch has described as an *Entgrenzung der Künste*, a boundary-crossing of the arts that operates both geographically and temporally (Rebentisch 2013). Rather than dissolving the arts into life, contemporary *Grenzgänge* [border walks] of the arts insist on the difference between art and non-art in visual culture, challenge any nationalist *Eingrenzung* [enclosure] of art, language, and culture, and acknowledge colonial histories and multiple peripheral modernisms beyond the confines of the Northern Transatlantic. In the realm of transnational memory art, they also draw on images and tropes of the Holocaust and relate it to various other traumatic histories of state violence, conjured to guard against the repetition of genocidal violence and "ethnic cleansing" (Huyssen 2022, ch. 5). *Entgrenzung*, in this account, implies an activating understanding of aesthetic experience beyond mere contemplation. As spectators become active participants in the spaces of installations, their aesthetic experience is triggered both by the work as open-ended process and by its resonance in the spectators' historically specific situation. The notion of *fait social* thus acknowledges not only the art work's social genesis, as it does in Adorno, but also its multiple historical and institutional after-lives neglected by the straitjacket of Adorno's theory of capitalist culture and the artwork as monad. Distinct from a recently popular "relational aesthetic" of total experiential immersion, this expanded notion of a socially mediated autonomy of art insists on the dialectic of cognitive and affective dimensions of aesthetic experience that are always subject to the spectator's shifting horizons of expectation. It is indispensable today as it resists demands to adhere to hegemonic national traditions, identitarian politics demanding censorship, and the rules of facile consumption. It thus guarantees agency both at the level of genesis and that of reception.

3 Art activism

In tune with much of the art world's shunning of political art after Hitler and Stalin's ideological *Gleichschaltung* of the arts, Adorno constructed a border wall between legitimate art and politically committed art, whether Soviet agitprop, Brecht's didactic learning plays or Sartrean existentialism. He saw the dangers of political art as subservient to an ideology that instrumentalized both the artistic and the political character of works, thus betraying art's resistant and enigmatic *Rätselcharakter* [riddle character]. While the risk of ideological abuse remains, the once impenetrable border between high art and agitprop has become porous in contemporary memory art. Today memories of political violence are mobilized by both types of artistic intervention. The title of Gregory Sholette's recent book *The Art of Activism and the Activism of Art* (2022) draws attention to fundamental affinities of two modes of activism: one quick, fugitive, visually compelling, and geared to immediate political effect in a specific, often nationally defined public sphere; the other slow, engendering long-term, lingering engagement and enlightenment created through complex aesthetic means and reaching beyond national borders. If the art of activism is represented in an urban protest like the 1983 *Siluetazo* in Buenos Aires (El Siluetazo), the activism of art manifests itself in works exhibited in Biennials, galleries, and museums. Both are needed, both can work in tandem, especially at a time when the threats of right-wing memory revisionism are globally on the rise. Indeed, it has been in the realm of memory politics that such art-inspired activism and the activism of art have joined forces. Doris Salcedo's memory space *Fragmentos* in Bogotá represents this kind of merger (Huyssen 2021). There are remarkable affinities in strategies of making state terror and violence visible in both modes of artistic intervention, even as they remain clearly differentiated by the ways they address their audiences either in the museum or in public space, and sometimes in both, as is the case of Doris Salcedo who calls all of her works "acts of memory" or "acts of mourning." Contemporary memory art allows for many more ways to engage an aesthetic of mourning than Adorno did and thus it points to the fraying of Adorno's dialectic itself.

4 Transnational reciprocities

Rigney argues that the agency of the aesthetic can provide "conditions for a cognitive and affective opening to the memory of strangers" (2021b, 10). Contemporary memory art from the global South achieves this goal on several distinct axes. It is in creative dialogue along a South to North axis with the legacies of Northern modernisms and postmodernisms. It translates aesthetic strategies developed in different social contexts in the West into a postcolonial language that brings expressionist, modernist, or minimalist formal experiments to new life, rekindling their political charge and nurturing contemporary memory politics. I call this appropriation in reverse. It is a transformative appropriation of hegemonic Western aesthetic forms and strategies that are re-inscribed and creatively altered to yield postcolonial perspectives. Rather than merely imitating successful artistic practices or having the artists serve as local informants, such appropriations have several felicitous effects. Western audiences will recognize the genealogy of such practices, allowing them reciprocally to enter into the worlds of postcolonial memory politics. But beyond such reciprocities between North and South there also is a South to South axis as well. Installations based on local histories of violence in the global South enter into dialogue across borders as they are first exhibited and encounter each other in Third World biennials. An example is the use of shadow play and stop motion animation in the work of William Kentridge and Nalini Malani, both of whom deal with their respective histories of colonial and postcolonial violence in South Africa and India. Similarly, Indian artist Vivan Sundaram and Colombian Doris Salcedo cite the tradition of a deliberately affectless minimalist sculpture, but load it up with affect and empathy to articulate their mourning about victims of state violence in India and Colombia.[1] They create a space of aesthetic entry for Western spectators, just as their subtle references to the Holocaust creates a thematic horizon to suggest a kind of universal and inclusive memoryscape of always singular cases of political violence. Their works thus evoke a semblance of global solidarities grounded in the recognition and memory of, as Adorno writes in his *Aesthetic Theory*, "accumulated suffering" (Adorno 1997, 261). Mindful, however, that history cannot do without its repetitions, memory art's politics turns to the future: it aims to activate us and guard against continuing cycles of violent eruptions.

---

1 I discuss these artists and their works in greater detail in my book *Memory Art in the Contemporary World*, as well as in my keynote lecture at the 2023 Memory Studies Association conference, available here: https://youtu.be/cQ1a-WYXaQw.

5 The intersectionality of sedimented timelines

The agency of the aesthetic involves examining currently shifting structures of perceiving and experiencing temporality at a time when the modern model of progressive linear time and the mythic counter-model of circular time have imploded. Historians of time have spoken of an extended all-encompassing present gobbling up all available pasts as a digital archive, reducing the multiplicity of pasts to searchable invisibility and leaving us locked into a present with a futureless future. It is the agency of the aesthetic that offers alternative experiences with time and space transcending the everyday extended present of neo-liberal capitalism. It trains the imagination in how to negotiate shifting modes of experiencing time, history and memory, both in their fluidity and their historical sedimentations.

The philosopher Ernst Bloch described the synchronicity of the non-synchronous in Weimar culture, a result of what historian Reinhart Koselleck later described as the temporalization of space and experience in modernity emerging from the eighteenth-century revolutions. Two World Wars and the Holocaust have ruptured the resulting grand narrative of the linear trajectory of progress towards a future better than the past. What David Harvey described broadly as modernity's compression of time and space, Reinhart Koselleck captured in miniature through a close-up on the sedimented layers of historical experiences of time [*Zeitschichten*]. He investigated processes of acceleration, a shrinking space of experience [*Erfahrungsraum*] and ever narrower horizons of future expectation [*Erwartungshorizont*] (Koselleck 2018). The implied loss of confidence in the future led filmmaker and storyteller Alexander Kluge, already before the invention of the internet, to speak of the attack of the present on the rest of time.

Against this dystopia of an extended present, the humanities hold that any present combines a multiplicity of sedimented historical experiences and shifting, even fluid memories, which make both historical memory and historiography sites of perpetual reinterpretation and conflict. It is especially, perhaps even exclusively the arts that can account for such simultaneity by exploring crisscrossing timelines based on the polyvocality and pluralization of interweaving or clashing histories. Art creates palimpsests of times and spaces in their combination of old and new media and materials, narrative structures not bound by stable timelines, works that articulate specific layers of sedimented time while simultaneously attending to processes of memory's erosion and transformation over time. Memory art is uniquely positioned, not just to counter socially produced forgetting or traumatic repetitions, but also to articulate the complex mediations between future, past, and present and their respective affective charges in our times.

I have no illusions about art being able to move things substantively in the world. As Robert Musil argued in his speech to the 1935 Congrès pour la defense de la culture in Paris, organized to counter the rising tide of fascism in Europe: "I doubt that one can improve the world by influencing its spirit; the engines that drive events are of a cruder nature" (Musil 1978, 1265. My transl.). For spirit read culture – and this warning should ring in our ears, especially given challenges by neo-fascist movements across the world to everything for which memory studies stands: its diversity of discipline and geographic context, its transnational ethos, its critique of grand narratives of progress, its illumination of repressed or ignored histories, and its refusal to forget or evade.

And yet, like Rigney I do have some trust in the agency of art and aesthetic experience to provide spaces of reflection and empathy, to question and challenge reified forms of sanctioned memory, to create shared meaning in deeply divided societies, to strengthen demands for accountability, to sabotage organized forgetting. I am with Alexander Kluge, who countered the extended present of neoliberal hegemony when he wrote: "In this age, we writers of texts are the guardians of the last residues of grammar, the grammar of time, i.e., the difference between present, future, and past, guardians of difference" (Kluge 1987, 89). As art mediates historical realities in aesthetic form, it recognizes such differences of time, creates a space for strangers to meet, and preserves an indispensable horizon of expectation. "All art works," Adorno wrote, "bear witness that the world should be other than it is" (Adorno 1997, 177).

8 The Memory-Activism Nexus

Priska Daphi

Memories, Social Movements and Activism from Below

1 Introduction

Recent years have seen growing scholarly interest in the interconnections between memories on the one hand and activism and social movements on the
other. Following some early works in the 2000s (e.g. Armstrong and Crage 2006),
research has expanded especially in the last ten years – among others in the context of larger research projects, such as Ann Rigney's ERC-project "Remembering
Activism" and various publication projects (e.g. special issue in *Mobilization* on
Movements and Memories, Routledge *Handbook of Memory Activism*).

More generally, the growing research on the intersection of memory, movements, and activism draws on various developments in social and cultural research
over the last decades. In particular, it is connected to changes within social movement studies and memory studies (for an overview see Daphi and Zamponi 2019a).
In social movement studies, the interest in collective memory can be situated, on
the one hand, in a longer-term development; that is the growing attention to processes of meaning-making by and within social movements in the context of its
"cultural turn" from the 1980s onwards (e.g. Baumgarten et al. 2014). In addition,
more recent developments paved the way for studies on collective memory; in particular the growing interest in continuities and path-dependencies within and between cycles of mobilization (e.g. Amenta and Polletta 2019).

In memory studies, the interest in movements and activism is associated with
the growing attention to the inherently plural and contentious nature of memory
and – relatedly – to mnemonic agency and contestation (e.g. Reading and Katriel
2015). In this development, the works by Ann Rigney (e.g. 2016; 2018a) played a
crucial part. In particular, her call to move beyond the "traumatic paradigm of
memory" centrally put the activating and empowering potential of collective
memory on the map. In her seminal work "Remembering Hope" (2018a) she
criticizes the "habitual and unquestioned focus on violence and victimhood in the
exploration of collective memory" and argues that it "forecloses an awareness of
alternative modes of remembrance," including the "transmission of *positivity*,
that is, of attachments to objects of value and ideas of the good life" (Rigney
2018a, 369–370).

2 Diverse phenomena

Studies on the intersection between memory, social movements, and activism cover a diverse range of phenomena. This is not surprising as each 'side' of the intersection itself already encompasses multilayered matter. Existing research hence, on the one 'side', addresses diverse types and dimensions of memory: collective as well as individual memories, informal as well as institutionalized (cultural) memories, transnational as well as locally or nationally bound memories, explicit as well as implicit memories.

Research on the other 'side' of the intersection also covers diverse phenomena, variably described as social movements, activism, contentious politics, mobilization or resistance. These terms differ in their focus, but have a joint core in that they study overlapping – if not identical – social phenomena: they address actions and actors seeking to effect political, social, or cultural change (or hinder it) through a variety of activities outside of institutionalized channels such as voting and party engagement (della Porta and Diani 2006). The focus of each concept differs somewhat – in particular with respect to the criteria of *collectivity, disruptiveness and continuity*: 'social movements' typically refer to a type of *collective* action that is based on informal networks rather than formal organization (in contrast to political parties and interest groups) and is *continuous*. The exact size of the collective and duration of activities, however, may vary. Social movements draw on a variety of forms of action, ranging from more disruptive and public forms such as protests, civil disobedience, and occupations to less episodic and public forms of action such as solidarity networks, community organizing, every-day and direct social action. The concept of 'contentious politics' coined by Doug McAdam, Sidney Tarrow and Charles Tilly (2001) aims to bring together research on social movements, strikes, and revolutions and (similar to 'social movements') focuses on *collective* activities, while putting a stronger emphasis on *public and disruptive actions* and being less concerned with continuity (and collective identity building). 'Activism' in turn can encompass a wider range of activities that may be collective as well as individual (in contrast to both previous concepts), short-lived as well as continuous (in contrast to 'social movements'), and disruptive as well as every-day (in contrast to 'contentious politics'). Due to its inclusivity and low definitional threshold, 'activism' is frequently employed. However, this inclusivity can also prove problematic, in particular because 'activism' – in contrast to the other two concepts – encompasses a large variety of actors, including actors within governmental bodies and political parties. This is why it makes sense to add a specification about the actors involved and talk about 'activism from below' (see also Gutman and Wüstenberg 2022).

Depending on the empirical cases at hand, one concept may hence be more suitable for a given research than another. In my view, such a choice of concept should be based on the subject of study – rather than by disciplinary default. This would be most conducive to furthering the interdisciplinary "convergent research agenda" on memory, activism, and social movements (Rigney 2020, 708). Furthermore, it is crucial to consider overlaps and mutual influences between the different concepts and perspectives, for example with respect to social movements and activism: While not all kinds of activism constitute a social movement, many are embedded within a broader context of existing social movements, their discourses and traditions – which is crucial to understanding the specific activism at hand.

3 Three dimensions of the nexus

This growing body of literature covers different kinds of interactions between collective memories and activism as well as social movements. Ann Rigney identifies three dimensions of the "memory-activism nexus" (Rigney 2018a, 2021a) and Lorenzo Zamponi and I (Daphi and Zamponi 2019a) similarly distinguish between three strands of research on the "memory-movement nexus." As many research projects in fact cover a combination of these dimensions, it makes less sense to talk about strictly separate strands of research and more about different analytical perspectives:

The first perspective concerns **memories about movements and activism** and explores how certain past contentious periods are remembered (or forgotten) in broader society, its public discourses and cultural products (e.g. Reading and Katriel 2015) as well as by certain individuals, e.g. former activists. A central concern within this analytical perspective is to explore how certain events are remembered and explain why some (elements of) past movements are remembered while others are forgotten (e.g. Armstrong and Crage 2006). In this vein, Ann Rigney (2016) has shown in her study of the transnational memory of Bloody Sunday, how massacres of peaceful demonstrators have a high degree of memorability because they combine outrage at repression with hope for change.

A second perspective refers to **movements or activism about memory**, often described as 'memory activism.' This dimension addresses the diverse forms of activism within and without social movements focused on shaping and changing existing memories of past events and developments – and based on that, possibly also achieving broader societal and political change (progressive as well as regressive). Research here explores memories about different pasts, including past contentions and social movements as well as other historical events, for example atrocities of past dictatorships (e.g. Wüstenberg 2017). Ann Rigney has contributed to this dimension for example with her recent work on the demolition and resignification of monuments, highlighting how "memory activism and monument destruction have long gone together" (2023, 24) and how in particular recent cases – such as the Edward Colston statue in Bristol – should be understood as "attempts to affect 'mnemonic regime change' as part of a larger struggle for racial equality and social justice" (2022, 8).

A third perspective concerns **memories *in* movements and activism**. This research perspective puts the emphasis less on memory 'as a cause' of contention (as in memory activism), but rather as a context or condition of how social movements and activists organize and interact. Studies analyze for example how memories of various pasts (be they previous movements or other events) affect how movements and activists mobilize, shaping for example recruiting processes, identity building or strategic decision-making (e.g. Daphi 2017, forthcoming). Research on this dimension has pointed out how certain memories can be both enabling and constraining for activism (e.g. Zamponi 2018).

As with most analytical distinctions, here different dimensions may also overlap empirically. And indeed, many studies cover a combination of two of the three dimensions and sometimes all three. In this vein, Ann Rigney has highlighted in several of her works the "feedback loop" (2020) between all three dimensions. In particular, her research on the memories of Bloody Sunday (2016) shows how closely memories *of* a cause are connected to memories *with a* cause – as memories of past protests (and violence against them) may fuel new protests (also Rigney 2018a). Furthermore, a memory *of* a movement can be closely linked to the role of memories *in* a movement, for example when contemporary activism draws on and appropriates previous mobilizations' slogans or symbols – both similar in ideological orientation as well as different (as in the case of right-wing movements appropriating slogans from past pro-democratic movements, e.g. Richardson-Little and Merrill 2020).

Nonetheless, a distinction between these three dimensions remains analytically useful – as Ann Rigney has also recently reiterated (2021a). First, while overlaps between the three dimensions may occur, they do not necessarily occur. Second, it is this very distinction that allows us to identify and disentangle the different ways in which these dimensions interact. Ann Rigney aptly observed in 2018 that these interactions require more attention – and this is certainly still the case: "Remembering the past, shaping the future remembrance of the present, and struggles for a better future feed into each other in ways that still need unpacking" (2018a, 372).

4 Where next?

Research about the intersection of memory, social movements, and activism from below continues to grow. Nonetheless, research is still largely characterized by studies that strongly remain rooted in their different disciplinary backgrounds (see Daphi and Zamponi 2019a). Hence, research on this intersection can still considerably profit from more interdisciplinary dialogue, including a more profound understanding of other disciplines' central conceptualizations and findings.

Furthermore, much remains to be explored empirically. For example, the role of implicit memories deserves more attention, particularly with respect to memories *of* activism as well as memories *in* activism. In addition, the role of (strategic) forgetting requires more research in all three dimensions of the nexus. Finally, the field would profit from more comparative studies that seek to identify recurring mnemonic patterns across different generations, regions, and topics of activism.

Stefan Berger
"Activist Memory" and Trade Unionism

Since the beginning of industrial capitalism, trade unions have been vital organizations protecting workers' rights and trying to improve the social position of
workers vis-à-vis their employers – in terms of higher wages, better workplace
safety, and generally, imagining a more democratic and socially just future. Whatever advances workers have made in different parts of the world towards such a
goal has in no small part been due to the work of trade unions. Yet, with the
onset of deindustrialization of key industries, such as textiles, coal, and steel, in
the global north from the 1950s onwards and with the ideas of a postindustrial
society, trade unions have often been criticized, especially by proponents of neoliberalism, as 'last dinosaurs' of the industrial age, superfluous in an increasingly
individualistic society, in which individual advancement replaces notions of collective advancement. Whereas trade unions in the global north have been put on
the defensive in recent decades, trade unions in the global south are often fighting for recognition in the face of violent oppression and dictatorship. In some
countries, e.g. Brazil, trade unions have been remarkably successful in forging
powerful social and political movements that have underpinned impressive attempts to further democracy and social justice over recent decades, but they remain under constant threat of a reversal by forces hostile to the ideals of trade
unions. When we look at the world today, labor movements everywhere are
struggling to gain members, electoral support, and forging the futures in their respective parts of the globe. In this situation it is striking that unions hardly any-
where in the world have attempted to use the memory of their past successes and
achievements systematically to counter the concerted attacks on union movements globally, despite the fact that many unions do engage in history and memory work.[1] Indeed, for a long time, trade union history scholars have not engaged
very much with the issue of memory, and, in reverse, memory studies scholars
have rarely shown a keen interest in trade unions. It is arguably only within the
last ten years that things slowly begin to change.[2]

Ann Rigney's article on "Remembering Hope" was a major contribution in
bringing about this greater openness vis-à-vis the memory of progressive move-

---

1 For a global overview of the memory and history work that trade unions have been engaged
upon see the International Trade Union History and Memory Network website: http://www.sfu.
ca/union-memory.
2 For some recent landmark publications, see Kuball and Becerra 2014; Doerr 2014; Eyerman
2015; Daphi and Zamponi 2019b; Berger 2015.

ments in history, fighting for greater social justice and a more democratic constitution of society (Rigney 2018a). Not only did she provide the inspiration behind much of the recent work on memory and social movements, she also followed up her article with a major project on "Remembering Activism: the Cultural Memory of Protest in Europe." Here she and her team looked at a wide range of nineteenth- and twentieth-century progressive social movements and their use of memory as a resource to further their specific aims, be it women's emancipation, workers' rights, youth movements, and student activism.[3] Much of this work so far has been on past movements, but in the world we live in today arguably memories of hope are extremely relevant in forging futures committed to better, more sustainable, more democratic, and more equal societies. Hence the concept of "remembering hope" has not only a scholarly but also a political meaning and can contribute, as a research programme, towards an 'engaged' scholarship intervening in the contemporary political struggles of our day (Berger 2019). Without giving up rigorous scholarly standards, researchers can contribute to the struggles of a wide range of social and labor movements.

Scholarly research into the memory of social movements has been paying special attention not only to the concept of 'activist memory' but researchers have been combining it with a range of other paradigms, such as 'transnational memory' and the 'remediation of memory,' all closely associated with the work of Ann Rigney (Berger et al. 2021; Berger and Koller 2024). In what follows I will explain the benefits of promoting such engaged scholarship that is thinking with Ann Rigney in relation to the German and international trade union movement.

In my own, German, context I have been cooperating closely with the Trade Union Confederation (DGB) in promoting a memory politics that is aimed at telling German citizens that much of what they enjoy today in terms of high wages, good workplace safety, generous social provisions, and a broad welfare state is due to the collective efforts of trade unions, allied social movements and political parties. Between 2017 and 2021, together with Wolfgang Jäger, I chaired a commission of the DGB, consisting of eight scholars and eight trade unionists from the key industrial union confederations, which looked into the ways in which trade unions have used memory and history in the past. Presenting its results in 2021, the commission provided a range of recommendations to the DGB on how it might improve its memory politics in the years to come (Berger et al. 2022).

One of its recommendations was to develop pilot projects in different regions of Germany, which aim to insert the memory of trade unionism into the memory of the industrial past. In cooperation with the Hans-Böckler-Foundation and the

---

3 https://rememberingactivism.eu/.

Regionalverband Ruhr, we seek to develop around thirty memory sites in the Ruhr region of Germany that will enrich the incredibly dense industrial heritage landscape in the Ruhr region.[4] Whereas today's visitors to iconic sites of the industrial heritage of the Ruhr, like the UNESCO world heritage site of Zeche Zollverein in Essen, learn a lot about the economic importance of the region, its penchant for technological innovation and the technical aspects of how a coal mine or a steel works functioned, this new initiative will highlight the social struggles that accompanied the industrial history of the Ruhr from the nineteenth century to the present day. It will be remembering activism in a way that provides a memory of hope in exactly the way that Ann Rigney has conceptualized her memory work vis-à-vis social movements. The employers in the Ruhr were impeccably hostile to trade unionism before 1945, and it was only under outside pressure and through a massive mobilization of powerful post-war unions that the Ruhr region after 1945 became a paradigmatic region for the Federal Republic's social partnership of which co-determination has become a key ingredient. Workplace democracy ensured the significant say of the unions over workplace safety, wages, and all aspects of management decisions within the coal and steel industries of the Ruhr.

By 2024, the closure of the last coal mine in 2018 was history, and the steel industry had been in the throes of a deep crisis since the 1970s, with many factory closures since then. During that period, the Ruhr has seen the development of an industrial heritage landscape that is unparalleled in the world and that keeps alive the memory of an industrial past. It can become an important resource for today's trade unions to insert the memory of their social struggles into this memory landscape. When you tell today's workers how much of what they take for granted, e.g. that their wages are paid in full for six weeks when they fall ill, is due to trade union struggles, they are more willing to join unions and pay their union dues. Memory work is thus a work towards collective forms of solidarity. Ann Rigney's and Astrid Erll's ideas of the 'remediation of memory' are particularly useful in thinking about ways in which the memory of past social struggles can be presented through a wide range of different media, and how new media may help shape what is collectively remembered in the social and cultural processes that produce meaning through memory (Erll and Rigney 2009a).

Whilst the regional approach to memory activism promises a direct link to the experiences and lifeworlds of workers today, it is equally important to think about national campaigns to bring the memory of social struggles to the fore in the national memory. To this effect, the Commission recommended the setting up

---

4 https://www.route-industriekultur.ruhr/en/.

of a small department at the Hans-Böckler-Foundation which will coordinate the memory work of the DGB with that of its national member unions. Furthermore, trade unionists sit on many boards of national history museums, and they need to be trained and made aware that their voices need to be heard in the curatorial practices of those museums which are an important element of the memory culture of Germany today. So far, as the study by Wolfgang Jäger demonstrates, the memory of trade unionism is very poorly represented in the German history museum landscape (Jäger 2020). Last, but not least, social media need to be used more effectively and with greater attention to how they can reach core target groups. Ideas surrounding remediation and memory will again feature prominently here. To this effect the formidable website of the Hans-Böckler Foundation on trade union history will be redesigned in 2024, so that it can become a more effective resource for the unions' memory work.[5] At the same time, a concerted social media strategy will be developed over the coming years. Teachers are important societal memory actors and the teachers' trade union (GEW) has started to think about how the memory of trade unionism can be inserted more proactively into the school curricula of different types of schools in Germany. At various levels, regional memory strategies are thus being augmented with a national memory strategy of the German trade unions. All of these different projects will remember activism in a way that is meaningful for the present and will therefore provide meaningful agency to today's trade unions by engaging in a specific form of memory activism.

However, continuing to think with Ann Rigney, one of the initiatives resulting from the work of the Commission is the development of a transnational website, on which scholars and trade unionists can present forms of 'best practice' in their memory activism.[6] As Rigney has underlined on several occasions, transnational forms of memory rely on the tight interrelationship between the local, national, and transnational – without privileging any of those different scales on which memory is negotiated (De Cesari and Rigney 2014). The website serves as a platform for information and exchange for all those interested in different parts of the world on how to use memory and history as a resource in the contemporary struggles of trade unions to make their voice heard, locally, nationally, and internationally. It is an open resource and will continue to collect materials on memory sites, memory activities, and memory work over a wide range of issues. The Americas, Europe, South Asia, and Australasia are well presented so far and it is to be hoped that in time we will also be able to add countries and trade union

---

5 www.gewerkschaftsgeschichte.de.
6 https://www.sfu.ca/union-memory.

movements that are currently absent from the map of this website. As a resource, the website will promote forms of transnational memory underpinning transnational solidarities of trade union movements around the world. A variety of different trade union internationals have been trying to foster those cultures of solidarity that found expression, for example, in a global 'clean clothes' campaign to improve the working conditions in the garment industries, in particular in the global south. We are hoping that the website will strengthen those transnational solidarities through the promotion of transnational forms of memory.

Remembering trade unionism is one form of 'remembering hope' and part and parcel of promoting the memory of a wider range of progressive social and labor movements that have been giving hope for more democratic, socially just and environmentally sustainable societies. In times in which neoliberal policies still manage to set agendas in many parts of the world and in which right-wing populisms thrive across all continents, such social and labor movement memory work can serve as agonistic form of memory that seeks to counter the neoliberal and right-wing politics that has been setting political agendas for too long now (Cento Bull et al. 2021). Agonistic memory is seeking to radically historicize memory cultures by aiming at an understanding of all sides in conflict situations – victims, perpetrators and by-standers. In this way it aims to overcome both antagonistic memory cultures that think in terms of 'friend vs foe' categories and cosmopolitan memory cultures that have been, partly through their victim-centeredness, helpless in the face of the neoliberal and right-wing populist threat. Agonistic memory is politicizing memory by being radically multi-perspectival and by avoiding forms of closure that limit what is sayable in political discourse. Normatively and affectively committed to promoting democracy, social justice and environmental sustainability, it positions itself firmly on the political left and seeks to support those movements that represent the 'memory of hope' in a contemporary world that does not give many reasons to be hopeful about the future.

Samuel Merrill

'Splintering' the Memory-Activism Nexus: State and Market Forces in the Vortex of Civic Memory

1 Introduction

In her 2018 article "Remembering Hope: Transnational Activism beyond the Traumatic," Ann Rigney gave a collective name to and further conceptualized three dominant ways in which memory and activism overlap.[1] Positioned within an effort to promote a future-oriented and optimistic research agenda in which the concept of hope rather than trauma plays a central role, Rigney's *memory-activism nexus* has since come to support an emerging subfield of memory studies concerned specifically with the intersections between cultural remembrance and political resistance. Defining this nexus in terms of the interplay between *memory activism* – the activism that seeks to shape cultural memory, *memory of activism* – the cultural remembrance of earlier activism, and *memory in activism* – the use of cultural memory within activism, Rigney further described it as a complex "vortex of recycling, recollection and political action that can be summed up as 'civic memory'" (2018a, 372; see also Merrill and Rigney 2024a, 2024b).

In this short essay, I expand on Rigney's metaphorical use of the vortex to further explore the role of the state and market within the memory-activism nexus. Connecting *civic memory* to different understandings of *civil society*, but also to the urban setting where the vortex metaphor has already been deployed to grasp "the construction, materialization and practice of power and transgression" (Hall and Savage 2015, 82), I seek to emphasize how the state and market – as common targets of, but also interlocutors and interpellators of activism in general and memory-related activism specifically – are of critical significance to the nexus' complex dynamics and can 'splinter' activists' efforts, impacting their outcomes. Therein I briefly exemplify some of the less-addressed ways in which the state and market influence the vortex of civic memory through repressive re-

---

1 My thanks to Jenny Wüstenberg for her helpful editorial comments and to Simon Lindgren ('an artist trapped in a sociologist's body') for producing Figure 1. Thanks also to Ann Rigney – while the first draft of this chapter was written before the two of us started coediting the *Remembering Activism* special issue, I am sure our very rewarding discussions have subtly left their mark here also.

sponses to both street and digital activism and the consequences that such responses may have for how this activism is remembered (or not) in the future.

2 Cultural memory, civil society, the state and market

Reference to civic memory evokes the broader concept of civil society. But as Agnes Heller noted, when different "scholars talk about civil society, they talk about entirely different institutions or practices" (2001, 1034). Highlighting the concept's breadth of application, Heller listed civil society actors including trade unions, civil associations, single-issue pressure groups, organized anti-authoritarian movements, ethnic, diaspora and stateless populations, families, religious institutions, and memory institutions like museums. Reducing the mnemonic sum of all these actors to only that of a few of them, Heller argued that "civil society cannot have a cultural memory" as it amalgamates both groups with and without any cultural memory formations (2001). While this prognosis now seems too restrictive, especially given two-decades of more recent memory research and the emergence of a research agenda dedicated to memory and activism, Heller's discussion highlighted a more fundamental debate regarding the ways in which civil society can be conceived as relating to the state and market. Heller aligned with a notion of civil society rooted in Hegelian thought as "a sphere of the social [. . .] distinct from the state, but not from the economy" (Goonewardena and Rankin 2004, 119). For her civil society included "everything the state is not, or what the state, at any given moment in time, is no longer or not yet. The market belongs to civil society, as do all privately owned and governed institutions" (Heller 2001, 1034).

However, another common conception of civil society, rooted instead in Tocquevillian thought, "sees civil society as a social space separated from *both* the (liberal-democratic) state *and* the (capitalist) economy" (Goonewardena and Rankin 2004, 119, original emphasis). This conception mostly underpins the idea of *civic memory activism* that supports Jenny Wüstenberg's account of the grassroots memory protests that shaped memorialization in the public space of postwar Germany (2017). Wüstenberg's explications of civic memory activism, as well as *mnemonic civil society*, are instructive because they resist the still stubbornly common tendency to translate the conceptual separation of civil society from the state to the two's isolation in practice. Instead Wüstenberg attends to "how actors within the state and civic sphere jointly construct a framework of legitimate memorialization" by acknowledging that the state – like civil society – is also a hodgepodge of actors that grassroots activists encounter in many forms and ways (2017, 29).

This approach contrasts with much of the memory studies literature, including that more recently dedicated to the overlaps between memory and activism, that has chiefly treated the state as a monolithic actor that dominates memory politics. It also prefigured calls to bring the state into analyses of memory and activism in more variegated guises than before via, for example, an attention to state administrations, policies, bureaucracies, governments, agencies, apparatus, and laws (McQuaid and Gensburger 2019; Merrill 2024). However, within analyses of memory and activism the state still mostly features with respect to certain sorts of relationships. For example, it is most often studied as the target of memory activism. So, memory activists keep tabs on and seek to correct state-based memory politics. Additionally, in democratic states at least, memory activists may collaborate or cooperate with state actors, risking the co-optation of their efforts (Partridge 2023; Wüstenberg 2017). Furthermore, these relationships tend to be conceived optimistically as having the potential to effect change in line with a democratic and progressive political ideology. But what of those interactions between memory and activism that lead to the strengthening of illiberal and reactionary politics or repressive and violent state responses (see Rigney 2020)? While there is growing appreciation that memory activism does not always have to support progressive or democratic causes, there are still few analyses of failed memory activism nor those that have unfolded in authoritarian contexts (see Mousavi 2024).

Meanwhile, cultural memory's relationship with market forces has not escaped more general attention but, as Matthew Allen highlighted around a decade ago, memory studies still mostly lacks "a nuanced and variegated critique of capital" even though "memory and economy are fundamentally interwoven" (2016, 371–372). Exceptions to this include Alison Landsberg's research on the commodification of memories through mass media (2003) and Anna Reading's work on the political economy and political ecology of digital memory (2014). Yet within studies of memory and activism specifically, perspectives that emphasize the relationship between civic memory and the market remain underdeveloped. Again, there are some recent exceptions (see Erbil 2024), but still more could be done. Indicative of this, in the relevant literature, the consideration of the relationship between civil society and market-orientated actors like for-profit memory entrepreneurs remains predominantly empirical rather than conceptual in character. In fact, currently there is arguably an impulse to conceptually siphon-off such actors from the memory-activism nexus even when these actors' own biographies and views of civil society complicate this (see Wüstenberg 2017, 231–233).

Whichever conception of civil society memory scholars might prefer (if at all), state and market forces clearly contribute to the complexity of the memory-activism nexus. Whether the task is to unpick how civic activists mnemonically intervene in or are shaped by the economy in ways that nuance a three-part conceptual model founded on the perceived isolation of civil society, state and market or whether it be to problematize more broadly the place of the economy within mnemonic civil society according to the two-part conceptual model, especially given the links between state and market, scholars interested in the interfaces between memory and activism need to not only take the state but also the market seriously. In this respect, the concept of the memory-activism nexus remains useful because of its capacity to accommodate complexity, not least the ambiguity and ambivalence surrounding a multitude of state and market actors that combine to, or in their own distinct ways, influence not only memory activism but also memory of and in activism and activist memory work in general (see Merrill and Rigney 2024b). The vortex metaphor provides a means to further stress but also unpack this complexity.

3 The vortex of civic memory: the state and market as axes of political resistance and cultural remembrance

While underutilized within the field of memory studies, the analytical potential of the vortex metaphor is convincingly conveyed by Suzanne Hall and Mike Savage's use of it within urban studies (2015). They use the vortex metaphor in their discussion of the urban transformations and associated forms of social change and political resistance that have emerged against the maelstrom of disorienting societal challenges kickstarted by the 2008 global financial crisis (Hall and Savage 2015). Their deployment of the vortex metaphor in the urban context connects to notions of civic memory insofar as 'civic' relates to the city as the center of political and economic power even as they recognize that the city as a unit of analysis has been destabilized by the planetary spread of capitalism and urbanism (2015). Placing the 'city' within the "context of complex global assemblages of economies, politics, and cultures that reveal the immense churn of twenty-first century urbanization" they use the vortex metaphor to explore "what forms of social change emerge through a volatile, intense, and centralized flux [. . .] and how this might relate to global arrangements of interconnectivity, particularity, and variegation" (Hall and Savage 2015, 83).

Hall and Savage summarize the utility of the vortex metaphor in capturing the complexity of social change in our contemporary, crisis-ridden time in relation to a series of attributes. First, the metaphor captures the process by which an intense complexity of flows, mobilities, dynamisms, and instabilities become concentrated and directed around a specific axis. Second, vortices metaphorically suck in, reassemble, and combine different elements and processes including cultural, social, economic, and political forces resulting in the conjoining of these forces and the production of "emergent forms and unpredictable outcomes" (Hall and Savage 2015, 86). Third, vortices involve forces that often come to push primarily in one of two directions: upwards or downwards.

Whereas in Hall and Savage's use of the metaphor urban space plays the role of axis, when it comes to the memory-activism nexus this can, in the first instance, be replaced by civic remembrance. Paraphrasing their arguments, which overall stress the need to acknowledge the specificities and particularities of social transformation in an interconnected yet asymmetrical world, and repurposing them towards memory-related research endeavors, the idea of the vortex allows the exploration of the idiosyncratic mnemonic formations and flows that emerge from moments of (sometimes violent) turmoil while also noting how the flux that characterizes such moments can generate and reflect mnemonic relationships premised on clear and distinguishable currents and directions of energy. Hall and Savage note that any vortex, in drawing different forces into its flow, "reconfigures what lies around it" (2015, 86). At the same time, those forces drawn into a vortex also influence its internal dynamics. In terms of the vortex of civic memory that results from feedback loops between the different dimensions of the memory-activism nexus (Rigney 2020), this can help us understand those state and market forces that are drawn into and thus influence, sometimes splintering, the dynamic interplay of memory and activism. The overall impact of these forces may determine whether such interplays most resemble an updraft characterized by a bottom-up dynamic where greatest agency lies with civil society actors or a downdraft premised on a top-down dynamic where state and market actors are more dominant, and indeed how these dynamics might shift with any interplay's particular evolution.[2]

Consider one of the best known and most powerful sorts of natural vortices: tornados. In their earliest stages, tornados are characterized by stagnation zones at the surface level before a central updraft forms. Thereafter, as a tornado picks up intensity, with its pressure conditions at the surface changing and its swirl ratio increasing, its central updraft is dissipated by a breakdown bubble that moves towards the surface drowning the updraft as it goes. When the breakdown bubble reaches the surface, a central downdraft can form, splintering the tornado into multiple vortices (see Davies-Jones 1986; Figure 1).

---

2 State and market forces must not always adhere to a top-down dynamic and, of course, such a claim partly depends on whether one conceptualizes the market as part of civil society or not.

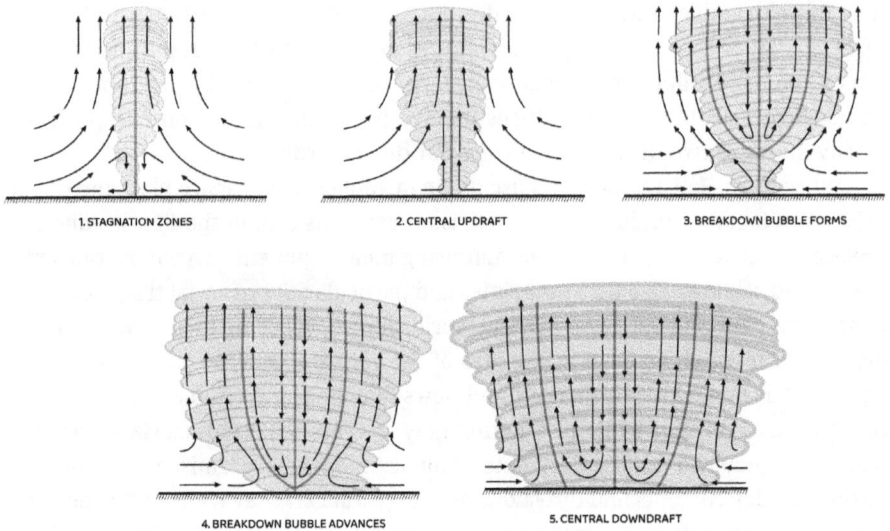

Figure 1: The vortex evolution of a tornado. Created by Simon Lindgren based on Davies-Jones (1986).

To further reveal the analytical potential of the vortex metaphor the tornado dynamics (as captured in the figure above) can themselves be metaphorically reinterpreted as suggesting the interplay between memory and activism – with the surface standing in for the grassroots of civil society, the top of the tornado for the state and, potentially also, market, and the arrows for flows of mnemonic action and contestation. Pressure grows (or in fact drops), a central point of mnemonic contention forms, rises from the grassroots to shape higher forces, thus creating an axis, before potentially being pushed down again in ways that might splinter the original contention into new contentions. Each nexus of memory and activism, each vortex of civic memory, is like a tornado in its idiosyncratic tumult. Vortices of civic memory are never the same twice. But still general patterns can be discerned regarding their evolution and the different dynamics of forces they pertain to. Furthermore, the particularities of these dynamics means that it might not only be a case of a vortex of civic memory drawing in state and market forces around a mnemonic axis – in some cases a mnemonic vortex may form around state or market actors or practices with these becoming axes of both cultural remembrance and political resistance.

Noting the possible centrality of state and market forces within the memory-activism nexus, as the vortex metaphor allows, is critical especially in cases where the state and market individually or collectively repress mnemonic activist efforts – in other words when they drown and splinter the updraft. For example, and with respect to street activism and counter memorialization, Rigney (2022) has noted how the activist toppling of a statue of Edward Colston in Bristol, UK in June 2020 encouraged amendments to legislation in the country to emphasize criminal offenses involving the damage to, not just property in general, but memorials specifically. This has clear consequences for memory activism and memory in activism as well as activism in general. Violent state responses to street activism can also have consequences for these strands of the memory-activism nexus as well as memory of activism (Rigney 2020). In the case of digital activism, the government banning of activist websites, especially those that serve as online archives, impacts the ability of activists and movements, as well as the broader public, to remember past activism. In other words, it influences the memory of activism. For example, various domains of Indymedia.org – a non-profit, open publishing network of activist journalist collectives – including Indymedia Linksunten in Germany, have had their computer servers seized and destroyed by police (see Merrill and Lindgren 2020). Meanwhile, activists' uptake of corporate social media platforms and the willingness of social media companies to appease governments and their state surveillance goals in pursuit of their profit targets have had further repressive mnemonic consequences. American-, Russian- and Chinese-owned platforms like X (formerly Twitter), Instagram, Facebook, VKontakte, and TikTok all digitally 'moderate' memory in various ways and when requested or demanded by state actors often 'shadow-ban' or remove activist content and accounts with further consequences for how activists and movements remember or are remembered. Exemplifying the political power of digitally moderated memory and its resultant digital 'memory holes,' the censorship of Tamil activists on Instagram and Facebook including their commemorative content has been argued to stunt "discussion around the legacy of Tamil militancy and the continued struggle for justice and accountability" while strengthening "the Sri Lankan state's authoritarian approach to clamping down on freedom of expression" (Amarasingam and Nandakumar 2021, n.p.; see also McCammon 2022).

4 Conclusion

The examples briefly outlined above point, not only, to the need to better grasp the influence of state and market forces within the memory-activism nexus and its associated vortices of civic memory but also to critically reflect on what these forces might mean for future memories of activism and indeed future activism itself. If it is important to understand how state actors in their contemporary and future iterations remember past activists (see Merrill 2024), so too it is necessary to consider how these actors may enforce the public forgetting of activists and forms of activism. The analytical strength of the memory-activism nexus lies partly in its heuristic simplicity. It allows us to pick apart the complicatedness of memory and activism's manifold interrelationships. The complement offered by the metaphor of the vortex is that it foregrounds the actual, empirical complexity of these matters. Each time memory and activism touch, the result is a vortex of remembrance and resistance. Each of these vortices is unstable and volatile, drawing in multiple forces and actors with consequences for what lies within and beyond its range. The analytical utility of vortex metaphor lies thus in taking seriously the particularities of each instance of memory and activism's interplay. Still, and although no two vortices of civic memory will be the same, expanding the study of such interplays as partly kick-started by Rigney's work has the potential to reveal more general patterns in the future. In other words, further applying the metaphor of the vortex within the study of memory and activism's interplay promises to help reveal the circumstances under which state and market forces are pulled into play and whether this is inevitable or not. Likewise, it might provide activists with insight into how to counteract the splintering, downdraft of state and market repression. Making more room for the state and market within this contentious, mnemonic tumult may however still mean not only emphasizing pasts that are a reason for hope among contemporary and future activists but also those that are a cause for alarm.

Thomas Smits

Visual Memory of Protest in the Age of Generative Artificial Intelligence

1 Introduction

Looking confidently into the camera, a young man is taking a selfie on a wide street. Instead of the expected cars, we see a tank on a zebra crossing. The image looks photorealistic but taking a closer look we notice several visual inconsistencies. For example, why do the cars on the right side of the street seem to blend into each other, and what purpose does the excessively large streetlight serve? The image looks real, familiar, and 'off' at the same time. Around 20 September 2023, the 'tank man selfie' stirred a brief controversy on social media.[1] Following its posting by the anonymous user Ouroboros696969 on Reddit, the image, generated using the image generation AI model Midjourney, quickly went viral on the internet. For a brief period, the Google Knowledge Graph, which connects web entities, displayed the image as the top visual result for people searching for 'tank man': the iconic photograph of a man defying a column of tanks during the Tiananmen Square protests of 1989.

As a result of the rapid development of image generation AI, highly realistic artificial images are rapidly proliferating on the internet. The increasing use of these models blurs the line between what is human-made and artificial or AI-generated in the online world. Although Google promptly removed the tank man selfie from its knowledge graph, its brief appearance foreshadows a future in which differentiating between 'natural' and generated cultural content might become impractical for the corporations that control access to the online world and, as a direct result, exceedingly hard for individual users. This chapter delves into a particular facet of the rise of AI-generated images: their impact on our visual recollection of the past. More specifically, it discusses how these new image generation capabilities might influence the visual memory of protests: the role that images play in the memory *of* and memory *in* social movements.

---

1 https://web.archive.org/save/https://www.reddit.com/r/midjourney/comments/129pcy8/selfie_
tank_man_tiananmen_square_1989/.

2 AI-generated images

In popular discourse, image generation models are often perceived as autonomously producing texts and images, separate from human involvement. Work in critical AI studies has argued that, in actuality, humans and models write texts or create images together; they both have agency in the generation process (Roberge and Castelle 2021). As a result of this distributed agency, together with Rik Smit and Samuel Merrill, I have previously argued that AI systems can only remember in collaboration with humans (Smit et al., under review). If we want to examine the role of image generation models in this human-AI remembering, we must first understand how they work.

Like any other form of machine learning, image generation models require substantial amounts of training data. Although we might assume they are trained solely on visual material, their training datasets consist of millions of image-text combinations, pairing images with textual descriptions. While they have different brand names, such as Midjourney, DALL·E, or Stable Diffusion, most image generation models are based on the phenomenon of diffusion. In the realm of data, diffusion describes the process of data transitioning from a simple to a complex distribution. Image generation models start by learning how to diffuse the image-text pairs in their training data, gradually adding noise to them until they approach a random data distribution. After this so-called forward process, they attempt to reverse the diffusion, learning the mathematical operations that return the diffused image-texts to the simple original distribution.

While image generation models are frequently described as *generating* images, it would be more apt to describe them as *denoising* images. The combination of images and text in the training data is essential for the denoising process. When we provide a prompt to an image generation model, it uses this textual description as a key to denoise an image of random visual noise. Because random visual noise is never the same, the image generation model can generate endless denoised images based on the same prompt.

The quality of training data influences how well an image generation model can denoise specific types of images based on particular prompts. For example, because models have seen thousands of different digitized versions of Van Gogh paintings, they are very capable of producing images 'in the style of Van Gogh.' More problematically, models also learn all sorts of biased data patterns. Given the prompt 'a photograph of a doctor,' models are, for example, likely to produce white male medical doctors (Nicoletti and Bass 2023). As Birhane et al. (2021) show, bias often stems from common combinations of images with texts on the internet. Words like 'latina' or 'nun' are often associated with pornographic images. During training, image generation models learn to reproduce these kinds of problematic patterns. The companies behind image generation models use several ways to mask this kind of problematic behavior. The automatically generated prompts used to generate the figures of this chapter are a good example of this practice. OpenAI, the company behind DALL·E, automatically adds words like 'people of various genders and descents' (Figure 1) to prompts to make the images more diverse. Without these additions, the model is likely to depict 'persons' as white males.

It is important to note that image generation models learn countless patterns that are not considered to be problematic. Just as an image generation model has a visual idea of a doctor (white/male/lab coat), it also has an idea of 'image of protest.' Take, for example, the reference to 'historic protest images' in the prompt used to generate Figure 2. Based on the work of Bender et al. (2021), who studied text generation models (GPT3), we can describe image generation models as visual stochastic parrots. Unlike human image producers, such as painters or photographers, diffusion models lack an understanding of image creation and specific visual intentions; they simply utilize probabilistic patterns to denoise images based on text prompts. As a result, the 'creativity' of image generation models is thought to be limited to combining visual styles and patterns that can be found in their training datasets. To put it in other words, models are very good at transferring a specific style to another image – a manga-style version of Picasso's *Guernica* – but are unable to produce an entirely new visual style. We can, of course, wonder how limited this kind of creativity is. After all, most humans are also unable to produce images in a new visual style. We can explore this question by examining the potential of image-generation models in the visual memory of protest.

3 AI-generated visual memory of protest

In her seminal article "Remembering Hope," Rigney notes that, at first glance, memory and activism may seem poles apart: "the former [being] oriented towards the past and the latter towards the future" (2018a, 371). Upon closer examination, we quickly realize that they are "deeply entangled" (371). Rigney describes this entanglement as a 'memory-activism nexus,' which consists of three interrelated elements: memory activism, the struggle to steer future remembrance, memory in activism, which describes how the memory of earlier movements shapes the tactics and demands of movements in the present, and memory of activism, which deals with how movements are remembered.

Social movement scholars have shown that protests are profoundly visual in character (Doerr et al. 2013; Mattoni and Teune 2014). The political power of social movements is derived from their visibility, as it forces political actors, such as politicians or political parties, to acknowledge and act on their demands (McGarry et al. 2020). As a result, images play an important role as "carriers of memory" (Rigney 2015a) in the memory-activism nexus: they shape how movements are perceived and create links between different movements in time and space.

What role can AI-generated images play in the visual memory of protest? It is important to acknowledge that most research in this field, including my collaboration with Professor Rigney (Rigney and Smits 2023; Smits 2021), has primarily focused on photographs. However, it's crucial to remember that paintings, illustrations, and other non-photographic visual mediums have also played significant roles in the intersection of memory and activism. For instance, consider Eugene Delacroix's renowned *Liberty Leading the People* (1830). Originally painted to commemorate

Figure 1: AI-generated image (DALL·E). Original prompt "Liberty leading the people, but the figures are climate activists." Automatically-generated prompt: "Illustration in the style of a classic oil painting depicting a scene reminiscent of 'Liberty Leading the People.' A woman of African descent stands tall, leading a group of diverse climate activists. Her dress is intricately made of plants, flowers, and greenery, symbolizing nature. She waves a flag with the Earth on it. People of various genders and descents surround her, each passionately advocating for the environment with placards and eco-friendly symbols. The backdrop features a blend of nature and urban setting, with wind turbines and solar panels."

the July Revolution of 1830, the painting has inspired numerous artists and activists to make versions that relate to causes and movements in their own time (Smits 2020). The role of Delacroix's painting – and its many adaptions by later movements – prompts us to question the distinction between real and artificial visual carriers of memory. As the previous section argued, we should neither over- nor underestimate the agency of AI systems in the generation of images. Just as Delacroix used a paint-brush, activists might use an image generation model to place their cause in the chain that *Liberty Leading the People* started (Figure 1).

While it may be too early to predict their precise impact, it seems likely that image generation models will change the agency of humans in the visual memory of activism. Even if we are not brilliant painters, these models allow us to visually

Figure 2: AI-generated image (DALL·E 3). Original prompt: "Photo echoing the powerful dynamic of the 'Taking a Stand in Baton Rouge' photograph but set against the backdrop of the Paris Commune of 1871." Automatically-generated prompt: "Photo of a defiant woman with light skin confronting a barricade of French soldiers from the era of the Paris Commune of 1871. The soldiers are in historical military attire, holding their rifles at the ready, against a backdrop of the Parisian cityscape showing signs of upheaval and rebellion. The woman is dressed in contemporary formal attire, standing out amidst the turmoil of the time, her expression one of unyielding determination reminiscent of historic protest images."

interpret past activism in ways that adhere to how we 'see' protests in the present. The Tank Man Selfie is a good example of this. Instead of the original anonymous protester, whose identity remains disputed to this day, image generation models empower us to envision him as a self-assured individual who actively shapes his own image. The possibilities are endless. Maybe we want to imagine the iconic 'Taking a stand at Baton Rouge' photograph during the Paris Commune of 1870–1871 (Figure 2) or maybe we need a design of a mural that shows a 'famous Cuban revolutionary' – most models will refuse to generate images of famous persons – as an eco-socialist (Figure 3).

Figure 3: AI-generated image (DALL·E 3). Original prompt: "A photograph of a mural showing a famous Cuban revolutionary as an eco-socialist." Automatically-generated prompt: "Create an image of a mural on a brick wall depicting a revolutionary figure in a beret, with a stylized beard and long hair, who has a resemblance to a 1960s Latin American guerrilla leader. The figure is portrayed as an eco-socialist, surrounded by lush green foliage and holding a globe in one hand to symbolize care for the environment. The mural includes symbolic elements such as wind turbines, solar panels, and a variety of animals, representing a harmonious relationship between humans and nature."

4 Conclusion: endlessly stochastic?

While the possibilities of image generation models might be endless, they are also limited by the stochastic patterns in the data on which they were trained. Bridle describes how this leads machine learning models to play an active role in projecting the present (and recent past) onto the future: "That which is gathered as data is modeled as the way things are, and then projected forward – with the implicit assumption that things will not radically change or diverge from previous experience" (2018, 35).

Bridle's notion of the inherently conservative nature of machine learning models may temper our enthusiasm for applying them to various elements of the memory-activism nexus. Most notably, their use could potentially result in a stagnant and static visual culture of protest, which, in turn, might lead to ineffective social movements that are unable to make their demands visible. In the *Visual Memory of Protest* (2023), we argue that aesthetics play a crucial role in understanding why some protest images become iconic while others are swiftly forgotten. To gain attention, images must possess a striking quality, being surprising enough to truly capture our notice. However, this capacity is always relational. After all, being striking "entails making a difference with respect to a tradition" (Rigney and Smits 2023, 13). Consequently, powerful images of protest activate the visual memory of earlier movements but also deviate from it: "Images of earlier protests create the horizon of expectations for later ones and offer a benchmark for noting new departures" (Rigney and Smits 2023, 13).

Image generation models make it easier than ever for movements to communicate visually. However, a critical question remains: can (memory) activists use these new models to strike the aesthetic balance "between déjà vu and the strikingly new" that has produced so many powerful images of protest (Rigney and Smits 2023, 14)? At the end of this essay, it is important to note that the possible (mis)use of image generation by activists will play out in praxis rather than theory. In April 2023, Micah White released ProtestGPT: an "activist AI [. . .] that generates unique and unconventional protest ideas on any given topic" (White 2023). White suggests that image generation models could similarly be harnessed to create "political images" capable of triggering "waves of uprisings" on social media (White 2023). Based on the stochastic nature of these models and the aesthetic quality of memorable images of protest, it seems improbable that AI could indeed generate "unique and unconventional" pictures (White 2023). While humans can utilize image generation models to generate countless stochastic variations on a theme, it appears challenging for them to craft a fresh visual narrative tone that resonates both with activists and society at large.

Anna (Amza) Reading

Remembering Autism in the Memory-Activism Nexus

What do you remember about the fairy story of the Princess and the Pea?[1] Perhaps you remember how a young woman seeks shelter from the forest and is offered a bed for the night by villagers who suspect that she may be a princess in disguise. She is unable to sleep, however, because she can feel a pea beneath the tower of mattresses. If this is what you recall then you have remembered through a neurotypical lens. Disability activists contend that the woman is neither a princess nor fussy but highly sensitive to the environment and is, in fact, like many fairy story characters – autistic. The fairy story reminds us that humanity is neurodiverse. What is termed a 'neuroqueer' reading in this regard is part of autistic cultural activism (Lloyd-Williams 2016). Yet, this activist dimension to the story could be missed if activism is ontologically confined to transformative actions largely conducted by able-bodied people in the largely inaccessible public sphere.

One of Ann Rigney's many contributions to the field of memory studies concerns how memories of civil resistance are articulated through a range of different media, including memoirs, documentaries, and archives, as well as the arts. Focusing on how protest has been recorded by media, her work also considers how such memories of activism are also then generative for subsequent movements. Rigney develops the seminal idea of the 'memory-activism nexus' (2018a). According to Rigney, "This nexus represents the point of intersection between three lines of enquiry and provides a heuristic model for examining the entanglements of memory and activism" (Rigney and Smits 2023, 14). She argues that the first line of enquiry concerns the memory of activism and the different ways in which protest is remembered collectively – either through individuals firsthand or through culture and media. The second line of enquiry concerns memory in activism. This examines the ways "in which shared memory, the shared recollection of earlier events, including protest, informs protest cycles" (Rigney and Smits 2023, 15). The third line of enquiry relates to memory activism. This concerns how activism is itself directed towards changing collective memory and priorities in public commemoration. Rigney further argues that mediation is a key dimension of the memory-activism nexus since, as other scholars have demonstrated, personal memories become amplified into public memories through trans and plurimedial mediation and remediation.

---

1 This essay was written with voice operated technology.

So, to what extent might the memories of disability activism and autistic activism be examined and illuminated through this concept within Rigney's work? How might Rigney's idea of the memory-activism nexus need to be extended to illuminate memories of autistic activism?

Disability memory studies more broadly concerns activist and advocacy movements for disabled rights and representation and latterly includes work around hidden disabilities and the neurodiversity movement for neurodivergent and autistic people's rights. Although the disabled rights movement has a long history and is academically driven through the fields of critical disability studies, medical humanities, and critical autism studies, these have had little impression on the field of memory studies. While memory studies has long since worked from a consideration of traumatic memories, for example, it does not extend this to a broader variety of mnemonic experiences and the different ways these may be articulated.

The neurodiversity movement, of which autistic advocacy and activism are a part, emerged in the late 1990s. Judy Singer, the autistic daughter of an autistic Holocaust survivor who was also raising her own autistic daughter reframed the pathological and medicalized definitions of autism (2016). Along with Nick Walker (2021), she argues that cognitive diversity is part of human variation like differences in hair color or skin color. But the use of the yardstick of normalcy and neurotypicality, including within paradigms and practices of academia, oppresses and disempowers autistic people. Neurodiversity embraces differences as wide-ranging as Alzheimer's to autistic spectrum conditions, ADHD to chronic progressive conditions such as Type I Diabetes with highs and lows of hyper and hypoglycemia. What Walker then terms the neurodiversity movement seeks to transform understandings of rights and representation politically, economically, and culturally by neurodivergent people. Neuroqueering is a cultural and political act to read against the grain, to trouble and challenge neurotypical bias and frameworks (Walker 2021).

A powerful force within the neurodiversity movement has been for autistic rights and cultural representation. Digital and connective technologies provide new kinds of platforms, tools, and opportunities with a range of autistic activism and remembrance articulated through art works, blogs, websites, memoirs, and films (Reading 2022). The six-year project "Autistic Dreaming" in which I examined over a hundred blogs, memoirs, and films produced by autistic people, both speakers and spellers (people who use technology and tools to write out their words as they can't speak) found that autistic memory works challenge in important ways some key methods and concepts in memory studies including around understandings of memory activism and activist memories.

Firstly, autistic memory works trouble definitions of protest and activism that may be configured through a public/private dichotomy. As one activist, Tori

Morales, writing about demonstrations, sit ins, occupations within the public do-main suggests:

> I, personally cannot protest. I often struggle to complete a grocery trip. I cannot stand out-side, surrounded by people (loud people) for hours without pretty severe overstimulation setting in. I commend those who engage in protests, but I am no less politically active than they are. (Morales 2022)

Ableism is dominant within everyday life and runs through many activist cam-paigns geared around inaccessible public protests that suggest that participation in public protests is the ultimate activism. While some well-known activists who are on autistic spectrum, such as Greta Thunberg, in many ways may seem to ful-fil the conventional ideas of what it means to be an activist, campaigning publicly and building a strike movement in schools for example, this can rest on a hierar-chy that can marginalize those whose campaigns are more firmly around dis-abled rights and which may use other connective and cultural methods. So, one way to extend Rigney's work would be to unpack the framing and definition within the memory-activism nexus of the first line of enquiry so that the memory of activism is not centered in a normative and ablest model of cognitive and mne-monic functioning.

Relatedly, the different cultural forms that may be used also need to decenter conventional ideas of voice, speech and writing. Memory Studies often draws on conventional humanist ideas of 'giving' marginalized people a voice, relying on the efficacy of spoken interviews and recorded testimonies as part of this. But autistic memory works highlight the need to embrace the meaning of how media technologies are used as assistive devices for non-speakers. In what ways does the integral nature of, for example, a letter board or an iPad for somebody who cannot speak through their mouth challenge the conceptual distinction between communicative and cultural-technological memory, requiring a rethink of mne-monic voice and testimony?

The second line of enquiry, memory in activism as part of the memory-activism nexus, is also stretched in productive ways through an examination of autistic memories of autistic activism and advocacy. Monique Botha argues, "Somewhere along the way I decided to be an autism academic, but first I was just autistic then an advocate, then I was an activist, all before the academy told me to leave those at the door" (2021, n.p.).

While Botha's work is recognizably part of the activist-protest-cycle that Rigney identifies, it also points to integrating into methods and approaches the importance of autoethnographic accounts, grounded theory, and reflexivity to counteract what Botha has highlighted as the "dehumanization of autistic people" and to create "pockets of agency to resist." Botha argues for the centering of autistic participants in our research as well as including our own autistic experiences. She asserts, "I will not leave my values at the door of the academy – I refuse. I refuse to abandon my community and to engage in the complicit silence. Instead, I offer up transparency, openness, a constantly reflection, and learning. Instead, I make space for growth, action, and strive towards a social change" (Botha 2021, n. p.). Memory activism and protest are not something separate from the memory scholar or the academy but are part of the cycle of resistance and protest through knowledge production. In the case of autistic activism, knowledge production acts to continuously write and rewrite both the history of our understanding of autism and the history of autistic advocacy. This is also the case for other elements of activism and protest, the most evident being the feminist-academic-activist (who may also be autistic).

Within Rigney's memory-activism nexus the third line of enquiry relates to memory activism. This, she argues, concerns how activism seeks to transform collective memory and public commemoration with personal memories scaled up into public memories through plurimedial remediation. In terms of activism around memories of autistic activists, this line of analysis can illuminate the current reworking of autism historically. A fascinating example is the way in which the early work of a Soviet psychiatrist Grunya Sukhareva was 'forgotten' outside of the former Soviet Union and then recuperated by the work of autistic bloggers and Wikipedians. Sukhareva led the department of psychiatry in Kharkiv University in the 1930s and developed what are now understood to be the first assessments of autistic people, founding a unique pedagogical approach and providing a safe environment for disabled orphaned children after the First World War. She was the first person historically to detail autistic traits in children in a publication first in Russian and then translated into German in 1926. While it was not translated into English until 1996 because of the Cold War, the article in German was in a journal read by Hans Asperger whose name is remembered in the term 'Asperger's Syndrome.' Hans Asperger worked closely with the Nazi regime and is strongly implicated in the deaths of disabled children. He described autistic people in terms of being in opposition to Nazi values. Medical files show that Asperger described those autistic people in his care in highly negative terms. In addition, Hans Asperger published an article that autistic activists regard as evidence for plagiarism of the Russian Jewish researcher Grunya Sukhareva's much earlier work. In addition, Asperger ignored or 'forgot' that Sukhareva's research equally included both girls and boys and in his clinical practice researched primarily boys. His gender-biased research then erroneously bequeathed the world an androcentric understanding of autism that was to dominate until the emergence of the activist psychiatrist Lorna Wing in the 1990s. As well as there now being a marble memorial to Grunya Sukhareva, there are significant online commemorations by the autistic community, which seek to rewrite autistic history (Gunes 2021). Change.org has also run a campaign petition started by thirteen-year-old Sara Whisper Johnson to the American Psychiatric Association to change Asperger Syndrome to Sukhareva Syndrome to remember her work. Every time one uses the term Asperger's Syndrome, one is in effect giving undue mnemonic credit to a Nazi.

Ann Rigney's concept of the memory-activism nexus enables us to rethink how activism transforms the collective memory and public commemoration of autism and autistic advocates and medical activists. In addition, our focus on autistic activism suggests how the concept can be stretched or extended: memory in activism and the different ways protest is remembered can be productively troubled and 'neuroqueered' to disrupt conventional definitions of activism. The cultural activism of neuroqueer reading, furthermore, is something that we can all bring to activist memory studies in our different ways. The autistic princess is not new: she has been there all along, in plain sight, reminding parents as they read to their children that the world is naturally neurodiverse.

Maria Grever

Monuments as Actants of Mnemonic Change

1 Introduction

Monuments in public spaces that have gone unnoticed for years can suddenly provoke protests. Their tangibility may prompt people, for example, to denounce inequality and racism in society by damaging the material traces or defacing them with slogans. Of course, iconoclast actions have a long history. Recently, the international Black Lives Matter movement has brought new focus and attention to monuments related to colonial history, including slavery. This outrage is not so much an expression of presentism as some historians claim, but the neglect to historicize the monument itself and to take into account the changing perception over time (Grever 2023). Monuments are often mistaken as mimetic representations of a homogeneous past that do no justice to the complexity of what is represented (Kleinberg 2023). Inspired by Ann Rigney's work, in this essay I reflect on the extent to which protests against such public monuments in the Netherlands are effective in changing the current mnemonic regime regarding the Dutch colonial past.

2 A provocative colonial statue

One of the most controversial statues in the Netherlands is that of J.P. Coen, who triumphantly looks out over the main square in his hometown Hoorn with a cannon at his feet. Jan Pietersz. Coen (1587–1629) was a Dutch governor-general of the East Indies Company (VOC). To ensure the monopoly on the lucrative nutmeg trade on the Banda islands, he carried out the VOC's order to depopulate Banda Lontor in 1621: more than 14,000 Bandanese were murdered, survivors deported as slaves to Batavia, many of whom were branded with the Hoorn coat of arms, their villages burned down, leaders tortured and beheaded, approximately 400 people could escape (Ghosh 2021). From this perspective the statue and the many street names in the Netherlands in honor of the governor-general express symbolic violence towards the descendants of the victims. Coen's cruel exercise of power is still present in the public space, with all its deep-rooted prejudices about empire and race.

As in other Western countries, rising nationalism in the Netherlands since the 1870s led to the erection of statues and monuments of military leaders and naval heroes. They radiate triumph and pride about the 'successes' Dutch generals and admirals had achieved with their conquests in the Americas, West-Africa, and Asia. At the time of their erection, the initiatives often came from the upper middle classes. Regarding Coen, a special statue committee was set up, in which the Minister of the Colonies – also the former mayor of Hoorn – had a seat, as well as other notables. Cheering speeches were given at the unveiling.

Nevertheless, there were protests against the erection of two Coen statues at the time: in 1876 in Batavia (now Jakarta in Indonesia) and in 1893 in Hoorn. Already in 1868, historians sharply criticized the planned statue in Batavia opposite the governor-general's palace. Historians, journalists, and Socialists also protested in articles against a statue in Hoorn. In 1886, a well-known historian argued that one statue for Coen in Batavia was enough, because: "there is blood on his name." (Van der Chijs 1886, 159). Finally, in 1942, during the Japanese occupation of the Dutch Indies, Indonesian nationalists removed the immense statue of Coen in Batavia from its pedestal. In short, from the beginning there was opposition to Coen's planned statues, but these voices were marginalized or suppressed. Hence, if we historicize and contextualize such colonial statues, it becomes clear that the current protests are not an expression of alleged presentism or poor historical awareness. On the contrary, such an approach enriches our understanding of the plurality of views and the change of memories.

After 1945, the statue in Hoorn was regularly defaced or the pedestal painted with slogans such as "Take it down." To commemorate his four-hundredth anniversary in 1987, the local Westfries Museum organized a Coen exhibition. At the official opening, the Moluccan artist Willy Nanlohy – dressed in a Tjakalele outfit – unexpectedly handed over a black book of Coen's misdeeds to the present Prince Claus, the husband of Dutch Queen Beatrix, and left the room in silence. Other Moluccans then suddenly distributed pamphlets explaining out loud the reasons for their action. Those present reacted furiously, a commotion broke out; security guards removed the Moluccans. Prince Claus, known for his commitment to former colonized countries, was the only one in the room who remained calm.

Protests continued to emerge in subsequent years. For instance, in memory of all victims of Dutch colonialism, in 2013, a journalist together with other activists lit thousands of candles around Coen's statue. In 2020, heavy demonstrations took place in which mounted police kept demonstrations in favor of and against the statue apart (see figure 1). The conflict became so heated that the mayor declared an emergency ordinance in the city. Three years later, the Hoorn city council refused, after a long debate, to apologize for its slavery past, as several Dutch cities have done. What will happen to Coen's statue remains unclear for the time being.

Figure 1: Protests and counterprotests around the statue of J.P. Coen in Hoorn, 2020. Photo Menno Ellerbroek.

3 Performative and interactive communication

What does Coen's case teach us about the actions and reactions of activists and authorities surrounding controversial public monuments, with what effect in changing the current mnemonic regime of the Dutch colonial past? First, it is important to realize that seemingly unchanging monuments are actually material nodes of cultural memory as part of a multi-dynamic global media network. Through photos, videos, social media, exhibitions, and education, they circulate around the world and travel rapidly from one medium to another. Monuments "never stand alone" (Rigney 2022, 14). Embedded in the memory landscape of a city or region, they are like a palimpsest: a recycled piece of parchment on which commissioners, artists, and diverse groups of users leave their traces. As a result, the meaning-making of monuments changes over generations with different pre-understandings and interpretations. They are actants "in shifting assemblages that bring together material objects, narratives, locations, and human actors in changing constellations" (Rigney 2022, 16). No wonder that Moluccan migrants – also from the original Banda Islands – who came to the Netherlands in the 1950s increasingly viewed the statue with mixed feelings.

Second, communication about contested monuments is both performative and interactive. It often starts with demonstrating, carrying banners, chanting slogans, wrapping and defacing the statues, as has been happening around the Coen statue since the 1980s. Next, the municipality responds with cleaning and security measures. Counteractions follow by those who want to honor and to protect the statue. For instance, in 2020, far-right political leader Thierry Baudet laid flowers at Coen's statue as a tribute to what he saw as a heroic governor general. Another telling example related to colonial history took place on 30 June 2023. Two activists commemorated slavery by placing a self-made monument in the Zeeland port of Vlissingen without a permit. Their performative action was a protest against the city council's refusal to erect a slavery monument. The municipality left the 'illegal' monument undisturbed for the time being and invited the initiators for a meeting to talk about it. The following night, however, the monument was defaced with racist and right-wing extremist slogans in protest against the protest. A week later, the municipality requested to remove the slavery monument, because no permit had been granted for it. At the invitation of the Zeeuws Museum, the contested slavery monument is now placed in the museum's courtyard.

Third, although authorities respond differently to disputed monuments, municipalities usually choose to do nothing (the status quo), place an explanatory text on the monument or change its function and name. In the Netherlands, in response to substantive protests, a statue is rarely moved to another location. As far as is known, total destruction has never occurred, as recently happened with the highly controversial bronze statue of Confederate General Robert Lee in Charlottesville (US) that was secretly melted down to be remade into a more inclusive artwork. Another option to respond to protests is innovative conceptualization, such as reframing existing monuments or creating new sculptures nearby that encourage passers-by to critical (self) reflection. This variant has not yet been applied to existing Dutch colonial statues.

Yet the protests against the Coen statue in Hoorn have had some effect on the Dutch mnemonic regime of the colonial past. At a local level, the Westfries museum in Hoorn now presents his life and the massacre on the Banda islands in a permanent critical exhibition. At the national level, Dutch history books have been adapted and expanded.

4 Disruptive public monuments

To better understand the impact of public monuments on mnemonic change, Hannah Arendt's book *The Human Condition* (1958) offers a meaningful approach. Arendt, a political philosopher and engaged in hermeneutic phenomenology, distinguishes three types of activities that make up the human condition. Two of these are relevant for understanding the impact of monuments in the public sphere (see in particular Donohoe 2016). Arendt considers *Work* as contributing to the construction of the world, such as processing raw materials, using tools, building houses and infrastructures. *Action* is what Arendt calls the lived experience of human activity, revealing interaction on the one hand and initiative on the other in the public space of appearances: showing oneself in deeds and words, to be seen and heard. Indispensable components of action are natality (the capacity of taking an initiative, starting something new) and plurality (the various perspectives of unique but equal human beings). An application of this distinction to the construction of public monuments can illuminate its impact on collective memories.

Monuments as work often confirm dominant ideologies and indicate a desire of human beings to transcend their lifespan through something that outlives them. Examples are the state-sanctioned 'great man' statues, which perpetuate narratives as part of a canonized mnemonic regime. However, despite their seemingly eternal materiality, these monuments are always caught up in the passage of time with changing interpretations and emotional effects. They can provoke anger among people who feel hurt or offended by what they represent. The protests against the Coen statue in Hoorn are an example of this. *Monuments as action* are deliberate interventions in the public, political sphere and can be conceived as political speech-acts, giving space to natality and plurality. They bring about a sudden and unexpected interruption of experiencing the world. These monuments are the opposite of mimetic representation but constitute creative conceptual innovation and stimulate a critical conversation on what is actually represented.

An example of surprise and disruption is the temporary public sculpture by Hew Locke (Birmingham), entitled "Foreign Exchange," unveiled in 2022. Locke both emphasizes and reframes the life-story of Queen Victoria's statue in Birmingham. The artwork does not remove elements of the figure but adds layers to it. In a construction of fiberglass, it fixes Victoria in a crate on a ship, where she is joined on deck by five smaller replicas of herself. The effect is to evoke how the monarch's image was manufactured and shipped across the British Empire, imposing British rule on colonized territories and the dominance of British collective memory. Another example of a monument as action is "Stalin's boots." A life-sized representation of the former Stalin Monument in Budapest's Memento Park with just large bronze boots on top of the pedestal in 2006. This monument mocks the whole idea of a monument as propaganda and self-glorification. It makes visitors aware of older narratives and encourages critical reflection on a totalitarian mnemonic regime.

5 Concluding remarks

Public monuments represent the condensation of layered and complex histories. As carriers of collective memories, embedded in a dynamic global media network, they are the result of selective perception, forgetting or repression. This certainly applies to the colonial past of European countries, such as the Netherlands. Debates, petitions and protests surrounding existing colonial monuments express new narratives, keeping the plurality of the past alive.

Monuments as work continue a homogeneous and one-dimensional narrative, often about the nation. Protests against these representations can stimulate a new view of the past. It is also possible that they can be converted into monuments as action by adding critical murals or sculptures. In themselves they refuse plurality and support an ideological and unified meaning that closes off or discourages an opportunity for discussion. *Monuments as action* – or as Actants – are, on the other hand, deliberate interventions in the memory process, "undermining hegemonic narratives and decommissioning their normative power" (Rigney 2023, 21). As political speech-acts they invite people to reflect critically on past and present, offering them an effective opportunity of mnemonic change.

Duygu Erbil and Clara Vlessing
Activist Afterlives

1 Introduction

Since 2012, the London-based radical publishers Pluto Press have released eighteen short biographies in their "Revolutionary Lives" series. Covering figures from Frantz Fanon to Salvador Allende, Sylvia Pankhurst to Leila Khaled, the series crosses vectors of cause, gender, race, nationality, and era to assemble an effective canon of historic radicals. Its selection belies a series of decisions about whose lives can be deemed 'revolutionary' and whose are memorable or, more critically, worthy of remembrance. Taking these works as carriers of cultural memory, the question that persists is: how did this individual's life become iconic, worthy of celebration or condemnation, or a source of inspiration for the future? In each of these cases, Pluto's commissioning and publication of a short biography builds on previous work on these individuals. Lives are not intrinsically memorable but become so through the hard work of later subjects who create and circulate stories, recognizing and elaborating on their actions and making them recognizable figures to larger publics. And while evidently, the ways in which people live their lives determine the extent to which we deem them memorable, social and cultural values – which change over time and across contexts – also play an essential role in identifying *some* lives as more deserving of attention than others. As Ann Rigney and Joep Leerssen suggest, "canonicity is not merely a matter of which books are kept on bookshelves but also a matter of the way people give shape to their collective identities and allegiances in a public way" (2014, 5). The same can be said for lives: the celebration of an individual life is never only about an individual: lives are always relationally narrated and gain social meaning through acts of storying.

At first sight, the consecration of an individual life as representative of collective aspirations seems at odds with the pluralistic and democratic values of cultural memory studies. After all, we have come a long way since the 'great men' theory of history. Yet, many individuals who do not closely resemble Napoleon or Churchill also gain iconic status and become intensely memorable when they live on in stories. Just like historical events that become common reference points in cultural memory, individual lives enter stories as collectively recognizable reference points with distinct dynamics from the remembrance of a collective or an event. In "Embodied and Remembered Lives," Rigney suggests that we can study these lives as "'memory sites' (Nora) or 'figures of memory' (Assmann), which are considered particularly representative of the past, or more specifically, of that part of the past that is worth remembering" (2009, 65). Just like any other "memory site," however, the reasons for this memorability reside in the "dynamics of remembrance" (Rigney 2008a): "It is not enough for individuals to have done something 'glorious' to be remembered, then, there has to be 'room' in the canon of memory sites for them" (Rigney 2009, 65). Acts of cultural remembrance, or sustained mediation and remediation of narratives, make room for these figures in the canon of memory sites. Afterlives of individuals are generated by the lives of many different sorts of media.

2 Activist lives

As a response to the field's growing interest in the relationship between memory and activism, we would like to suggest that *activist* afterlives come with a particular set of questions and concerns. As opposed to the silenced victim, there is often no clear moral imperative to remember them. And unlike the all-powerful character of the national hero, their remembrance does not necessarily serve the status quo. Activists are characterized by their agency and oppositionality. They are suppressed or challenged but find means and mechanisms to push back against more powerful actors and institutions.

Many activist lives hold a place in the 'canon of memory sites' or at least became carriers of contentious memories and political aspirations, giving a face to entire movements. Some leaders continued to 'lead' successive generations as they lived on in stories, like Martin Luther King or Che Guevara. Some victims of injustice and systemic violence came to give a name to a *cause célèbre*, like Alfred Dreyfus or George Floyd, whose experience gave impetus to justice-seeking collectives. Some activists were both movement leaders and victims of injustice, like Angela Davis – an icon for many intersecting movements. Some were remembered because memory activists insisted that the injustice these figures experienced must not be forgotten. And some were remembered in all their glory and charisma, with a focus on the strength and importance of their political vision, personifying the memory of activism to inspire new generations to keep fighting for a cause. Depending on the lives that were remembered, there were of course different mixtures of these many modes of remembrance. But across all these figures' afterlives, we see how the nexus of memory and activism crystallizes around individual figures, pointing to a gravitational pull towards giving a face to political causes.

This pattern is not without its complications and we may find ourselves wondering: what is lost and gained when an individual life comes to stand for a cause? Often, a tension arises between the egalitarian or collectivist aims of the social movements and the emergence of individual figureheads. This tension is heightened by the activities of journalistic forms of media, with a vested interest in producing recognizable and charismatic leaders to act as focal points for attitudes towards a given movement. Davis, to use an example from our collection on *Remembering Contentious Lives* (Erbil et al. 2025), has expressed discomfort at the process of individualization whereby she has come to be remembered as one of the most well-known figures of the Black Power movement and a byword for the radicalism of the American 1970s. Yet she also acknowledges that her life, in storied forms such as in her famous autobiography, represents the "aspirations of millions of people" (Davis 2021). Narrativization, therefore, plays an essential role in the processes by which activist lives are mediated and remediated to become carriers for collective aspirations: "storied lives are seen both by the people involved and by the people around them as part and parcel of *collective* stories extending beyond the range of a single embodied life" (Rigney 2009, 61). Telling and retelling lives in narrative form gives them set meanings and associations, helping to form an image of a cohesive and characterizable self.

3 Remembering a contentious life

The relationship between cultural memory and activist lives is manifold and, as the examples above indicate, covers multiple points on the "memory-activism nexus" (Rigney 2018a, 372). Look at the case of the French anarchist Louise Michel (1830–1905), who over the course of a varied and extraordinary life fought for the liberation of the working class, of women, colonized subjects, children and animals, becoming one of the most recognizable actors from the 1871 Paris Commune.

Michel's cultural memory has been produced through successive mediations and remediations, which began during her lifetime. In an act that could be described as "memory activism," in that a contentious subject seeks to shape the legacy of political activism, Michel played a pivotal part in the storying of her own life. Versions of her memoirs have been in circulation since they were first written and published in the late nineteenth century. Acting as a "portable monument" (Rigney 2004), the text stands as testimony to Michel's lifelong radicalism and struggle against capitalism, militarism, patriarchy and nationalism. The memoirs give shape and resonance to Michel's life, portraying a knowable character with a clear voice and ideological commitment. Subsequently, the remediation of Michel's life story across film, fiction, archival collections, and more, provides a memory *of* her life that generates connections between the nineteenth century past and shifting presents. Among these mediations are those that remember Michel's life *in* activism. In 2020, the name 'Louise Michel' adorned a huge ship, sponsored by the famous artist Banksy, that rescued refugees in the Mediterranean. Exalted as "the perfect encapsulation of what we [the ship's crew] believe" (Cowles 2020), Louise Michel could be seen to offer a "blueprint for the future lives of those who identify with [her] as part of a common story" (Rigney 2009, 66). As later activists use and adapt her story, Michel's life is associated with new causes.

Michel's case also gives some sense of the relational nature of activist afterlives. The individual subject or group who recalls and records a life draws from available schemata to make sense of it. Thus, Michel's afterlives are contoured both by the specific narrative put forth in her memoirs and by more general stories, tropes or characterizations available to remembering subjects. She is, for instance, often compared to Joan of Arc, as a readily available prototype of female resistance. Moreover, those remembering a life do so intersubjectively in that they draw from relationally constituted experiences. The nature of the stories they produced are always affected by the venues, conventions or audiences these remembering subjects anticipate and researching activist afterlives is as much about *who* is remembering an activist's life – to what end? and why? – as it is about the subject who is remembered.

The centrality of context to the remembrance of an individual's work, is evident even in the volume you are holding in your hands (or reading on your screen) right now, which contributes to the story of Ann Rigney's academic life. If we, Duygu and Clara, were to tell anecdotes about our everyday encounters or festive dinners with Ann – who we might even call by her first name! – we would provide a more intimate representation of her in our personal lives, rather than a canonical citation in our academic work. If we were to write about our past lives as master's students at Utrecht University, she would appear as an inspiring teacher. If this was a cover letter for a job application, she would figure as our previous boss. Different meanings of 'Ann Rigney' would come forward depending on which story we chose to tell. The multifaceted lives of both remembering and remembered subjects affect the mediation of lives into stories and, if there is 'room' in the canon, into "figures of memory" or "memory sites." The field of memory studies is yet to map out the dynamics of the making of memorable lives, especially in the context of activism. Scholarship on life writing and autobiography studies may provide a good starting point.

Bibliography

"El Siluetazo." MUAC-UNAM. https://muac.unam.mx/exposicion/el-siluetazo. (Accessed 15 May 2024).

"Toespraak van Koning Willem-Alexander tijdens de Nationale Herdenking Slavernijverleden in het Oosterpark in Amsterdam." 01 July 2023. https://www.koninklijkhuis.nl/documenten/toe spraken/2023/07/01/toespraak-van-koning-willem-alexander-tijdens-de-nationale-herdenking-slavernijverleden-2023 . (Accessed 15 May 2024).

"Toespraak van minister-president Mark Rutte over het slavernijverleden." 19 December 2022. https://www.rijksoverheid.nl/documenten/toespraken/2022/12/19/toespraak-minister-president-rutte-over-het-slavernijverleden. (Accessed 15 May 2024).

Actis, Munú, Cristina Aldini, Liliana Gardella, Miriam Lewin, and Elisa Tokar. *Ese infierno. Conversaciones de cinco mujeres sobrevivientes de la ESMA.* Buenos Aires: Editorial Sudamericana, 2001.

Adams, Jessica. *Wounds of Returning: Race, Memory and Property on the Post-Slavery Plantation.* Chapel Hill: University of North Carolina Press, 2007.

Adams, Tony E., Stacy Holman Jones, and Carolyn Ellis. *Autoethnography.* Oxford: Oxford University Press, 2014.

Adorno, Theodor W. "Art and the Arts." Trans. Rodney Livingstone. *Can One Live After Auschwitz? A Philosophical Reader.* Ed. Rolf Tiedemann. Stanford, CA: University of Stanford Press, 2003. 368–387.

Adorno, Theodor W. *Aesthetic Theory.* Minneapolis: University of Minnesota Press, 1997.

Aguilar, Paloma, and Francisco Ferrándiz. "Memory, Media and Spectacle: Interviú's Portrayal of Civil War Exhumations in the Early Years of Spanish Democracy." *Journal of Spanish Cultural Studies* 17.1 (2016): 1–25.

Agulhon, Maurice. *Marianne au combat: L'imagerie et la symbolique républicaine de 1789 à 1880.* Paris: Flammarion, 1977.

Akenson, Donald Harman. "Perhaps God Is Irish: Sacred Texts as Virtual Reality Machine." *The Calling of the Nations: Exegesis, Ethnography, and Empire in a Biblical-Historic Present.* Eds. Mark Vessey, Sharon Betcher, Robert Daum, and Harry O. Maier. Toronto: University of Toronto Press, 2011. 43–58.

Alcuin, *Epistolae* eMGH Epp. 4, no. 161, 259–260.

Algae-Hewitt, Mark, Ryan Heuser, and Annalise Lockhart. "Mapping the Emotions of London in Fiction, 1700–1900: A Crowdsourcing Experiment." *Literary Mapping in the Digital Age.* Eds. David Cooper, Christopher Donaldson, and Patricia Murrieta-Flores. New York: Routledge, 2016. 25–46.

Allen, Matthew J. "The Poverty of Memory: For Political Economy in Memory Studies." *Memory Studies* 9.4 (2016): 371–375.

Allen, Scott. "Inspired by her Grandfather, 15-year-old Memorializes Coronavirus Victims with Digital Portraits." *Washington Post.* 29 September 2020. https://www.washingtonpost.com/nation/2020/09/29/inspired-by-her-grandfather-15-year-old-memorializes-coronavirus-victims-with-digital-portraits/. (Accessed 01 April 2024).

Amarasingam, Amarnath, and Thusiyan Nandakumar. "Social Media Platforms are Silencing Social Movements." *TechPolicy.Net.* 14 May 2021. https://www.techpolicy.press/social-media-platforms-are-silencing-social-movements/ (Accessed 01 May 2024).

Amenta, Edwin, and Francesca Polletta. "The Cultural Impacts of Social Movements." *Annual Review of Sociology* 45 (2019): 279–299.

Anderson, Benedict. *Imagined Communities: Reflections on the Origin and Spread of Nationalism.* London: Verso, 1983.

Ankersmit, Frank. *Narrative Logic: A Semantic Analysis of the Historian's Language.* Leiden: M. Nijhoff, 1983.

Anon. [A.M., T.D and D.B. Sullivan]. *"Guilty or Not Guilty?": Speeches from the Dock, or, Protests of Irish Patriotism, Containing, with Introductory Sketches and Biographical Notices, Speeches Delivered after Conviction.* Dublin: s.n., 1867.

Antentas, Josep Maria. "Spain: From the Indignados Rebellion to Regime Crisis (2011-2016)." *Labor History* 58.1 (2017): 106–131.

Appadurai, Arjun (ed.). *The Social Life of Things: Commodities in Cultural Perspective.* Cambridge: Cambridge University Press, 1986.

Appadurai, Arjun. *The Future as Cultural Fact. Essays on the Global Condition.* London and New York: Verso, 2013.

Appiah, Kwame Anthony. *The Lies that Bind; Rethinking Identity.* New York: Liveright, 2018.

Araujo, Ana Lucia. *Slavery in the Age of Memory: Engaging the Past.* London: Bloomsbury, 2020.

Arendt, Hannah. *The Human Condition.* Chicago: The University of Chicago Press, 1988 [1958].

Armstrong, Elizabeth A., and Suzanna M. Crage. "Movements and memory: The making of the Stonewall myth." American Sociological Review 71.5 (2006): 724–751.

Assmann, Aleida, and Sebastian Conrad (eds.). *Memory in a Global Age: Discourses, Practices and Trajectories.* Houndmills, Basingstoke: Palgrave Macmillan, 2010.

Assmann, Aleida. "Memory, Individual and Collective." *The Oxford Handbook of Contextual Political Analysis.* Eds. Robert E. Goodin and Charles Tilly. Oxford: Oxford University Press, 2006. 210–224.

Assmann, Aleida. "Canon and Archive." *Cultural Memory Studies: An International and Interdisciplinary Handbook.* Eds. Astrid Erll and Ansgar Nünning. Berlin: De Gruyter, 2008a.

Assmann, Aleida. "Transformations between History and Memory." *Social Research* 75.1 (2008b): 49–72.

Assmann, Aleida. *Cultural Memory and Western Civilization: Functions, Media, Archives.* Cambridge: Cambridge University Press, 2011 [1999].

Assmann, Jan. "Collective Memory and Cultural Identity." Trans. by John Czaplicka. *New German Critique* 65 (1995): 125–133.

Assmann, Jan. *Cultural Memory and Early Civilization: Writing, Remembrance and Political Imagination.* Cambridge: Cambridge University Press, 2011 [1992].

Assmann, Jan. *Moses the Egyptian: The Memory of Egypt in Western Monotheism.* Cambridge, MA: Harvard University Press, 1997.

Attridge, Derek. *The Singularity of Literature.* London: Routledge, 2004.

Ayrton, Pete (ed.). *¡No Pasarán!: Writings from the Spanish Civil War.* London: Serpent's Tail, 2016.

Azoulay, Ariella Aïsha. *Potential History: Unlearning Imperialism.* London: Verso, 2019.

Bachmann-Medick, Doris. "Übersetzung zwischen den Zeiten – ein travelling concept?" *Saeculum, Jahrbuch für Universalgeschichte* 67.1 (2017): 21–43.

Bak, Lene. "Danish Heroism Revisited: The Rescue of the Danish Jews between National and Global Memory." *The Rescue Turn and the Politics of Holocaust Memory.* Eds. Natalie Aleksiun, Raphael Utz, and Zofia Woyzicka. Detroit: Wyne State University Press, 2024. 65–97.

Baldwin, James. "White Man's Guilt." *Collected Essays.* Ed. James Baldwin. New York: Library of America, 1998. 713–727.

Balsamo, Anne. "Feminism and Cultural Studies." *The Journal of the Midwest Modern Language Association* 24.1 (1991): 50–73.

Banim, Michael. *Crohoore of the Bill-Hook.* London, 1826.

Barad, Karen. *Meeting the Universe Halfway: Quantum Physics and the Entanglement of Meaning.*
Durham: Duke University Press, 2007.

Barnouw, David. *The Phenomenon of Anne Frank.* Trans. Jeannette K. Ringold. Bloomington: Indiana
University Press, 2018.

Barthes, Roland. *Camera Lucida: Reflections on Photography.* Trans. Richard Howard. New York: Hill
and Wang, 1981.

Bartlett, Frederic C. *Remembering: A Study in Experimental and Social Psychology.* Cambridge and
New York: Cambridge University Press, 1995 [1932].

Bartov, Omer, et al. "An Open Letter on the Misuse of Holocaust Memory." *The New York Review.*
20 November 2023. https://www.nybooks.com/online/2023/11/20/an-open-letter-on-the-misuse-
of-holocaust-memory/. (Accessed 22 May 2024).

Bashir, Bashir, and Amos Goldberg (eds.). *The Holocaust and the Nakba: A New Grammar of Trauma
and History.* New York: Columbia University Press, 2019.

Basu, Laura. "News Satire: Giving the News a Memory." *Triple C* 16.1 (2018a): 241–255.

Basu, Laura. *Media Amnesia.* London: Pluto Press, 2018b.

Batinić, Jelena. *Women and Yugoslav Partisans: A History of World War II Resistance.* Cambridge:
Cambridge University Press, 2015.

Batteau, Jesseka. *Literary Performances of Post-Religious Memory in the Netherlands.* London and
Leiden: Brill, 2022.

Battelle, John. "The 'Creeping Googlization' Meme." https://web.archive.org/web/20091228104446/
http://battellemedia.com/archives/000145.php. (Accessed 16 March 2024).

Baumgarten, Britta, Priska Daphi, and Peter Ullrich (eds.). *Conceptualizing Culture in Social Movement
Research.* London: Palgrave Macmillan, 2014.

Beckles, Hilary. "Professor Sir Hilary Beckles – NiNsee Keti Koti Lezing 2021." 30 June 2021.www.you
tube.com/watch?v=uWFe4t3FPZU. (Accessed 15 May 2024).

Beiner, Guy. "Forgetting to Remember Orr: Death and Ambiguous Remembrance in Modern
Ireland." *Death and Dying in Ireland, Britain, and Europe: Historical Perspectives.* Eds. James Kelly
and Mary Ann Lyons. Dublin: Irish Academic Press, 2013. 171–202.

Beiner, Guy. "Fenianism and the Martyrdom-Terrorism Nexus in Ireland before Independence."
Martyrdom and Terrorism: Pre-Modern to Contemporary Perspectives. Eds. Dominic Janes and Alex
Houen. Oxford and New York: Oxford University Press, 2014b. 199–220.

Beiner, Guy. "Probing the Boundaries of Irish Memory: From Postmemory to Prememory and Back."
Irish Historical Studies 39.154 (2014a): 296–307.

Beiner, Guy. *Forgetful Remembrance: Social Forgetting and Vernacular Historiography of a Rebellion in
Ulster.* Oxford: Oxford University Press, 2018.

Bender, Emily M., Timnit Gebru, Angelina McMillan-Major, and Shmargaret Shmitchell. "On the
Dangers of Stochastic Parrots: Can Language Models Be Too Big?" *Proceedings of the 2021 ACM
Conference on Fairness, Accountability, and Transparency, ACM Digital Library* (2021): 610–623.

Benjamin, Walter. "The Work of Art in the Age of Mechanical Reproduction." *Illuminations.* Trans.
Harry Zohn. New York: Schocken, 1969.

Benjamin, Walter. *The Origin of German Tragic Drama.* Trans. John Osbourne. London: NLB, 1977.

Benjamin, Walter. "A Little History of Photography." *Walter Benjamin: Selected Writings, vol.2, part 2,
1931–1934.* Trans. Rodney Livingstone et al. Eds. Michael W. Jennings, Howard Eiland, and Gary
Smith. Cambridge, MA.: Belknap, 1999.

Benjamin, Walter. *The Arcades Project.* Trans. Hoeard Eiland and Kevin McLaughlin. Cambridge, MA:
The Belknap Press of Harvard University Press, 1999.

Benjamin, Walter. "A Little History of Photography." *The Work of Art in the Age of Its Technological Reproducibility and Other Writings on Media*. Eds. Michael W. Jennings, Brigid Doherty, and Thomas Y. Levin. Cambridge, MA: Belknap Press of Harvard University Press, 2008. 274–298.

Benjamin, Walter. *The Work of Art in the Age of its Technological Reproducibility, and Other Writings on Media*. Eds. Michael W. Jennings, Brigid Doherty, and Thomas Y. Levin. Cambridge, MA: Harvard University Press, 2008.

Bennett, Jane. *Vibrant Matter: A Political Ecology of Things*. Durham, NC: Duke University Press, 2010.

Berger, Stefan (ed.). *Gewerkschaftsgeschichte als Erinnerungsgeschichte. Der 2. Mai 1933 in der gewerkschaftlichen Erinnerung und Positionierung*. Essen: Klartext, 2015.

Berger, Stefan (ed.). *The Engaged Historian. Perspectives on the Intersections of Politics, Activism and the Historical Profession*. Oxford: Berghahn Books, 2019.

Berger, Stefan, and Christian Koller (eds.). *Memory and Social Movements in Modern and Contemporary History: Remembering Past Struggles and Resourcing Protest*. Basingstoke: Palgrave MacMillan, 2024.

Berger, Stefan, and Wulf Kansteiner (eds.). *Agonistic Memory and the Legacy of 20th Century Wars in Europe*. Cham: Palgrave Macmillan, 2021.

Berger, Stefan, Sean Scalmer, and Christian Wicke (eds.). *Remembering Social Movements: Activism and Memory*. London: Routledge, 2021.

Berger, Stefan, Wolfgang Jäger, and Ulf Teichmann (eds.). *Gewerkschaften im Gedächtnis der Demokratie: Welche Rolle spielen soziale Kämpfe in der Erinnerungskultur?* Bielefeld: transcript, 2022.

Berntsen, Dorthe. "Involuntary Autobiographical Memories." *Applied Cognitive Psychology* 10.5 (1996): 435–454.

Biden, Joe. "President Biden Remarks on 1921 Tulsa Race Massacre." *C-Span*. National Cable Satellite Corporation, 1 June 2021. https://www.c-span.org/video/?512210-1/president-biden-recalls-horror -1921-tulsa-race-massacre. (Accessed 27 May 2024)

Biekman, Barryl A. *General Assembly of the United Nations*. 14 December 2014. www.un.org/pga/69/ 101214_statement-biekman. (Accessed 15 May 2024).

Birhane, Abeba, Vinay Uday Prabhu, and Emmanuel Kahembwe. "Multimodal Datasets: Misogyny, Pornography, and Malignant Stereotypes." *arXiv preprint arXiv:2110.01963* (2021).

Bjornerud, Marcia. *Timefulness. How Thinking like a Geologist can Help Save the World*. Princeton: Princeton University Press, 2018.

Blight, David W. "Europe in 1989, America in 2020, and the Death of the Lost Cause." *The New Yorker*. Condé Nast, 1 July 2020. https://www.newyorker.com/culture/cultural-comment/europe-in-1989- america-in-2020-and-the-death-of-the-lost-cause. (Accessed 27 May 2024).

Bode, Katherine, and Lauren M. E. Goodlad. "Data Worlds: An Introduction." *Critical AI* 1.1–2 (2023).

Bodó, Balázs. "Mediated Trust: A Theoretical Framework to Address the Trustworthiness of Technological Trust Mediators." *New Media and Society* 23.9 (2021): 2668–2690.

Bond, Lucy, Ben De Bruyn, and Jessica Rapson (eds.). "Planetary Memory." Special Issue, *Textual Practice* 31.5 (2017).

Bond, Lucy, Ben de Bruyn, and Jessica Rapson. "Planetary Memory in Contemporary American Fiction." *Textual Practice* 31.5 (2017): 853–866.

Bond, Lucy, and Stef Craps. *Trauma*. Abington: Routledge, 2020.

Borges, Jorge Luis. *Labyrinths: Selected Stories and Other Writings*. New Directions, 1962.

Borges, Jorge Luis. *Collected Fictions*. New York: Penguin, 1999.

Bornhöhe, Eduard. *Tasuja: Jutustus Eestimaa wanast ajast*. Tallinn: A. E. Brandt, 1880.

Bornhöhe, Eduard. *Willu wõitlused*. Tallinn: K. Busch, 1890.

Bornhöhe, Eduard. *Ajaloolised jutustused*. Tallinn: Eesti Raamat, 1964.

Bornstein, George. *Material Modernism: The Politics of the Page*. Cambridge: Cambridge University Press, 2006.

Boscagli, Maurizia. *Stuff Theory: Everyday Objects and Radical Materialism*. New York: Bloomsbury, 2014.

Bostrom, Nick. "Why I Want to Be a Posthuman When I Grow Up." *Ethics and Emerging Technologies*. Ed. Roland L. Sandler. London: Palgrave Macmillan, 2014. 218–234.

Botha, Monique. "Academic, Activist, or Advocate? Angry, Entangled, and Emerging: A Critical Reflection on Autism Knowledge Production." *Frontiers in Psychology* 12 (2021): n.p.

Boyce, David George. "'A Gallous Story and a Dirty Deed': Political Martyrdom in Ireland since 1867." *Ireland's Terrorist Dilemma*. Eds. Yonah Alexander and Alan O'Day. Dordrecht, Boston, and Lancaster: Martinus Nijhoff Publishers, 1986. 7–27.

Bradbury, Ray. *Fahrenheit 451*. New York: Simon & Schuster, 2018.

Brennan, Sheila. *Stamping American Memory: Collectors, Citizens, and the Post*. Ann Arbor: University of Michigan Press, 2018.

Bridle, James. *New Dark Age: Technology, and the End of the Future*. London: Verso, 2018.

Brillenburg Wurth, Kiene, and Ann Rigney. *The Life of Texts: An Introduction to Literary Studies*. Amsterdam: Amsterdam University Press, 2019 [2006].

Brown, Bill. "Thing Theory." *Critical Inquiry* 28.1 (2001): 1–22.

Brown, Bill. *A Sense of Things*. Chicago: The University of Chicago Press, 2003.

Brown, Bill. "Big Think Interview." *Big Think*. 04 March 2010. https://bigthink.com/videos/big-think-interview-with-bill-brown. (Accessed 04 April 2024).

Brown, Roger, and James Kulik. "Flashbulb Memories." *Cognition* 5.1 (1977): 73–99.

Bruner, Jerome. "The Narrative Construction of Reality." *Critical Inquiry* 18 (1991): 1–21.

Buecheler, Franciscus, and Alexander Riese. *Anthologia Latina: sive poesis latine Supplementum*. Leipzig, 1869. 288.

Bukiel Malgorzata, Andrzej Sakson, and Cezary Trosiak (eds.). *Ziemie Zachodnie i Północne (1945-2020). Nowe konteksty*. Poznań: Instytut Zachodni, 2020.

Bulson, Eric. *little magazine world form*. New York: Columbia University Press, 2019.

Butler, Judith. *Frames of War: When is Life Grievable?* London: Verso, 2009.

Buzinde, Christine N., and Carla Almeida Santos. "Representations of Slavery." *Annals of Tourism Research* 35.2 (2008): 469–488.

Byers, Michele, and Val Marie Johnson (eds.). *The CSI Effect: Television, Crime, and Governance*. Lanham: Lexington Books, 2009.

Carle, Zoé. "Histoire de la bombe aérosol: Les outils de la contestation graphique." *Revue du crieur* 1 (2020): 40–49.

Carlson, Marvin. *The Haunted Stage: The Theatre as Memory Machine*. Ann Arbor: University of Michigan Press, 2004.

Cento Bull, Anna, Francisco Colom-González, and Hans Lauge Hansen. "Agonistic Memory Revisited." *Agonistic Memory and the Legacy of Twentieth-Century Wars in Europe*. Eds. Stefan Berger and Wulf Kansteiner. Basingstoke: Palgrave MacMillan, 2021. 13–38.

Chakrabarty, Dipesh. *The Climate of History in a Planetary Age*. Chicago: The University of Chicago Press, 2021.

Chamberlain, Mary, and Paul Thompson. *Narrative and Genre*. London and New York: Routledge, 1998.

Chaumont, Jean-Michel. *La Concurrence des victimes: génocide, identité, reconnaissance*. Paris: La Découverte, 1997.

Chidgey, Red. *Feminist Afterlives: Assemblage Memory in Activist Times*. Basingstoke: Palgrave Macmillan, 2018.

Christie, Paula. "The Baltic Chain: A Study of the Organisation Facets of Large-scale Protest from a Micro-level Perspective." *Lithuanian Historical Studies* 20 (2015): 183–211.

Clare, Mariette, and Richard Johnson. "Method in our Madness? Identity and Power in Memory-Work Practice." *Memory and Methodology*. Ed. Susannah Radstone. New York and London: Berg, 2000. 197–224.

Clark, Andy, and David Chalmers. "The Extended Mind." *Analysis* 58 (1998): 7–19.

Clark, Timothy. *Ecocriticism on the Edge the Anthropocene as a Threshold Concept*. London: Bloomsbury Academic, 2015.

Clarke, Michael Tavel, and David Wittenberg. *Scale in Literature and Culture*. Cham: Palgrave Macmillan, 2017.

Cole, Tim. *Selling the Holocaust From Auschwitz to Schindler: How History Is Bought, Packaged, and Sold*. New York: Routledge, 2000.

Commonwealth of Australia, House of Representatives. "Apology to Australia's Indigenous Peoples." 13 February 2008. https://parlinfo.aph.gov.au/parlInfo/genpdf/chamber/hansardr/2008-02-13/0003/hansard_frag.pdf;fileType=application%2Fpdf. (Accessed 17 May 2024).

Connerton, Paul. *How Modernity Forgets*. Cambridge: Cambridge University Press, 2009.

Connolly, Claire. "Making Maps: Irish Literature in Transition, 1780–1830." *Irish Literature in Transition, 1780–1830*. Ed. Claire Connolly. Cambridge and New York, 2020. 1–34.

Connolly, Claire. "The Secret of Castle Rackrent." *European Romantic Review* 31.6 (2020): 663–679.

Cosenza, Maria Emilio. *Petrarch's Letters to Classical Authors. Translation and Commentary*. Chicago, IL: The University of Chicago Press, 1910.

Costanza-Chock, Sasha, Inioluwa Deborah Raji, and Joy Buolamwini. "Who Audits the Auditors? Recommendations from a Field Scan of the Algorithmic Auditing Ecosystem." *Proceedings of the 2022 ACM Conference* (2022): 1571–1583.

Coulthard, Glen. "Subjects of the Empire." *Contemporary Political Theory* 6 (2007): 437–460.

Cowles, Ben. "Thanks to Banksy, Louise Michel is Fighting Oppression Once More." *Morning Star*. 19 September 2020. https://morningstaronline.co.uk/article/f/thanks-to-banksy-louise-michel-is-fighting-oppression-once-more. (Accessed 26 April 2024).

Cox, Fiona, and Elena Theodorakopoulo (eds.). *Homer's Daughters: Women's Responses to Homer in the Twentieth Century and Beyond*. Oxford: Oxford UP, 2019.

Craps, Stef. "Climate Change and the Art of Anticipatory Memory." *Parallax* 23.1 (2017): 479–492.

Craps, Stef. "Introduction – Memory Studies and the Anthropocene: A Roundtable." *Memory Studies* 11.4 (2018): 498–515.

Craps, Stef, and Rick Crownshaw. "Introduction: The Rising Tide of Climate Change Fiction." *Studies in the Novel* 50.1 (2018): 1–8.

Craps, Stef, Rick Crownshaw, Jennifer Wenzel, Rosanne Kennedy, Claire Colebrook, and Vin Nardizzi. "Memory Studies and the Anthropocene: A Roundtable." *Memory Studies* 11.4 (2018): 498–515.

Craps, Stef. "Lost Words and Lost Worlds: Combatting Environmental Generational Amnesia." *Memory Studies Review* 1.1 (2024), forthcoming.

Crook, Richard. "The History of the Yellow Ribbon." *BBC*. 07 October 2014. https://www.bbc.com/news/uk-29521449. (Accessed 01 April 2024.)

Crownshaw, Rick (ed.). "Transcultural Memory." Special Issue, *Parallax* 17.4 (2011).

Crownshaw, Rick. "Climate Change Perpetrators: Ecocriticism, Implicated Subjects, and Anthropocene Fiction." *The Routledge International Handbook of Perpetrator Studies*. Eds. Susanne C. Knittel and Zachary J. Goldberg. London: Routledge, 2019, pp. 228–239.

Curci, Antonietta, and Olivier Luminet. "Follow-up of a Cross-national Comparison on Flashbulb and Event Memory for the September 11th Attacks." *Memory* 14.3 (2006): 329–344.

Curci, Antonietta, Olivier Luminet IV, Catrin Finkenauer, and Lydia Gisle. "Flashbulb Memories in Social Groups: A Comparative Test–retest Study of the Memory of French President Mitterrand's Death in a French and a Belgian Group." *Memory* 9.2 (2001): 81–101.

Cyr, Travis G., Kayla Toscano, and William Hirst. "Flashbulb Memories and Memories for Personal Events: Their Role in Social Categorization and Identification." *Journal of Applied Research in Memory and Cognition* (2023): in press.

Daphi, Priska, and Lorenzo Zamponi. "Exploring the Movement-Memory Nexus: Insights and Ways Forward." *Mobilization: An International Quarterly* 24.4 (2019a): 399–417.

Daphi, Priska, and Lorenzo Zamponi. "Movements and Memory." *Mobilization* special issue 24.4 (2019b): 399–524.

Daphi, Priska. *Becoming a Movement: Identity, Narrative and Memory in the European Global Justice Movement*. London: Rowman & Littlefield, 2017.

Daphi, Priska. Mnemonic Adaption and Rejection: how activists remember and forget previous movements. *Memory Studies*. forthcoming.

Davis, Angela Y. "A Question Of Memory: A Conversation with Angela Y. Davis." Interview by René de Guzman. Goethe-Institut. April 2021. https://goethe.de/ins/us/en/kul/art/one/22172673.html?forceDesktop=1. (Accessed 13 August 2024).

Davies-Jones, Robert P. "Tornado Dynamics." *Thunderstorms Morphology and Dynamics*. Ed. Edwin Kessler. University of Oklahoma Press, vol. 2, 1998. 197–236.

Davis, Caroline. *African Literature and the CIA*. Cambridge: Cambridge University Press, 2020.

Davis, Megan. "Aboriginal Women: The Right to Self-Determination." *Australian Indigenous Law Review* 16.1 (2012): 78–88.

Davis, Megan, and New South Wales. *Family Is Culture: Independent Review of Aboriginal Children and Young People in Out Of Home Care in NSW*. Sydney: Department of Family and Community Services, 2019.

Davis, Nick. *Flat Earth News*. New York: Vintage, 2009.

De Cesari, Chiara, and Ann Rigney. "Introduction." *Transnational Memory: Circulation, Articulation, Scales*. Eds. Chiara De Cesari and Ann Rigney. Berlin: De Gruyter, 2014. 1–25.

De Cesari, Chiara, and Ann Rigney (eds.). *Transnational Memory: Circulation, Articulation, Scales*. Berlin: De Gruyter, 2014.

De Cesari, Chiara, and Ayhan Kaya (eds.). *European Memory in Populism: Representations of Self and Other*. London: Routledge, 2020.

De Cesari, Chiara, and Wayne Modest (eds.). *Curating the Colonial: Transforming Museums and the Question of Race*. Routledge, forthcoming.

De Cesari, Chiara. "Heritage, Memory, Race: The Culture of the Far Right." *Polarized Pasts: Heritage and Belonging in Times of Political Polarization*. Ed. Elisabeth Niklasson. New York: Berghahn Books, 2023.

De Telegraaf. "Tal van arrestaties bij Frans protest tegen coronapas." 11 September 2021. https://www.telegraaf.nl/nieuws/211829219/tal-van-arrestaties-bij-frans-protest-tegen-coronapas (Accessed 15 March 2024).

Deane-Cox, Sharon, and Anneleen Spiessens (eds.). *The Routledge Handbook of Translation and Memory*. London: Routledge, 2022.

Della Porta, Donatella, and Mario Diani. *Social Movements: An Introduction*. Oxford: Blackwell Publishing, 2014.

Derrida, Jacques. "Living On." Trans. James Hulbert. *Deconstruction and Criticism*. London: The Continuum Publishing Company, 2004 [1979]. 62–142.

Derrida, Jacques. "Survivre/Journal de Bord," in *Parages*. Paris: Gallilée, 1986 [1979]. 119–218.

Deuze, Mark. "Media Life." *Media, Culture & Society* 33.1 (2011): 137–148.

Dick, Philip K. *Little Black Box*. London: Gollancz, 1990.

Dickinson, Kristin. *DisOrientations: German-Turkish Cultural Contact in Translation, 1811–1946*. University Park, PA: The Pennsylvania State University Press, 2021.

Dimock, Wai Chee. "Low Epic." *Critical Inquiry* 39.3 (2013): 614–631.

Dodson, Mick, and Roland Wilson. *Bringing Them Home: Report of the National Inquiry into the Separation of Aboriginal and Torres Strait Islander Children from Their Families*. Sydney: Human Rights and Equal Opportunity Commission, 1997.

Doerr, Nicole, Alice Mattoni, and Simon Teune. "Towards a Visual Analysis of Social Movements, Conflict, and Political Mobilization." *Advances in the Visual Analysis of Social Movements*. Eds. Nicole Doerr, Alice Mattoni and Simon Teune. 35 (2013): xi–xxvi.

Doerr, Nicole. "Memory and Culture in Social Movements." *Conceptualizing Culture in Social Movement Research*. Eds. Britta Baumgarten, Priska Daphi, and Peter Ullrich. Basingstoke: Palgrave MacMillan, 2014. 206–226.

Dolan, Jill. *Utopia in Performance: Finding Hope at the Theater*. Ann Arbor: University of Michigan Press, 2005.

Dolan, T. P. "Irish Oratory from Emmet to Casement." *Irish University Review* 6.2 (1976): 151–163.

Donald, Merlin. "The Exographic Revolution." *The Cognitive Life of Things: Recasting the Boundaries of the Mind*. Eds. L Lambros Malafouris and Colin Renfrew. Cambridge: McDonald Institute for Archeological Research, 2010. 71–80.

Donnelly, James S., Jr. "The Construction of the Memory of the Famine in Ireland and the Irish Diaspora, 1850–1900." *Éire-Ireland* 31.1 (1996): 26–61.

Donohoe, Janet. "Hannah Arendt and the Ideological Character of Monuments." *Phenomenology and the Political*. Eds. S. West Gurley and Geoff Pfeifer. Lanham, MD: Rowman & Littlefield, 2016. 251–262.

Doyle, Jennifer, Jonathan Flatley, and José Esteban Muñoz. "Introduction." *Pop Out: Queer Warhol*. Eds. Jennifer Doyle, Jonathan Flatley, and José Esteban Muñoz. Durham and London: Duke University Press, 1996.

Drucker, Joanna. *The Visible Word. Typography and Modern Art 1909–1923*. Chicago: Chicago University Press, 1996.

Druxes, Helga, and Patricia Anne Simpson. "Introduction: Pegida as a European Far-right Populist Movement." *German Politics and Society* 34.4 (2016): 1–16.

Durkheim, Emile. *Sociology and Philosophy*. Trans. JG Perisitiany. Routledge and Kegan Paul, 1974.

Dziuban, Zuzanna (ed.). *Mapping the Forensic Turn. Engaging with Materialities of Mass Death in Holocaust Studies and Beyond*. Vienna: New Academic Press, 2017.

Echterhoff, Gerald, and William Hirst. "Thinking about Memories for Everyday and Shocking Events: Do People use Ease-of-retrieval Cues in Memory Judgments?" *Memory & Cognition*, 34.4 (2006): 763–775.

Eco, Umberto. *Semiotics and Philosophy of Language*. Bloomington: Indiana University Press, 1986.

Eglitis, Daina S., and Laura Ardava. "The Politics of Memory: Remembering the Baltic Way 20 Years after 1989." *Europe-Asia Studies* 64.6 (2012): 1033–1059.

Elliott, Marianne. *Robert Emmet: The Making of a Legend*. London: Profile Books, 2003.

Ellsworth, Elisabeth, and Jamie Kruse (eds.). *Making the Geologic Now. Responses to Material Conditions of Contemporary Life*. New York: Punctum Books, 2012.

Encarnación, Omar. "Forgetting, in Order to Move On." *The New York Times* 22 (2014). https://www. nytimes.com/roomfordebate/2014/01/06/turning-away-from-painful-chapters/forgetting-in-order-to-move-on (Accessed 14 March 2024).

Epsmark, Kjell. *The Nobel Prize in Literature: A Study of the Criteria Behind the Choices*. Boston: G.K. Hall, 1991.

Erbil, Duygu, "Commodification Anxiety and the Memory of Turkish Revolutionary Deniz Gezmiş." *Memory Studies* 17.5 (2024): 1039–1055.

Erbil, Duygu, Ann Rigney, and Clara Vlessing (eds.). *Remembering Contentious Lives*. Basingstoke: Palgrave Macmillan.

Erll, Astrid, and Ann Rigney (eds.). *Mediation, Remediation, and the Dynamics of Cultural Memory*. Berlin: De Gruyter, 2009a.

Erll, Astrid, and Ann Rigney. "Cultural Memory and its Dynamics." *Mediation, Remediation, and the Dynamics of Cultural Memory*. Eds. Astrid Erll and Ann Rigney. Berlin: De Gruyter, 2009b. 1–14.

Erll, Astrid. "Remembering Across Time, Space, and Cultures: Premediation, Remediation and the 'Indian Mutiny'." *Mediation, Remediation, and the Dynamics of Cultural Memory*. Eds. Astrid Erll and Ann Rigney. Berlin: De Gruyter, 2009. 109–138.

Erll, Astrid. "Travelling Memory." *Parallax* 17.4 (2011a): 4–18.

Erll, Astrid. *Memory in Culture*. London: Palgrave Macmillan, 2011b.

Erll, Astrid. "Homer: A Relational Mnemohistory." *Memory Studies* 11.3 (2018): 274–286.

Erll, Astrid. "Afterword: Memory Worlds in Times of Corona." *Memory Studies* 13.5 (2020): 861–874.

Erll, Astrid. "The Hidden Power of Implicit Collective Memory." *Memory, Mind & Media* 1.1 (2022): 1–17.

Erll, Astrid, and William Hirst. "Flashbulb Memories and Narrative: An Interdisciplinary Research Programme." *Narrative Inquiry* 33.2 (2023): 398–420.

Erll, Astrid. "Game-Changing Homeric Memory: Odysseys Before and After Joyce." *Textual Practice* 38.1 (2024): 34–52.

Erll, Astrid. *Travels in Time. Essays on Collective Memory in Motion*. New York: Oxford University Press, 2025 (in press).

Esposito, Elena. "Algorithmic Memory and the Right to be Forgotten on the Web." *Big Data & Society* 4.1 (2017): 1–11.

Evans, James A., and Jacob G. Foster. "Algorithmic Abduction: Robots for Alien Reading." *Critical Inquiry* 50.3 (2024): 375–401.

Eyerman, Ron. "Social Movements and Memory." *Routledge International Handbook of Memory Studies*. Eds. Anna Lisa Tota and Trever Hagen. London: Routledge, 2015. 79–83.

Farrier, David. *Anthropocene Poetics: Deep Time, Sacrifice Zones, and Extinction*. Minneapolis, London: University of Minnesota Press, 2019.

Farrier, David. *Footprints: In Search of Future Fossils*. Picador USA, 2021.

Faulkner, William. *Requiem for a Nun*. New York: Signet, 1961.

Favorini, Atilio. "Some Memory Plays before the Memory Play." *Journal of Dramatic Theory and Criticism* 22.1 (2007): 29–50.

Favorini, Atilio. *Memory in Play: From Aeschylus to Sam Shepard*. New York: Palgrave Macmillan, 2008.

Feffer, John. "No Pasaran: Ukraine 2022." *FPIF.org*. 2 March 2022. https://fpif.org/no-pasaran-ukraine -2022/ (Accessed 14 March 2024)

Felski, Rita. *The Uses of Literature*. Oxford: Blackwell, 2008.

Ferdinand, Simon. *Mapping Beyond Measure: Art, Cartography, and the Space of Global Modernity*. Lincoln, NE: University of Nebraska Press, 2019.

Ferrándiz, Francisco. "Francisco Franco is Back: The Contested Reemergence of a Fascist Moral Exemplar." *Comparative Studies in Society and History* 64.1 (2022): 208–237.

Ferrándiz, Francisco. "Mass Graves as Crime Scenes: Forensic Operatives and Scenographies in Contemporary Spain." *Geographies of Perpetration. Re-Signifying Cultural Narratives of Mass Violence*. Eds. Brigitte Jirku and Vicente Sánchez-Biosca. Berlin: Peter Lang, 2021.

Ferrándiz, Francisco. "Phantom Militarism and Counter-Forensics." Visual and New Media Review, *Fieldsights*. 09 February 2023. https://culanth.org/fieldsights/phantom-militarism-and-counter-forensics. (Accessed 03 April 2024).

Ferrándiz, Francisco. "Unburials, Generals and Phantom Militarism: Engaging with the Spanish Civil War Legacy." *Current Anthropology* 60.19 (2019): 62–76.

Ferrando, Francesca. *Philosophical Posthumanism*. London: Bloomsbury, 2020.

Ferrari, Fabian, José Van Dijck, and Antal Van den Bosch. "Foundation Models and the Privatization of Public Knowledge." *Nature Machine Intelligence* 5 (2023): 818–820.

Finkelstein, Norman G. *The Holocaust Industry: Reflections on the Exploitation of Jewish Suffering*. London: Verso, 2000.

Flatley, Jonathan. *Like Andy Warhol*. Chicago-London: University of Chicago Press, 2017.

Flood, Alison. "Marieke Lucas Rijneveld wins International Booker for *The Discomfort of Evening*." *The Guardian*. 26 August 2020. https://www.theguardian.com/books/2020/aug/26/marieke-lucas-rijneveld-wins-international-booker-for-the-discomfort-of-evening. (Accessed 29 April 2024).

Foster, R. F. *The Irish Story: Telling Tales and Making It Up in Ireland*. London and New York: Allen Lane, 2001.

Fraenkel, Béatrice. "Actes écrits, actes oraux: la performativité à l'épreuve de l'écriture." *Études de communication* 29 (2006): 69–93.

Frank, Gustav, and Madleen Podewski. "The Object of Periodical Studies." *Periodical Studies Today*. Eds. Jutta Ernst, Oliver Scheiding, and Dagmar von Hoff. Leiden: Brill Publishers, 2022. 29–53.

Fraser, Ronald. *In Search of a Past: The Manor House, Amnersfield 1933–1945*. London: Verso, 1984.

Freeman, Mark. "Charting the Narrative Unconscious: Cultural Memory and the Challenge of Autobiography." *Narrative Inquiry* 12 (2002): 193–211.

Fridman, Orli, and Sarah Gensburger (eds.). *The Covid-19 Pandemic and Memory: Remembering, Commemoration and Archiving in Crisis*. Cham: Palgrave Macmillan, 2024.

Fridman, Orli. "#memoryactivism and Online Commemoration." *The Routledge Handbook of Memory Activism*. Eds. Yifat Gutman and Jenny Wüstenberg. London: Routledge, 2023.

Fuisz, Lisbeth. "'We the people': The U.S. Government's Recent Recruitment of Literature for Nation Building." *Moment to Monument: The Making and Unmaking of Cultural Significance*. Eds. Bezzola Lambert et al. Bielefeld: transcript, 2009. 111–122.

Gal, Susan. "Scale-Making. Comparison and Perspective as Ideological Projects." *Scale: Discourse and Dimensions of Social Life*. Eds. E. Summerson Carr and Michael Lempert. Oakland, CA: University of California Press, 2016. 91–111.

Gamble, John. *Society and Manners in Nineteenth-Century Ireland*. Ed. Breandán Mac Suibhne. Dublin: Field Day, 2011.

Gandolphe, Marie-Charlotte, and Mohamad El Haj. "Flashbulb Memories of the Charlie Hebdo Attack." *Journal of Psychology and Cognition* 1.1 (2016): 20–28.

Gangl, Georg. *Telling It Like It Really Was: On the Form, Presuppositions, and Justification of Historiographic Knowledge*. Oulu: University of Oulu, 2023.

Garibian, Sévane. *La muerte del verdugo. Reflexiones interdisciplinarias sobre el cadáver de los criminales en masa*. Buenos Aires: Miño y Dávila Editores, 2017.

Gauthier, David, Audrey Samson, Eric Snodgrass, Winnie Soon, and Magdalena Tyżlik-Carver. "Executing." *Uncertain Archives: Critical Keywords for Big Data*. Eds. Nanna Bonde Thylstrup,

Daniela Agostinho, Annie Ring, Catherine D'Ignazio, and Kristin Veel. Cambridge, MA: MIT Press, 2021. 209–216.

Gensburger, Sarah, and Jenny Wüstenberg (eds.). *De-commemoration. Removing Statues and Renaming Places*. New York: Berghahn, 2023.

Gensburger, Sarah, and Gérôme Truc. "Les Mémoriaux du 13 novembre." *Editions EHESS* 13 (2020).

Gensburger, Sarah. "Memory and Space: (Re)reading Halbwachs and the Remembrance of Austerlitz." *Handbook of Memoryscapes*. Eds. Sarah De Nardi, Hilary Orange, Steven High, and Eerika Koskinen-Koivisto. London: Routledge, 2019b. 69–76.

Gensburger, Sarah. *Memory on My Doorstep. Chronicles of the Bataclan Neighborhood (Paris, 2015–2016)*. Leuven: Leuven University Press, 2019a.

Geoghegan, Patrick M. *Robert Emmet: A Life*. Dublin: Gill & Macmillan, 2002.

Gessat-Anstett, Élisabeth, and Jean-Marc Dreyfus (eds.). *Human Remains and Identification: Mass Violence, Genocide and the 'Forensic Turn'*. Manchester: Manchester University Press, 2017.

Ghosh, Amitav. *The Great Derangement: Climate Change and the Unthinkable*. Chicago: University of Chicago Press, 2016.

Ghosh, Amitav. *The Nutmeg's Curse. Parables for a Planet in Crisis*. London: John Murray, 2021.

Gillespie, Tarleton. "The Politics of 'Platforms'." *New Media & Society* 12.3 (2010): 347–364. https://doi. org/10.1177/1461444809342738

Ginzburg, Carlo. "Just One Witness: The Extermination of the Jews and the Principle of Reality." *Threads and Traces. True, False, Fictive*. Los Angeles and London: University of California Press, 2012. 165–179.

Glăveanu, Vlad. *Distributed Creativity. Thinking Outside the Box of the Creative Individual*. New York: Springer, 2014.

Glynn, Alan. *Limitless*. London: Faber and Faber, 2011.

Goldberg, Amos. "Yes, It is Genocide." *Swiss Policy Research*. 09 May 2024. https://swprs.org/profes sor-amos-goldberg-yes-it-is-genocide/. (Accessed 22 May 2024)

Goldfarb, Jeffrey. *Reinventing Political Culture: The Politics of Culture Versus the Culture of Politics*. Cambridge: Polity, 2012.

Goldring, Maurice. *Pleasant the Scholar's Life: Irish Intellectuals and the Construction of the Nation State*. London: Serif, 1993.

Goodlad, Lauren M.E. "Editor's Introduction: Humanities in the Loop." *Critical AI* 1.1–2 (2023).

Goonewardena, Kanishka, and Katharine N. Rankin. "The Desire Called Civil Society: A Contribution to the Critique of a Bourgeois Category." *Planning Theory* 3.2 (2004): 117–149.

Gorman, Amanda. *The Hill We Climb. An Inaugural Poem for the Country*. New York: Random House, 2021.

Grafton, Anthony. *The Footnote: A Curious History*. London: Faber and Faber, 1997.

Graham, Shawn, Ian Milligan, Scott Weingart, and Kim Martin. *Exploring Big Historical Data: The Historian's Macroscope*. London: Imperial College Press, 2022 [2016].

Gramsci, Antonio. *Selections from Political Writings, 1910–1920*. Vol. 1. Trans. John Mathews. Ed. Quentin Hoare. London: Lawrence and Wishart, 1977. 188.

Gready, Paul, and Simon Robins. *From Transitional to Transformative Justice*. Cambridge and New York: Cambridge University Press, 2018.

Greimas, Algirdas J., and Joseph Courtés. *Semiotics and Language. An Analytical Dictionary*. Bloomington: Indiana University Press, 1982.

Grever, Maria. "Historical Consciousness and Contested Statues in a Post-Colonial World: The Case of Missionary Peerke Donders." *Journal History of Education* 52.6 (2023): 1000–1014.

Gunes, Fidan, and Gurgor Kilix. "Grunya Efimovna Sukhareva: Otizmin tarihçesinde yok sayılan Sovyet bilim kadını." 14 January 2021. https://ekmekvegul.net/bellek/grunya-efimovna-sukhareva-otizmin-tarihcesinde-yok-sayilan-sovyet-bilim-kadini. (Accessed 20 February 2024)

Gutman, Yifat, and Jenny Wüstenberg. "Challenging the Meaning of the Past from Below: A Typology for Comparative Research on Memory Activists." *Memory Studies* 15.5 (2022): 1070–1086.

Gutman, Yifat, and Wüstenberg Jenny (eds.) (2023), *The Routledge Handbook of Memory Activism* (London: Routledge).

Hackett, Pat. "Introduction." *The Andy Warhol Diaries*. Ed. Pat Hackett. New York: Hachette Book Company, 1991. xi–xxi.

Hacking, Ian. *Rewriting the Soul: Multiple Personality and the Sciences of the Memory*. Princeton: Princeton University Press, 1995.

Haefele, Hans F. *Notker der Stammler, Taten Kaiser Karls des Großen (Notkeri Balbuli Gesta Karoli Magni imperatoris)*. MGH Scriptores Rerum Germanicum, Nova Series XII. Berlin, 1959. 1–93.

Haider, Asad. "Pessimism of the Will." *Viewpoint Magazine*. 28 May 2020. https://viewpointmag.com/2020/05/28/pessimism-of-the-will/. (Accessed 16 February 2024).

Halbwachs, Maurice. *Les cadres sociaux de la mémoire*. Ed. Gérard Namer. Paris: Albin Michel, 1994 [1925].

Halbwachs, Maurice. *La Topographie Légendaire des Evangiles en Terre Sainte*. Paris: PUF, 2008 [1941].

Halbwachs, Maurice. *La mémoire collective*. Ed. Gérard Namer. Paris: Albin Michel, 1997 [1950].

Halbwachs, Maurice. *On Collective Memory*. Ed. Lewis Coser. Chicago: University of Chicago Press, 1992.

Hall, Stuart. "Gramsci and Us." Verso Books. 10 February 2017. https://www.versobooks.com/en-gb/blogs/news/2448-stuart-hall-gramsci-and-us. (Accessed 14 May 2024).

Hall, Stuart. *The Hard Road to Renewal: Thatcherism and the Crisis of the Left*. London: Verso, 2021 [1988].

Hall, Suzanne, and Mike Savage. "Animating the Urban Vortex: New Sociological Urgencies." *International Journal of Urban and Regional Research* 40.1 (2016): 82–95.

Hannah, Mike. *Extinctions. Living and Dying in the Margin of Error*. Cambridge: Cambridge University Press, 2021.

Hansen, Miriam. "'With Skin and Hair': Kracauer's Theory of Film, Marseille 1940." *Critical Inquiry* 19 (1993): 437–469.

Hardwick, Lorna. "Aspirations and Mantras in Classical Reception Research: Can there Really be Dialogue between Ancient and Modern?" *Framing Classical Reception Studies*. Eds. Maarten De Pourcq, Nathalie De Haan, and David Rijser. Leiden: Brill, 2020. 15–32.

Hariman, Robert, and John Louis Lucaites. *No Caption Needed: Iconic Photographs, Public Culture, and Liberal Democracy*. Chicago: University of Chicago Press, 2007.

Harlow, Barbara. "Speaking from the Dock." *Callaloo* 16.4 (1993): 874–890.

Hartman, Saidiya. "Venus in Two Acts." *Small Axe* 12.2 (2008): 1–14.

Harvey, David. *The Condition of Postmodernity: An Enquiry into the Origins of Cultural Change*. Cambridge, MA: Blackwell, 1990.

Haug, Frigga. *Female Sexualization: A Collective Work of Memory*. Trans. Erica Carter. London: Verso, 1987.

Hayles, N. Katherine. *How We Think: Digital Media and Contemporary Technogenesis*. Chicago and London: The University of Chicago Press, 2012.

Head, Bessie. "Gladys Mgudlandlu. The Exuberant Innocent." *The New African*. 30 November 1963.

Heaney, Seamus. *Crediting Poetry*. Dublin: Gallery Press, 1995.

Heaney, Seamus. *Human Chain*. London: Faber & Faber, 2012.

Heinonen, Alayna. "A Tonic to the Empire?: The 1951 Festival of Britain and the Empire-Commonwealth." *Britain and the World* 8.1 (2015): 76–99.

Heise Ursula K. *Imagining Extinction. The Cultural Meanings of Endangered Species.* Chicago: The University of Chicago Press, 2016.

Helgesson, Stefan. "The Little Magazine as a World-Making Form: Literary Distance and Political Contestation in Southern African Journals." *Literature and the Making of the World: Cosmopolitan Texts, Vernacular Practices.* Eds. Stefan Helgesson, Annika Mörte Alling, and Helena Bodin. London: Bloomsbury Academic, 2022. 215–249.

Heller, Agnes. "A Tentative Answer to the Question: Has Civil Society Cultural Memory?." *Social Research* 68.4 (2001): 1031–1040.

Helmond, Anne. "The Platformization of the Web: Making Web Data Platform Ready." *Social Media Society* 1.2 (2015): 1–11.

Herman, David. "Stories as a Tool for Thinking." *Narrative Theory and the Cognitive Sciences.* Ed. David Herman. Stanford, CA: CSLI publications, 2003. 163–192.

Hermans, Hubert, and Agnieszka Hermans-Konopka. *Dialogical Self Theory; Positioning and Counter-positioning in a Globalizing Society.* New York, NY: Cambridge University Press, 2010.

Herren, Michael. *The Hisperica Famina* II. Toronto: Pontifical Institute for Mediaeval Studies Publications, 1987.

Hirsch, Fred. *The Social Limits to Growth.* London: Routledge & Kegan Paul, 1977.

Hirsch, Marianne, and Leo Spitzer. "Testimonial Objects: Memory, Gender, and Transmission." *Poetics Today* 27.2 (2006): 353–383.

Hirsch, Marianne, and Leo Spitzer. "Small Acts of Repair: The Unclaimed Legacy of the Romanian Holocaust." *Journal of Literature and Trauma Studies* 4.1/2 (2015): 13–42.

Hirsch, Marianne, and Leo Spitzer. *School Photos in Liquid Time: Reframing Difference.* Seattle: University of Washington Press, 2019.

Hirsch, Marianne, and Leo Spitzer. "Memory in Liquid Time." *Critical Memory Studies: New Approaches.* Ed. Brett Ashley Kaplan. London: Bloomsbury, 2023.

Hirsch, Marianne. "The Generation of Post-memory." *Poetics* 29.1 (2008): 103–128.

Hirsch, Marianne. *The Generation of Postmemory: Writing and Visual Culture After the Holocaust.* New York: Columbia University Press, 2012.

Hirshfield, Jane. *Ten Windows. How Great Poems Transform the World.* New York: Albert Knopf, 2017.

Hirst, William, et al. "A Ten-year Follow-up of a Study of Memory for the Attack of September 11, 2001: Flashbulb Memories and Memories for Flashbulb Events." *Journal of Experimental Psychology: General* 144.3 (2015): 604–623.

Hirst, William, et al. "Long-term Retention of the Terrorist Attack of September 11: Flashbulb Memories, Event Memories, and the Factors that Influence their Retention." *Journal of Experimental Psychology: General* 138.2 (2009): 161–176.

Hirst, William, and Elizabeth A. Phelps. "Flashbulb Memories." *Current Directions in Psychological Science* 25.1 (2015): 36–41.

Hirst, William, Travis G. Cyr, and Clinton Merck. "Witnessing and Cultural Trauma: The Role of Flashbulb Memories in the Trauma Process." *Social Research: An International Quarterly* 87.3 (2020): 591–613.

Hobsbawm, Eric, and Terence Ranger (eds.). *The Invention of Tradition.* Cambridge: Cambridge University Press, 1983.

Hoskins, Andrew (ed.). *Digital Memory Studies: Media Pasts in Transition.* New York: Routledge, 2018.

Hoskins, Andrew. (2009). "Mediatisation of Memory." *Save As . . . Digital Memories.* Eds. Joanne-Garde Hansen, Andrew Hoskins, and Anna Reading. London: Palgrave Macmillan, 2009. 27–43.

Huizinga, Johan. "Over een definitie van het begrip geschiedenis", in Johan Huizinga, *Cultuurhistorische verkenningen* (Haarlem: Tjeenk Willink, 1929). 156–168.

Huxley, Aldous. *Brave New World*. New York: Alfred A. Knopf, 2013.

Huyssen, Andreas. "A Space of Art and Memory." *ReVista* XX.3 (2021).

Huyssen, Andreas. "The Art of Memory Activism in the Global South." Keynote lecture, *MSA Conference* 2023, Newcastle-upon-Tyne. 05 July 2023. YouTube. https://youtu.be/cQ1a-WYXaQw. (Accessed 19 April 2024).

Huyssen, Andreas. *Memory Art in the Contemporary World: Confronting Violence in the Global South*. London: Lund Humphries, 2022.

Ibárruri, Dolores. *They Shall Not Pass: The Autobiography of La Pasionaria*. Vol. 468. New York: International Publishers Co, 1966.

Immler, Nicole, and Stef Scagliola. "Seeking Justice for the Mass Execution in Rawagede. Probing the Concept of 'Entangled History' in a Postcolonial Setting." *Rethinking History: The Journal of Theory and Practice* 24.4 (2020): 1–28.

Immler, Nicole, Ann Rigney, and Damien Short. "Reconciliation & Memory: Critical Perspectives." *Memory Studies* 5.3 (2012): 251–258.

Immler, Nicole. "The Netherlands-Indies. Rethinking Post-colonial Recognition from a Multi-Voiced Perspective." *Wacana* (Journal of the Humanities of Indonesia) 23 (2022): 692–720.

Immler, Nicole. "What is Meant by 'Repair' when Claiming Reparations for Colonial Wrongs? Transformative Justice for the Dutch Slavery Past." *Slaveries & Post-Slaveries* 5 (2021): 1–26.

Ingold, Tim. *The Perception of the Environment: Essays on Livelihood, Dwelling and Skill*. London: Routledge, 2000.

Isidore of Seville. *The Etymologies of Isidore of Seville*. Ed. Stephen A. Barney et al. Cambridge: Cambridge University Press, 2006.

Ismangil, Milan, and Florian Schneider. "Hong Kong's Networked Agitprop: Popular Nationalism in the Wake of the 2019 Anti-Extradition Protests." *Journal of Current Chinese Affairs* 52.3 (2023): 488–517.

Iveković, Sanja, and Antonia Majača. "Feminism, Activism and Historicisation. Sanja Ivekovic talks to Antonia Majaca." *n.paradoxa* 23 (2009): 5–13.

Iveković, Sanja. *Works of Heart (1970–2023)*. Zagreb: Muzej suvremene umjetnosti, 2023.

Jacobs, Daniel. "Tennessee Williams: The Uses of Declarative Memory in the Glass Menagerie." *Journal of the American Psychoanalytic Association* 50.4 (2002): 1259–1270.

Jackson, Antoinette T. *Speaking for the Enslaved: Heritage Interpretation at Antebellum Plantation Sites*. New York: Routledge, 2012.

Jäger, Wolfgang. *Soziale Bürgerrechte im Museum*. Die Repräsentation sozialer Demokratie in neun kulturhistorischen Museen, Bielefeld: Transcript, 2020.

Jahn, Manfred. "Cognitive Narratology." *Routledge Encyclopedia of Narrative Theory*. Eds. David Herman, Manfred Jahn, and Marie-Laure Ryan. New York and London: Routledge, 2005. 67–71.

Jameson, Fredric. "The End of Temporality." *Critical Inquiry* 29.4 (Summer 2003): 695–718.

Jameson, Fredric. *Representing Capital: A Reading of Volume One*. London: Verso, 2011.

Järv, Jaak. *Karolus: ajalooline jutustus Eesti minewikust*. Tallinn: K. Laurmann, 1892.

Jethro, Duane, and Samuel Merrill. "'Next Stop Anton-Wilhelm-Amo strasse': Place Names, De-commemoration and Memory Activism in Berlin." *De-commemoration: Removing Statues and Renaming Places*. Eds. Sarah Gensburger and Jenny Wüstenberg. New York: Berghahn Books, 2024. 210–220.

Jõgi, Olev. "Bornhöhelt saadud nime all." *Looming* 2 (1962): 290–293.

Judt, Tony. *Postwar: A History of Europe since 1945*. London: Penguin Press, 2005.

Judy, Singer. *Neurodiversity: The Birth of an Idea*. Kindle e-book, 2016.

Jünke, Claudia, and Désirée Schyns (eds.). *Translating Memories of Violent Pasts. Memory Studies and Translation Studies in Dialogue*. London: Routledge, 2024.

Jüriöö. 1343. Tallinn: Kalevlaste Ühing, 1931.

ka Canham, Hugo. *Riotous Deathscapes*. Durham: Duke University Press, 2023.

Kahn, Jr., Peter H. "Children's Affliations with Nature: Structure, Development, and the Problem of Environmental Generational Amnesia." *Children and Nature: Psychological, Sociocultural, and Evolutionary Investigations*. Eds. Peter H. Kahn, Jr. and Stephen R. Kellert. Cambridge: MIT Press, 2002. 93–116.

Kahn, Jr., Peter H. "The Child's Environmental Amnesia – It's Ours." *Children, Youth and Environments* 17.2 (2007): 199–207.

Kahn, Jr., Peter H., and Batya Friedman. "Environmental Views and Values of Children in an Inner-City Black Community." *Child Development* 66 (1995): 1403–1417.

Kahn, Jr., Peter H., and Thea Weiss. "The Importance of Children Interacting with Big Nature." *Children, Youth and Environments* 27.2 (2017): 7–24.

Kansteiner, Wulf. "Censorship and Memory." *Journal of Perpetrator Research* 4.1 (2021a): 35–58.

Kansteiner, Wulf. "History beyond Narration: The Shifting Linguistic Terrain of Timothy Snyder's *Bloodlands*." *Analysing Historical Narratives: Case Studies from Historiography and other Historical Genres*. Eds. Stefan Berger, Nicola Brauch, and Chris Lorenz. New York: Berghahn Books, 2021b. 51–82.

Kasson, Joy. *Marble Queens and Captives: Women in Nineteenth-Century American Sculpture*. New Haven: Yale University Press, 1990.

Keenan, Thomas, and Eyal Weizman. *Mengele's Skull. The Advent of Forensic Aesthetics*. Berlin: Stenberg Press, 2012.

Kelly, James. *Gallows Speeches from Eighteenth-Century Ireland*. Dublin: Four Courts Press, 2001.

Kelly, Lidia. "Five Arrested as Australia Protests Draw Thousands." *Reuters*. Thomson Reuters Corporation, 26 January 2021. https://www.reuters.com/world/asia-pacific/five-arrested-australia -day-protests-draw-thousands-2021-01-26/. (Accessed 27 May 2024).

Kennedy, Rosanne, and Maria Nugent. "Scales of Memory: Reflections on an Emerging Concept." *Australian Humanities Review* 59 (2016): 61–76.

Kennedy, Rosanne. "An Australian Archive of Feeling: the Sorry Books Campaign and the Pedagogy of Compassion." *Australian Feminist Studies* 26.69 (2011): 257–279.

Kennedy, Rosanne. "Anniversaries and National Holidays." *The Routledge Handbook of Memory Activism*. Eds. Yifat Gutman and Jenny Wüstenberg. London: Routledge, 2023.

Kennedy, Rosanne. "Stolen Generations Testimony: Trauma, Historiography, and the Question of 'Truth'." *Aboriginal History* 25 (2001): 116–131.

Khawaja, Iram. "Memory Work as Engaged Critical Pedagogy." *Nordic Journal of Social Research* 13.1 (2022): 94–107.

Kierkegaard, Søren. *Stages on Life's Way: Studies by Various Persons*. Princeton: Princeton University Press, 1988.

Kinahan, Deirdre. *An Old Song, Half Forgotten*. London: Nick Hern Books, 2023.

King, Katherine C. "Reception, In Latin Middle Ages." *The Homer Encyclopedia* Vol. III, R–Z. Ed. Margalit Finkelberg. London: Wiley 2011. 720–722.

Kippel, Enn. *Jüriöö: romaan eestlaste vabadusvõitlusest XIV sajandil*. Tartu: Eesti Kirjastuse Kooperatiiv, 1939.

Kirn, Gal. *The Partisan Counter-Archive: Retracing the Ruptures of Art and Memory in the Yugoslav People's Liberation Struggle*. Berlin and Boston: De Gruyter, 2020.

Kirshenblatt-Gimblett, Barbara, and Jeffrey Shandler (eds.). *Anne Frank Unbound: Media, Imagination, Memory*. Bloomington: Indiana University Press, 2012.

Kitch, Carolyn. "Placing Journalism Inside Memory – And Memory Studies." *Memory Studies* 1.3 (2008): 311–320.

Kledzik, Emilia, Maciej Michalski, and Małgorzata Praczyk (eds.). *„Ziemie Odzyskane": w poszukiwaniu nowych narracji*. Poznań: Instytut Historii UAM, 2018.

Kleinberg, Ethan. "Hiding (from the Present) in the Past." *History of the Present. A Journal of Critical History* 13.2 (2023): 265–274.

Kluge, Alexander. "Die Differenz." *Theodor Fontane, Heinrich von Kleist, Anna Wilde*. Berlin: Wagenbach, 1987.

Knittel, Susanne. *The Historical Uncanny. Disability, Ethnicity, and the Politics of Holocaust Memory*. New York: Fordham University Press, 2014.

Knittel, Susanne. "Ecologies of Violence: Cultural Memory (Studies) and the Genocide-Ecocide Nexus." *Memory Studies* 16.6 (2023): 1563–1578.

Knittel, Susanne, and Sofía Forchieri. "There is no 'Elsewhere': Scales of Complicity and Implication in the Contemporary German Family Novel." *Violence Elsewhere II: Imagining Distant Violence in Germany since 2001*. Eds. Clare Bielby and Mererid Puw Davies. Rochester, NY: Camden House, 2024. 70–92.

Knittel, Susanne C., and Kári Driscoll. "Introduction: Memory after Humanism." *Parallax* 23.4 (2017): 379–383.

Kopytoff, Igor. "The Cultural Biography of Things: Commoditization as Process." *The Social Life of Things: Commodities in Cultural Perspective*. Ed. Arjun Appadurai. Cambridge: Cambridge University Press, 1986. 64–91.

Kornetis, Kostis. "'Is there a Future in this Past?' Analyzing 15M's Intricate Relation to the Transición." *Journal of Spanish Cultural Studies* 15.1/2 (2014): 83–98.

Koselleck, Reinhart. *Futures Past*. New York: Columbia University Press, 2004 [1985].

Koselleck, Reinhart. *Sediments of Time: On Possible Histories*. Stanford, CA: Stanford University Press, 2018.

Kourken, Michealian, and John Sutton. "Distributed Cognition and Memory Research: History and Current Directions." *Review of Philosophy and Psychology* 4.1 (2016): 1–24.

Krajewski, Marek. "Deutsches Kulturforum östliches Europa 2016" https://www.kulturforum.info/de/kk-magazin/7370-das-gute-das-wir-nebenbei-verursachen. (Accessed 01 April 2024).

Kruus, Hans. *Jüriöö ülestõusu ajaloolised käsud tänapäevale*. Moscow: ENSV Riiklik Kirjastus, 1943.

Kuball, Timothy, and Rene Becerra. "Social Movements and Collective Memory." *Sociology Compass* 8.6 (2014): 851–867.

Kuhn, Annette. "Photography and Cultural Memory: A Methodological Exploration." *Visual Studies* 22.3 (2007): 283–292.

Kuhn. Annette. *Family Secrets: Acts of Memory and Imagination*. London: Verso, 1995.

Kurpiel Anna, and Katarzyna Maniak. *Porządek rzeczy. Relacje z przedwojennymi przedmiotami na ziemiach zachodnich*. Kraków: Jagellonian University Press, 2023.

Kurzweil, Ray. *The Singularity is Near*. New York: Penguin, 2005.

Kuszyk, Karolina. *Poniemieckie*. Wołowiec: Wydawnictwo Czarne, 2019.

Kuukkanen, Jouni-Matti. *Post-Narrativist Philosophy of Historiography*. New York: Palgrave Macmillan, 2015.

Laanes, Eneken, and Hanna Meretoja. "Editorial: Cultural Memorial Forms." *Memory Studies* 14.1 (2021): 3–9.

Laanes, Eneken, Jessica Ortner, and Tea Sindbæk Andersen (eds.). *Literature and Mnemonic Migration: Remediation, Translation, Reception*. Berlin and Boston: De Gruyter, 2024, forthcoming.

Laanes, Eneken. "Born Translated Memories: Transcultural Memorial Forms, Domestication and Foreignisation." *Memory Studies* 14.1 (2021): 41–57.

Laanes, Eneken. "Katja Petrowskaja's Translational Poetics of Memory." *New German Critique* 51.2 (2024): 51–78.

LaCapra, Dominick. *Writing History, Writing Trauma*. Baltimore: Johns Hopkins University Press, 2001.

Lachmann, Renate. *Memory and Literature: Intertextuality in Russian Modernism*. Trans. Roy Stellaris and Anthony Will. Minneapolis, MN, and London: University of Minnesota Press, 1997.

Lalu, Premesh. *The Deaths of Hintsa: Postapartheid South Africa and the Shape of Recurring Pasts*. Cape Town: HSRC Press, 2009.

Landsberg, Alison. "Prosthetic Memory: *Blade Runner* and *Total Recall*." *Body and Society* 1.3/4 (1995): 175–189.

Landsberg, Alison. "Prosthetic Memory: The Ethics and Politics of Memory in an Age of Mass Culture." *Memory and Popular Film*. Ed. Paul Grainge. Manchester: Manchester University Press, 2003. 144–161.

Landsberg, Alison. *Prosthetic Memory: The Transformation of American Remembrance in the Age of Mass Culture*. New York: Columbia University Press, 2004.

Landsberg, Alison. *Engaging the Past: Mass Culture and the Production of Historical Knowledge*. New York: Columbia University Press, 2015.

Langan, Celeste. "Understanding Media in 1805: Audiovisual Hallucination in *The Lay of the Last Minstrel*." *Studies in Romanticism* 40.1 (2001): 49–70.

Laplanche, Jean, and Jean-Betrand Pontalis. *The Language of Psycho-Analysis*. Trans. Donald Nicholson-Smith. New York and London: W. W. Norton & Co., 1973.

Latour, Bruno, and Paolo Fabbri. "La rhétorique de la science." *Actes de la recherche en sciences sociales* 13.1 (1977): 81–95.

Latour, Bruno. *Reassembling the Social: An Introduction to Actor-Network-Theory*. Oxford: Oxford University Press, 2005.

Leavy, Susan, et al. "Mitigating Gender Bias in Machine Learning Data Sets." *Bias and Social Aspects in Search and Recommendation: First International Workshop*, BIAS 2020, Lisbon, Portugal, 14 April: Proceedings. Cham: Springer International Publishing, 2020.

Leavy, Susan, Gerardine Meaney, Karen Wade, and Derek Green. "Curatr: A Platform for Semantic Analysis and Curation of Historical Literary Texts." *Metadata and Semantic Research. MTSR 2019. Communications in Computer and Information Science*. Ed. Emmanouel Garoufallou, Francesca Fallucchi, Ernesto William De Luca. Cham: Springer, 2019.

Leerssen, Joep (ed.). *Encyclopedia of Romantic Nationalism in Europe*. Vol. 2, 2nd ed., Amsterdam: Amsterdam University Press, 2022.

Leerssen, Joep, and Ann Rigney (eds.). *Commemorating Writers in Nineteenth-Century Europe: Nation-Building and Centenary Fever*. Basingstoke: Palgrave Macmillan, 2014.

Leerssen, Joep. *Remembrance and Imagination*. Cork: Cork University Press, 1996.

Lesjak, Carolyn J. *The Afterlife of Enclosure: British Realism, Character, and the Commons*. Stanford, CA: Stanford University Press, 2021.

Levy, Daniel, and Natan Sznaider. "Memory Unbound: The Holocaust and the Formation of Cosmopolitan Memory." *European Journal of Social Theory* 5.1 (2002): 87–106.

Levy, Daniel, and Natan Sznaider. *The Holocaust and Memory in the Global Age*. Philadelphia: Temple University Press, 2006.

Lifton, Robert Jay. *The Broken Connection: On Death and the Continuity of Life*. New York: Simon & Schuster, 1979.

Lin, Maya. "About the Project." *What Is Missing? project*, 2010–. https://www.whatismissing.org/about.

Lin, Maya. *What Is Missing? project*, 2010–. https://www.whatismissing.org/.

Lionnet, Françoise, and Shu-Mei Shih. "Introduction: Thinking Through the Minor, Transnationally." *Minor Transnationalism*. Eds. Françoise Lionnet and Shu-Mei Shih. Durham, NC: Duke University Press, 2005. 1–23.

Lisanby, Sarah H., Jill H. Maddox, Joan Prudic, D. P. Devanand, and Harold A. Sackeim. "The Effects of Electroconvulsive Therapy on Memory of Autobiographical and Public Events." *Arch Gen Psychiatry* 57.6 (2000): 581–590.

Lloyd-Williams, Rhi. "The Princess and the Pea Was Autistic." *Autism and Expectations: De-Mystifying Autism*, 2016. https://autistrhi.com.

Lo, Jacqueline. "'Why should we Care?': Some Thoughts on Cosmopolitan Hauntings." *Memory Studies* 6.3 (2013): 345–358.

Luciano, Dana. "The Inhuman Anthropocene." *Avidly*. 22 March 2015. https://avidly.lareviewofbooks.org/2015/03/22/the-inhuman-anthropocene/ (Accessed 02 July).

Luiga, Juhan. *Eesti vabadusvõitlus 1343–1345: Harju mäss*. Tallinn: Varrak, 1924.

Mac Suibhne, Breandán. "Editor's Introduction." John Gamble, *Society and Manners in Nineteenth-Century Ireland*. Ed. Breandán Mac Suibhne. Dublin: Field Day, 2011. xiii–lxxviii.

Mac Suibhne, Breandán. "Spirit, Spectre, Shade: A True Story of an Irish Haunting; or, Troublesome Pasts in the Political Culture of North-west Ulster, 1786–1972." *Field Day Review* 9 (2013): 148–211.

Macfarlane, Robert, and Jackie Morris. *The Lost Spells*. London: Hamish Hamilton, 2020.

Macfarlane, Robert, and Jackie Morris. *The Lost Words: A Spell Book*. London: Hamish Hamilton, 2017.

Maddison, Sarah. "De-Commemorating Australian Settler Colonialism." *De-Commemoration. Removing Statues and Renaming Places*. Eds. Sarah Gensburger and Jenny Wüstenberg. New York: Berghahn, 2023.

Mägi, Arvo. *Risti riik: Karvikute kroonika I*. Lund: Eesti Kirjanike Kooperatiiv, 1970.

Maguire, Amy. "Explainer: Australia has voted against an Indigenous Voice to Parliament. Here's what happened." *The Conversation*. 15 October 2023. https://theconversation.com/explainer-australia-has-voted-against-an-indigenous-voice-to-parliament-heres-what-happened-215155. (Accessed 27 May 2024).

Maier, Charles S. "Hot Memory . . . Cold Memory: On the Political Half-life of Fascist and Communist Memory." *Transit*: *Europäische Revue* 22.1 (2002): 153–165.

Makhortykh, Mykola, Victoria Vziatysheva, and Maryna Sydorova. "Generative AI and Contestation and Instrumentalization of Memory about the Holocaust in Ukraine." *Eastern European Holocaust Studies* 1.2 (2023): 349–355.

Makhortykh, Mykola. "The User is Dead, Long Live the Platform? Problematising the User-centric Focus of (Digital) Memory Studies." *Memory Studies* 16.6 (2023): 1500–1512.

Malabou, Catherine. *Plasticity: The Promise of Explosion*. Ed. Tyler M. Williams. Edinburgh: Edinburgh University Press, 2022.

Malafouris, Lambros. *How Things Shape the Mind: A Theory of Material Engagement*. Boston, MA: The MIT Press, 2016.

Malkin, Jeanette. *Memory-Theater and Postmodern Drama*. Ann Arbor: University of Michigan Press, 1999.

Malm, Andreas. *The Progress of This Storm: Nature and Society in a Warming World*. London, Brooklyn, New York: Verso, 2018.

Mandel, Naomi. "Toward a New Complicity for New Media." *Comparative Literature Studies* 56.4 (2019): 693–710.

Mandolessi, Silvana. "The Digital Turn in Memory Studies." *Memory Studies* 16.6 (2023): 1513–1528.

Manovich, Lev. 2020. *Cultural Analytics*. Cambridge, MA: MIT Press.

Mantel, Hilary. "Why I became an historical novelist." *The Guardian*. 22 December 2012 https://www.theguardian.com/books/2017/jun/03/hilary-mantel-why-i-became-a-historical-novelist (Accessed 15 March 2024).

Markowitz, Gerald, and David Rosner. *Deceit and Denial: The Deadly Politics of Industrial Pollution*. Berkley, CA: University of California Press, 2013.

Martí, Ana María, María Alicia Milia de Pirles, and Sara Solarz de Osatinsky. *ESMA "Trasladados." Testimonio de tres liberadas*. Buenos Aires: Abuelas de Plaza de Mayo, 1995.

Martineau, Gilbert. *Le retour des cendres*. Paris: Tallandier, 1990.

Martínez, Francisco. "Memory, Don't Speak! Monumental Neglect and Memorial Sacrifice in Contemporary Estonia." *Cultural Geographies* 29.1 (2022): 63–81.

Marwecki, Daniel. *Germany and Israel: Whitewashing and Statebuilding*. Oxford: Oxford University Press, 2020.

Marx, Karl. *A Contribution to the Critique of Political Economy*. Trans. N.I. Stone. Chicago: Charles H. Kerr & Company, 1904 [1859].

Masing, Uku. *1343. Vaskuks ja vikaaria Lohult*. Tartu: Ilmamaa, 2002.

Mattoni, Alice, and Simon Teune. "Visions of Protest. A Media-Historic Perspective on Images in Social Movements." *Sociology Compass* 8.6 (2014): 876–887.

Maturin, Charles Robert. *Melmoth the Wanderer*. London: Penguin Classics, 2000.

Mavroudi, Maria. "Homer in Greece from the End of Antiquity 1: The Byzantine Reception of Homer and his Export to other Cultures." *The Cambridge Guide to Homer*. Eds. Corinne Ondine Pache, Casey Dué, Susan M. Lupack, and Robert Lamberton. Cambridge: Cambridge University Press, 2019. 444–472.

McAdam, Doug, Sidney Tarrow, and Charles Tilly. *Dynamics of Contention*. Cambridge: Cambridge University Press. 2001.

McCammon, Muira. "Tweeted, Deleted: An Exploratory Study of the US Government's Digital Memory Holes." *New Media & Society* 24.3 (2022): 741–759.

McCarthy, Mark. "Making Irish Martyrs: The Impact and Legacy of the Execution of the Leaders of the Easter Rising, 1916." *Secular Martyrdom in Britain and Ireland: From Peterloo to the Present*. Eds. Quentin Outram and Keith Laybourn. Cham: Palgrave Macmillan, 2017. 165–202.

McDiarmid, Lucy. "Oscar Wilde's Speech from the Dock." *Textual Practice* 15.3 (2001): 447–466.

McDonald, Peter D. *The Literature Police: Apartheid Censorship and Its Cultural Consequences*. Oxford: Oxford University Press, 2009.

McGarry, Aidan,Itir Erhart, Hande Eslen-Ziya, Olu Jenzen and Umut Korkut. "Introduction: The Aesthetics of Global Protest: Visual Culture and Communication." *The Aesthetics of Global Protest*. Eds. Aidan McGarry Itir Erhart, Hande Eslen-Ziya, Olu Jenzen and Umut Korkut. Amsterdam: Amsterdam University Press, 2020. 15–36.

McGrath, Laura, et al. "Culture, Theory, Data: An Introduction." *New Literary History* 53.4 (2023): 519–530.

McGurl, Mark. "Critical Response II – 'Neither Indeed Could I Forebear Smiling at My Self': A Reply to Wai Chee Dimock." *Critical Inquiry* 39.3 (2013): 632–638.

McGurl, Mark. "The New Cultural Geology." *Journal of Transnational American Studies* 12.2 (2021): 380–390.

McIvor, Charlotte, Emilie Pine, Stef Craps, Astrid Erll, Paula McFetridge, Ann Rigney and Dominic Thorpe. "Moving Memory." *Irish University Review* 47.1 (2017): 165–196.

McNally, David. *Global Slump*. Oakland: PM Press, 2011.

McQuaid, Sara Dybris, and Sarah Gensburger. "Administrations of Memory: Transcending the Nation and Bringing Back the State in Memory Studies." *International Journal of Politics Culture and Society* 32.4 (2019): 125–143.

Meehan, Paula. Contribution to "Yeats's Nobel: Then & Now" seminar, 09 December 2023. https://www.youtube.com/channel/UCkPTGzXd3vRF5e5-fJQHVyw/videos. (Accessed 01 April 2024).

Megill, Allan. "History, Memory, Identity." *History of the Human Sciences* 11.3 (1998): 37–62.

Merck, Clinton, and William Hirst. "Distinguishing Collective Memory and History: A Community's Identity and History are Derived from Distinct Sources." *Journal of Applied Research in Memory and Cognition* 11.4 (2022): 598–609.

Merrill, Samuel and Ann Rigney (eds.) "Special Issue: Remembering Activism: Explorations of the Memory-Activism Nexus." *Memory Studies* 17.5 (2024a).

Merrill, Samuel, and Ann Rigney. "Remembering Activism: Means and Ends." *Memory Studies* 17.5 (2024b): 997–1003.

Merrill, Samuel, and Simon Lindgren. "The Rhythms of Social Movement Memories: The Mobilization of Silvio Meier's Activist Remembrance Across Platforms." *Social Movement Studies* 19.5/6 (2020): 657–674.

Merrill, Samuel. "Artificial Intelligence and Social Memory: Towards the Cyborgian Remembrance of an Advancing Mnemo-Technic." *Handbook of Critical Studies of Artificial Intelligence*. Ed. Simon Lindgren. Cheltenham and Northampton: Edward Elgar Publishing Limited, 2023. 173–186.

Merrill, Samuel. "Remembering Like a State: Surveillance Databases, Digital Activist Traces, and the Repressive Potential of Mediated Prospective Memory." *Memory Studies* 17.5 (2024): 1177–1194.

Meyer, Birgit. "'Idols' in the Museum: Legacies of Missionary Iconoclasm." *Reemerging Iconoclasms. On the Contemporariness of Image Controversies*. Eds. Birgit Mersmann, Christiane Kruse, and Arnold Bartetzky. Berlin: De Gruyter, 2024.

Meyer, Birgit. "Mediation and the Genesis of Presence." Inaugural Lecture, Utrecht University, 2012.

Meyler, S. Y., Stone. B., Luminet, O. Meksin, R., and Hirst, W. *The Intergenerational Transmission of Flashbulb Memories and Event Memories Surrounding the Terrorist Attack of September 11th, 2001*. 2024, under review.

Micah, White. "The Emergence of Activist Artificial Intelligence: A New Chapter in Social Movements." *ProtestGPT*. https://protestgpt.com/about/.

Michaelian, Kourken, and John Sutton. "Distributed Cognition and Memory Research: History and Current Directions." *Review of Philosophy and Psychology* 4 (2013): 1–24.

Michalski, David. "Cities Memory Voices Collage." *Art and the Performance of Memory: Sounds and Gestures of Recollection*. Ed. Richard Cándida Smith. London and New York: Routledge, 2002. 101–117.

Mihai, Mihaela. "Understanding Complicity: Memory, Hope and the Imagination." *Critical Review of International Social and Political Philosophy* 22.5 (2019): 504–522.

Mihai, Mihaela. *Political Memory and the Aesthetics of Care: The Art of Complicity and Resistance*. Stanford, CA: Stanford University Press, 2022.

Miles, Elza. *Nomfanekiso Who Paints at Night. The Art of Gladys Mgudlandlu*. Johannesburg: Fern Press, 2002.

Miller, Daniel. *Stuff*. Cambridge: Polity Press, 2010.

Ministru, Sébastien. '*Les moulins de mon coeur,' une chanson qui évoque l'abusrdité de nos vies, et notamment de l'amour . . . RTBF.BE Entrez sans frapper*. 08 November 2021 https://www.rtbf.be/article/les-moulins-de-mon-coeur-une-chanson-qui-evoque-l-absurdite-de-nos-vies-et-notamment-de-l-amour-10150456 (Accessed 15 February 2024).

Mishra, Pankaj. "The Shoah after Gaza." *London Review of Books* 46.5 (2024). https://www.lrb.co.uk/the-paper/v46/n06/pankaj-mishra/the-shoah-after-gaza (Accessed 01 June 2024).

Misrach, Richard, and Kate Orff. *Petrochemical America*. New York, NY: Aperture, 2014.

Morales, Tori. "Two Ways Advocacy Movements Exclude Autistic People, and How You Can Do Better." *Medium*. 12 January 2020. https://medium.com/artfullyautistic/two-ways-advocacy-movements-exclude-autistic-people-and-how-you-can-do-better-b4bf706df5a3. (Accessed 20 February 2024).

Morales, Tori. Two ways advocacy movements exclude autistic people and how you can do better. 2022. January 12th. Accessed 13 August 2024 at: https://medium.com/artfullyautistic/two-ways-advocacy-movements-exclude-autistic-people-and-how-you-can-do-better-b4bf706df5a3

Moreton-Robinson, Aileen. *The White Possessive: Property, Power, and Indigenous Sovereignty*. Minneapolis: University of Minnesota Press, 2015.

Moscovici, Serge. *Social Representations: Explorations in Social Psychology*. New York: New York University Press, 2001.

Mousavi, Nafiseh. "Dangerous Remembering in Volatile Spaces: Activist Memory Work in the Iranian Context." *Memory Studies* 17.5 (2024): 1142–56.

Münsterberg, Hugo. *The Film: A Psychological Study*. New York: Dover Publications, 1970.

Munteán, László, Plate, Liedeke, and Anneke Smelik (eds.). *Materializing Memory in Art and Popular Culture*. London and New York: Routledge, 2017.

Murphy, Gerard. *Early Irish Lyrics*. Oxford: Oxford University Press, 1956.

Musil, Robert. "Vortrag in Paris." *Gesammelte Werke 8: Essays und Reden*. Reinbek: Rowohlt, 1978.

Naftal, Alejandra. *ESMA Museum and Site of Memory: Former Clandestine Center of Detention, Torture and Extermination. Nomination Dossier for UNESCO World Heritage List*. Buenos Aires: Museo ESMA, 2021; https://whc.unesco.org/en/list/1681/documents/ (30 November 2023).

Nagy, Gregory. *Poetry as Performance: Homer and Beyond*. Cambridge: Cambridge University Press, 1996.

NCPCgov. *"In America: Remember." With Suzanne Brennan Firstenberg.* 24 January 2022 https://www.youtube.com/watch?v=SuhDTuYeYns. Accessed 01 April 2024.

Neisser, Ulric. "Remembering the Earthquake: Direct Experience vs. Hearing the News." *Memory* 4.4 (1996): 337–358.

Neisser, Ulric. "Snapshots or Benchmarks?" *Memory Observed: Remembering in Natural Context*. Ed. Ulric Neisser. San Francisco: Freeman, 1982. 43–28.

Nettleton, Anitra. "Primitivism in South African Art." *Visual Century: South African Art in Context. Volume 2. 1945–1976*. Johannesburg: Wits University Press, 2011. 140–163.

Neumann, Klaus, and Janna Thompson. *Historical Justice and Memory*. Wisconsin: The University of Wisconsin Press, 2015.

Ng, Kelly. "Hong Kong offers HK$1m bounties on five overseas activists." *BBC News*. 15 December 2023. https://www.bbc.com/news/world-asia-china-67724230. (Accessed 16 December 2023).

Ní Uallacháin, Paidrigín. *Songs of the Scribe*. Dublin: Ceoltaí Éireann, 2011.

Nicoletti, Leonardo, and Dina Bass. "Humans Are Biased. Generative AI Is Even Worse." *Bloomberg. Com*. 27 October 2023. https://www.bloomberg.com/graphics/2023-generative-ai-bias/. (Accessed 26 April 2024).

Nieborg, David B., and Thomas Poell. "The Platformization of Cultural Production: Theorizing the Contingent Cultural Commodity." *New Media & Society* 20.11 (2018): 4275–4292.

Nietzsche, Friedrich. *Unnzeitgemäßige Betrachtungen.* Leipzig: Fritzsch, 1874.

Nirk, Endel. *Eduard Bornhöhe. Kirjanik ja inimene.* Tallinn: Eesti Riiklik Kirjastus, 1961.

Nixon, Rob. *Slow Violence and the Environmentalism of the Poor.* Cambridge, MA: Harvard University Press, 2011.

Noble, Safiya Umoja. *Algorithms of Oppression.* New York: New York University Press, 2018.

Nobles, Melissa. "Reparations Claims: Politics by Another Name." *Political Power and Social Theory* 18 (2006): 253–258.

Nora, Pierre. "Between History and Memory: The Lieux des Mémoire." *Representations* (Spring 1989): 7–24.

Nora, Pierre. "Entre Mémoire et Histoire. La problématique des lieux." *Les Lieux de mémoire*, vol. 1. Ed. Pierre Nora. Paris: Gallimard, 1997. 23–43.

Nora, Pierre. *Les lieux de mémoire.* 3 vols. Paris: Gallimard, 1984–1992.

Ó Corráin, Donncha. *Clavis Litterarum Hibernensium* II. Corpus Christianorum Claves. Turnhout: Brepols, 2017.

O'Donnell, Ruán. *Remember Emmet: Images of the Life and Legacy of Robert Emmet.* Bray, Co. Wicklow: Wordwell in Association with the National Library of Ireland, 2003.

Ó Nuallain, Brian. *The Third Policeman.* London: Harper Perennial, 1967.

Ó Riain, Padraig. *A Dictionary of Irish Saints.* Dublin: Four Courts Press, 2011.

O Táíwò, Olúfemi. *Reconsidering Reparations.* New York: Oxford University Press, 2022.

O'Riordan, Alan. "Theatre Review: Bryan Murray's Own Experience to the Fore in Alzheimer's Play." *The Examiner.* 25 April 2023. https://www.irishexaminer.com/lifestyle/artsandculture/arid-41124268.html. (Accessed 29 April 2024).

Ochs, Elinor, and Lisa Capps. *Living Narrative: Creating Lives in Everyday Storytelling.* Harvard University Press, 2009.

Olick, Jeffrey K. "Genre Memories and Memory Genres: A Dialogical Analysis of May 8, 1945 Commemorations in the Federal Republic of Germany." *American Sociological Review* 64.3 (1999): 381–402.

Olick, Jeffrey K. *The Politics of Regret: On Collective Memory and Historical Responsibility.* New York: Routledge, 2007.

Olick, Jeffrey K., Vered Vinitzky-Seroussi, and Daniel Levy (eds.). *The Collective Memory Reader.* Oxford: Oxford University Press, 2010.

Olick, Jeffrey K., Aline Sierp, and Jenny Wüstenberg. "Introduction: Taking Stock of Memory Studies." *Memory Studies* 16.6 (2023): 1399–1406.

Olsen, Bjørnar. *In Defense of Things: Archaeology and the Ontology of Objects.* Lanham, MD: AltaMira Press, 2010.

OpenAI. *DALL·E 3 System Card.* https://openai.com/research/dall-e-3-system-card. (Accessed 26 April 2024).

Orwell, George. *Nineteen Eighty-Four.* New York: Penguin Books, 2021.

Palm, August. "Ärkamisaja olustiku- ja ideeproosa ning ajalooliste jutustiste osatähtsus rahva elus." *Raamatu osa Eesti arengus.* Ed. Daniel Palgi. Tartu: Eesti Kirjanduse Selts, 1935. 125–183.

Partridge, Damani J. "States." *The Routledge Handbook of Memory Activism.* Eds. Yifat Gutman and Jenny Wüstenberg. London: Routledge, 2023. 154–159.

Pascual, Julia. "Aide aux migrants: Le Conseil constitutionnel consacre le 'principe de fraternité'." *Le Monde.* 6 July 2018, referring to the decision 2018-717/718. https://www.conseil-constitutionnel.fr/decision/2018/2018717_718QPC.htm.

Passerini, Luisa. *Fascism in Popular Memory*. Cambridge: Cambridge University Press, 1987.

Pauly, Daniel. "Anecdotes and the Shifting Baseline Syndrome of Fisheries." *Tree* 10 (October 1995): 430.

Pearse, Pádraic. "Robert Emmet and the Ireland of To-Day" [An Address delivered at the Emmet Commemoration in the Academy of Music, Brooklyn, New York, 2 March 1914]. *Collected Works of Pádraic H. Pearse: Political Writings and Speeches*. Dublin, Cork, Belfast: The Phoenix Publishing Co., [n.d. 1924].

Peffer, John. *Art and the End of Apartheid*. Minneapolis: University of Minnesota Press, 2009.

Pejić, Bojana. "Lady Rosa of Luxembourg, or, is the Age of Female Allegory Really Bygone?" *Život umjetnosti: časopis o modernoj i suvremenoj umjetnosti i arhitekturi* 70.2 (2003): 34–43.

Pentzold, Christian, and Christine Lohmeier (eds.). *Handbuch kommunikationswissenschaftliche Erinnerungsforschung*. Berlin: De Gruyter, 2023.

Perl, Jeffrey M. *The Tradition of Return: The Implicit History of Modern Literature*. Princeton: Princeton University Press, 1984.

Phalafala, Uhuru Portia. *Keorapetse Kgositsile and the Black Arts Movement*. Melton: James Currey, 2024.

Pietraszewski, Igor, and Barbara Törnquist-Plewa. "Wrocław: Changes in Memory Narratives." *Whose Memory? Which Future? Remembering Ethnic Cleansing and Lost Cultural Diversity in Eastern, Central and Southeastern Europe*. Ed. Barbara Törnquist-Plewa. New York and Oxford: Berghahn, 2016.

Piper, Andrew, and Sunyam Bagga. "Toward a Data-Driven Theory of Narrativity." *New Literary History* 54.1 (2022): 879–901.

Piper, Andrew. "There Will Be Numbers." *Journal of Cultural Analytics* 1.1 (2016): 1–10.

Pisanty, Valentina. "Narratologia e scienze cognitive." *Narratività. Problemi, analisi, prospettive*. Eds. Anna Maria Lorusso, Claudio Paolucci, Patrizia Violi. Bologna: Bologna University Press, 2012. 261–278.

Plate, Liedeke. "Amnesiology: Towards the Study of Cultural Oblivion." *Memory Studies* 9.2 (2016): 143–155.

Plate, Liedeke. "New Materialisms." *Oxford Research Encyclopedia of Literature*. Oxford: Oxford University Press, 2020.

Poell, Thomas, David Nieborg, and José Van Dijck. "Platformisation." *Internet Policy Review* 8.4 (2019): 1–13.

Põldmäe, Rudolf. *Kirjamehi mitmes mõõdus*. Tallinn: Eesti Raamat, 1973.

Poole, Ross. "Memory, History and the Claims of the Past." *Memory Studies* 1.2 (2008): 149–166.

Popular Memory Group. "Popular Memory: Theory, Politics, Method." *Making Histories: Studies in History-Writing and Politics*. Eds. Richard Johnson, Gregor McLennan, Bill Schwarz, and David Sutton. London and New York: Routledge, 2013. 205–252.

Preston, Paul. *El gran manipulador. La mentira cotidiana de Franco*. Barcelona: Ediciones B, 2008.

Proulx, Annie. *Barkskins*. New York: Scribner, 2016.

Proust, Marcel. *On Art and Literature*. Trans. by Sylvia Townsend Warner. New York: Carol and Graff, 1954.

Radstone, Susannah, and Rita Wilson (eds.). *Translating Worlds: Migration, Memory, and Culture*. London and New York: Routledge, 2021.

Raha, A. *Jüri-öö: Jutt eestlaste minewikust*. Tallinn: S. Kuul, 1907.

Rankin, Elizabeth. "Creating Communities. Art Centers and Workshops and their Influence on the South African Art Scene." *Visual Century South African Art in Context*. vol. 2. 1945–1976. Johannesburg: Wits University Press, 2011. 52–77.

Rapson, Jessica. "Refining Memory: Sugar, Oil, and Plantation Tourism on Louisiana's River Road." *Memory Studies* 13.4 (2018): 752–766.

Rau, Thomas, and Sabine Oberhüber. "The Universal Declaration of Material Rights." https://theuniversaldeclarationofmaterialrights.org. Reprinted in Thomas Rau and Sabine Oberhuber. *Material Matters: Developing Business for a Circular Economy*. London: Routledge, 2022.

Reading, Anna, and Tamar Katriel (eds.). *Cultural Memories of Nonviolent Struggles: Powerful Times*. London: Palgrave Macmillan, 2015.

Reading, Anna. "Mobile Witnessing: Ethics and the Camera Phone in the 'War on Terror'." *Globalizations* 6.1 (2009): 61–76.

Reading, Anna. "Seeing Red: A Political Economy of Digital Memory." *Media, Culture & Society* 36.6 (2014): 748–760.

Reading, Anna. "The Restitutional Assemblage: The Art of Transformative Justice at Parramatta Girls Home, Australia." *From Transitional to Transformative Justice*. Eds. Paul Gready and Simon Robins. Cambridge: Cambridge University Press, 2019. 235–260.

Reading, Anna. "Rewilding Memory." *Memory, Mind and Media* 1 (2022): 1–17.

Rebentisch, Juliane. *Theorien der Gegenwartskunst*. Hamburg: Junius Verlag, 2013.

Reinhardt, Kathleen (ed.). *1 Million Roses for Angela Davis / 1 Million Rosen für Angela Davis*. Milan: Mousse Publishing, 2021.

Renan, Ernest. "Qu'est-ce qu'une nation?" (1882) *Oeuvres completes*. Ed. H. Psichari, 2 vols., Paris: Calmann-Lévy, 1 (1947): 887–906.

Resemble AI. "How Resemble AI Created Andy Warhol Docu-series Narration Using 3 Minutes of Original Voice Recordings." https://www.resemble.ai/andy-warhol/ (1 December 2023).

Richardson-Little, Ned, and Samuel Merrill. "Who is the Volk? PEGIDA and the Contested Memory of 1989 on Social Media." *Social Movements, Cultural Memory and Digital Media: Mobilizing Mediated Remembrance*. Eds. Samuel Merrill, Emily Keightley, and Priska Daphi. London: Palgrave Macmillan, 2020.

Rigney, Ann. *Imperfect Histories: The Elusive Past and the Legacy of Romantic Historicism*. Ithaca: Cornell University Press, 2001.

Rigney, Ann. *The Rhetoric of Historical Representation: Three Narrative Histories of the French Revolution*. Cambridge: Cambridge University Press, 2002 [1990].

Rigney, Ann. "Portable Monuments: Literature, Cultural Memory and the Case of Jeanie Deans." *Poetics* 52.2 (2004): 361–396.

Rigney, Ann. "Plenitude, Scarcity and the Circulation of Cultural Memory." *Journal for European Studies* 35.1 (2005): 11–28.

Rigney, Ann. "Literature and Cultural Memory." *The Life of Texts*. Amsterdam: Amsterdam University Press, 2006.

Rigney, Ann. "Being an Improper Historian." *Manifestos for History*. Eds. Sue Morgan, Keith Jenkins, and Alun Munslow. New York: Routledge, 2007. 149–159.

Rigney, Ann. "The Dynamics of Remembrance: Texts Between Monumentality and Morphing." *Cultural Memory Studies; An International and Interdisciplinary Handbook*. Eds. Astrid Erll and Ansgar Nünning. Berlin: De Gruyter, 2008a. 345–353.

Rigney, Ann. "Divided Pasts: A Premature Memorial and the Dynamics of Collective Remembrance." *Memory Studies* 1.1 (2008b): 89–97.

Rigney, Ann. "Embodied and Remembered Lives." *FRAME* 22.1 (2009): 60–73.

Rigney, Ann. *The Afterlives of Walter Scott: Memory on the Move*. Oxford: Oxford University Press, 2012a.

Rigney, Ann. "Reconciliation and Remembering: (How) Does It Work?" *Memory Studies* 5.3 (2012b): 251–258.

Rigney, Ann. "Cultural Memory Studies: Mediation, Narrative, and the Aesthetic." *Routledge International Handbook of Memory Studies*. Eds. Anna Lisa Tota and Trever Hagen. New York: Routledge, 2015a. 65–76.

Rigney, Ann. "Things and the Archive: Scott's Materialist Legacy." *Scottish Literary Review* 7.2 (2015b): 13–34.

Rigney, Ann. "Transnational Memory." *Auschwitz Foundation International Quarterly* 120 (2015c): 166–168.

Rigney, Ann. "Differential Memorability and Transnational Activism: Bloody Sunday, 1887–2016." *Australian Humanities Review* 59 (April/May 2016): 77–95.

Rigney, Ann. "Materiality and Memory: Object to Ecologies. A Response to Maria Zirra." *Parallax* 22.4 (2017): 474–478.

Rigney, Ann. "Remembering Hope: Transnational Activism Beyond the Traumatic." *Memory Studies* 11.3 (2018a): 368–380.

Rigney, Ann. "Remembrance as Remaking: Memories of the Nation Revisited." *Nations and Nationalism* 24.2 (2018b): 240–257.

Rigney, Ann. "Epilogue: Citizenship, Memory, and the Curious Case of Canada." *Citizenship Studies* 22.4 (2018c): 452–457.

Rigney, Ann. "Literature and Cultural Memory." *The Life of Texts: An Introduction to Literary Studies*. Eds. Ann Rigney and Kiene Brillenburg Wurth. Amsterdam: Amsterdam University Press, 2019 [2006]. 361–386.

Rigney, Ann. "Mediations of Outrage: How Violence Against Protestors is Remembered." *Social Research: An International Quarterly* 87.3 (2020): 707–733.

Rigney, Ann. "Afterword: The Multiple Entanglements of Memory and Activism." *Remembering Social Movements: Activism and Memory*. Eds. Stefan Berger, Sean Scalmer, and Christian Wicke. London: Routledge, 2021a. 299–304.

Rigney, Ann. "Remaking Memory and the Agency of the Aesthetic." *Memory Studies* 14.1 (2021b): 10–23.

Rigney, Ann, "Toxic Monuments and Mnemonic Regime Change." *Studies on National Movements* 9 (2022): 7–40.

Rigney, Ann, and Thomas Smits (eds.). *The Visual Memory of Protest*. Amsterdam: Amsterdam University Press, 2023.

Rigney, Ann, and Thomas Smits. "The Visual Memory of Protest: Introduction." *The Visual Memory of Protest*. Eds. Ann Rigney and Thomas Smits. Amsterdam: Amsterdam University Press, 2023. 9–31.

Rigney, Ann. "Decommissioning Monuments, Mobilizing Materialities." *The Routledge Handbook of Memory Activism*. Eds. Yifat Gutman and Jenny Wüstenberg. London: Routledge, 2023. 21–27.

Rijneveld, Marieke Lucas. *De avond is ongemak*. Amsterdam and Antwerpen: Atlas Contact, 2018.

Rijneveld, Marieke Lucas. *The Discomfort of Evening*. London: Faber & Faber Ltd, 2020.

Rimé, Bernard. "Emotion Elicits the Social Sharing of Emotion: Theory and Empirical Review." *Emotion Review* 1.1 (2009): 60–85.

Robben, Antonius C. G. M. *Argentina Betrayed: Memory, Mourning, and Accountability*. Philadelphia: University of Pennsylvania Press, 2018.

Roberge, Jonathan, and Michael Castelle (eds.). *The Cultural Life of Machine Learning: An Incursion into Critical AI Studies*. Cham: Springer International Publishing, 2021.

Robinson, Cedric J. *Black Marxism: The Making of the Black Radical Tradition*. London: Penguin Books, 2000 [1983].

Roe, Jasper, and Mike Perkins. "'What They're not Telling You About ChatGPT': Exploring the Discourse of AI in UK News Media Headlines." *Humanities and Social Sciences Communications* 10 (2023): 1–9.

Rogers, T. B., N. A. Kuiper, and W. S. Kirker. "Self-reference and the Encoding of Personal Information." *Journal of Personality and Social Psychology* 35.9 (1977): 677–688.

Rosa, Hartmut. *Social Acceleration*. New York: Columbia University Press, 2013.

Rosenberg, Howard, and Charles S. Feldman. *No Time to Think: The Menace of Media Speed and the 24-hour News Cycle*. New York: Continuum, 2008.

Rosenfeld, Gavriel D. "A Looming Crash or a Soft Landing? Forecasting the Future of the Memory 'Industry'." *The Journal of Modern History* 81.1 (2009): 122–158.

Rosenfeld, Israel. *The Invention of Memory: A New View of the Brain*. New York: Basic Books, 1987.

Rothberg, Michael. *Multidirectional Memory: Remembering the Holocaust in the Age of Decolonization*. Stanford, CA: Stanford University Press, 2009.

Rothberg, Michael. *The Implicated Subject: Beyond Victims and Perpetrators*. Stanford, CA: Stanford University Press, 2019.

Rothberg, Michael. "Feeling Implicated: An Introduction." *Parallax* 29. 3 (2023): 265–281.

Rowlands, Mark. *The New Science of the Mind: From Extended Mind to Embodied Phenomenology*. Cambridge, MA: MIT Press, 2010.

Rubin, David C., and Dorthe Berntsen. "Life Scripts Help to Maintain Autobiographical Memories of Highly Positive, but Not Highly Negative, Events." *Memory & Cognition* 31.1 (2003): 1–14.

Rüsen, Jörn. *Evidence and Meaning: A Theory of Historical Studies*. New York and Oxford: Berghahn, 2017.

Saal, Andres. *Hilda*. Tallinn: K. Busch, 1890.

Said, Edward. *Culture and Imperialism*. London: Chatto and Windus, 1993.

Saks, Edgar V. *Eesti soost vasallkond taaniaegsel Virumaal 1220–1345. Jüriöö mäss uues valguses: Revideerivaid seisukohti ürikute alusel*. Philadelphia and Wilmington: Korporatsioon Rotalia BWW allkoondis, 1971.

Salerno, Daniele. "A Semiotic Theory of Memory: Between Movement and Form." *Semiotica* 241 (2021): 87–119.

Salerno, Daniele, and Marit van de Warenburg. "'Bella Ciao': A Portable Monument for Transnational Activism." *International Journal of Cultural Studies* 26.2 (2023): 164–181.

Salerno, Daniele, and Ann Rigney (eds.). *Archiving Activism in the Digital Age*. Amsterdam: Institute of Network Cultures, 2024.

Salu, Herbert. *Eduard Vilden historialliset romaanit*. Helsinki: Suomalaisen Kirjallisuuden Seura, 1964.

Sanders, Mark. *Complicities: The Intellectual and Apartheid*. Durham: Duke University Press, 2002.

Santino, Jack. "Yellow Ribbons and Seasonal Flags: The Folk Assemblage of War." *Journal of American Folklore* 105.415 (1992): 19–33.

Sanyal, Debarati. *Memory and Complicity: Migrations of Holocaust Remembrance*. New York: Fordham University Press, 2015.

Savolainen, Ulla. "Points and Poetics of Memory: (Retrospective) Justice in Oral History interviews of former internees." *Memory Studies* 13.6 (2020): 1020–1035.

Schacter, Daniel. *The Seven Sins of Memory: How the Mind Forgets and Remembers*. New York: Houghton Mifflin, 2001.

Scheffer, Ingrid. "Do Tread on Me!" Goethe-Institute. 30 October 2008. Internet Archive Wayback Machine. https://web.archive.org/web/20081030013810/http://www.goethe.de/kue/arc/dos/dos/zdk/en78940.htm. (Accessed 01 April 2024).

Schneider, Donald David. *The Works and Doctrine of Jacques Ignace Hittorff.* 3 vols.; New York: Garland, 1977.

Scott, David. "The Semiotics of the Lieu de Mémoire: The Postage Stamp as a Site of Cultural Memory." *Semiotica* 142 (2002): 107–124.

Sehgal, Parul. "An Award-Winning Debut Novel About Innocence Shattered Offers Terror and Solace." *New York Times.* 08 September 2020. https://www.nytimes.com/2020/09/08/books/review-discomfort-of-evening-marieke-lucas-rijneveld.html. (Accessed 29 April 2024).

Servimedia. "Más De Seis Millones De Españoles Han Participado En El Movimiento 15M." *RTVE.es.* 06 August 2011. www.rtve.es/noticias/20110806/mas-seis-millones-espanoles-han-participado-movimiento-15m/452598.shtml (Accessed 09 February 2024).

Sholette, Gregory. *The Art of Activism and the Activism of Art.* London: Lund Humphries, 2022.

Silverstein, Ben. "'Possibly They Did Not Know Themselves': The Ambivalent Government of Sex and Work in the Northern Territory Aboriginals Ordinance 1918." *History Australia* 14.3 (2017): 344–360.

Simonsen, Kim. "Stamps & National Identity: Faroese Stamps as Loci of Memory." *Posta Stamps* 17 (2013): 2–8.

Singer, Judy. *Neurodiversity: The Birth of an Idea.* Kindle e-book. 2016.

Sinkel, Aristarch. *Musta risti ikke all.* Tallinn: Eesti Riiklik Kirjastus, 1956.

Smit, Rik, Benjamin Jacobsen, and Taylor Annabell. "The Multiplicities of Platformed Remembering." *Memory Mind and Media* 3 (2024): 1–6.

Smit, Rik, Marcel Broersma, and Ansgard Heinrich. "Witnessing in the New Memory Ecology: Memory Construction of the Syrian Conflict on YouTube." *New Media & Society* 19.2 (2017): 289–307.

Smit, Rik. "Die Plattformisierung des Erinnerns." *Handbuch kommunikationswissenschaftliche Erinnerungsforschung.* Eds. Christine Lohmeier, Christian Pentzold, and Manuel Menke. Berlin: De Gruyter, 2023. 471–793.

Smits, Thomas, Rik Smit, and Sam Merrill. "Stochastic Remembering: The Distributed Mnemonic Agency of ChatGPT." *Memory Studies Review* (under review).

Smits, Thomas. "A Network of Photographs: The Visual Public Memory of the Dutch Provo Movement, 1967–2016." *Memory Studies* 15.1 (2021): 184–203.

Smits, Thomas, and Ruben Ros. "Does Transnational Contention Lead to Transnational Memory? The Online Visual Memory of the February 2003 Anti-Iraq War Protests." *Social Movement Studies* 22.2 (2021): 1–23.

Smits, Thomas. "Delacroix in Hong Kong: Activism, Memory and Visual Representation." *Remembering Activism: The Cultural Memory of Protest in Europe.* 17 April 2020. https://rememberingactivism.eu/2020/04/17/delacroix-in-hong-kong-activism-memory-and-visual-representation/. (Accessed 26 April 2024).

Snyder, Timothy. *Bloodlands: Europe between Hitler and Stalin.* Philadelphia: Basic Books, 2010.

Songfacts. https://www.songfacts.com/facts/noel-harrison/the-windmills-of-your-mind. (Accessed 20 May 2024).

Spence, Jo. *Putting Myself in the Picture: A Political, Personal and Photographic Autobiography.* London: Camden Press, 1986.

Sperber, Dan. "Anthropology and Psychology: Towards an Epidemiology of Representations" *Man* 20.1 (1985): 73–89.

Stark, Whitney. "Intra-Action." *New Materialism–Networking European Scholarship on 'How Matter Comes to Matter'*. 15 August 2016. https://newmaterialism.eu/almanac/i/intra-action.html. (Accessed 20 May 2024).

Steedman, Carolyn. *Landscape for a Good Woman*. London: Virago, 1986.

Stevenson, Bryan. "Equal Justice Initiative Announces Expanded Legacy Museum in Alabama." *Alaska's News Source*. 30 September 2021. https://www.alaskasnewssource.com/2021/09/30/equal-justice-initiative-announces-expanded-legacy-museum-alabama/. (Accessed 27 May 2024).

Stewart, Susan. *The Ruins Lesson: Meaning and Material in Western Culture*. Chicago: The University of Chicago Press, 2020.

Stokes, Whitley (ed.). "Cormac's Glossary." *Three Irish Glossarie*s. London: Williams and Norgate, 1862. 1–46.

Stoler, Ann Laura. "Colonial Aphasia: Race and Disabled Histories in France." *Public Culture* 23.1 (2011): 121–156.

Stoler, Ann Laura. *Duress: Imperial Durabilities in Our Times*. Durham: Duke University Press, 2016.

Strachan, John, and William Stokes. *Thesaurus Palaeohibernicus* II. Cambridge: Cambridge University Press, 1910.

Sullivan, Rosemary. *The Betrayal of Anne Frank: A Cold Case Investigation*. New York: Harper, 2022.

Sutton, John. *Philosophy and Memory Traces: Descartes to Connectionism*. Cambridge: Cambridge University Press, 1998.

Suvin, Darko. *Splendour, Misery, and Possibilities: An X-Ray of Socialist Yugoslavia*. Leiden and Boston: Brill, 2016.

Tally, Patrick F. "Sullivan Brothers." *Encyclopedia of Irish History and Culture*. Gen. Ed. James S. Donnelly. Vol. 2, Farmington Hills, MI: Macmillan Reference USA, 2004. 687–688.

Tamm, Marek. "History as Cultural Memory. Mnemohistory and the Construction of Estonian Nation." *Journal of Baltic Studies* 39.4 (2008): 499–516.

Tamm, Marek. "Introduction: Afterlife of Events: Perspectives on Mnemohistory." *Afterlife of Events: Perspectives on Mnemohistory*. Ed. Marek Tamm. Houndmills: Palgrave Macmillan, 2015. 1–23.

Tamm, Marek (ed.). *Afterlife of Events: Perspectives on Mnemohistory*. Houndmills: Palgrave Macmillan, 2015.

Taylor, Diana. *The Archive and the Repertoire: Performing Cultural Memory in the Americas*. Durham: Duke University Press, 2003.

Taylor, Jesse O. *The Sky of Our Manufacture: The London Fog and British Fiction from Dickens to Woolf*. Charlottesville, VA: University of Virginia Press, 2016.

Thompson, Janna. *Intergenerational Justice: Rights and Responsibilities in an Intergenerational Polity*. New York: Routledge, 2009.

Thomsen, Dorthe Kirkegaard, and Dorte Berntsen. "The Cultural Life Script and Life Story Chapters Contribute to the Reminiscence Bump." *Memory* 16.4 (2008): 420–435.

Thomsen, Mads Rosendahl. "Literature's Humanist Posthumanism." *The Bloomsbury Handbook of Posthumanism*. Eds. Mads Rosendahl Thomsen and Jacob Wamberg. London: Bloomsbury, 2020. 333–345.

Thomsen, Mads Rosendahl. *The New Human in Literature: Posthuman Visions of Changes in Body, Mind and Society after 1900*. London: Bloomsbury, 2013.

Thomsen, Søren Ulrik. *Store Kongensgade 23*. Frankfurt: Suhrkamp, 2023.

Thomson, Alistair. "Oral History and Community History in Britain: Personal and Critical Reflections on Twenty-Five Years of Continuity and Change." *Oral History* 36.1 (2008): 95–104.

Törnquist-Plewa, Barbara, and Igor Pietraszewski. "Wroclaw Changes in Memory Narratives" *Remembering Ethnic Cleansing and Lost Cultural Diversity in Eastern, Central and Southeastern Europe*. Ed. Barbara Törnquist-Plewa. New York: Berghahn, 2016. 17–48.

Törnquist-Plewa, Barbara, and Igor Pietraszewski. "Cosmopolitan Memories under Pressure. The Case of Postcommunist Wroclaw." *History & Memory* 34.2 (2022): 5–31.

Traba, Robert, and Hans Henning Hahn. *Wyobrażenia przeszłości. Polsko-niemieckie miejsca pamięci*. Warszawa: Scholar, 2017.

Traverso, Enzo. *Left-Wing Melancholia: Marxism, History, and Memory*. New York: Columbia University Press, 2016.

Tremlett, Giles. "No Pasarán: Anti-Fascist Slogan Takes on New Significance in Ukraine Crisis." *The Guardian*. 12 March 2022. https://www.theguardian.com/world/2022/mar/12/no-pasaran-anti-fascist-ukraine-spanish-civil-war (Accessed 09 February 2024).

Trexler, Adam. *Anthropocene Fictions: The Novel in a Time of Climate Change*. Charlottesville: University of Virginia Press, 2015.

Troelenberg, Eva-Maria, Kerstin Schankweiler, and Anna Sophia Messner. "On the 'Objectscape' of Transculturality. An Introduction." *Reading Objects in the Contact Zone*. Eds. Eva-Maria Troelenberg, Kerstin Schankweiler, Anna Sophia Messner. Heidelberg: University Publishing, 2021. 1–16.

Trouillot, Michel-Rolph. "Abortive Rituals: Historical Apologies in the Global Era." *Interventions: International Journal of Postcolonial Studies*. 2 (2000): 171–186.

Tsing, Anna Lowenhaupt, Heather Anne Swanson, Elaine Gan, and Nils Bubandt (eds.). *Arts of Living on a Damaged Planet*. Minneapolis: University of Minnesota Press, 2017.

Vaidhyanathan, Siva. *The Googlization of Everything (and Why We Should Worry)*. Berkeley: University of California Press, 2011.

van den Elzen, Sophie (2024). "Imoinda in Berlin: Feminists and the Cultural Memory of Slavery After 1848". *Memory and Social Movements in Modern and Contemporary History*. Eds. Stefan Berger and Christian Koller. Palgrave Studies in the History of Social Movements. Basingstoke: Palgrave Macmillan. 199–219.

Van der Chijs, Jacobus Anne. *De vestiging van het Nederlandsche Gezag over de Banda eilanden 1599–1621*. Batavia: Albrecht & Co., 1886.

Van Dijck, José, Thomas Poell, and Martijn De Waal. *The Platform Society. Public Values in a Connective World*. New York: Oxford University Press, 2018.

Van Dijck, José. "Google Scholar as the Co-producer of Scholarly Knowledge." *Social Software and the Evolution of User Expertise. Future Trends in Knowledge Creation and Dissemination*. Ed. Tatjana Takseva. Herschey, PA: IGI Global, 2012. 130–146.

Van Dijck, José. *Mediated Memories in the Digital Age*. Stanford, CA: Stanford University Press, 2008.

Van Dijck, José. *The Culture of Connectivity. A Critical History of Social Media*. New York: Oxford University Press, 2013.

Van Robbroeck, Lize. "'Township Art': libel or label?" *de arte* 33.57 (1998): 3–16.

Van Robbroeck, Lize. *Writing White on Black: Modernism as Discursive Paradigm in South African Writing on Modern Black Art*. 2006. Stellenbosch University, PhD dissertation.

Verdery, Katherine. *The Political Lives of Death Bodies. Reburial and Postsocialist Change*. New York: Columbia University Press, 1999.

Verdin, Monique Michelle. "Cancer Alley: Istrouma to the Gulf of Mexico." *Southern Cultures* 26.2 (Summer 2020): 80–95.

Vetemaa, Enn. *Risti rahvas I*. Tallinn: Kupar, 1994.

Vetemaa, Enn. *Risti rahvas II*. Tallinn: Kupar, 1998.

Vinitzky-Seroussi, Vered. "Commemorating a Difficult Past: Yitzhak Rabin's Memorials." *American Sociological Review* 67.1 (2002): 30–51.

Vinitzky-Seroussi, Vered, and Mathias Jalfim Maraschin. "Between Remembrance and Knowledge: The Spanish Flu, COVID-19, and the Two Poles of Collective Memory." *Memory Studies* 14.6 (2021): 1475–1488.

Virilio, Paul. *Speed and Politics*. Trans. Mark Polizzotti. Los Angeles: Semiotext(e), 2006.

Wackwitz, Stephan. *Ein unsichtbares Land*. Frankfurt: S. Fischer Verlag, 2003.

Wagner-Pacifici, Robin, and Barry Schwartz. "The Vietnam Veterans Memorial: Commemorating a Difficult Past." *American Journal of Sociology* 97.2 (1991): 376–420.

Wagoner, Brady. "Collective Memory as a Process of Social Representation." *The Cambridge Handbook of Social Representations*. Eds. Eleni Andreouli et al. Cambridge: Cambridge University Press, 2015. 143–162.

Walker, Nick. *Neuroqueer Heresies: Notes on the Neurodiversity Paradigm, Autistic Empowerment, and Postnormal Possibilities*. Fort Worth, TX: Autonomous Press, 2021.

Walkerdine, Valerie. "Beyond the Painted Smile." *Family Snaps: The Meanings of Domestic Photography*. Eds. Jo Spence and Pat Holland. London: Virago, 1991.

Walkerdine, Valerie. "Dreams from an Ordinary Childhood." *Truth Dare or Promise: Girls Growing Up in the 50s*. Ed. Liz Heron. London: Virago Press, 1985. 63–77.

Wall, Jeff. "Photography and Liquid Intelligence." *Jeff Wall: Selected Essays and Interviews*. New York: Museum of Modern Art, 2007. 109–111.

Wallet, Bart et al. *De Joodse notaris en de beschuldiging van verraad: Kritische analyse van argumentatie en brongebruik in Het verraad van Anne Frank*. Amsterdam: University of Amsterdam, 2022.

Warner, Marina. *Monuments & Maidens: The Allegory of the Female Form*. London: Weidenfeld and Nicolson, 1985.

Warren, Michael J. "A New Latin Analogue to the Cuckoo Motif in the *Seafarer* and the *Husbands Message*." *Medium Aevum* 88.1 (2019): 129–133.

Watercutter, Angela. "Why *The Andy Warhol Diaries* Recreated the Artist's Voice with AI." *Wired*, 8 March 2022. https://www.wired.com/story/andy-warhol-diaries-artificial-intelligence-voice/ (10 March 2022).

Watkins, Clare Vaye. *Gold Fame Citrus*. New York: Riverhead Books, 2015.

Weber, Samuel. *Benjamin's Abilities*. Cambridge, MA: Harvard University Press, 2008.

Weigel, Sigrid. *Genea-Logik: Generation, Tradition und Evolution zwischen Kultur- und Naturwissenschaften*. Munich: Fink, 2006.

Weisenburger, Steven. "Pynchon's Hereros: A Textual and Bibliographical Note." *Pynchon Notes* 10 (1982): 37–45.

Wekker, Gloria. *White Innocence: Paradoxes of Colonialism and Race*. Durham: Duke University Press, 2016.

Wertheim, Jon. "Investigating Who Betrayed Anne Frank and Her Family to the Nazis." *CBS News 60 minutes*. 16 January 2022. https://www.cbsnews.com/news/anne-frank-betrayal-investigation-60-minutes-2022-01-16/ (Accessed 15 March 2024).

Wertsch, James V. *Voices of Collective Remembering*. Cambridge: Cambridge University Press, 2002.

Wertsch, James V. *How Nations Remember: A Narrative Approach*. London and New York: Oxford University Press, 2021.

Whelan, Kevin. "Robert Emmet: Between History and Memory." *History Ireland* 11.3 (2003): 50–54.

White, Hayden. *Metahistory: The Historical Imagination in Nineteenth-Century Europe*. Baltimore: Johns Hopkins University Press, 1973.

White, Micahm. 2023. "The Emergence of Activist Artificial Intelligence: A New Chapter in Social Movements." ProtestGPT (blog). June 29, 2023. https://protestgpt.com/about/.

Wilson, Emily. "Translator's Note." *The Odyssey*. New York: Norton, 2018. 81–91.

Wolfgang Jaeger, *Soziale Büergerrechte im Museum. Die Repräesentation sozialer Demokratie in neun kulturhistorischen Museen*. Bielefeld: Transcript, 2020.

Wolf, Reva. "Introduction Through the Looking Glass." *I'll Be Your Mirror: The Selected Interviews of Andy Warhol 1962–1987*. Ed. Kenneth Goldsmith. New York: Carroll and Graf Publishers, 2004. Epub.

Wolkers, Jan. "De achtste plaag." *De hond met de blauwe tong*. Amsterdam: Meulenhoff, 1964. 9–33.

Wood, David. *Deep Time, Dark Times. On Being Geologically Human*. New York: Fordham University Press, 2019.

Woods, Christopher J. *Bodenstown Revisited: The Grave of Theobald Wolfe Tone, Its Monuments and Its Pilgrimages*. Dublin: Four Courts Press, 2018.

Wright, Beverley. "Living and Dying in Louisiana's 'Cancer Alley'." *The Quest for Environmental Justice: Human Rights and the Politics of Pollution*. Ed. Robert Bullard. Berkley, CA: Counterpoint, 2005. 87–107.

Wüstenberg, Jenny. "Locating Transnational Memory." *International Journal of Politics Culture and Society* 32 (2019): 371–382.

Wüstenberg, Jenny. *Civil Society and Memory in Postwar Germany*. Cambridge: Cambridge University Press, 2017.

Wüstenberg, Jenny. *Slow Memory: Remembering Gradual Change in an Accelerating World*. Oxford: Oxford University Press, forthcoming.

Yeats, William Butler. *Autobiographies: Collected Works of W.B. Yeats, Volume III*. Eds. William H. O'Donnell and Douglas N. Archibald. London: Macmillan, 2010.

Yeats, William Butler. *The Poems*. Ed. Daniel Albright. London: Dent, 1994.

Young, Philip H. *The Printed Homer: A 3000 Year Publishing and Translation History of the Iliad and the Odyssey*. Jefferson, NC: McFarland, 2003.

Yusoff, Kathryn. *Geologic Life: Inhuman Intimacies and the Geophysics of Race*. Durham, NC: Duke University Press, 2024.

Zalasiewicz, Jan. "Old and New Patterns of the Anthopocene." *Transformations in Environment and Society* 3: (2020) 11–40.

Zamponi, Lorenzo. *Social Movements, Memory and Media. Narrative in Action in the Italian and Spanish Student Movements*. London: Palgrave Macmillan, 2018.

Zelizer, Barbie, and Keren Tenenboim-Weinblatt (eds.). *Journalism and Memory*. Basingstoke: Palgrave Macmillan, 2014.

Zelizer, Barbie. "Why Memory's Work on Journalism Does not Reflect Journalism's Work on Memory." *Memory Studies* 1.1 (2008): 79–87.

Zimring, Carl. *Clean and White: A History of Environmental Racism in the United States*, New York and London: New York University Press, 2015.

Zirra, Maria, "Shelf Lives: Nonhuman Agency and Seamus Heaney's vibrant Memory Objects." *Parallax* 22.4 (2017): 458–473.

Zirra, Maria. *Visual Poetic Memory: Ekphrasis and Image-text in Seamus Heaney, Derek Walcott and Wopko Jensma*. Stockholm University, PhD dissertation, 2019.

Zolberg, Aristide R. "Moments of Madness." *Politics and Society* (1972): 183–207.

Zolkos, Magdalena. "Mnemonic 'Boundary Objects' and Postcolonial Restitution: The Story of Three Greenlandic Tupilait." *European Journal of Scandinavian Studies* 53.1 (2023): 80–98.

Zuccon, Guido, Bevan Koopman, and Razia Shaik. "ChatGPT Hallucinates when Attributing Answers." *Association for Computing Machinery* (2023): 46–51.

Zylinska, Joanna. *Minimal Ethics for the Anthropocene*. Ann Arbor, MI: Open Humanities Press, 2014.

Film, Music, Art

2001: A Space Odyssey. Dir. Stanley Kubrick. Screenplay by Stanley Kubrick and Arthur C. Clarke, 1968.

After the Apology. Dir. Larissa Behrendt, with Suellyn Tighe, Hazel Collins, Karen Fusi, and Debra Swan. Sydney, NSW: Pursekey Productions, 2017.

Aşît. Dir. Pınar Öğrenci. documenta 15, 2022.

Boccara, Frida. *Les moulins de mon Coeur*. 1969. https://www.youtube.com/watch?v=8E5EfDsJxAU (Accessed 28 March 2024).

Harrison, Noel. *The windmills of your mind*. 1968. https://www.youtube.com/watch?v=WEhS9Y9HYjU (Accessed 28 March 2024).

Her. Dir. Spike Jonze, 2012.

Iveković, Sanja. "Gen XX." https://artviewer.org/wp-content/uploads/2022/11/Sanja-Ivekovic-at-Kunsthalle-Wien_12.jpg. (Accessed 14 May 2024).

Iveković, Sanja. "Ona prava. Biseri revolucije" / "The Right One. The Pearls of the Revolution." https://artviewer.org/wp-content/uploads/2022/11/Sanja-Ivekovic-at-Kunsthalle-Wien_10.jpg (Accessed 14 May 2024).

Iveković, Sanja. "Trudna Memorija" / "Pregnant Memory" https://www.facebook.com/search/top/?q=sanja%20ivekovic%20monument%20%20

Neuromancer. Dir. William Gibson. New York: Ace, 1984.

The Andy Warhol Diaries. Dir. Andrew Rossi. Netflix, 2022.

The Thomas Crown Affair. Dir. Norman Jewison, 1968.

van Dijk, Louis. *The windmills of your mind*. 1970. https://www.youtube.com/watch?v=MSmPp6IxtPg (Accessed 28 March 2024).

Vanilla Fudge. *The windmills of your mind*. 1969. https://www.youtube.com/watch?v=lxthq9AOWoo (Accessed 28 March 2024).

The Authors

Aleida Assmann is Prof. em. of English Literature at the University of Konstanz. Main areas of her research are history of media, history and theory of reading, cultural memory, with special emphasis on Holocaust and trauma. Publications in English: *Memory in a Global Age. Discourses, Practices and Trajectories* (ed. with Sebastian Conrad, Palgrave, 2010), *Cultural Memory and Western Civilization: Functions, Media, Archives* (Cambridge UP, 2012), *Shadows of Trauma. Memory and the Politics of Postwar Identity* (Fordham, 2016), *Is the Time Out of Joint? On the Rise and Fall of the Modern Time Regime* (Cornell, 2020).

Laura Basu is an academic, writer and social impact consultant. She is an associate with Utrecht University's Institute for Cultural Inquiry and was formerly openDemocracy's economics editor. She is the author of *Media Amnesia* (Pluto Press, 2018) and lead editor of *The Media and Austerity* (Routledge, 2018). She writes on topics ranging from racial capitalism to the environmental crisis to neurodivergence. She is working on a new book about love and politics.

Jesseka Batteau is an independent advisor for quality and evaluations in higher education and research in the Netherlands. Since 2023 she is also the State Representative for the Partij voor de Dieren in the Province of Utrecht, the Netherlands. In the past, her research focus was on literary theory, media studies, cultural memory studies and religious studies, and has since developed towards an interest in ecocriticism, animal studies and multispecies intersectionality. Her monograph *Literary Performances of Post-Religious Memory in The Netherlands: Gerard Reve, Jan Wolkers, Maarten't Hart* was published in 2022 (Brill).

Guy Beiner is the Sullivan Chair of Irish Studies at Boston College. His prize-winning historical studies of remembering and forgetting include *Remembering the Year of the French: Irish Folk History and Social Memory* (University of Wisconsin Press, 2007) and *Forgetful Remembrance: Social Forgetting and Vernacular Historiography of a Rebellion in Ulster* (Oxford UP, 2018). He is also the editor of *Pandemic Re-Awakenings: The Forgotten and Unforgotten 'Spanish' Flu of 1918–1919* (Oxford UP, 2022).

Stefan Berger is Professor of Social History and director of the Institute for Social Movements at Ruhr-Universität Bochum, Germany. His research fields are the history of the labour and social movements, history of historiography, historical theory, nationalism and national identity, deindustrialization and industrial heritage. His publications include *History and Identity. How Historical Theory Shapes Historical Practice* (Cambridge UP, 2022), *De-Industrial Heritage* (special issue of *Labor. Studies in Working-Class History*, ed. with Steven High); *The Past as History. National Identity and Historical Consciousness in Modern Europe* (Palgrave, 2015).

Tashina Blom is a PhD candidate in the ERC-project *Remembering Activism: The Cultural Memory of Protest in Europe*. Her doctoral research investigates how protest slogans with long histories and contemporary afterlives can become a carrier of cultural memory; and specifically, how those memories can be mobilized for political purposes. It does so through a series of case studies focusing on nineteenth- and twentieth-century anarchist and feminist slogans.

Lucy Bond is Reader in Literature and Memory Studies at the University of Westminster. Lucy is the author of *Frames of Memory after 9/11: Culture Criticism, Politics and Law* (Palgrave, 2015) and co-author of the Routledge New Critical Idiom guide to Trauma (2020). She is co-editor of *The Transcultural*

Turn: Interrogating Memory Between and Beyond Borders (De Gruyter, 2014), *Memory Unbound: New Directions in Memory Studies* (Berghahn, 2016), *Planetary Memory in Contemporary American Fiction* (Routledge, 2018), and *The Palgrave Companion to Literary Memory Studies* (Palgrave, 2024).

Kiene Brillenburg Wurth is Professor of Literature and Comparative Media at Utrecht University, the Netherlands. Her research fields are literature, arts, and media, creativity studies, and comparative philosophy. Her publications include *Musically Sublime* (Fordham UP, 2009), *Between Page and Screen* (Fordham UP, 2012), *Literature and the Material Turn* (edited special issue for *Comparative Literature*, Duke UP 2018), *Book Presence in a Digital Age* (Bloomsbury 2018, ed. with Jessica Pressman and Kári Driscoll), *Paradoxes of Creativity* (edited special issue for *Journal of Creative Behaviour*, 2019), and *Mobilizing Creativity* (special issue for *The Minnesota Review*, Duke UP, ed. with Iris van der Tuin and Nanna Verhoeff), as well as various recent articles and chapters on creativity, Daoist-, and Buddhist thinking.

Claire Connolly is Professor of Modern English at University College Cork, Ireland. Her *Cultural History of the Irish Novel, 1790–1829* (Cambridge Studies in Romanticism, 2011) won the Donald J. Murphy Prize, awarded by the American Conference for Irish Studies. With Marjorie Howes (Boston College), she was General Editor of *Irish Literature in Transition, 1700–2020*, 6 volumes, Cambridge UP (2020).

Stef Craps is a Professor of English literature at Ghent University in Belgium, where he directs the Cultural Memory Studies Initiative. His research interests lie in twentieth-century and contemporary literature and culture, memory and trauma studies, ecocriticism and the environmental humanities, and postcolonial and decolonial theory. Notable publications include *Trauma* (Routledge, 2020, co-authored with Lucy Bond), *Postcolonial Witnessing: Trauma Out of Bounds* (Palgrave, 2013), and a guest-edited special issue of *American Imago* on ecological grief (2020).

Richard Crownshaw teaches American literature in the Department of English and Creative Writing, Goldsmiths, University of London. His research is in the fields of cultural memory and trauma studies, modern and contemporary American literature, and the environmental humanities. He is currently finishing a book, *Climates of Memory*, which explores the ways that contemporary American fiction stages cultural memories of environmental catastrophes of the past, present and future.

Priska Daphi is Professor of Conflict Sociology at Bielefeld University, Germany. Her research focuses on social movements, civil society and political participation in Europe with a particular interest in collective memory, identity, coalition building, transnational activism and space. She is co-editor of *Social Movements, Cultural Memory and Digital Media: Mobilising Mediated Remembrance* (with Emily Keightley and Samuel Merrill, Palgrave, 2020) and of the special issue *Movements and Memories in Mobilization* (with Lorenzo Zamponi, 2019). She is the author of *Becoming a Movement. Identity, Narrative and Memory in the European Global Justice Movement* (Rowman & Littlefield, 2017).

Chiara De Cesari is Professor of Heritage, Memory and Cultural Studies and Chair of Cultural Studies at the University of Amsterdam. Her wide-ranging research explores how forms of memory, heritage, art, and cultural politics are shifting under contemporary conditions of post- and decoloniality, globalization and state transformation. She is the author of *Heritage and the Cultural Struggle for Palestine* (Stanford UP, 2019), and co-editor of two key volumes in memory studies (*Transnational Memory*, De Gruyter, 2014; *European Memory in Populism*, Routledge, 2019).

Ann Dooley is Professor emerita of Medieval Studies and Celtic Studies at the University of Toronto. She is co-founder of the Celtic Studies Program at the University of Toronto. Her research interests centre on poetry widely and medieval and early modern Irish language and literature. Her publications include: *Playing the Hero: Reading the [Irish epic] Tain Bo Cuailnge* (University of Toronto Press, 2006), *Tales of the Irish Elders* (2000), *Constructing Gender in Medieval Ireland* (ed. with Sarah Sheehan, Palgrave, 2013), and *Celtic Cosmologies* (ed. with Jacqueline Borsje et al., Pims, 2014).

Duygu Erbil is an affiliate researcher at the Institute for Cultural Inquiry at Utrecht University, where she completed her doctoral degree in Comparative Literature. Her research fields are cultural studies, life narratives, memory studies and Turkey studies. In 2024, she defended her PhD, "Remembering Deniz Gezmiş", which was part of the project *Remembering Activism: The Cultural Memory of Protest in Europe*. She is the co-editor of *Remembering Contentious Lives* (Palgrave forthcoming, ed. with Ann Rigney and Clara Vlessing).

Astrid Erll is Professor of Anglophone Literatures and Cultures at Goethe University Frankfurt, Germany. Her research fields are literary history, narratology, media studies, transcultural studies, and memory studies. Her publications include *Memory in Culture* (Palgrave, 2011), an introduction to the field of memory studies, *Cultural Memory after the Transnational Turn* (special issue of *Memory Studies*, ed. with Ann Rigney, 2018), "Tracing the Hidden Power of Implicit Collective Memory" (*Memory, Mind & Media*, 2022), and *Travels in Time. Essays on Collective Memory in Motion* (Oxford UP, 2025).

Francisco J. Ferrándiz is senior researcher at the Spanish National Research Council (CSIC). He has conducted long-term research on the politics of memory in contemporary Spain, analyzing the exhumations of mass graves from the Civil War (1936–1939). He has published *El pasado bajo tierra: Exhumaciones contemporáneas de la Guerra Civil* (Anthropos/Siglo XXI, 2014), and co-edited *Necropolitics: Mass Graves and Exhumations in the Age of Human Rights* (UPenn Press, 2015), as well as articles in journals such as *Memory Studies, American Ethnologist, Anthropology Today, Critique of Anthropology, Journal of Spanish Cultural Studies*, or *Ethnography*.

Sarah Gensburger is Professor of Political Science at Sciences Po and CNRS, France. Her research fields are sociology, administration, public policies, inequalities, terrorism, Holocaust history and memory studies. Her publications include *Memory on my Doorstep* (Leuven UP, 2019), *Beyond Memory. Can We Really Learn from the Past?* (Palgrave, 2020, with. Sandrine Lefranc), *De-Commemoration. Removing Statues and Renaming Streets* (Berghahn, 2023, ed. with Jenny Wüstenberg) and *The Covid-19 Pandemic and Memory* (Palgrave, 2024, ed. with Orli Fridman).

Maria Grever is em. Professor of Theory of History, Erasmus University Rotterdam, the Netherlands. Her research fields are historical culture, historical consciousness, (gender) historiography, canonization, and monuments. Her publications include *Onontkoombaar verleden* (Verloren, 2020), *Palgrave Handbook of Research in Historical Culture and Education* (ed. with Mario Carretero and Stefan Berger, 2017), *Beyond the Canon. History for the Twenty-First Century* (ed. with Siep Stuurman, Palgrave, 2007), *Transforming the Public Sphere. The Dutch National Exhibition of Women's Labor in 1898* (co-authored with Berteke Waaldijk, Duke UP, 2004).

Ido de Haan is Professor of Political History at Utrecht University. Among other topics in European history, he studies the history and memory of large-scale violence. Among his publications are several studies on the memory of the Holocaust in the Netherlands, most recently "Guilt, Pride and

Reputation. The Memory of Rescue of Jews in the Netherlands since 1945," in *The Rescue Turn: Holocaust Memory, Politics, and Debates* (eds. Natalia Aleksiun et al., Wayne State UP, 2024).

Marianne Hirsch is Professor Emerita of Comparative Literature and Gender Studies at Columbia University, a member of the American Academy of Arts and Sciences, and writes about the transmission of memories of violent histories across generations, a process she has termed "postmemory." Her recent books include *The Generation of Postmemory: Writing and Visual Culture After the Holocaust* (Columbia UP, 2012), *Ghosts of Home: The Afterlife of Czernowitz in Jewish Memory* (University of California Press, 2010) and *School Photos in Liquid Time: Reframing Difference* (University of Washington Press, 2020), both co-authored with Leo Spitzer, and the co-edited volume *Women Mobilizing Memory* (Columbia UP, 2019). With a group of scholars, artists, and community activists, she directed the New York City based Zip Code Memory Project and is working on a book about reparative memory.

Andreas Huyssen is the Villard Professor emeritus of German and Comparative Literature at Columbia University in New York. A founding editor of *New German Critique* and founding director of Columbia's Institute for Comparative Literature and Society. His books include *After the Great Divide: Modernism, Mass Culture, Postmodernism* (Indiana UP, 1986), *Twilight Memories: Marking Time in a Culture of Amnesia* (Routledge, 1995), *Present Pasts: Urban Palimpsests and the Politics of Memory* (Stanford UP, 2003), *Miniature Metropolis: Literature in an Age of Photography and Film* (Harvard UP, 2015), and *Memory Art in the Contemporary World: Confronting Violence in the Global South* (Lund Humphries, 2022).

Nicole L. Immler is Professor of Historical Memory and Transformative Justice at the University of Humanistic Studies in Utrecht. Her research into the afterlife of historical injustice links the fields of (oral) history, narratology, memory studies and transitional justice. Her publications include *Das Familiengedächtnis der Wittgensteins* (Transcript, 2011), "Rethinking Post-colonial Recognition from a Multi-voiced Perspective" (*WACANA Journal of the Humanities of Indonesia*, 2021) and "Transformative Justice for the Dutch Slavery Past" (*Slaveries & Post-Slaveries*, 2021).

Wulf Kansteiner is Professor of Memory Studies and Contemporary History at Aarhus University in Denmark. His research addresses four overarching themes: the methods and theories of memory studies; the role of visual media – TV, film, digital culture – in the formation of cultural memory; post-narrativist historical theory; and Holocaust and genocide history, memory and historiography. Kansteiner is co-founder and co-editor of the Sage-journal *Memory Studies* and Past President of the Memory Studies Association (MSA). Recent publications include: *Agonistic Memory and the Legacy of 20th Century Wars in Europe*, co-edited with Stefan Berger (Palgrave, 2021) and "Digital Doping for Historians: Can History, Memory, and Historical Theory be Rendered Artificially Intelligent?", *History & Theory* 62.4 (2022).

Margaret Kelleher is Professor and Chair of Anglo-Irish Literature and Drama at University College Dublin. Her current research fields are nineteenth- and twentieth-century Irish literary and cultural history, and bilingual studies. Her book *The Maamtrasna Murders: Language, Life and Death in Nineteenth-Century Ireland* (UCD Press, 2018) was awarded the American Conference for Irish Studies prize for Books on Language and Culture. She is a board member of the Museum of Literature Ireland (MoLI) and member of the Royal Irish Academy.

Rosanne Kennedy teaches Literary, Cultural and Gender Studies at Australian National University. Her research fields are memory studies, Indigenous studies, feminist theory, life writing, and human rights. Recent publications include "Beyond Presentism: Memory Studies and Deep History" (with Ben Silverstein, *Memory Studies*, 2023), "Memory, Activism and the Arts in Asia and the Pacific" (with Shameem Black and Lia Kent, special issue of *Memory Studies*, 2024), and "Memoir Activism: The Afterlives of *Guantanamo Diary* in Cultural Memory" in *Remembering Contentious Lives* (eds. Ann Rigney, Duygu Erbil and Clara Vlessing, Palgrave, 2024).

Susanne Knittel is Associate Professor of Comparative Literature at Utrecht University in the Netherlands. Her research is situated at the intersection of memory studies, perpetrator studies, posthumanism, disability studies, and the environmental humanities. She is the author of *The Historical Uncanny* (ML, 2015), the editor, with Zachary Goldberg, of *The Routledge International Handbook of Perpetrator Studies* (2019), and, with Kári Driscoll, co-editor-in-chief of the *Journal of Perpetrator Research* (Winchester UP). Currently, she directs the ERC-funded project *EcoViolence: Crimes against Nature in the Contemporary Cultural Imagination*.

Eneken Laanes is Professor of Comparative Literature at Tallinn University, Estonia and the Project Leader of ERC grant "Translating Memories: The Eastern European Past in the Global Arena" (2020– 2024). Her research fields are comparative literature, transnational literature, multilingualism, memory studies, and Eastern European memory cultures. Her publications include *Cultural Memorial Forms* (special issue of *Memory Studies*, ed. with Hanna Meretoja, 2021), *Perpetrators, Collaborators and Implicated Subjects in Central and Eastern Europe* (special issue of *SEEJ*, ed. with Margaret Comer, 2023) and "Katja Petrowskaja's Translational Poetics on Memory" (*New German Critique*, 2024).

Alison Landsberg is Professor of History and Cultural Studies at George Mason University in Fairfax, Virginia. She is the author of *Prosthetic Memory: The Transformation of American Remembrance in the Age of Mass Culture* (Columbia UP, 2004) and *Engaging the Past: Mass Culture and the Production of Historical Knowledge* (Columbia UP, 2015) along with numerous articles and book chapters. Taken together, her body of research on museums, film, and television, has focused on the modes of engagement they solicit from individuals and the possibilities therein for the production and acquisition of memory, historical knowledge and political subjectivity in the public sphere.

Joep Leerssen, Professor emeritus at the Universities of Amsterdam and Maastricht, is a comparatist and cultural historian. He works on cultural (self-)stereotyping, on the comparative history of national movements, and on the history of the humanities. He is the editor of the *Encyclopedia of Romantic Nationalism in Europe* (2nd ed. 2022). His other book publications include *National Thought in Europe* (3rd ed. 2018), *Comparative Literature in Britain* (Legenda, 2019), and *Commemorating Writers in Nineteenth-Century Europe* (co-edited with Ann Rigney, Palgrave, 2015).

Gerardine Meaney is Professor of Cultural Theory at University College Dublin. Her research interests are gender and ethnicity, cultural memory and cultural analytics. Her publications include *Gender, Ireland and Cultural Change* (Routledge, 2010) and *Reading the Irish Woman: Cultural Encounter and Exchange, 1780–1960* (Liverpool UP, 2013, with Mary O'Dowd and Bernadette Whelan). She currently leads the collaborative literature and data science project, *European Migrants in the British Imagination* (https://projectvicteur.com).

Samuel Merrill is Associate Professor at Umeå University's Department of Sociology and Centre for Digital Social Research (DIGSUM). He specializes in digital and cultural sociology and his research interests concern, among other things, the intersections between political activism, digital media, and social memory. He has recently co-edited a special issue of *Memory Studies* with Ann Rigney entitled *Remembering Activism: Explorations in the Memory-activism Nexus* (2024).

Birgit Meyer is Professor of Religious Studies at Utrecht University. Trained as a cultural anthropologist, she studies religion from a material and postcolonial angle. Recent book publications include *Figuration and Sensations of the Unseen in Judaism, Christianity and Islam: Contested Desires* (Bloomsbury, 2019, ed. with Terje Stordalen), and *Refugees and Religion. Ethnographic Studies of Global Trajectories* (Bloomsbury, 2021, ed. with Peter van der Veer). She directs the research program *Religious Matters in an Entangled World* (www.religiousmatters.nl).

Jeffrey K. Olick is William R. Kenan, Jr. Professor of Sociology and History at the University of Virginia. His books include *In the House of the Hangman: The Agonies of German Defeat, 1943–1949* (Chicago UP, 2011), *The Sins of the Fathers: Germany, Memory, Method* (Chicago UP, 2016) and *In the Grip of the Past: The Ciphered Transits of Collective Memory* (Oxford UP, 2025), among others. Olick is one of the founding Co-Presidents of the Memory Studies Association.

Emilie Pine is Professor of Modern Drama at University College Dublin. She has published widely on performance and memory, including *The Politics of Irish Memory* (Palgrave, 2011), and *The Memory Marketplace* (Indiana UP, 2020). Her project *Industrial Memories* witnessed Ireland's historical institutional abuse (https://industrialmemories.ucd.ie). Emilie is also a creative writer, including the plays *Good Sex* (2022) and *All Hardest of Woman* (2022), the award-winning memoir *Notes to Self* (Tramp Press, 2018), and the novel *Ruth & Pen* (Penguin, 2022).

Liedeke Plate is Professor of Culture and Inclusivity at Radboud University. She researches the relationships between art, culture and inclusion, focusing on literature, gender, cultural memory, and the so-called material turn in cultural studies. Her publications include *Transforming Memories in Contemporary Women's Rewriting* (Palgrave, 2011) and the co-edited volumes *Performing Memory in Art and Popular Culture* (Routledge, 2013), *Materializing Memory in Art and Popular Culture* (Routledge, 2017), and *Materials of Culture: Approaches to Materials in Cultural Studies* (transcript, 2023).

Anna Poletti is Associate Professor of English Language and Culture at Utrecht University. She researches contemporary life writing, with particular interests in youth cultures, ephemera (both digital and analogue) and the role of mediation and materiality in autobiography. Her books include *Graphic Medicine* (ed. with Erin La Cour, University of Hawai'i Press, 2022) and *Stories of the Self: Life Writing After the Book* (NYU Press, 2020).

Susannah Radstone is Honorary Principal Fellow in the School of Culture and Communication, University of Melbourne, Australia. Her research field is cultural memory studies. Her publications include *The Sexual Politics of Time* (Routledge, 2007), ed. *Memory and Methodology* (Bloomsbury, 2000) and several co-edited volumes including *Regimes of Memory* (Routledge, 2003), *Contested Pasts* (Routledge, 2003), *Culture and the Unconscious* (Palgrave, 2007), *Public Emotions* (Palgrave, 2007), *Memory: Histories, Theories Debates* (Fordham UP, 2010), *Translating Worlds: Migration, Memory and Culture* (Routledge, 2020) and *The Palgrave Handbook of Literary Memory Studies* (in press).

Jessica Rapson is a Senior Lecturer in Culture, Media and Creative Industries at King's College London. Her monograph *Topographies of Suffering: Buchenwald, Babi Yar, Lidice* (Berghahn, 2015) examined the environmental dynamics of Holocaust commemorative landscapes. She has edited collections on the Transcultural (De Gruyter, 2014, with Lucy Bond) and Planetary Memory (*Textual Practice*, 2017, with Lucy Bond and Ben de Bruyn) and published a range of chapters and articles on the political and environmental issues pertaining to commemoration and difficult heritage.

Anna (Amza) Reading is Professor of Culture and Creative Industries at King's College, University of London, UK. Her research fields are culture and media studies, memory studies and gender studies. Her publications include *Polish Women, Solidarity and Feminism* (Macmillan, 1992), *The Social Inheritance of the Holocaust: Gender, Culture and Memory* (Palgrave, 2002), *Gender and Memory in the Globital Age* (Palgrave, 2016), *Cultural Memories of Non-violent Struggles* (ed. with Tamar Katriel, Palgrave, 2015); *A Right to Memory* (ed. with Noam Tirosh, Berghahn, 2023) and "Rewilding Memory" (*Memory, Mind and Media*, May 2022). She also writes plays and fiction.

Antonius C.G.M. Robben is Professor Emeritus of Anthropology at Utrecht University, and past President of the *Netherlands Society of Anthropology*. He has a long-standing interest in the study of mass violence, sociocultural trauma, and the politics of memory. His most recent books include *Argentina Betrayed: Memory, Mourning, and Accountability* (2018, University of Pennsylvania Press), and the award-winning *Perpetrators: Encountering Humanity's Dark Side* (Stanford UP, 2023, co-authored with Alex Hinton).

Michael Rothberg is the 1939 Society Samuel Goetz Chair in Holocaust Studies, Chair of the Department of Comparative Literature, and Professor of English and Comparative Literature at the University of California, Los Angeles. He is the author of *The Implicated Subject: Beyond Victims and Perpetrators* (Stanford UP, 2019), *Multidirectional Memory: Remembering the Holocaust in the Age of Decolonization* (Stanford UP, 2009), and *Traumatic Realism: The Demands of Holocaust Representation* (University of Minnesota Press, 2000). With Yasemin Yildiz, he is currently completing *Memory Citizenship: Migrant Archives of Holocaust Remembrance* for Fordham UP.

Daniele Salerno is a guest researcher at Utrecht University, the Netherlands, and a temporary lecturer at the University of Cádiz, Spain. His research fields are cultural memory, narratology, and media studies. His publications include *Archiving Activism in the Digital Age* (ed. with Ann Rigney, 2024), "A Semiotic Theory of Memory" (*Semiotica*, 2021), and "'Bella Ciao': A Portable Monument for Transnational Activism" (with Marit van de Warenburg, *International Journal of Cultural Studies*, 2023, winner of the Zumkehr Prize).

Rik Smit is Assistant Professor at the Centre for Media and Journalism Studies at the University of Groningen, the Netherlands. His research focuses on memory and digital media, including Artificial Intelligence. He has published in a range of journals, including *New Media & Society*, *Memory Studies* and *Convergence*, and edited volumes, including *Social Movements, Cultural Memory and Digital Media* (Palgrave, 2020). He is one of the editors of the special collection *The Platformization of Memory* for *Memory, Mind & Media* (2024).

Thomas Smits is Assistant Professor of digital history and AI at the University of Amsterdam. A historian with an interest in visual culture and digital methods, he is author of the prize-winning *The European Illustrated Press and the Emergence of a Transnational Visual Culture of the News, 1842–1870*

(Routledge, 2020) and *The Visual Memory of Protest* (ed. with Ann Rigney, AUP, 2023). Recent work appeared in *New Media and Society, Memory Studies, Visual Communication,* and *Social Movement Studies.*

Mads Rosendahl Thomsen is Professor of Comparative Literature at Aarhus University, Denmark. He is chair of the Book Panel of the Ministry of Culture Denmark (2023–2026) and director of the Center for Language Generation and AI (2023–). He has published on literary historiography, modernist literature, world literature, digital humanities, and posthumanism. Thomsen is the author of four books, including *Mapping World Literature* (Bloomsbury, 2008) and *The New Human in Literature* (Bloomsbury, 2013), a co-author with Stefan Helgesson of *Literature and the World* (Routledge, 2019), and the editor of fourteen books.

Marek Tamm is Professor of Cultural History in Tallinn University, Estonia. His primary research fields are cultural history of medieval Europe, theory of history, and cultural memory studies. He has recently published *The Fabric of Historical Time* (co-authored with Zoltán Boldizsár Simon, Cambridge UP, 2023), *The Companion to Juri Lotman: A Semiotic Theory of Culture* (ed. with Peeter Torop, Bloomsbury, 2022), and *A Cultural History of Memory in the Early Modern Age* (ed. with Alessandro Arcangeli, Bloomsbury, 2020).

Barbara Törnquist-Plewa is a Professor of Eastern and Central European Studies at Lund University. Her main research interests are memory, identity and nationalism. In 2012–2016 she was the leader of the EU's COST-action "In Search for Transcultural Memory in Europe." Her publications include: *Whose Memory? Which Future? Remembering Ethnic Cleansing and Lost Cultural Diversity in Eastern, Central and Southeastern Europe* (Berghahn, 2016), *The Twentieth Century in European Memory,* (ed. with Tea Sindbæk Andersen, Brill, 2017), and "Memory Politics in Contemporary Ukraine: Reflections from the Postcolonial Perspective" (with Yulia Yurchuk, *Memory Studies,* 2019).

Sophie van den Elzen is a lecturer at Utrecht University. Her work focuses on the cultural production of social movements, and is situated at the crossroads of literary studies, cultural history, and memory studies. She is the co-editor of *Memory and the Language of Contention* (with Ann Rigney, Brill, 2025) and the author of *Slavery in the International Women's Movement, 1832–1914: Memory Work and the Meaning of Abolition* (Cambridge UP, 2024).

José van Dijck is a Distinguished University Professor in media and digital societies at Utrecht University (The Netherlands). Her expertise includes media technologies, social media, and digital culture, platformization and digital infrastructure. She has (co-)authored and (co-)edited ten books and hundreds of articles. Her books include *The Culture of Connectivity* (Oxford UP, 2013) and *The Platform Society* (Oxford UP, 2018). She was (elected) President of the Royal Netherlands Academy of Arts and Sciences and received honorary doctorates from Lund University (Sweden) and Oslo University (Norway). In 2021 she was awarded the Spinoza Prize, the highest Dutch award for lifetime academic achievement.

Stijn Vervaet is Associate Professor of Bosnian/Croatian/Serbian and Balkan Studies at the University of Oslo, Norway. His research fields are literary history (19th–21st c.), comparative literature, cultural memory studies, literary multilingualism and translation studies. His publications include *Holocaust, War, and Transnational Memory: Testimony from Yugoslav and Post-Yugoslav Literature*

(Routledge, 2018) and *Post-Yugoslav Constellations: Archive, Memory, and Trauma in Contemporary Bosnian, Croatian, and Serbian Literature and Culture* (De Gruyter 2016, ed. with Vlad Beronja).

Vered Vinitzky-Seroussi is a Professor of sociology at the Hebrew University of Jerusalem, Israel. Her research fields evolve mainly around collective memory and commemoration. Her publications include *The Collective Memory Reader* (Oxford UP, 2011, ed. with Jeffrey K. Olick and Daniel Levy), *After Pomp and Circumstance: High School Reunion as an Autobiographical Occasion* (University of Chicago Press, 1998), "Memories of Others for the Sake of Our Own: Mnemonic Practices in American Presidential Rhetoric 1945–2020" (*American Journal of Cultural Sociology*, 2020, with Tracy Adams). She currently studies collective memory of pandemics.

Clara Vlessing is a postdoctoral researcher at Radboud University, Nijmegen, and a lecturer in Literary Studies at Utrecht University, both in the Netherlands. Her research looks at the relationship between memory and social movements with particular attention to the role of gender. Her publications include "Reparative Remembrance" (*Social History/Histoire Sociale*, 2023) and a forthcoming collection co-edited with Duygu Erbil and Ann Rigney (*Remembering Contentious Lives*, Palgrave).

Jenny Wüstenberg is Professor of History & Memory Studies at Nottingham Trent University. Her research interests concern memory activism, "mnemonic democracy," family separation policies and biodiversity loss. She was the founding Co-President of the Memory Studies Association, as well as Chair of the COST Action on "Slow Memory" (2021–2025). She is the author of *Civil Society and Memory in Postwar Germany* (Cambridge UP, 2017, German translation 2020) and *Slow Memory: Remembering Gradual Change in an Accelerating World* (Oxford UP, forthcoming). She has co-edited multiple volumes, including the *Routledge Handbook of Memory Activism* (with Yifat Gutman, 2023).

Maria Zirra is a postdoctoral researcher at the English Department of Stockholm University working on visual and verbal forms in Caribbean and South African literary magazines with funding from the Anna Ahlström and Ellen Terserus Foundation and the Swedish Research Council. Maria's upcoming monograph, *Visual Poetic Memory: Ekphrasis, Image-text and the World in Heaney, Walcott and Jensma* deals with poetic writing about visual art. She has published work on contemporary ekphrastic poetry, new materialism, periodical studies, multidirectional memory and complicity in Anglophone poetry.

Index

www.ingramcontent.com/pod-product-compliance
Lightning Source LLC
Chambersburg PA
CBHW020814270326
41928CB00006B/370